Shojo Beat

Sweet Rein

1

Story & Art by Sakura Tsukuba

Sweet✲Rein

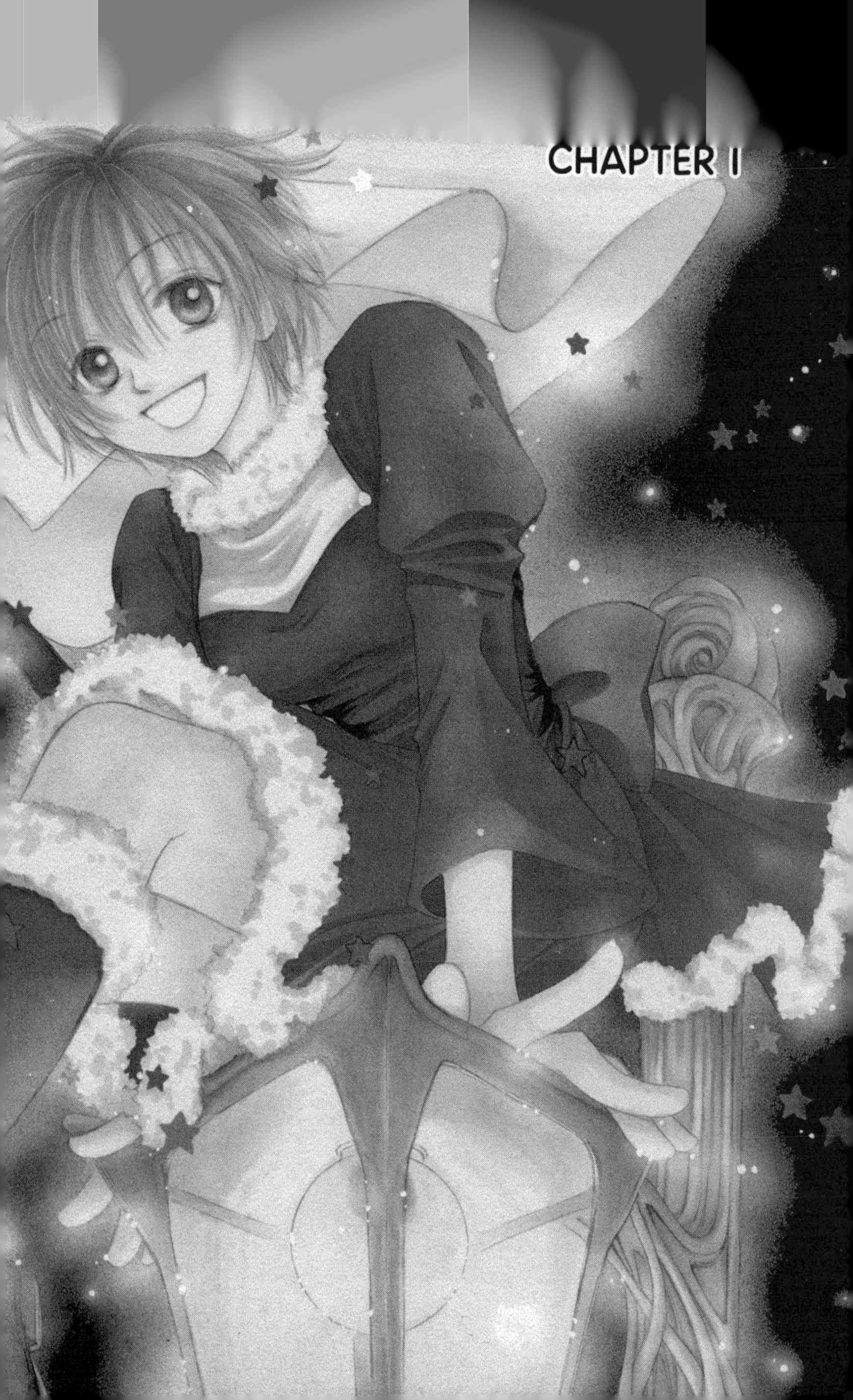
CHAPTER 1

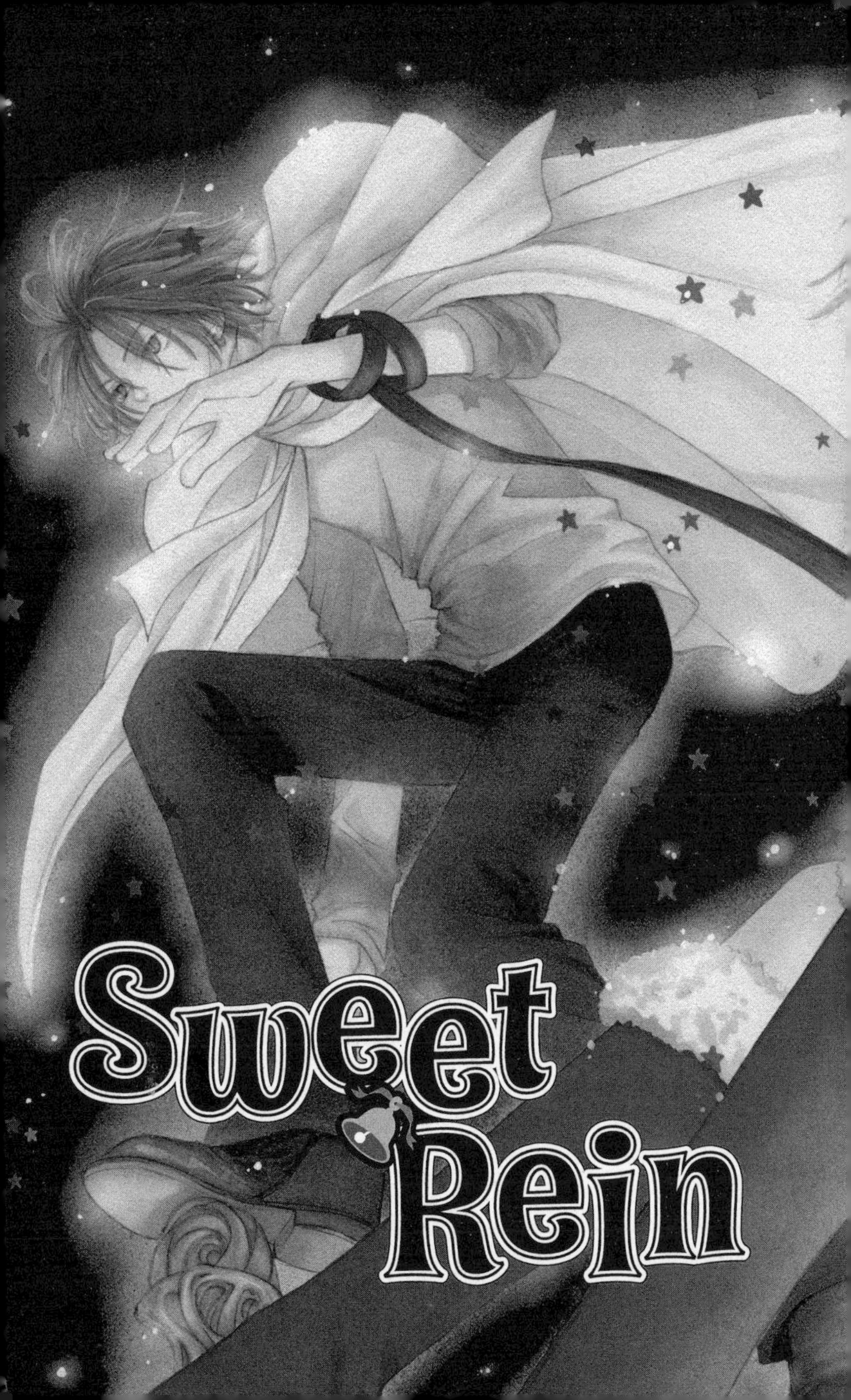
Sweet Rein

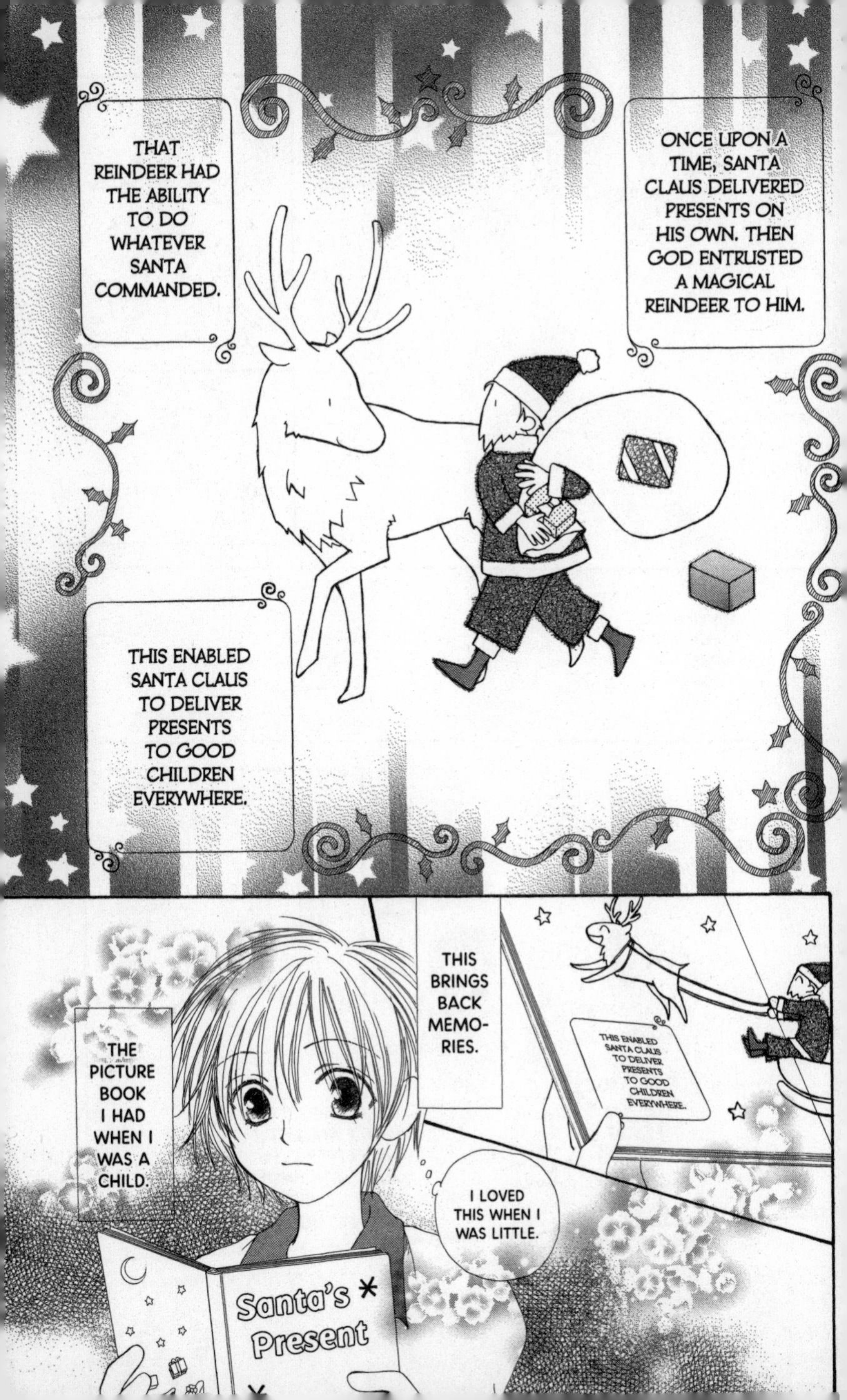
ONCE UPON A TIME, SANTA CLAUS DELIVERED PRESENTS ON HIS OWN. THEN GOD ENTRUSTED A MAGICAL REINDEER TO HIM.
THAT REINDEER HAD THE ABILITY TO DO WHATEVER SANTA COMMANDED.
THIS ENABLED SANTA CLAUS TO DELIVER PRESENTS TO GOOD CHILDREN EVERYWHERE.
THIS ENABLED SANTA CLAUS TO DELIVER PRESENTS TO GOOD CHILDREN EVERYWHERE.
THIS BRINGS BACK MEMO-RIES.
THE PICTURE BOOK I HAD WHEN I WAS A CHILD.
I LOVED THIS WHEN I WAS LITTLE.
Santa's Present

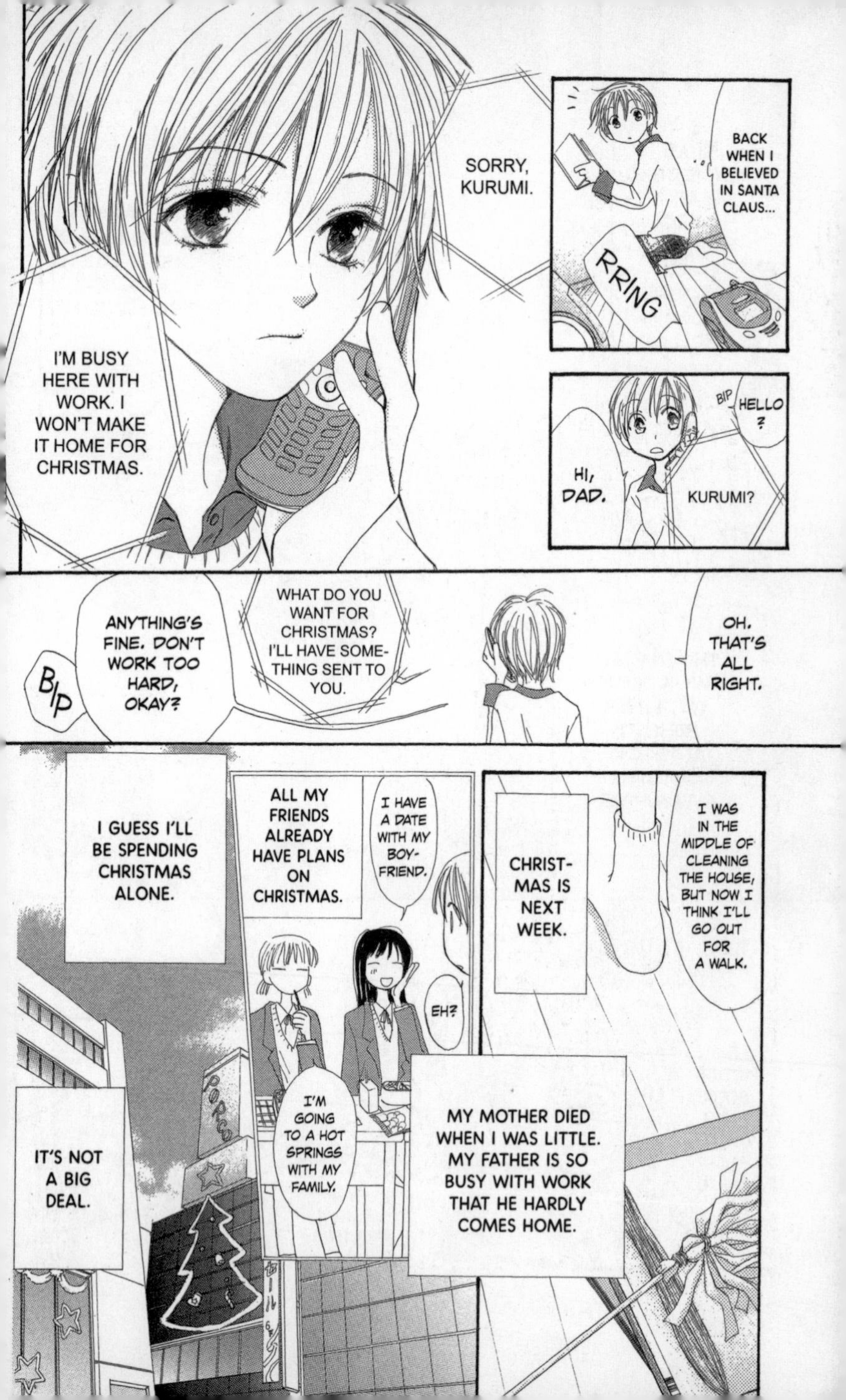
BACK WHEN I BELIEVED IN SANTA CLAUS...
RRING
BIP
HELLO?
KURUMI?
HI, DAD.
SORRY, KURUMI.
I'M BUSY HERE WITH WORK. I WON'T MAKE IT HOME FOR CHRISTMAS.
OH. THAT'S ALL RIGHT.
WHAT DO YOU WANT FOR CHRISTMAS? I'LL HAVE SOMETHING SENT TO YOU.
ANYTHING'S FINE. DON'T WORK TOO HARD, OKAY?
BIP
I WAS IN THE MIDDLE OF CLEANING THE HOUSE, BUT NOW I THINK I'LL GO OUT FOR A WALK.
CHRISTMAS IS NEXT WEEK.
MY MOTHER DIED WHEN I WAS LITTLE. MY FATHER IS SO BUSY WITH WORK THAT HE HARDLY COMES HOME.
I HAVE A DATE WITH MY BOYFRIEND.
ALL MY FRIENDS ALREADY HAVE PLANS ON CHRISTMAS.
EH?
I'M GOING TO A HOT SPRINGS WITH MY FAMILY.
I GUESS I'LL BE SPENDING CHRISTMAS ALONE.
IT'S NOT A BIG DEAL.

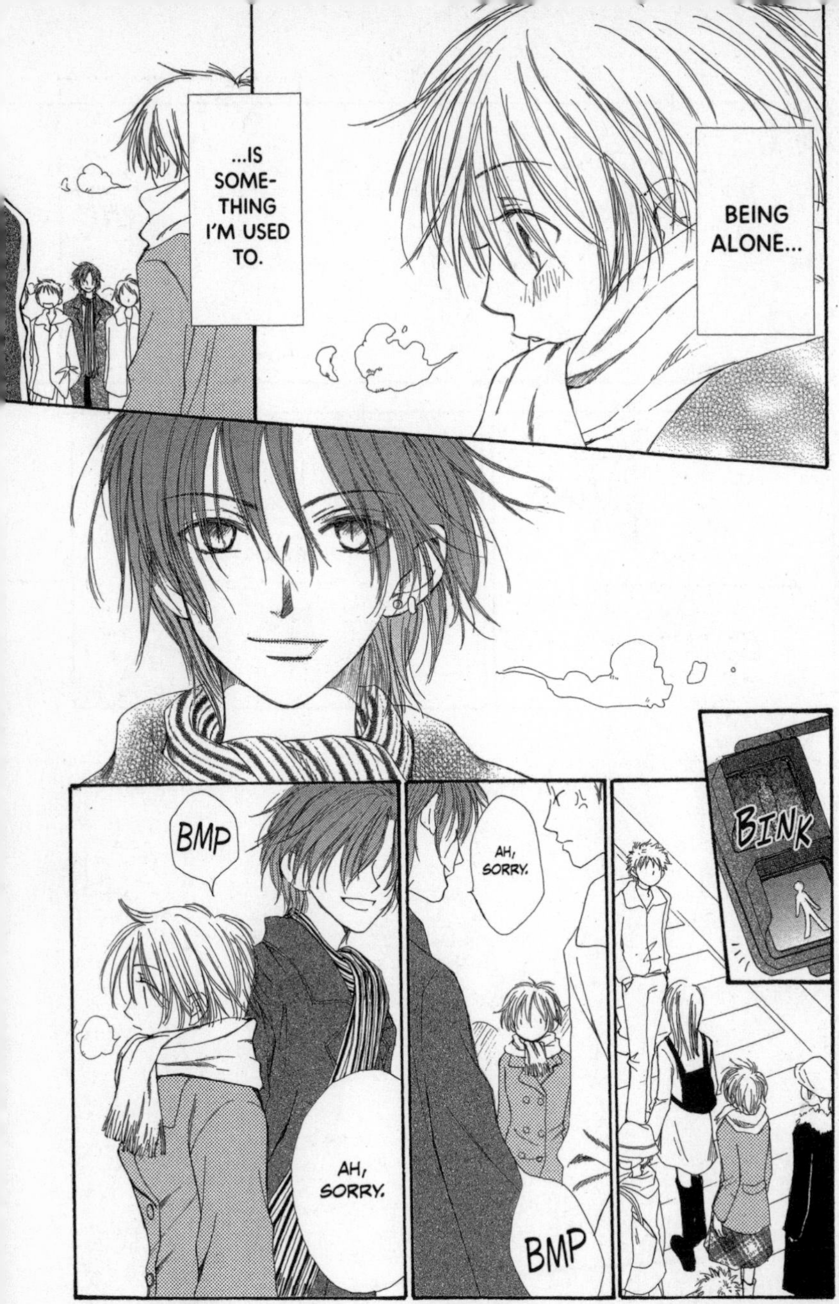
BEING ALONE...
...IS SOMETHING I'M USED TO.
BINK
AH, SORRY.
BMP
BMP
AH, SORRY.

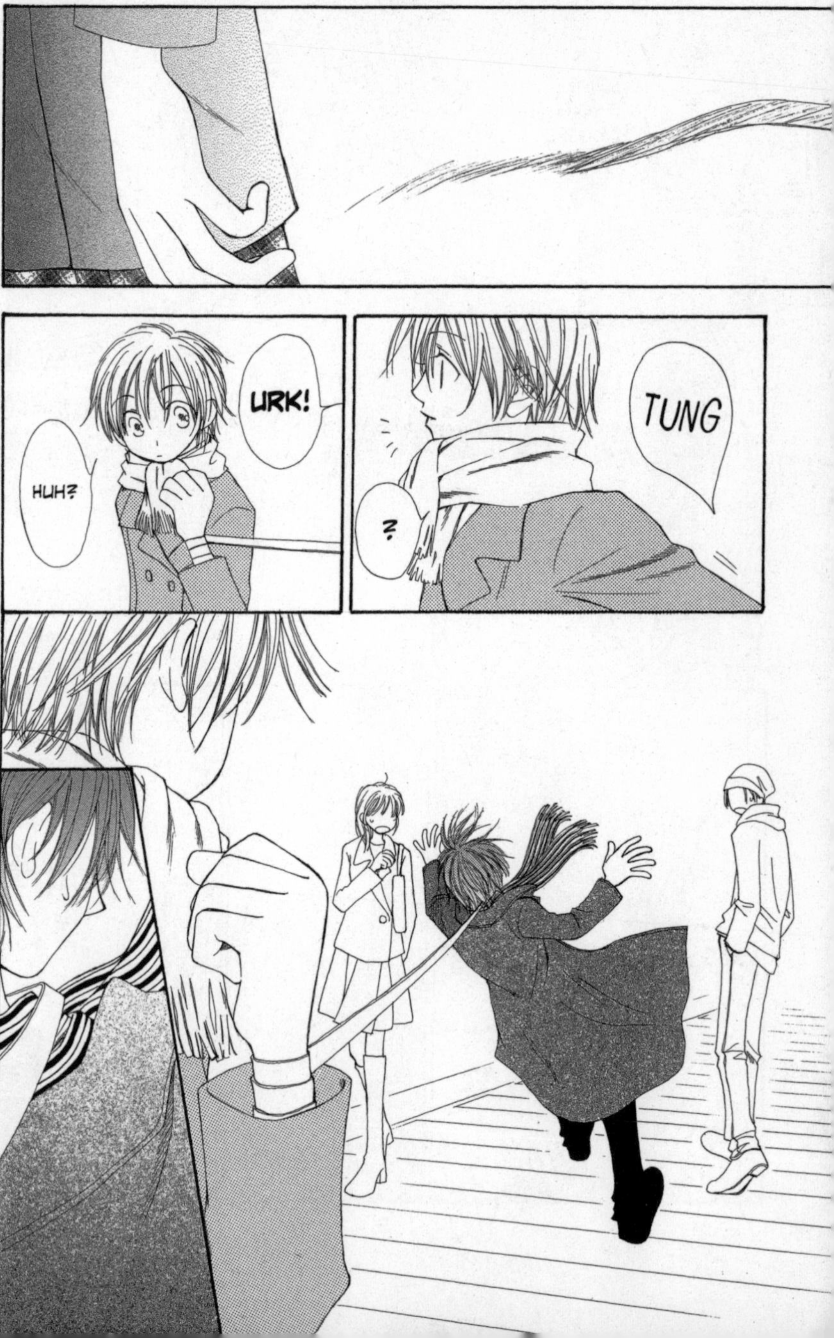
TUNG
?
URK!
HUH?

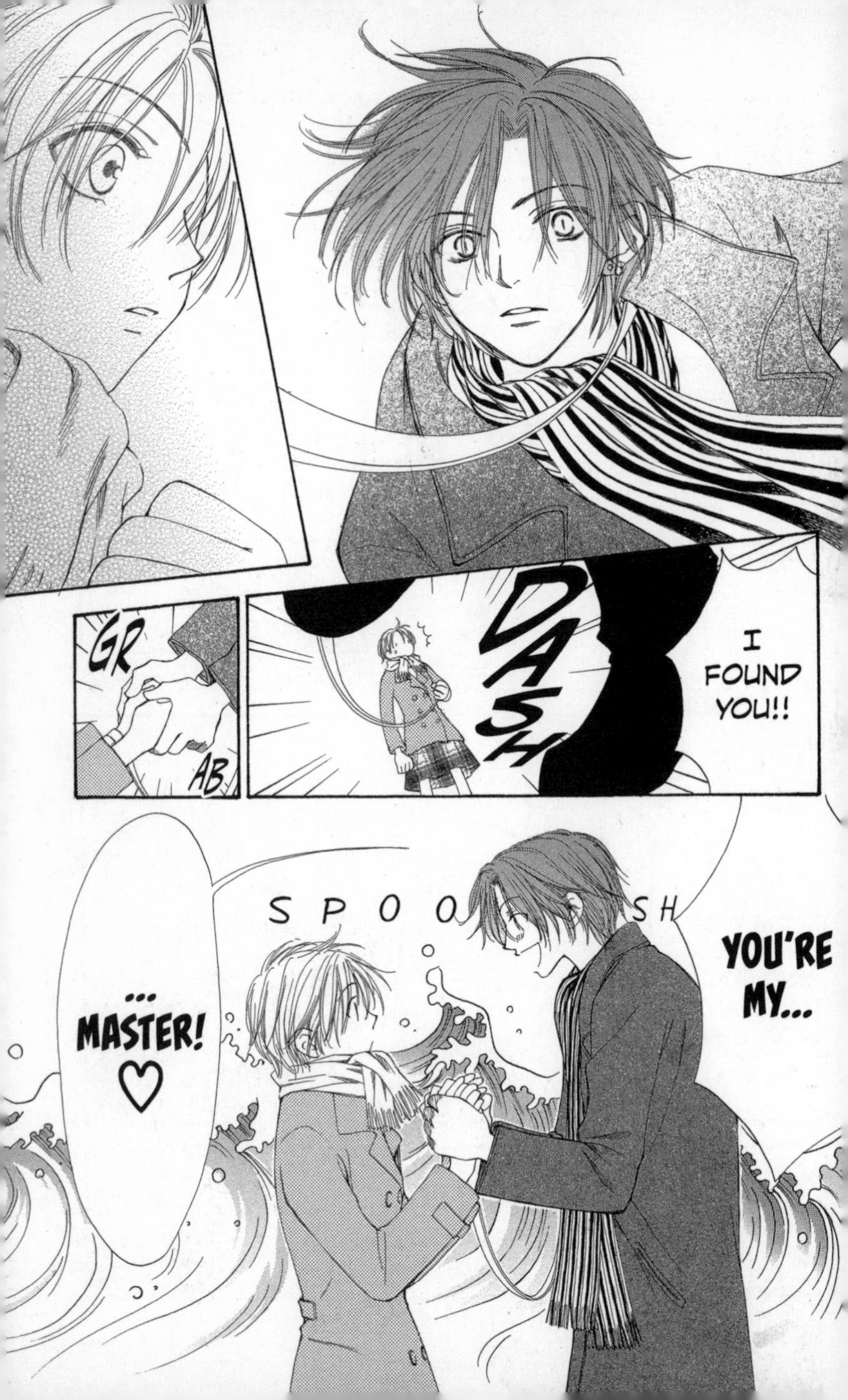

DASH
I FOUND YOU!!
GR
AB
YOU'RE MY...
SPOO SH
...MASTER! ♡

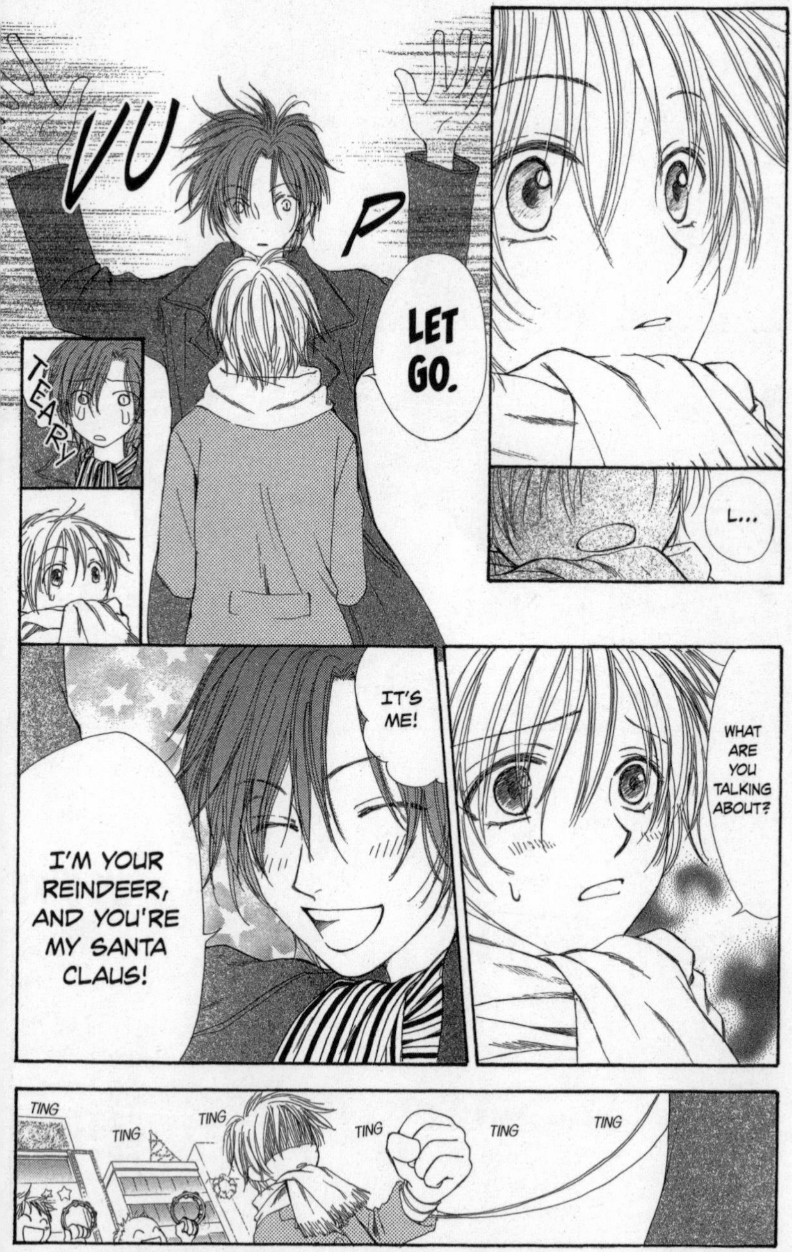
L...
VUP
LET GO.
TEARY
WHAT ARE YOU TALKING ABOUT?
IT'S ME!
I'M YOUR REINDEER, AND YOU'RE MY SANTA CLAUS!
TING TING TING TING TING TING

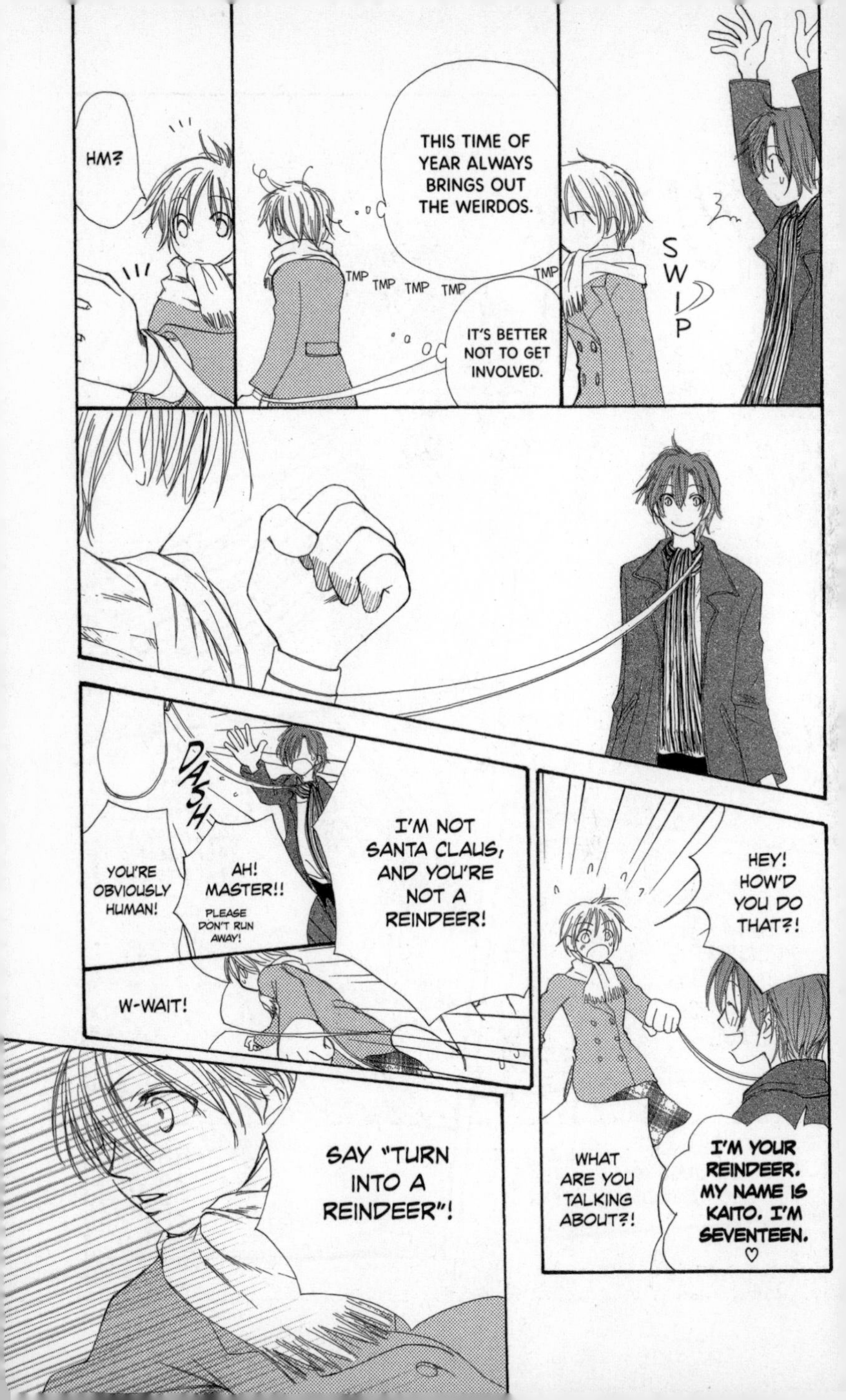
SWIP
TMP TMP TMP TMP TMP
THIS TIME OF YEAR ALWAYS BRINGS OUT THE WEIRDOS.
IT'S BETTER NOT TO GET INVOLVED.
HM?
HEY! HOW'D YOU DO THAT?!
I'M YOUR REINDEER. MY NAME IS KAITO. I'M SEVENTEEN. ♡
WHAT ARE YOU TALKING ABOUT?!
I'M NOT SANTA CLAUS, AND YOU'RE NOT A REINDEER!
DASH
AH! MASTER!!
PLEASE DON'T RUN AWAY!
YOU'RE OBVIOUSLY HUMAN!
W-WAIT!
SAY "TURN INTO A REINDEER"!

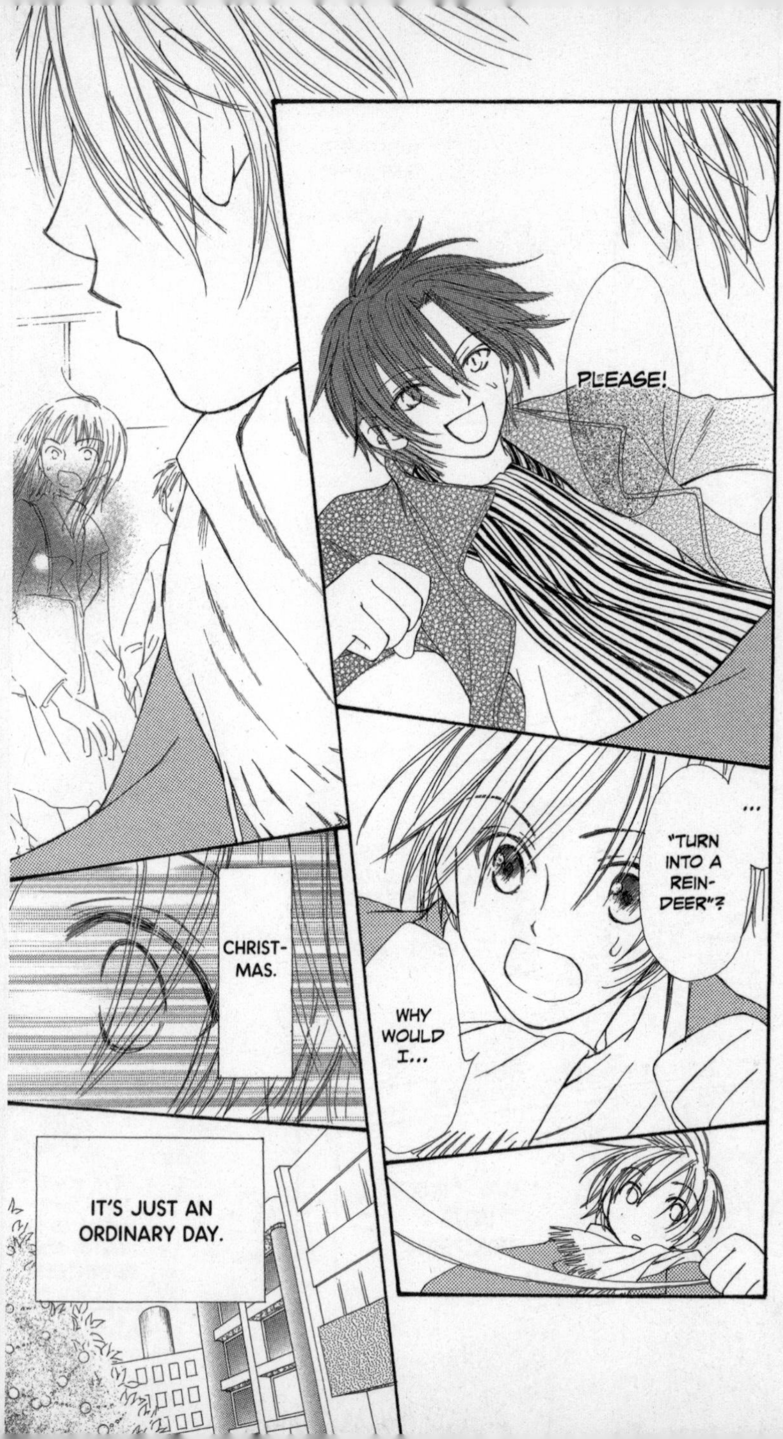
PLEASE!
...
"TURN INTO A REINDEER"?
WHY WOULD I...
CHRISTMAS.
IT'S JUST AN ORDINARY DAY.

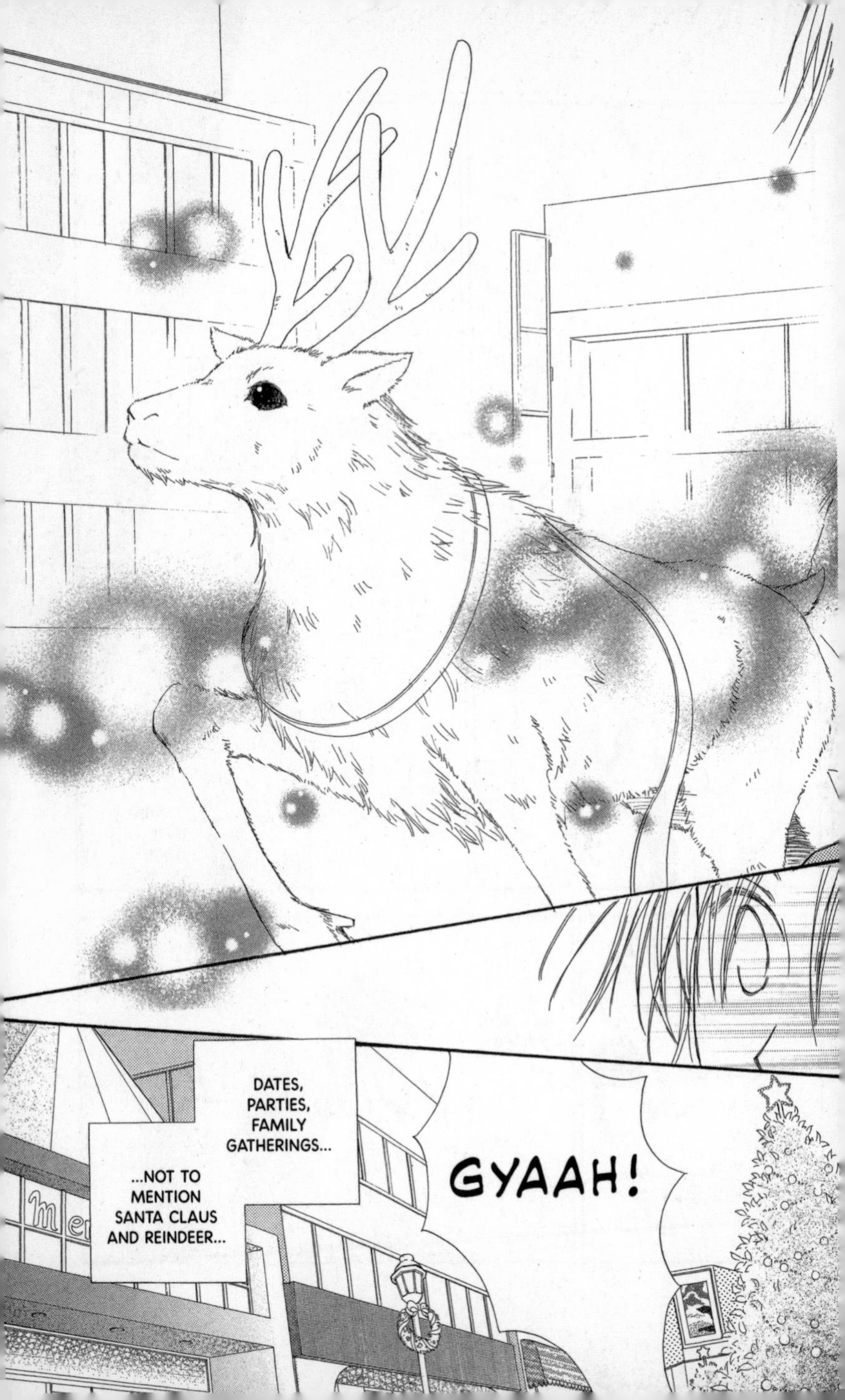
DATES, PARTIES, FAMILY GATHERINGS...
...NOT TO MENTION SANTA CLAUS AND REINDEER...
GYAAH!

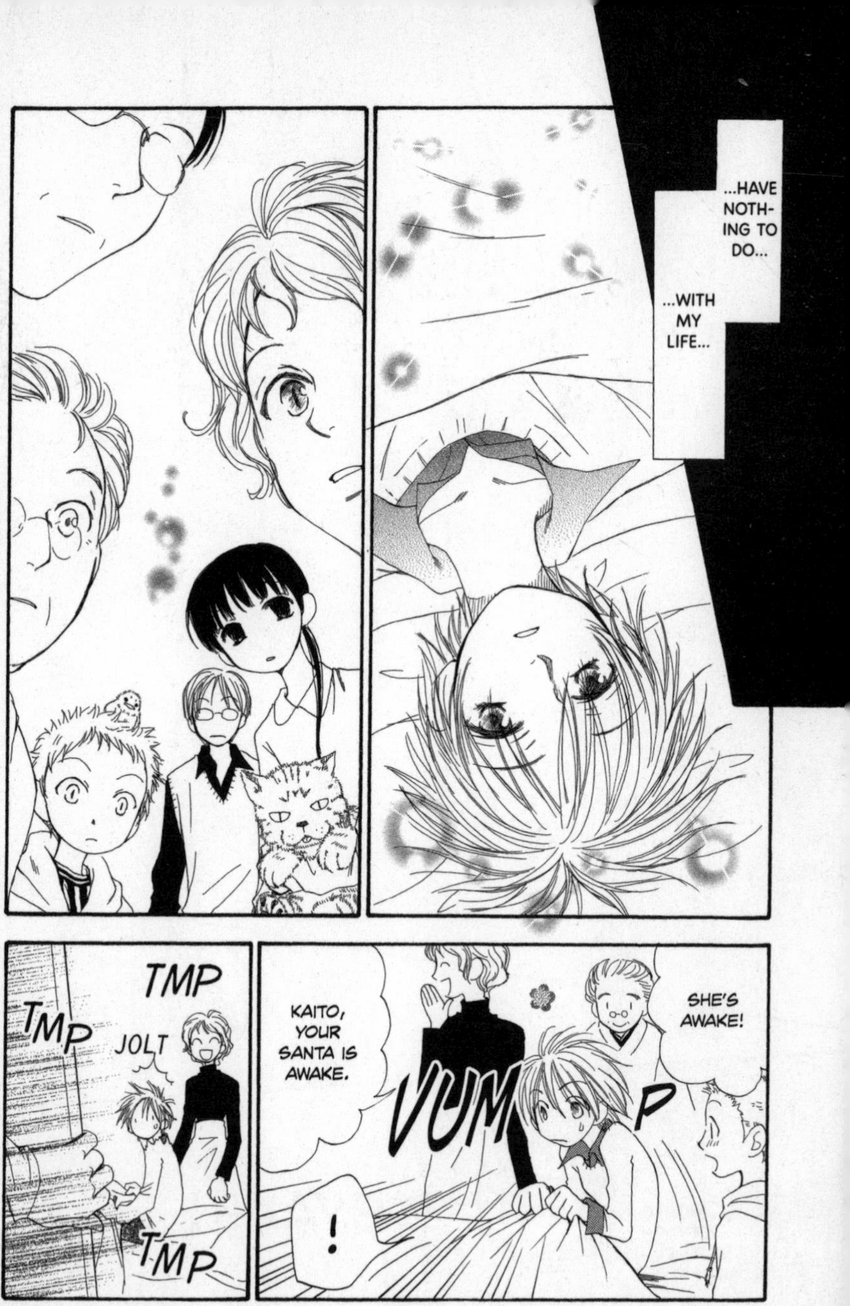
...HAVE NOTHING TO DO...
...WITH MY LIFE...
SHE'S AWAKE!
KAITO, YOUR SANTA IS AWAKE.
VUMP
!
TMP
TMP
JOLT
TMP

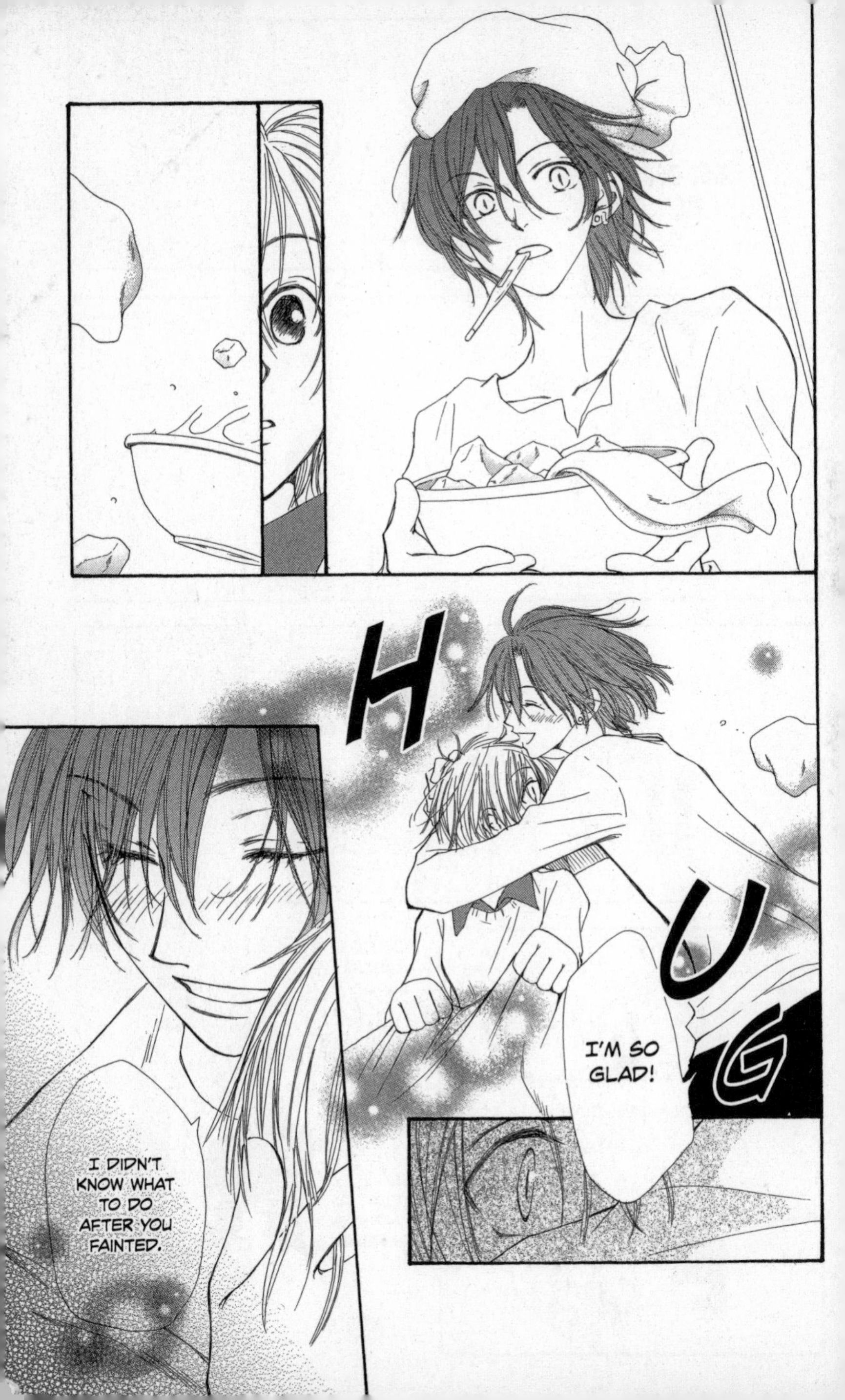
HUG
I'M SO GLAD!
I DIDN'T KNOW WHAT TO DO AFTER YOU FAINTED.

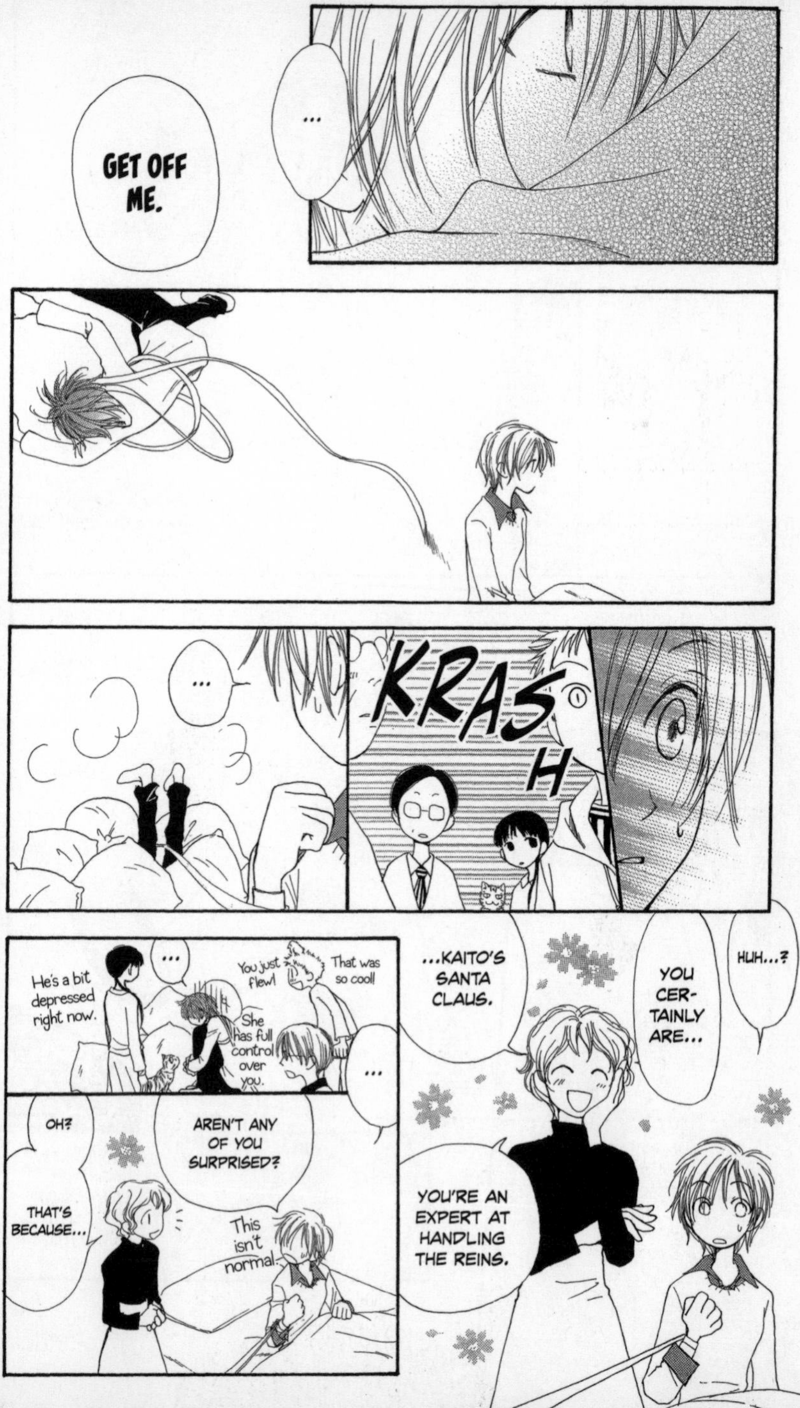
...
GET OFF ME.
KRASH
...
HUH...?
YOU CERTAINLY ARE...
...KAITO'S SANTA CLAUS.
YOU'RE AN EXPERT AT HANDLING THE REINS.
That was so cool!
You just flew!
...
He's a bit depressed right now.
She has full control over you.
...
AREN'T ANY OF YOU SURPRISED?
OH?
This isn't normal.
THAT'S BECAUSE...

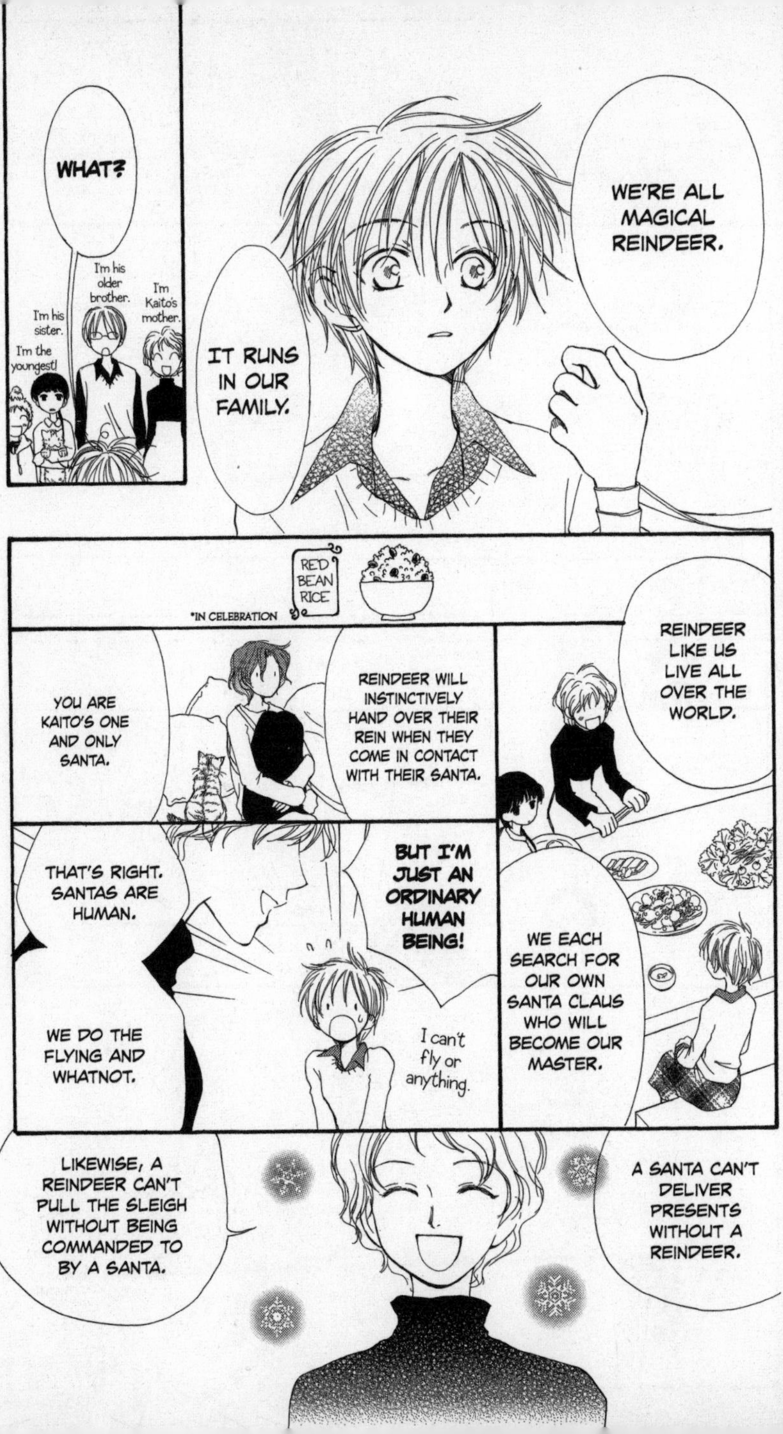

WE'RE ALL MAGICAL REINDEER.
IT RUNS IN OUR FAMILY.
WHAT?
I'm Kaito's mother.
I'm his older brother.
I'm his sister.
I'm the youngest!
REINDEER LIKE US LIVE ALL OVER THE WORLD.
WE EACH SEARCH FOR OUR OWN SANTA CLAUS WHO WILL BECOME OUR MASTER.
RED BEAN RICE
*IN CELEBRATION
REINDEER WILL INSTINCTIVELY HAND OVER THEIR REIN WHEN THEY COME IN CONTACT WITH THEIR SANTA.
YOU ARE KAITO'S ONE AND ONLY SANTA.
BUT I'M JUST AN ORDINARY HUMAN BEING!
I can't fly or anything.
THAT'S RIGHT. SANTAS ARE HUMAN.
WE DO THE FLYING AND WHATNOT.
A SANTA CAN'T DELIVER PRESENTS WITHOUT A REINDEER.
LIKEWISE, A REINDEER CAN'T PULL THE SLEIGH WITHOUT BEING COMMANDED TO BY A SANTA.

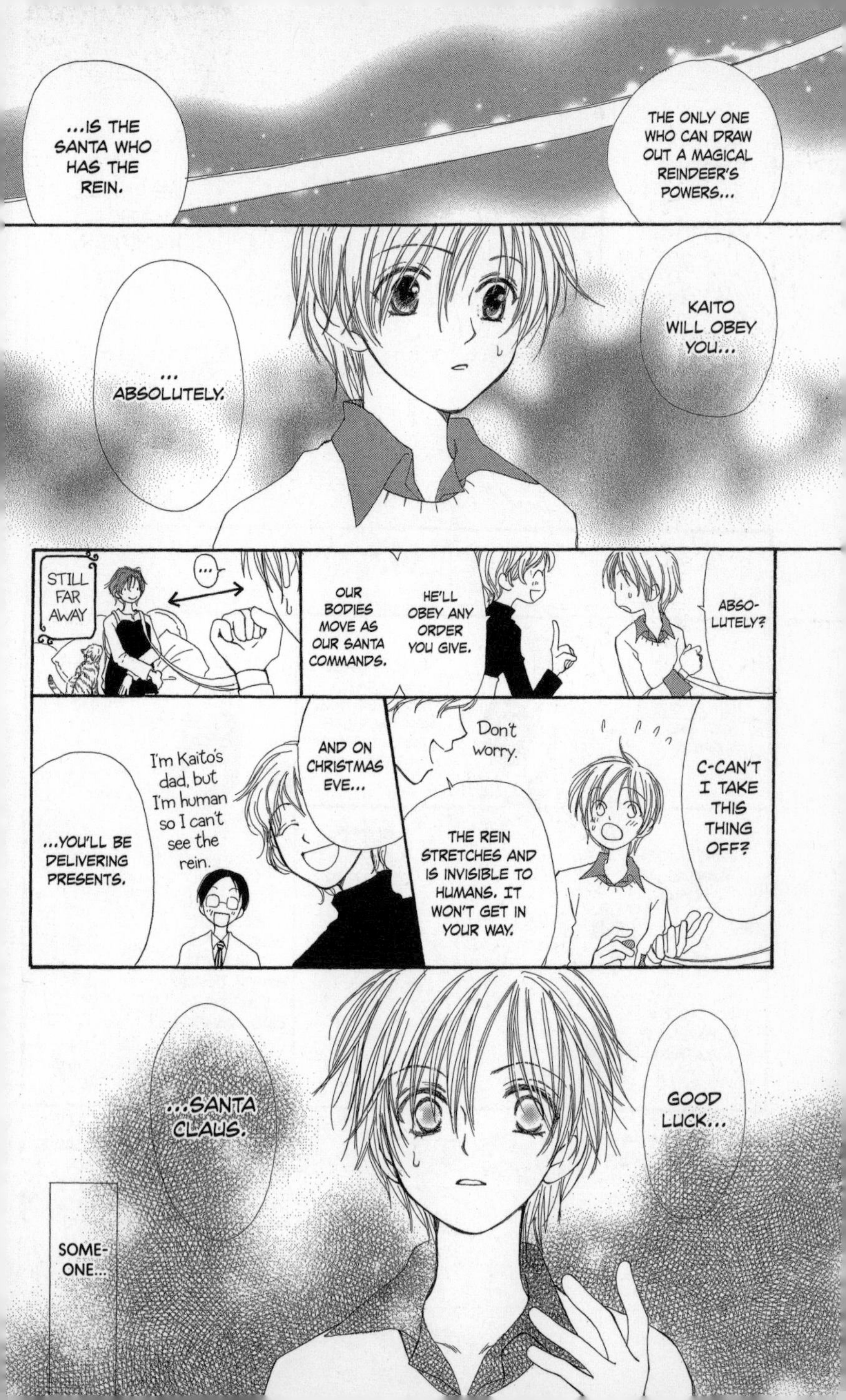
THE ONLY ONE WHO CAN DRAW OUT A MAGICAL REINDEER'S POWERS...
...IS THE SANTA WHO HAS THE REIN.
KAITO WILL OBEY YOU...
... ABSOLUTELY.
ABSO-LUTELY?
HE'LL OBEY ANY ORDER YOU GIVE.
OUR BODIES MOVE AS OUR SANTA COMMANDS.
....
STILL FAR AWAY
C-CAN'T I TAKE THIS THING OFF?
Don't worry.
THE REIN STRETCHES AND IS INVISIBLE TO HUMANS. IT WON'T GET IN YOUR WAY.
AND ON CHRISTMAS EVE...
I'm Kaito's dad, but I'm human so I can't see the rein.
...YOU'LL BE DELIVERING PRESENTS.
GOOD LUCK...
...SANTA CLAUS.
SOME-ONE...

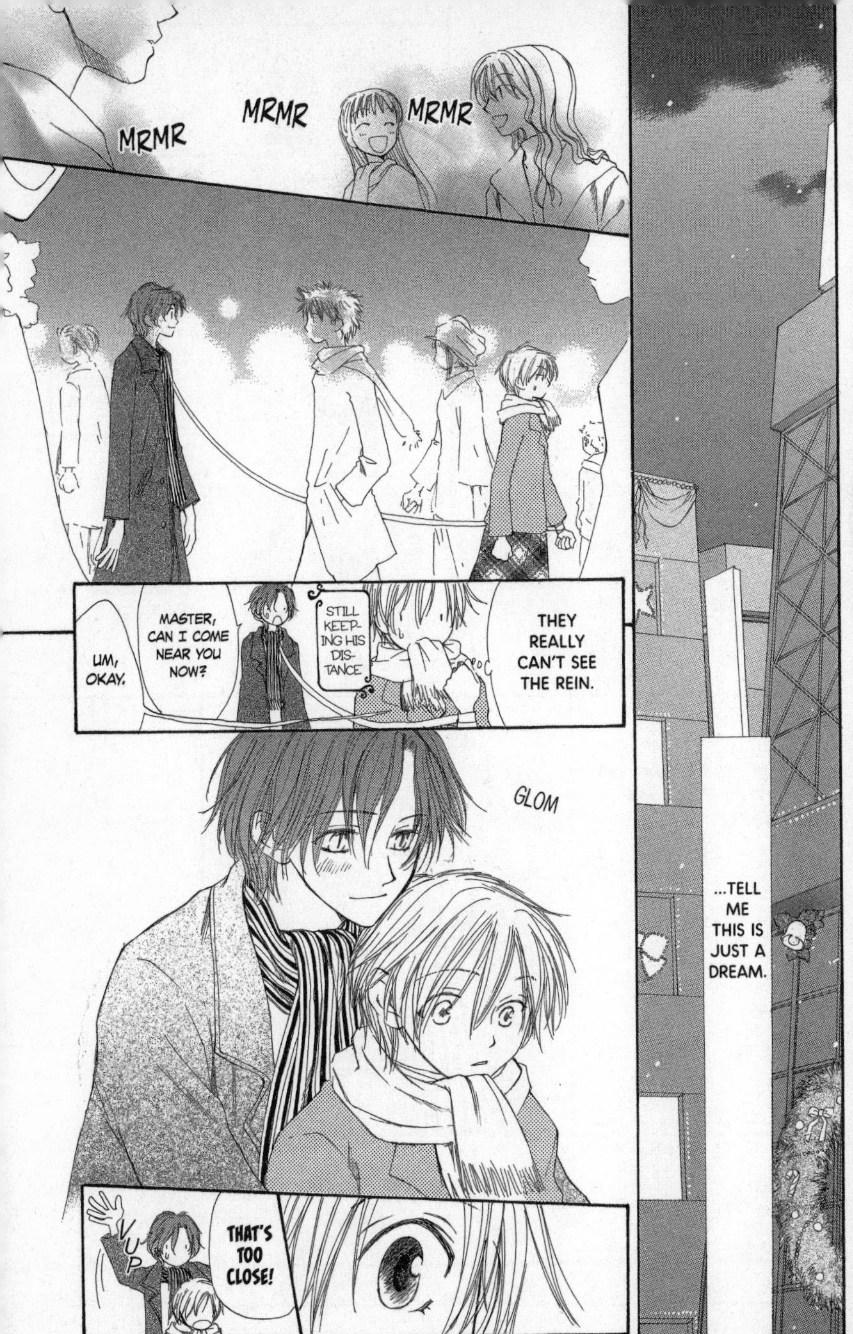
...TELL ME THIS IS JUST A DREAM.
MRMR
MRMR
MRMR
THEY REALLY CAN'T SEE THE REIN.
STILL KEEPING HIS DISTANCE
MASTER, CAN I COME NEAR YOU NOW?
UM, OKAY.
GLOM
THAT'S TOO CLOSE!
VUP

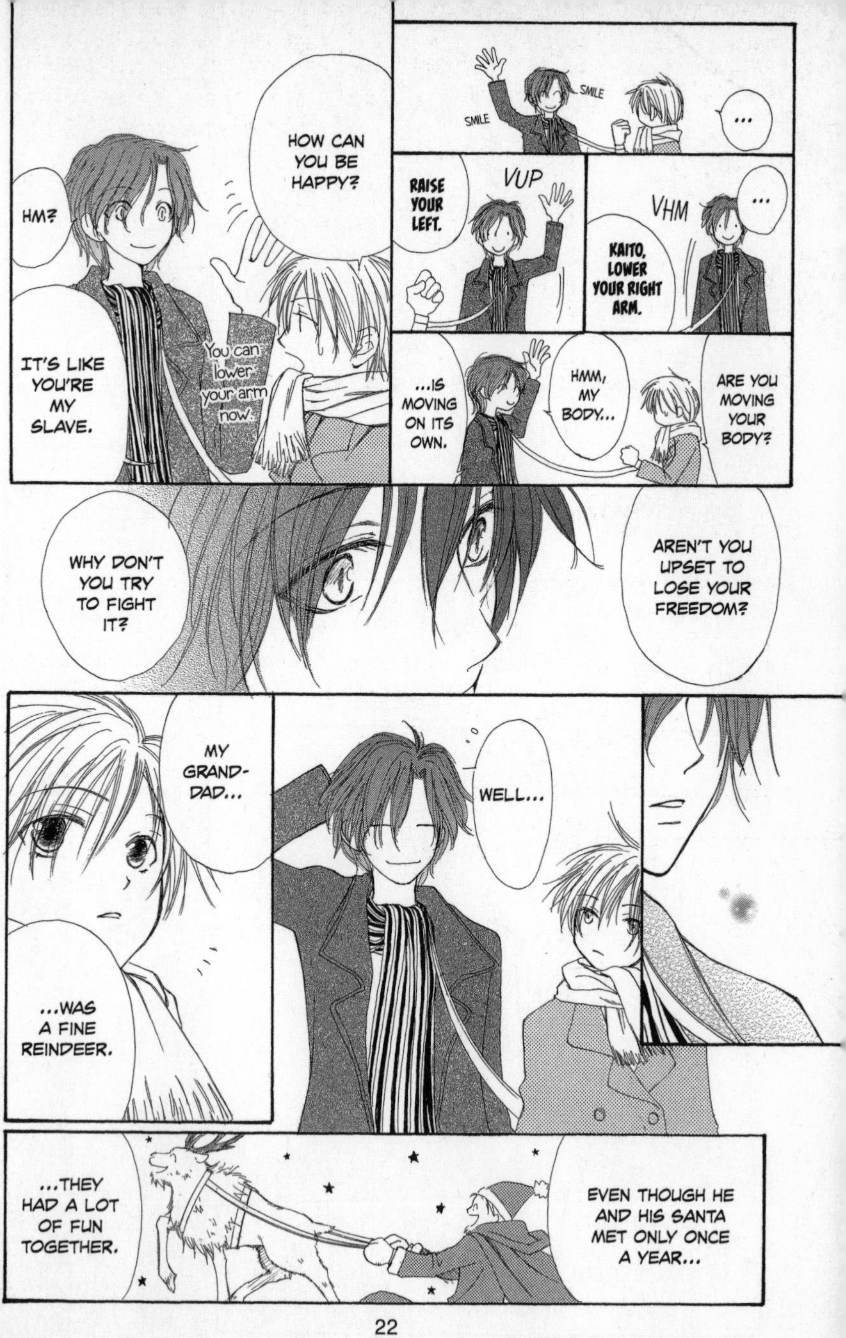
...
SMILE
SMILE
...
KAITO, LOWER YOUR RIGHT ARM.
VHM
RAISE YOUR LEFT.
VUP
ARE YOU MOVING YOUR BODY?
HMM, MY BODY...
...IS MOVING ON ITS OWN.
HOW CAN YOU BE HAPPY?
HM?
You can lower your arm now.
IT'S LIKE YOU'RE MY SLAVE.
AREN'T YOU UPSET TO LOSE YOUR FREEDOM?
WHY DON'T YOU TRY TO FIGHT IT?
WELL...
MY GRAND-DAD...
...WAS A FINE REINDEER.
EVEN THOUGH HE AND HIS SANTA MET ONLY ONCE A YEAR...
...THEY HAD A LOT OF FUN TOGETHER.

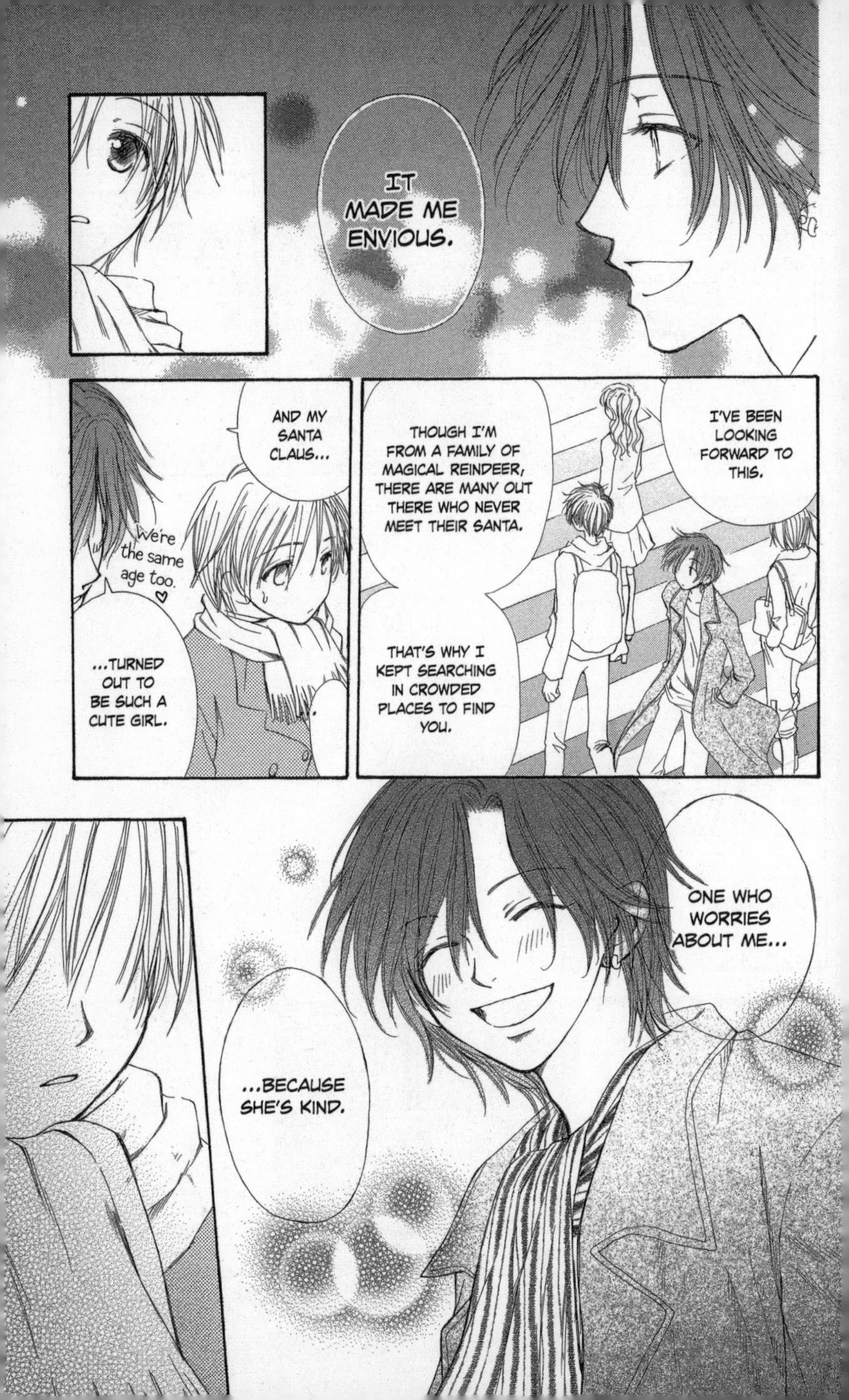
IT MADE ME ENVIOUS.
I'VE BEEN LOOKING FORWARD TO THIS.
THOUGH I'M FROM A FAMILY OF MAGICAL REINDEER, THERE ARE MANY OUT THERE WHO NEVER MEET THEIR SANTA.
THAT'S WHY I KEPT SEARCHING IN CROWDED PLACES TO FIND YOU.
AND MY SANTA CLAUS...
We're the same age too. ♥
...TURNED OUT TO BE SUCH A CUTE GIRL.
ONE WHO WORRIES ABOUT ME...
...BECAUSE SHE'S KIND.

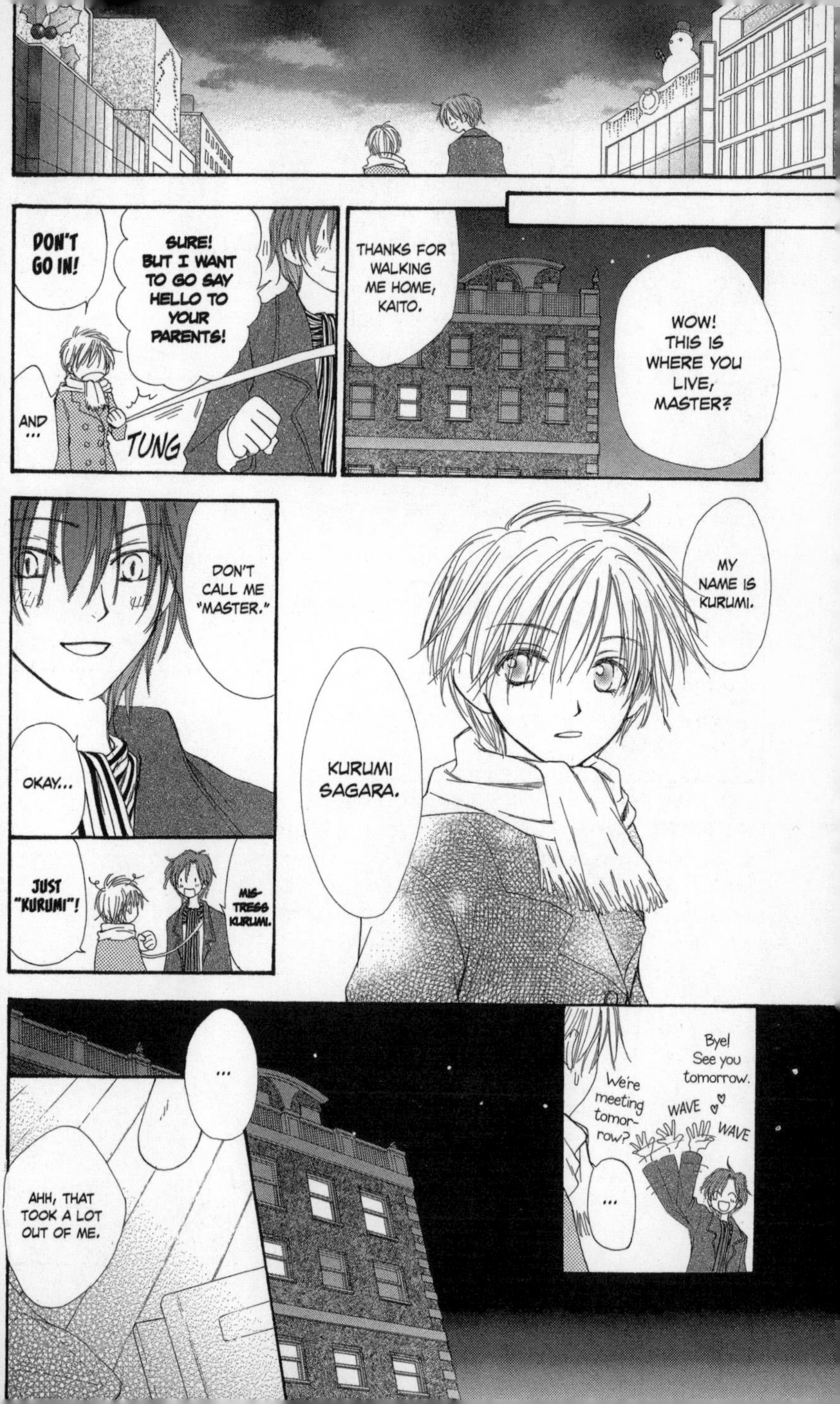
THANKS FOR WALKING ME HOME, KAITO.
WOW! THIS IS WHERE YOU LIVE, MASTER?
SURE! BUT I WANT TO GO SAY HELLO TO YOUR PARENTS!
DON'T GO IN!
AND ...
TUNG
MY NAME IS KURUMI.
KURUMI SAGARA.
DON'T CALL ME "MASTER."
OKAY...
MIS-TRESS KURUMI.
JUST "KURUMI"!
Bye! See you tomorrow.
WAVE
WAVE
We're meeting tomor-row?
...
...
AHH, THAT TOOK A LOT OUT OF ME.

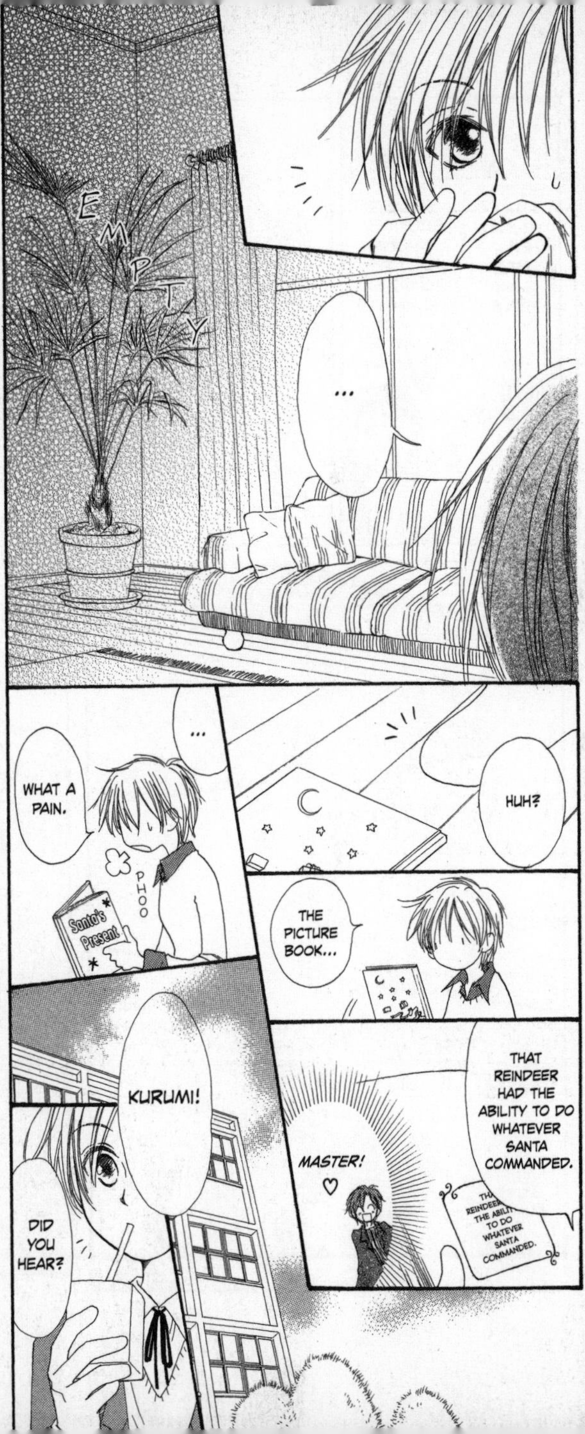
EMPTY
...
HUH?
...
WHAT A PAIN.
PHOO
Santa's Present
THE PICTURE BOOK...
THAT REINDEER HAD THE ABILITY TO DO WHATEVER SANTA COMMANDED.
THAT REINDEER HAD THE ABILITY TO DO WHATEVER SANTA COMMANDED.
MASTER!
KURUMI!
DID YOU HEAR?

1/4 Sakura Mail

Part 1

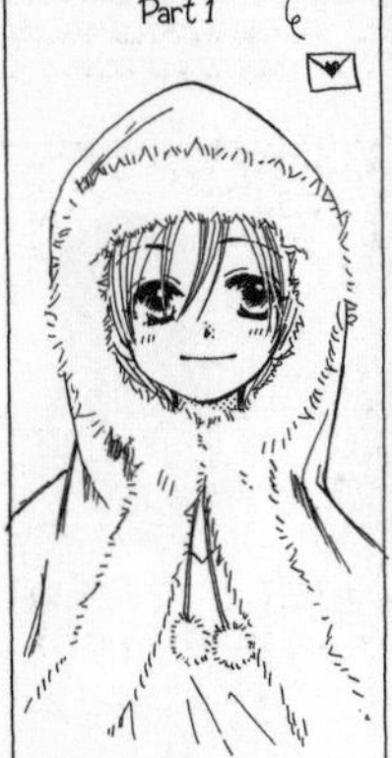

Greetings to all those who know me and to those who don't! I'm Sakura Tsukuba!! Thank you very much for picking up this volume. ♥SQUEE SQUEE♥ *Sweet 🔔 Rein.* I happily added a bell here after hearing I could do that. I even asked them to put the bell in the title of this manga too! Thank you very much for doing that. I think it's very cute. What do you think?

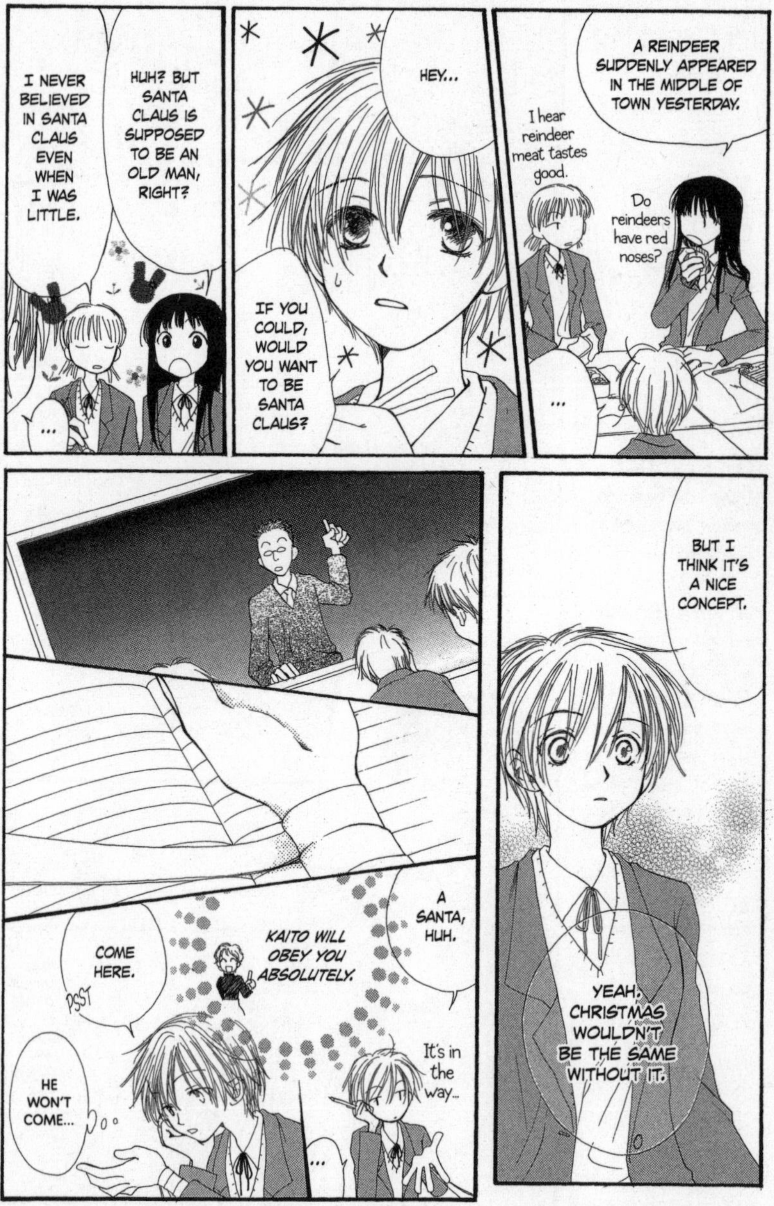
A REINDEER SUDDENLY APPEARED IN THE MIDDLE OF TOWN YESTERDAY.
Do reindeers have red noses?
I hear reindeer meat tastes good.
...
HEY...
IF YOU COULD, WOULD YOU WANT TO BE SANTA CLAUS?
HUH? BUT SANTA CLAUS IS SUPPOSED TO BE AN OLD MAN, RIGHT?
I NEVER BELIEVED IN SANTA CLAUS EVEN WHEN I WAS LITTLE.
...
BUT I THINK IT'S A NICE CONCEPT.
YEAH. CHRISTMAS WOULDN'T BE THE SAME WITHOUT IT.
A SANTA, HUH.
It's in the way...
...
KAITO WILL OBEY YOU ABSOLUTELY.
COME HERE.
PSST
HE WON'T COME...

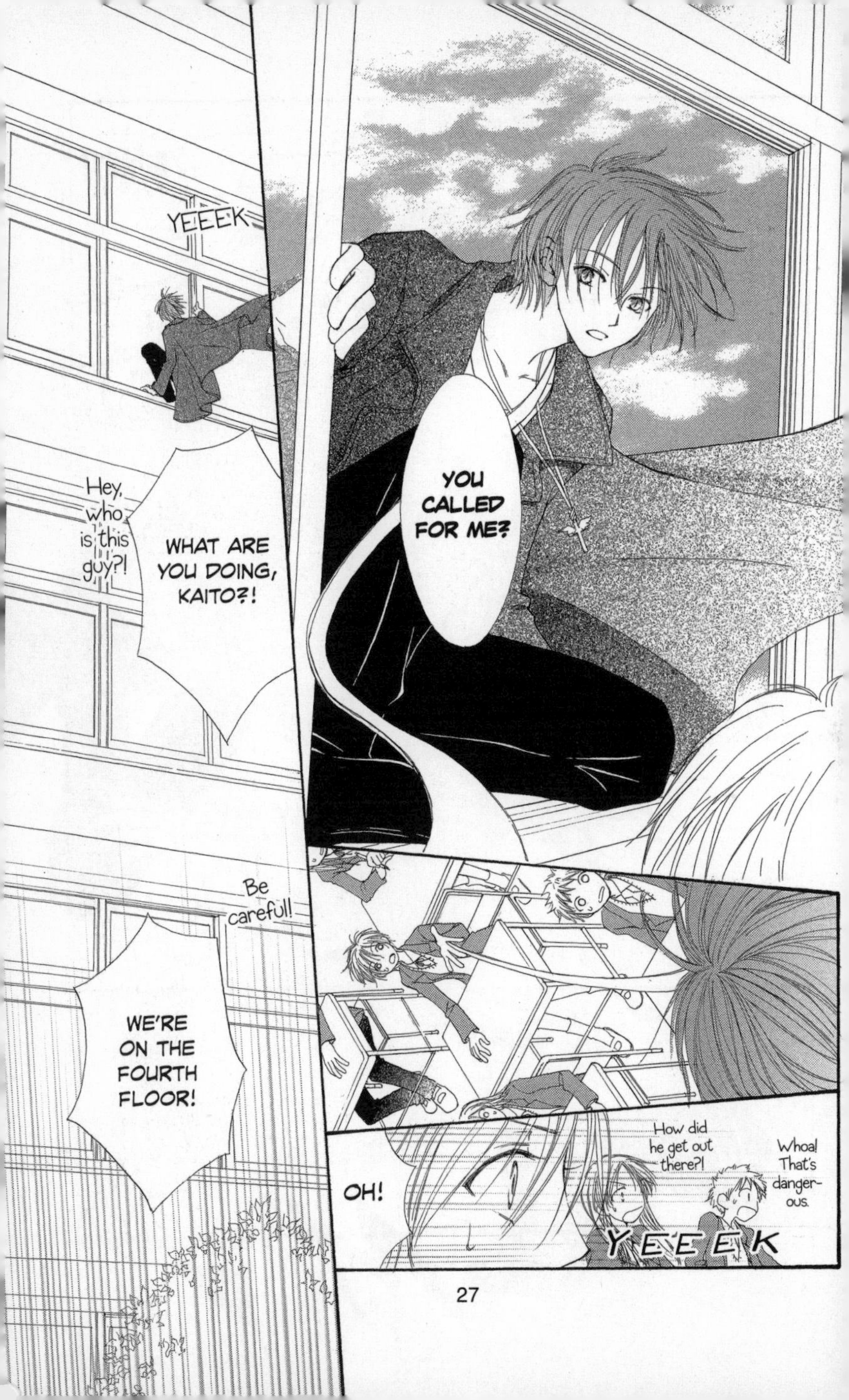
YOU CALLED FOR ME?
Whoa! That's danger-ous.
How did he get out there?!
OH!
YEEEK
YEEEK
WHAT ARE YOU DOING, KAITO?!
Hey, who is this guy?!
Be careful!
WE'RE ON THE FOURTH FLOOR!

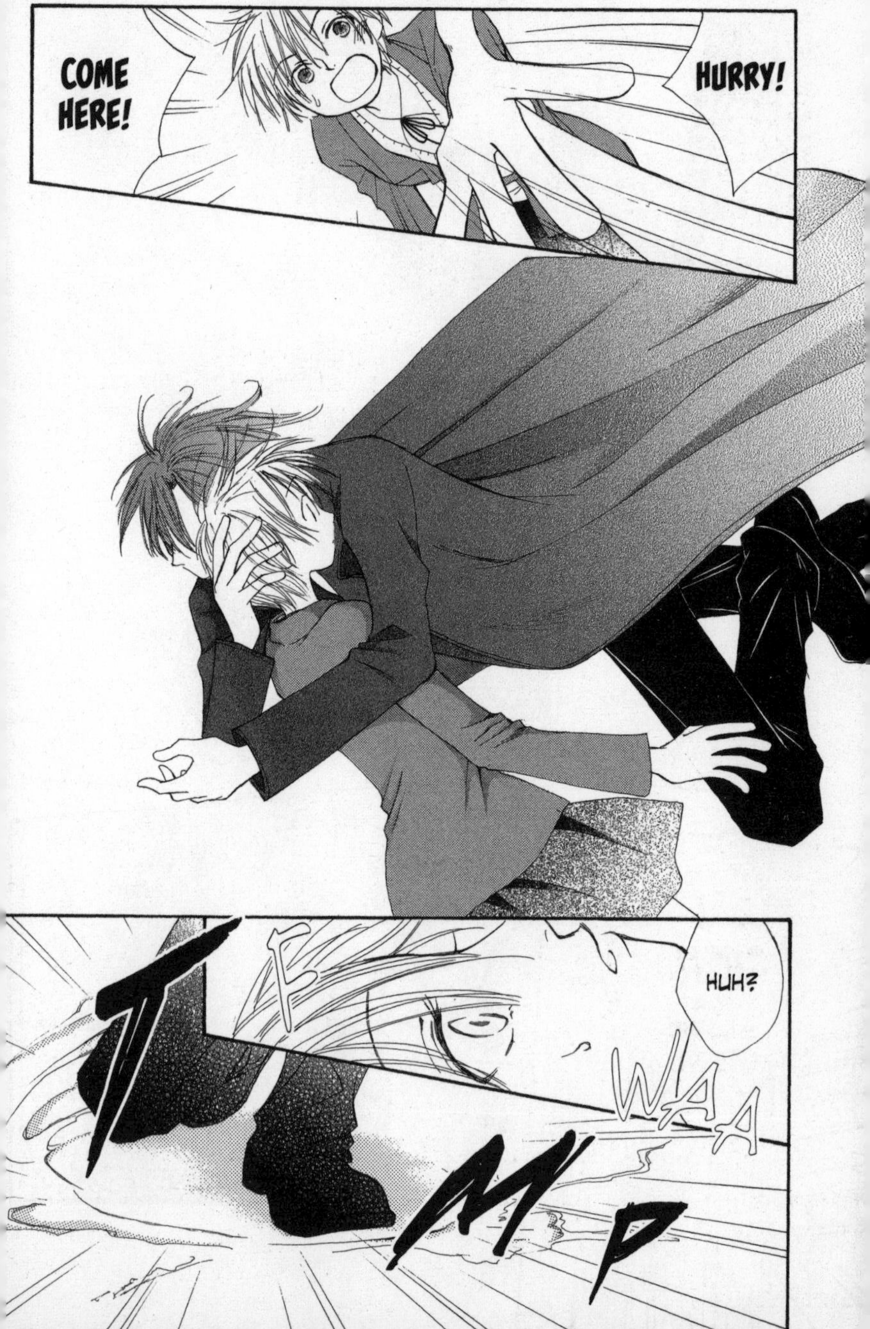
HURRY!
COME HERE!
HUH?
WAA

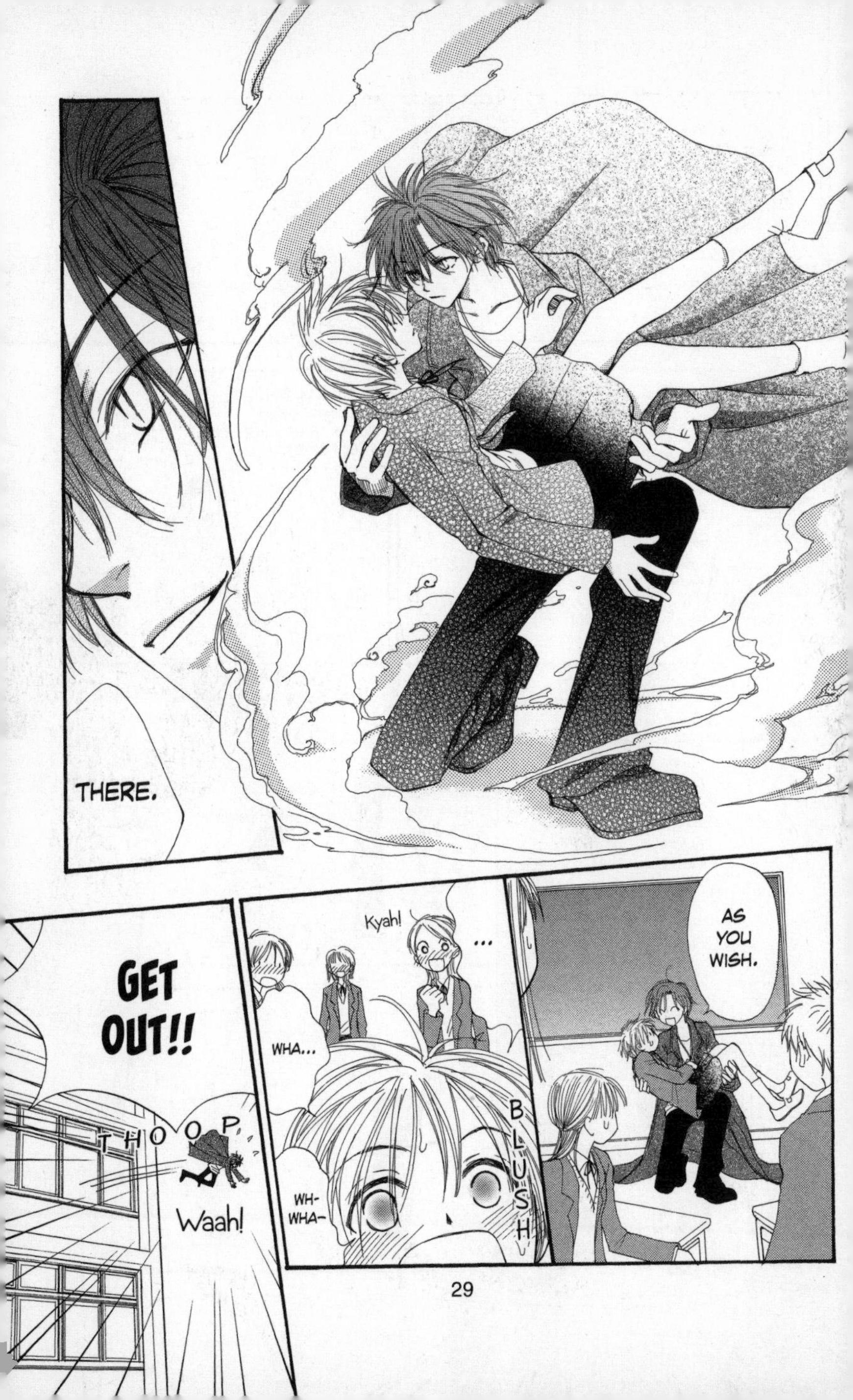
THERE.
AS YOU WISH.
...
Kyah!
BLUSH
WHA...
WH-WHA-
GET OUT!!
THOOP
Waah!

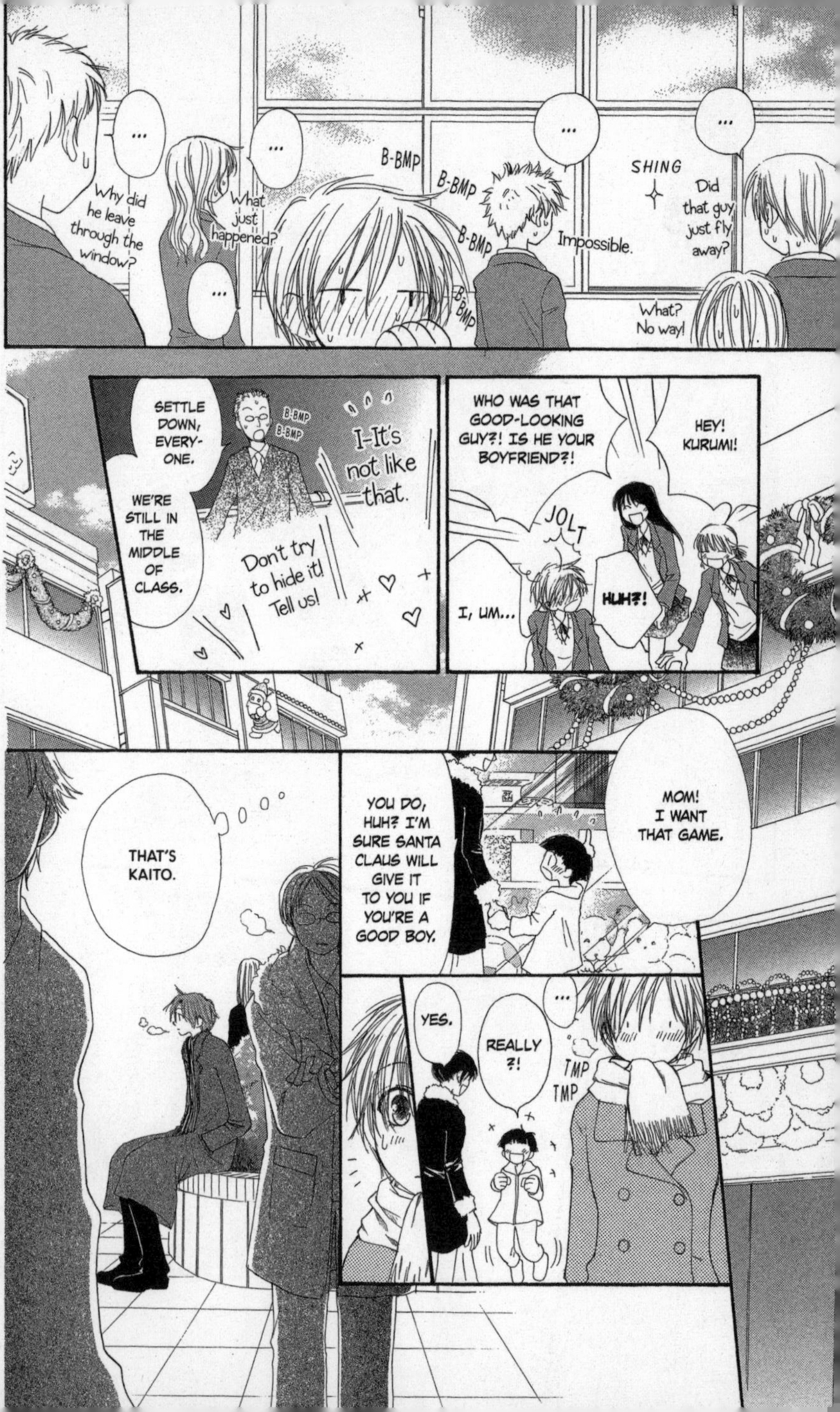
...
Did that guy just fly away?
What? No way!
SHING
...
Impossible.
B-BMP
B-BMP
B-BMP
B-BMP
...
What just happened?
...
Why did he leave through the window?
...
HEY! KURUMI!
WHO WAS THAT GOOD-LOOKING GUY?! IS HE YOUR BOYFRIEND?!
JOLT
HUH?!
I, UM...
I-It's not like that.
B-BMP B-BMP
SETTLE DOWN, EVERY-ONE.
WE'RE STILL IN THE MIDDLE OF CLASS.
Don't try to hide it! Tell us!
MOM! I WANT THAT GAME.
YOU DO, HUH? I'M SURE SANTA CLAUS WILL GIVE IT TO YOU IF YOU'RE A GOOD BOY.
...
TMP TMP
REALLY?!
YES.
THAT'S KAITO.

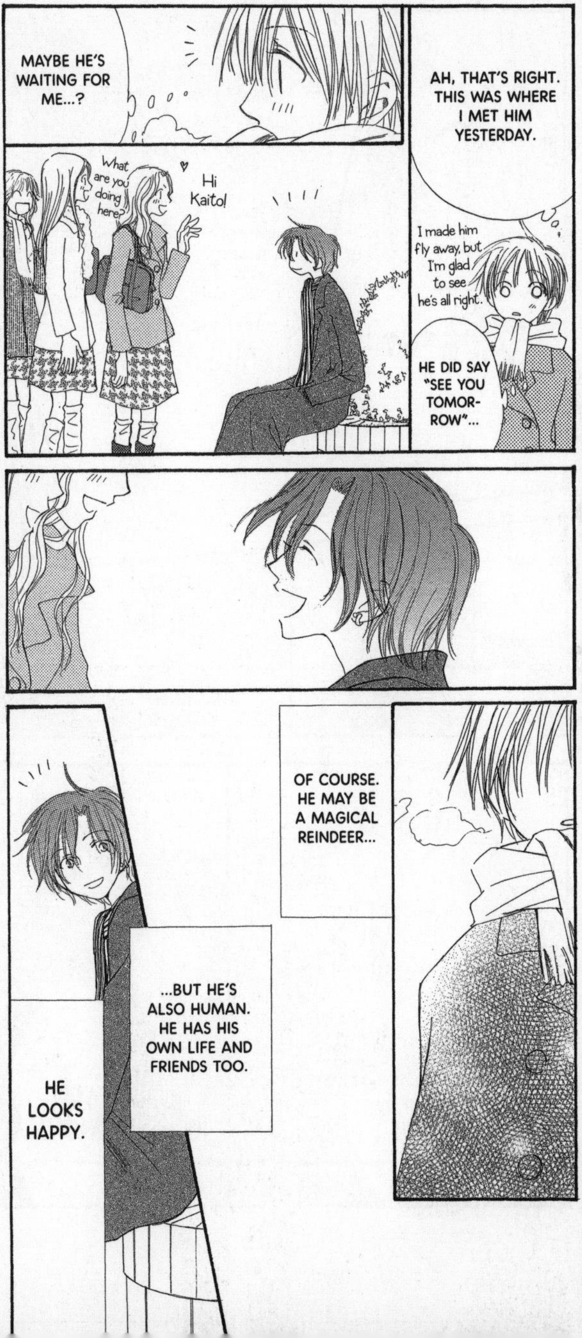
AH, THAT'S RIGHT. THIS WAS WHERE I MET HIM YESTERDAY.
I made him fly away, but I'm glad to see he's all right.
HE DID SAY "SEE YOU TOMOR-ROW"...
MAYBE HE'S WAITING FOR ME...?
Hi Kaito!
What are you doing here?
OF COURSE. HE MAY BE A MAGICAL REINDEER...
...BUT HE'S ALSO HUMAN. HE HAS HIS OWN LIFE AND FRIENDS TOO.
HE LOOKS HAPPY.

1/4 Sakura Mail

Part 2

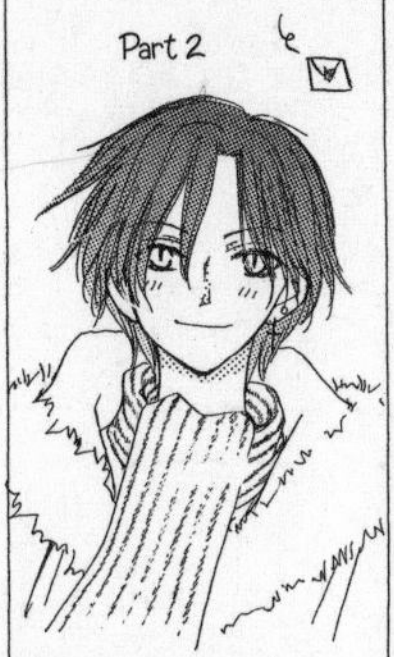

Before I started working on this series, I was thinking of what I wanted to draw that excites me... ♥ That's how I came up with the "master and servant" relationship. I decided to draw it when I was given the opportunity to do a one-shot, but I struggled with finding the exact relationship I wanted to depict. The one-shot was for an issue of the magazine that releases around Christmas, so I finally managed to come up with this idea. I thought, "Hey! There's a very famous master and servant(?) relationship connected to Christmas!!" That's how this story came into being.

I get to draw animals too, which makes me even happier. ♥

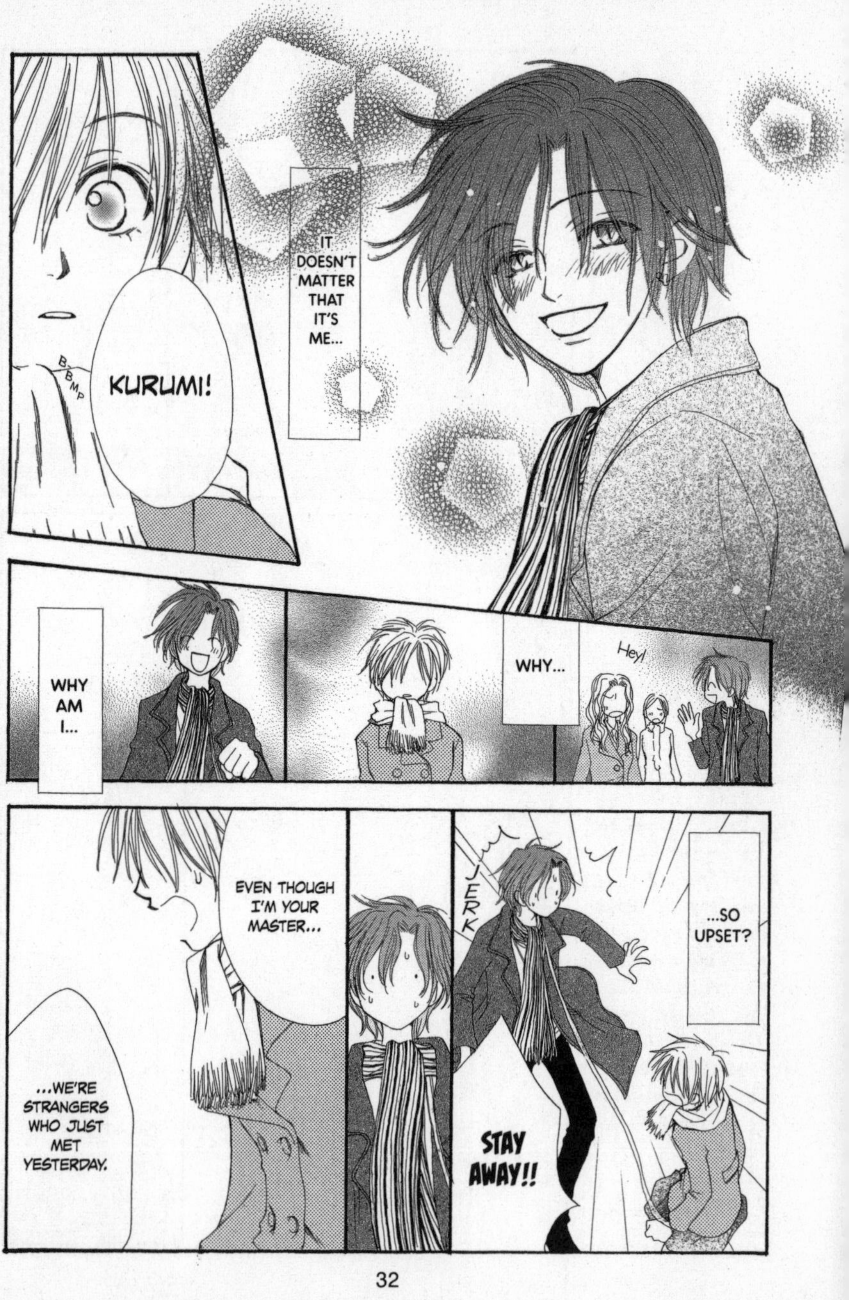
IT DOESN'T MATTER THAT IT'S ME...
KURUMI!
BBMP
WHY...
Hey!
WHY AM I...
...SO UPSET?
JERK
STAY AWAY!!
EVEN THOUGH I'M YOUR MASTER...
...WE'RE STRANGERS WHO JUST MET YESTERDAY.

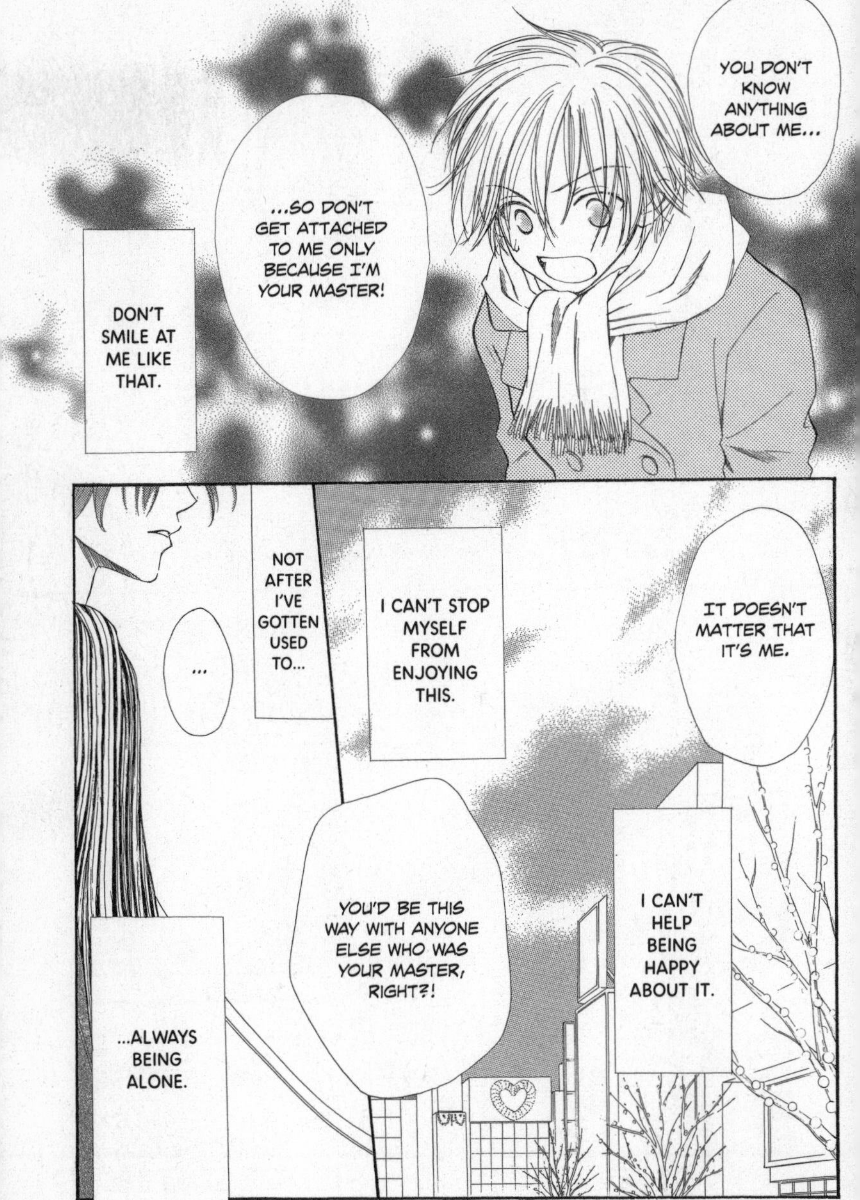
YOU DON'T KNOW ANYTHING ABOUT ME...
...SO DON'T GET ATTACHED TO ME ONLY BECAUSE I'M YOUR MASTER!
DON'T SMILE AT ME LIKE THAT.
IT DOESN'T MATTER THAT IT'S ME.
YOU'D BE THIS WAY WITH ANYONE ELSE WHO WAS YOUR MASTER, RIGHT?!
I CAN'T STOP MYSELF FROM ENJOYING THIS.
I CAN'T HELP BEING HAPPY ABOUT IT.
NOT AFTER I'VE GOTTEN USED TO...
...
...ALWAYS BEING ALONE.

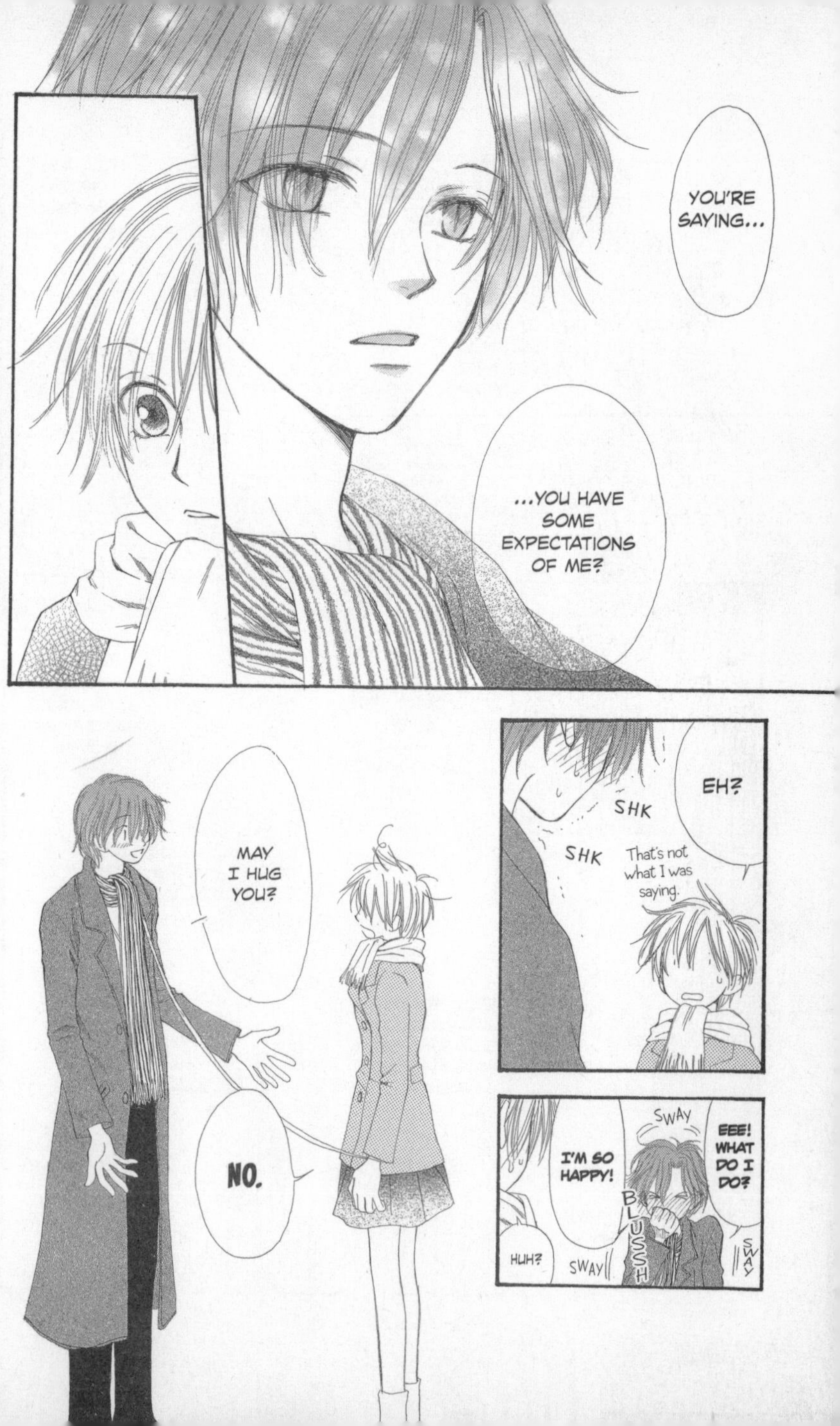
YOU'RE SAYING...
...YOU HAVE SOME EXPECTATIONS OF ME?
EH?
SHK
SHK
That's not what I was saying.
SWAY
EEE! WHAT DO I DO?
I'M SO HAPPY!
SWAY
BLUSSH
SWAY
HUH?
MAY I HUG YOU?
NO.

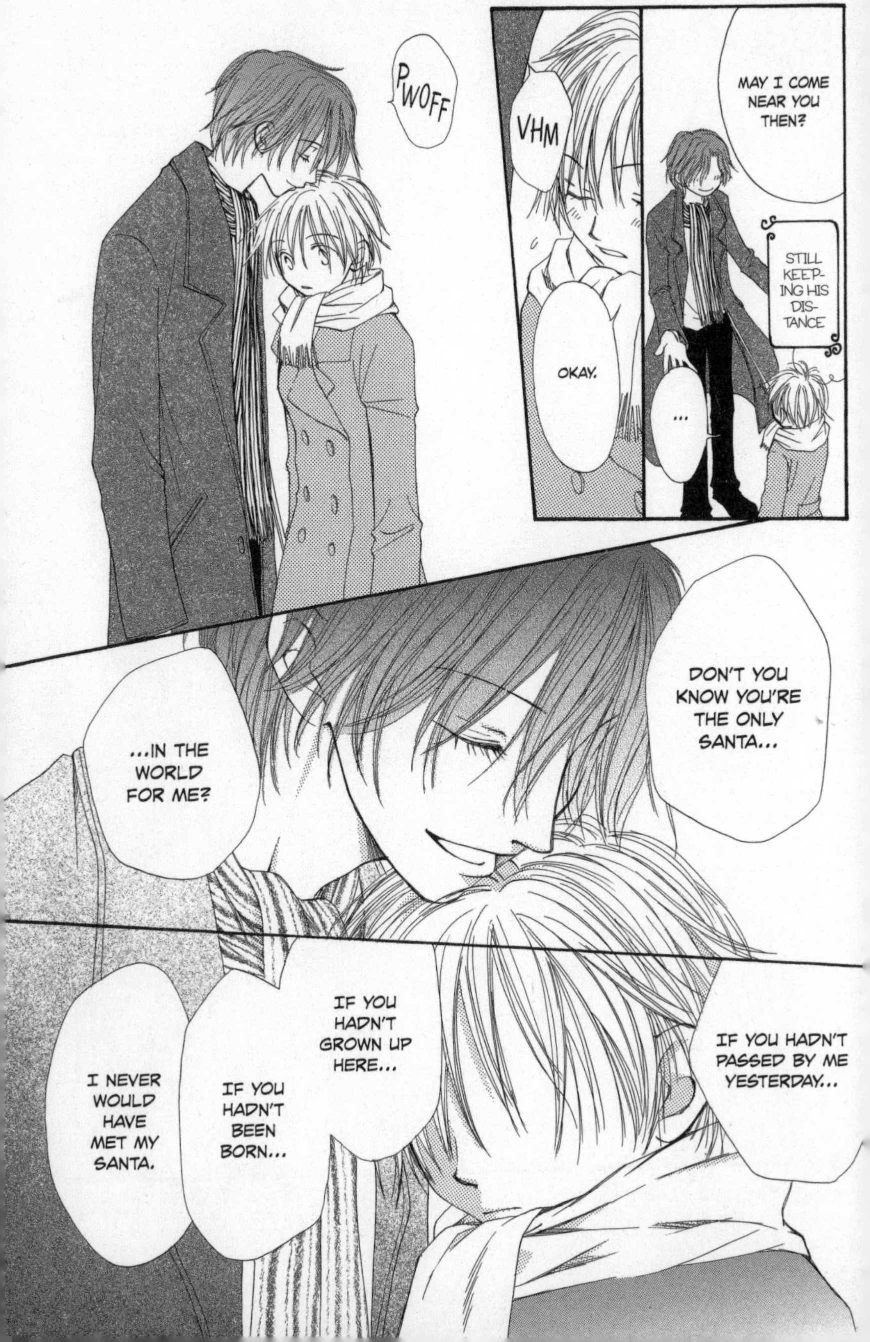
MAY I COME NEAR YOU THEN?
STILL KEEPING HIS DISTANCE
...
VHM
OKAY.
PWOFF
DON'T YOU KNOW YOU'RE THE ONLY SANTA...
...IN THE WORLD FOR ME?
IF YOU HADN'T PASSED BY ME YESTERDAY...
IF YOU HADN'T GROWN UP HERE...
IF YOU HADN'T BEEN BORN...
I NEVER WOULD HAVE MET MY SANTA.

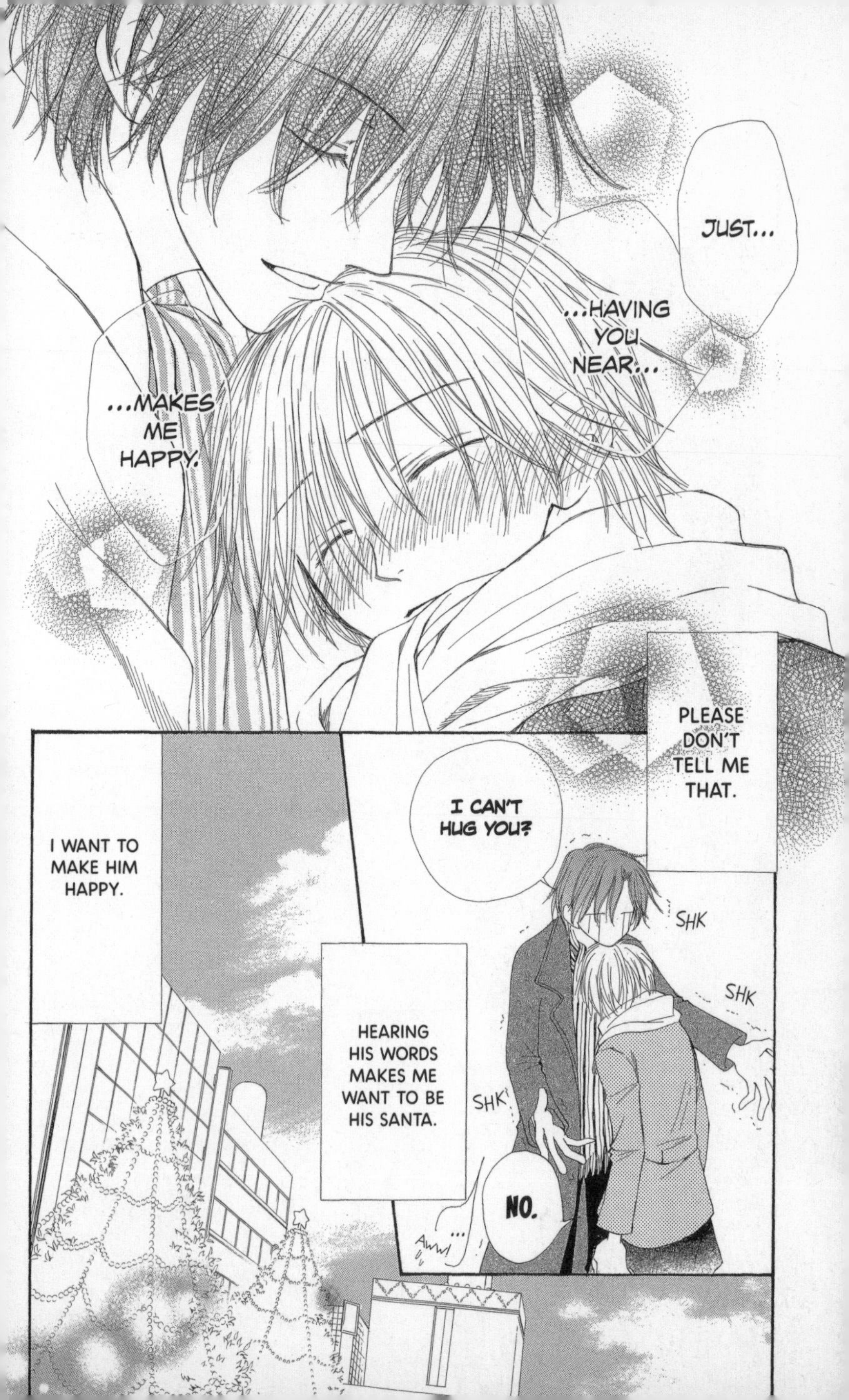
JUST...
...HAVING YOU NEAR...
...MAKES ME HAPPY.
PLEASE DON'T TELL ME THAT.
I CAN'T HUG YOU?
SHK
SHK
SHK
NO.
...
AWW!
HEARING HIS WORDS MAKES ME WANT TO BE HIS SANTA.
I WANT TO MAKE HIM HAPPY.

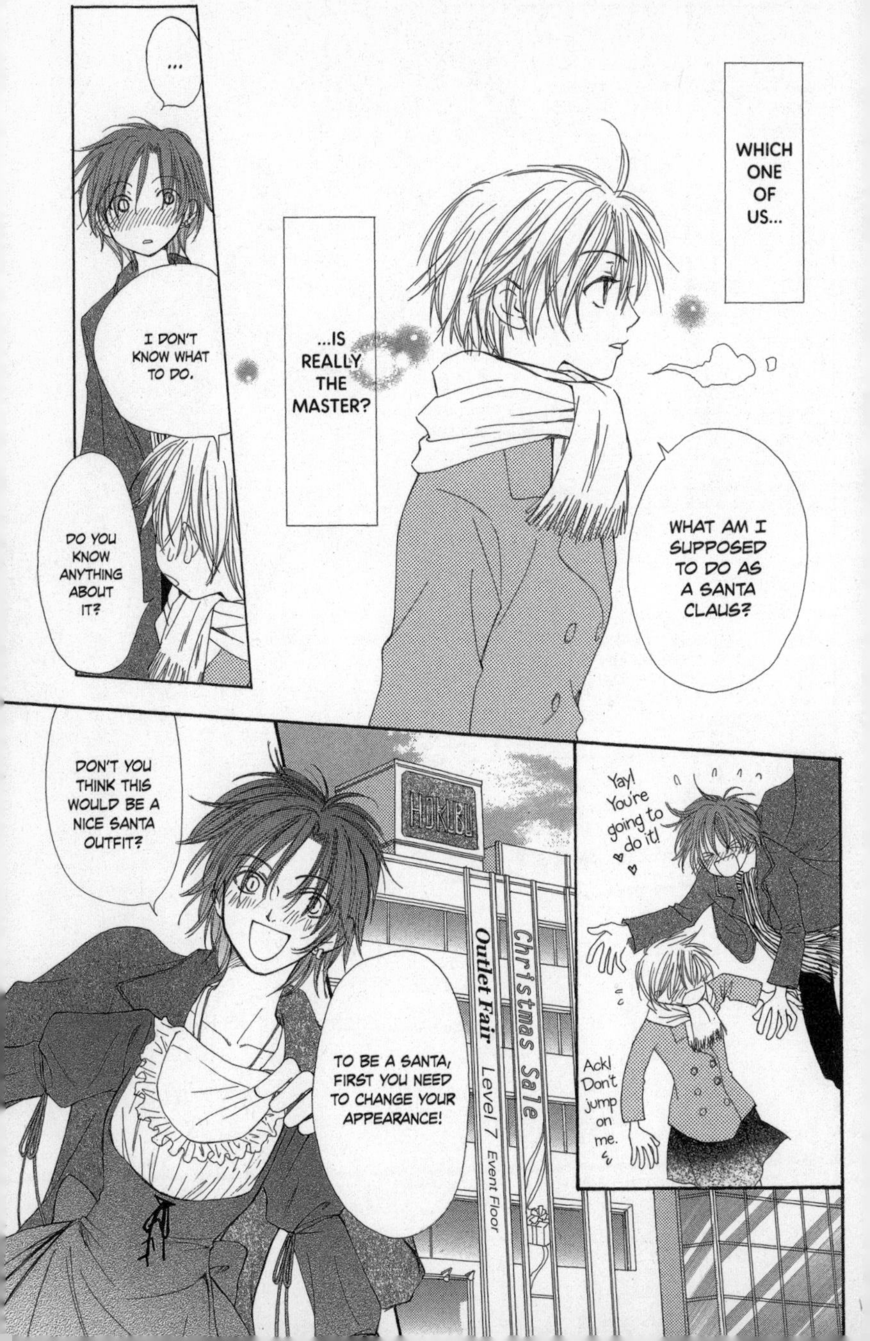
WHICH ONE OF US...
...IS REALLY THE MASTER?
WHAT AM I SUPPOSED TO DO AS A SANTA CLAUS?
...
I DON'T KNOW WHAT TO DO.
DO YOU KNOW ANYTHING ABOUT IT?
Yay! You're going to do it!
Ack! Don't jump on me.
DON'T YOU THINK THIS WOULD BE A NICE SANTA OUTFIT?
HOKUBU
Christmas Sale
Outlet Fair
Level 7 Event Floor
TO BE A SANTA, FIRST YOU NEED TO CHANGE YOUR APPEARANCE!

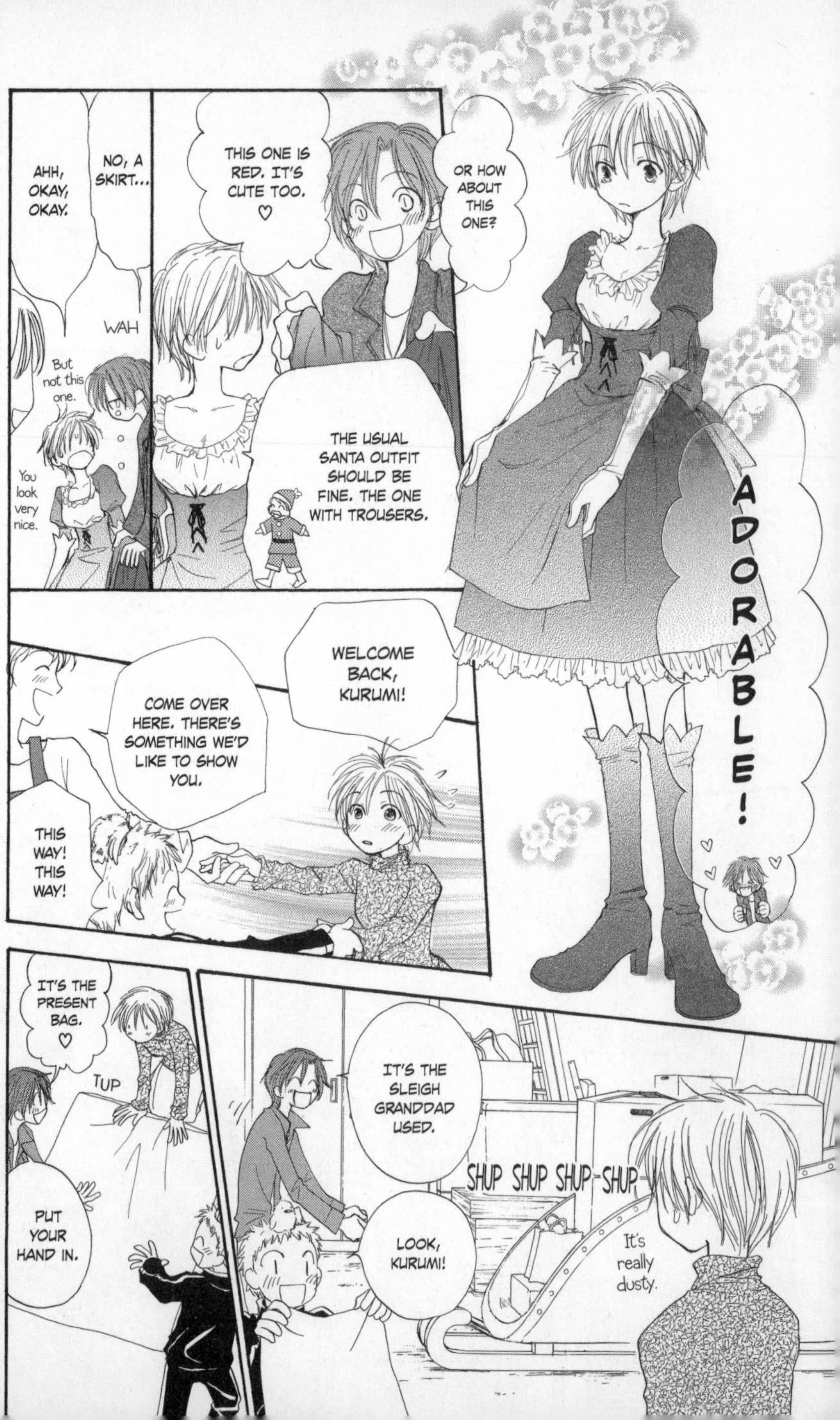
ADORABLE!
OR HOW ABOUT THIS ONE?
THIS ONE IS RED. IT'S CUTE TOO. ♡
THE USUAL SANTA OUTFIT SHOULD BE FINE. THE ONE WITH TROUSERS.
NO, A SKIRT...
AHH, OKAY, OKAY.
WAH
But not this one.
You look very nice.
WELCOME BACK, KURUMI!
COME OVER HERE. THERE'S SOMETHING WE'D LIKE TO SHOW YOU.
THIS WAY! THIS WAY!
It's really dusty.
SHUP SHUP SHUP SHUP
IT'S THE SLEIGH GRANDDAD USED.
LOOK, KURUMI!
IT'S THE PRESENT BAG. ♡
TUP
PUT YOUR HAND IN.

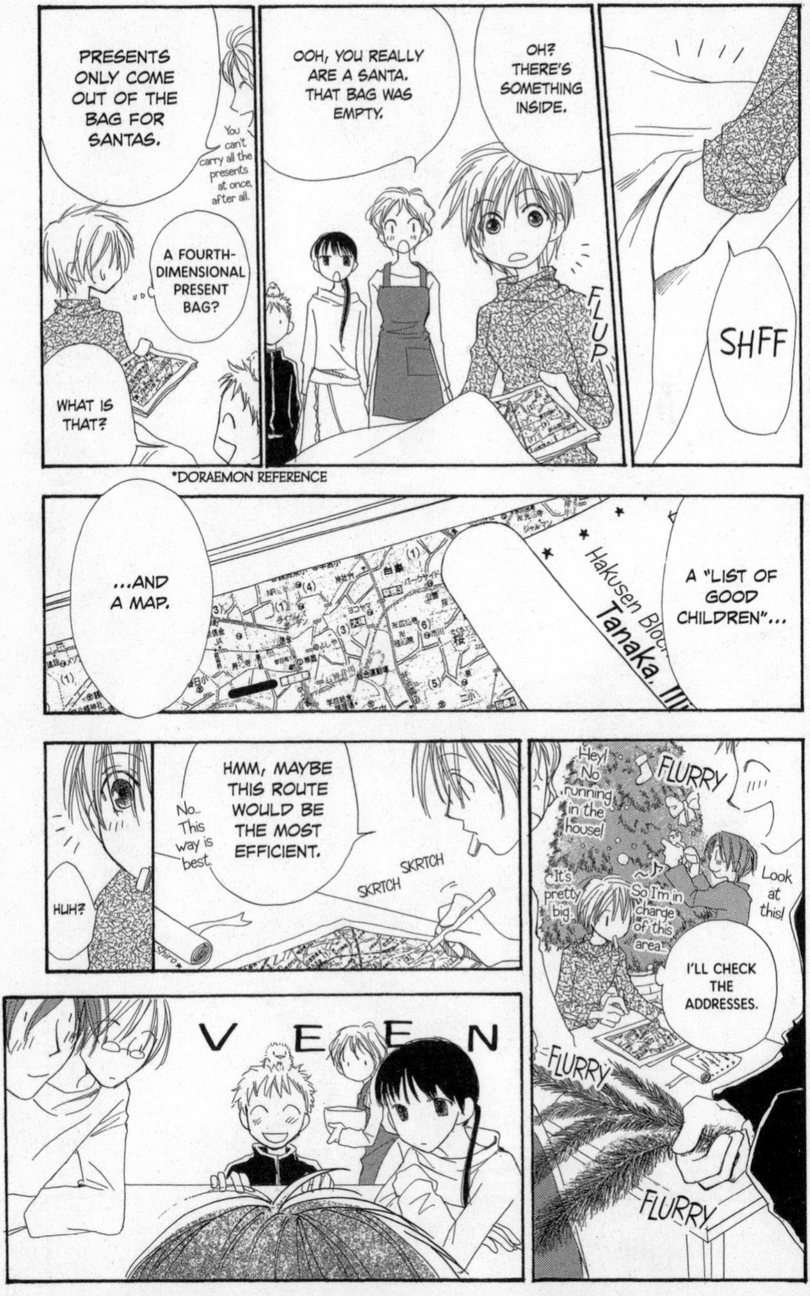
SHFF
OH? THERE'S SOMETHING INSIDE.
FLUP
OOH, YOU REALLY ARE A SANTA. THAT BAG WAS EMPTY.
PRESENTS ONLY COME OUT OF THE BAG FOR SANTAS.
You can't carry all the presents at once, after all.
A FOURTH-DIMENSIONAL PRESENT BAG?
WHAT IS THAT?
*DORAEMON REFERENCE
A "LIST OF GOOD CHILDREN"...
Hakusen Block
Tanaka.
...AND A MAP.
FLURRY
Hey! No running in the house!
Look at this!
So I'm in charge of this area.
It's pretty big.
I'LL CHECK THE ADDRESSES.
FLURRY
FLURRY
HMM, MAYBE THIS ROUTE WOULD BE THE MOST EFFICIENT.
SKRTCH
SKRTCH
No... This way is best.
HUH?
VEEN

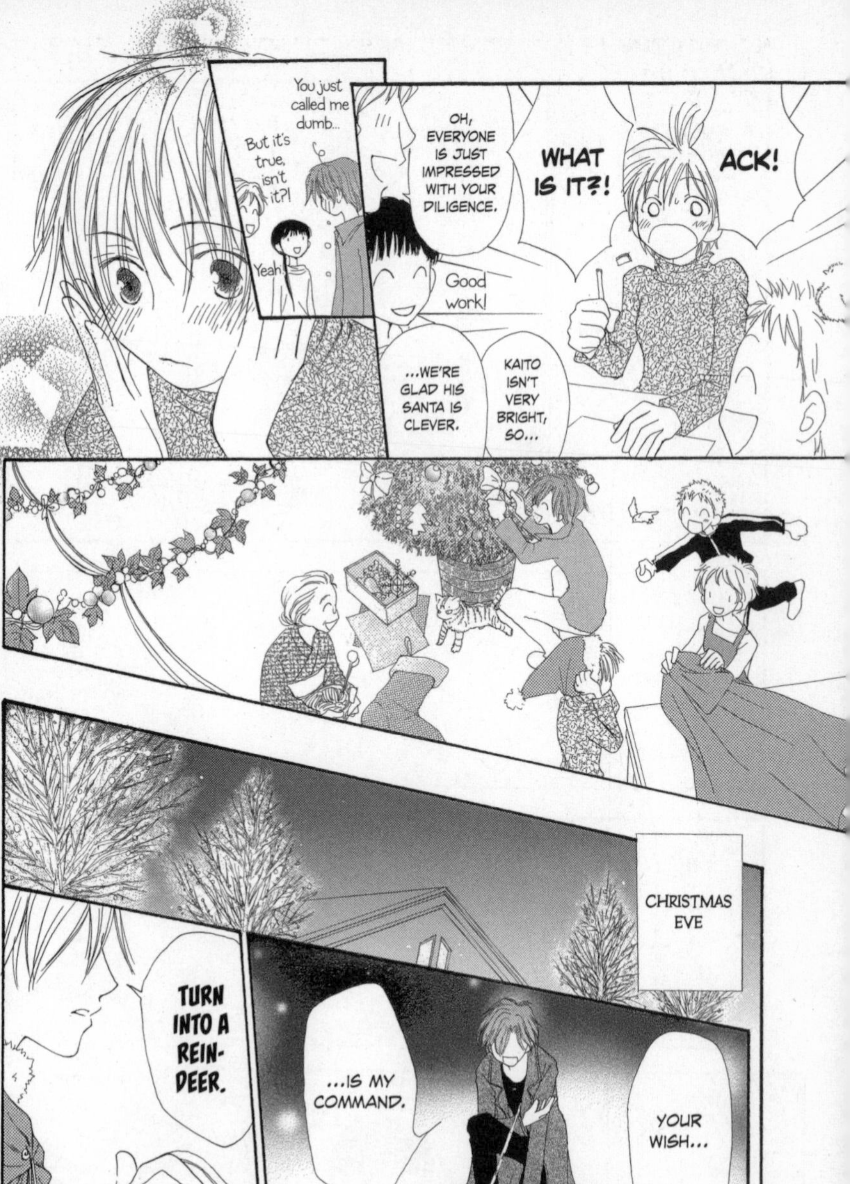
ACK!
WHAT IS IT?!
OH, EVERYONE IS JUST IMPRESSED WITH YOUR DILIGENCE.
Good work!
KAITO ISN'T VERY BRIGHT, SO...
...WE'RE GLAD HIS SANTA IS CLEVER.
You just called me dumb...
But it's true, isn't it?!
Yeah!
CHRISTMAS EVE
YOUR WISH...
...IS MY COMMAND.
TURN INTO A REIN-DEER.

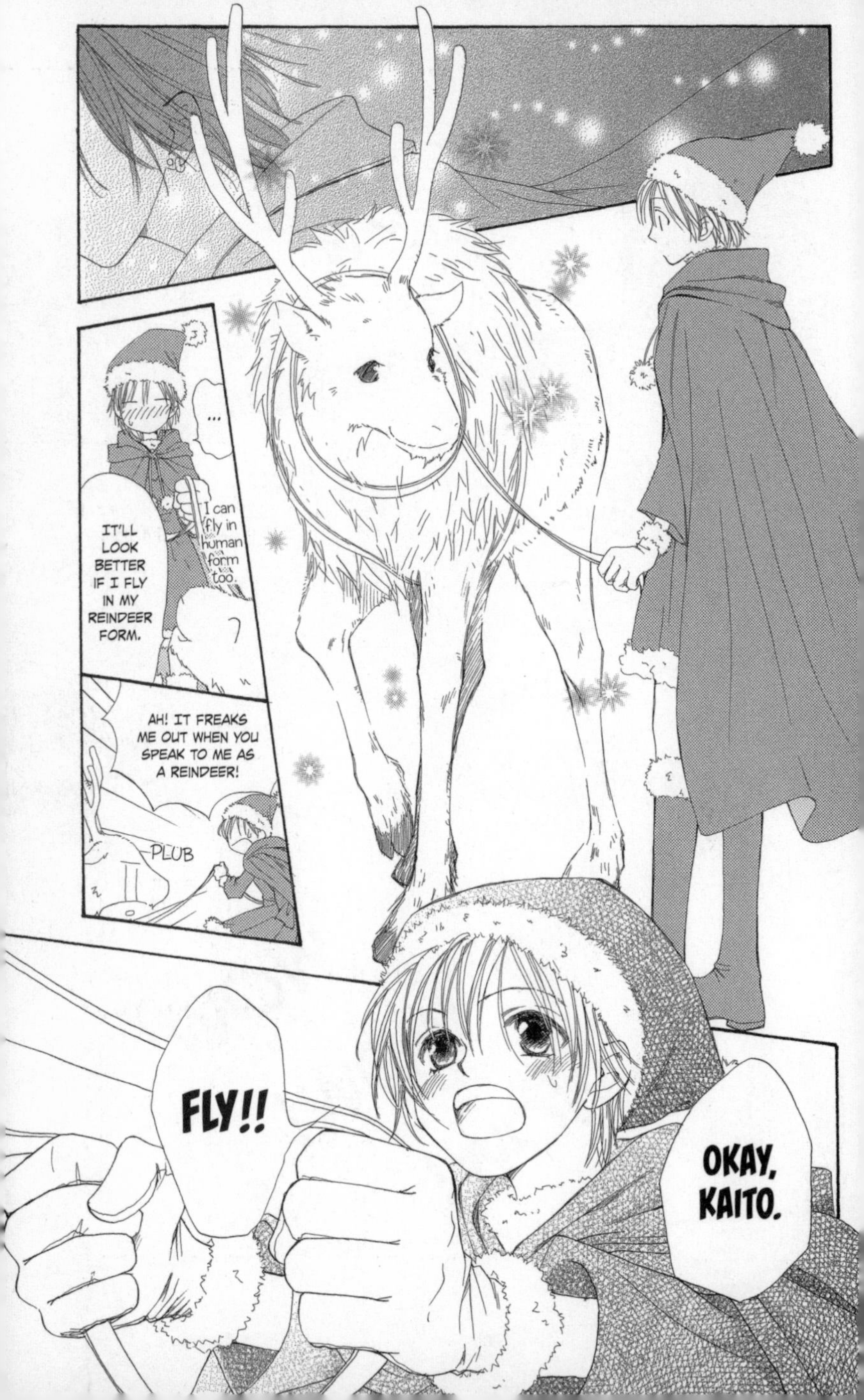
...
I can fly in human form too.
IT'LL LOOK BETTER IF I FLY IN MY REINDEER FORM.
AH! IT FREAKS ME OUT WHEN YOU SPEAK TO ME AS A REINDEER!
PLUB
OKAY, KAITO.
FLY!!

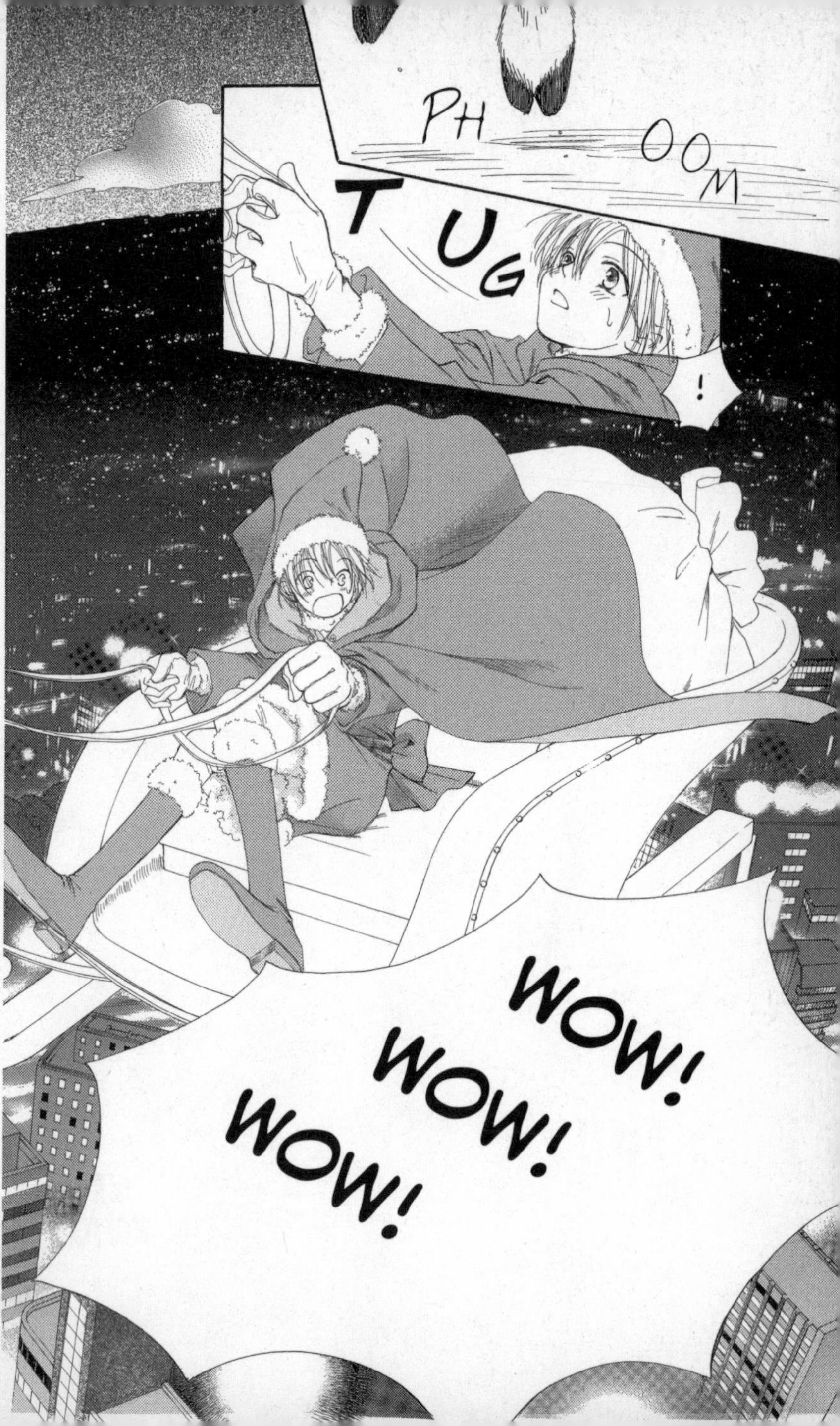
PH OOM
TUG
!
WOW! WOW! WOW!

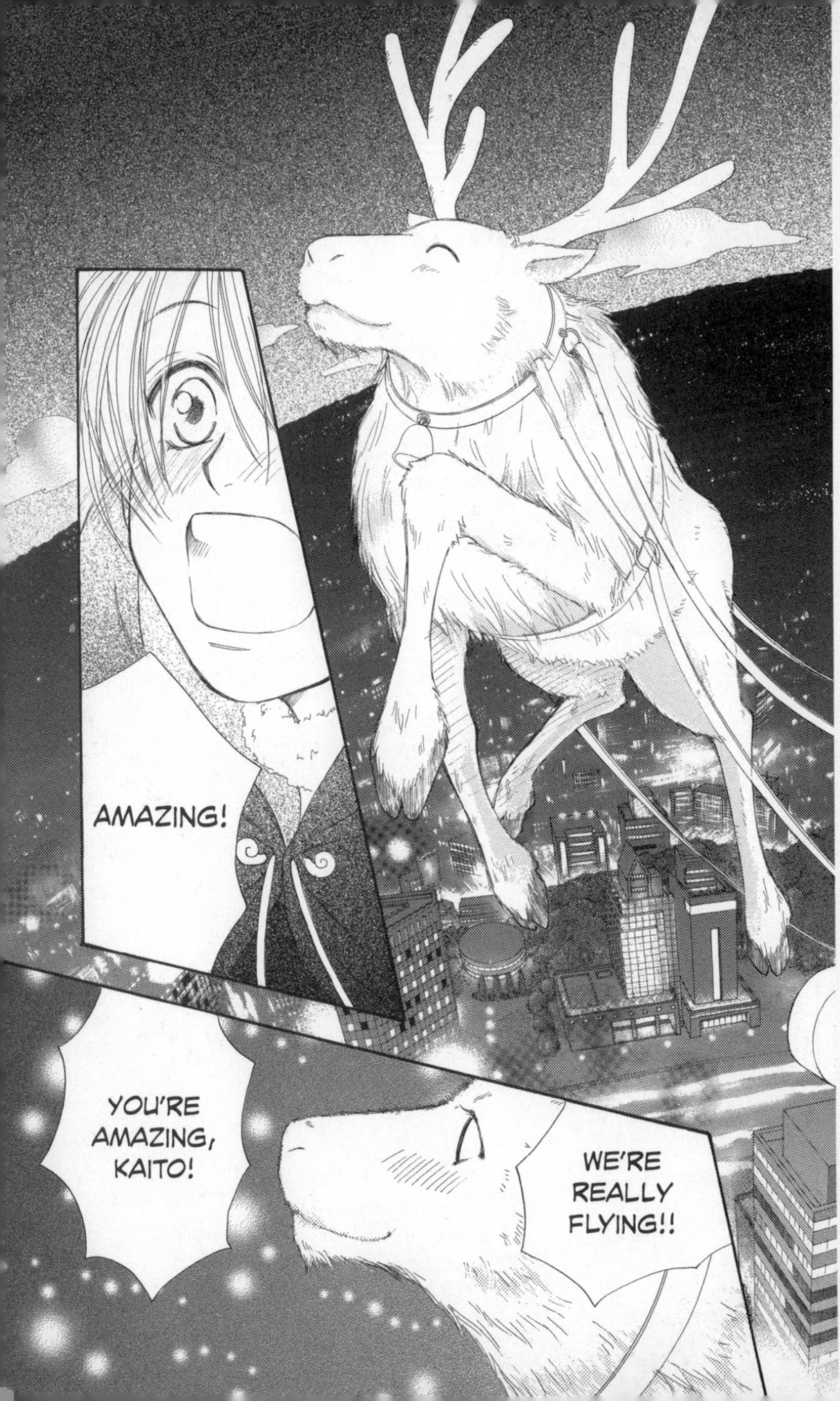
AMAZING!
WE'RE REALLY FLYING!!
YOU'RE AMAZING, KAITO!

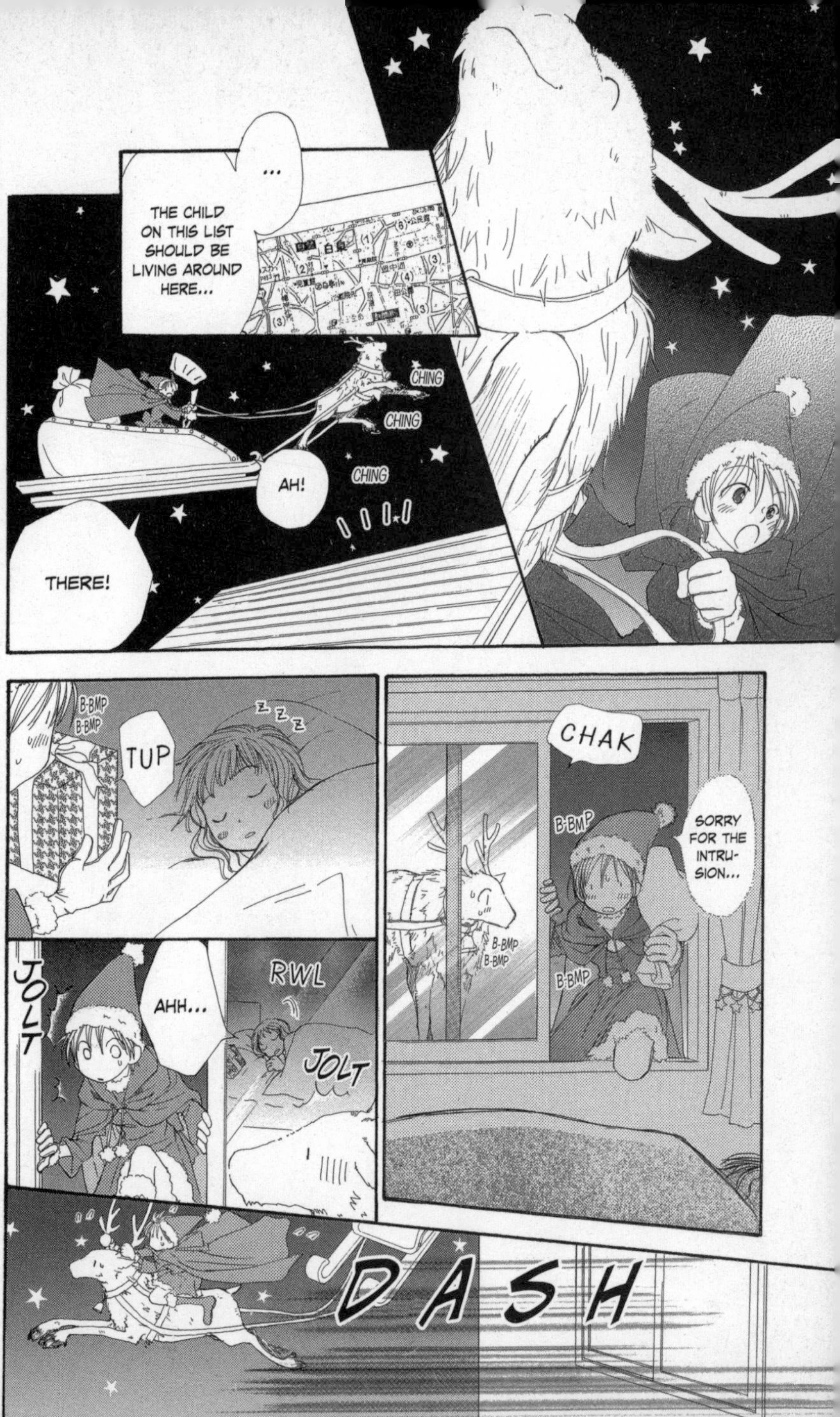
...
THE CHILD ON THIS LIST SHOULD BE LIVING AROUND HERE...
CHING
CHING
CHING
AH!
THERE!
CHAK
B-BMP
SORRY FOR THE INTRU-SION...
B-BMP
B-BMP
B-BMP
B-BMP
B-BMP
TUP
Z Z Z
RWL
JOLT
AHH...
JOLT
DASH

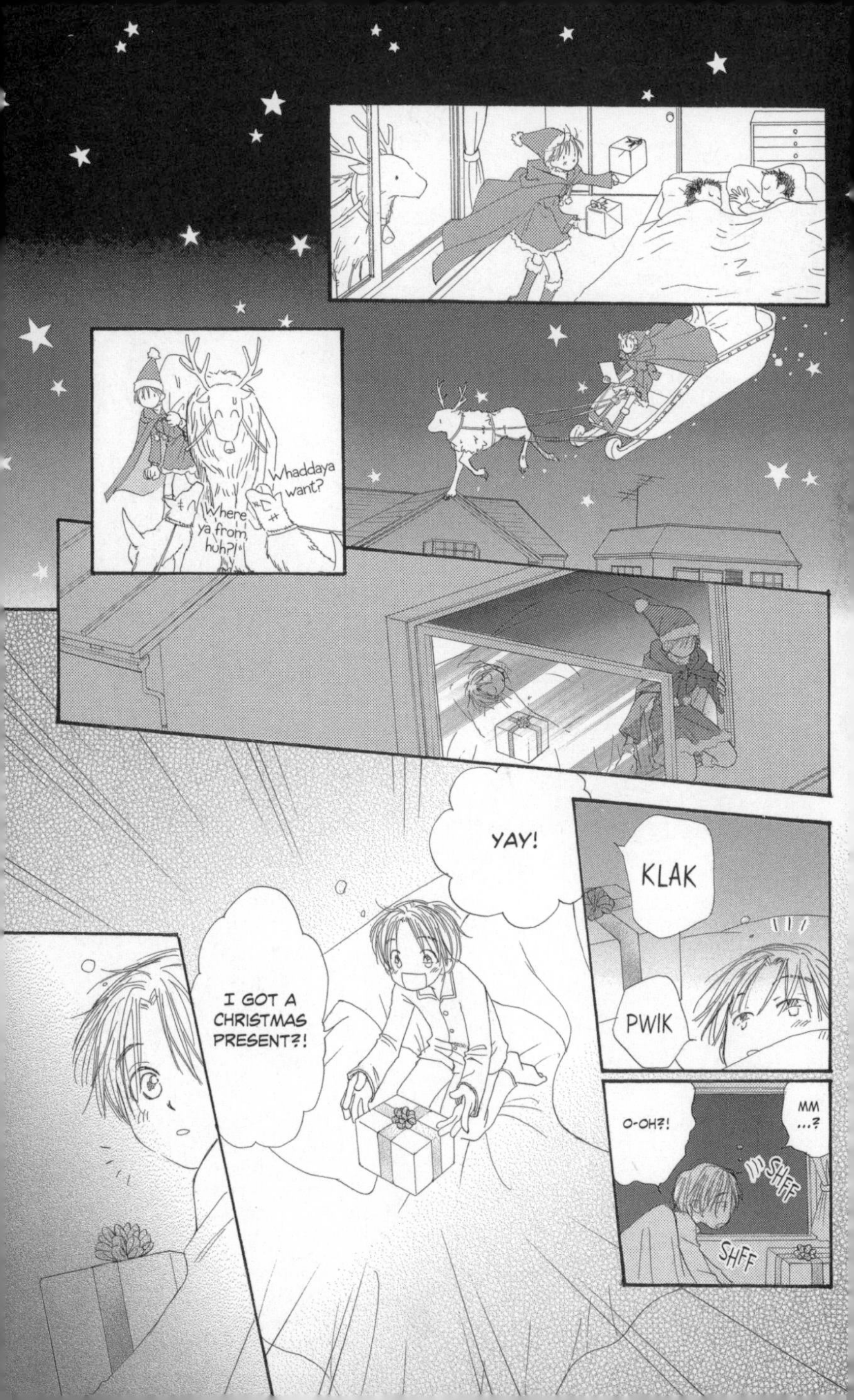
Whaddaya want?
Where ya from, huh?!
KLAK
PWIK
MM ...?
O-OH?!
SHFF
SHFF
YAY!
I GOT A CHRISTMAS PRESENT?!

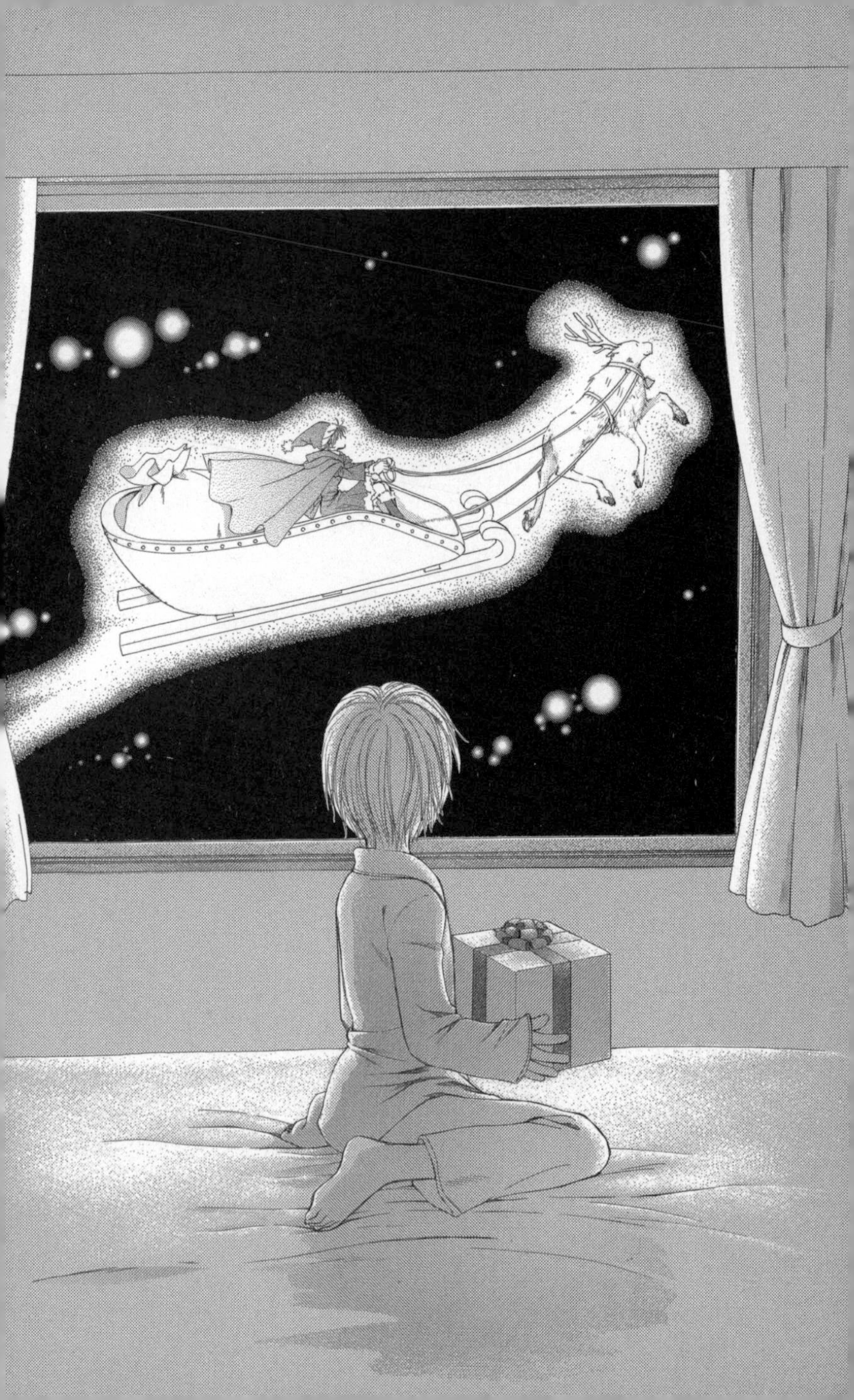

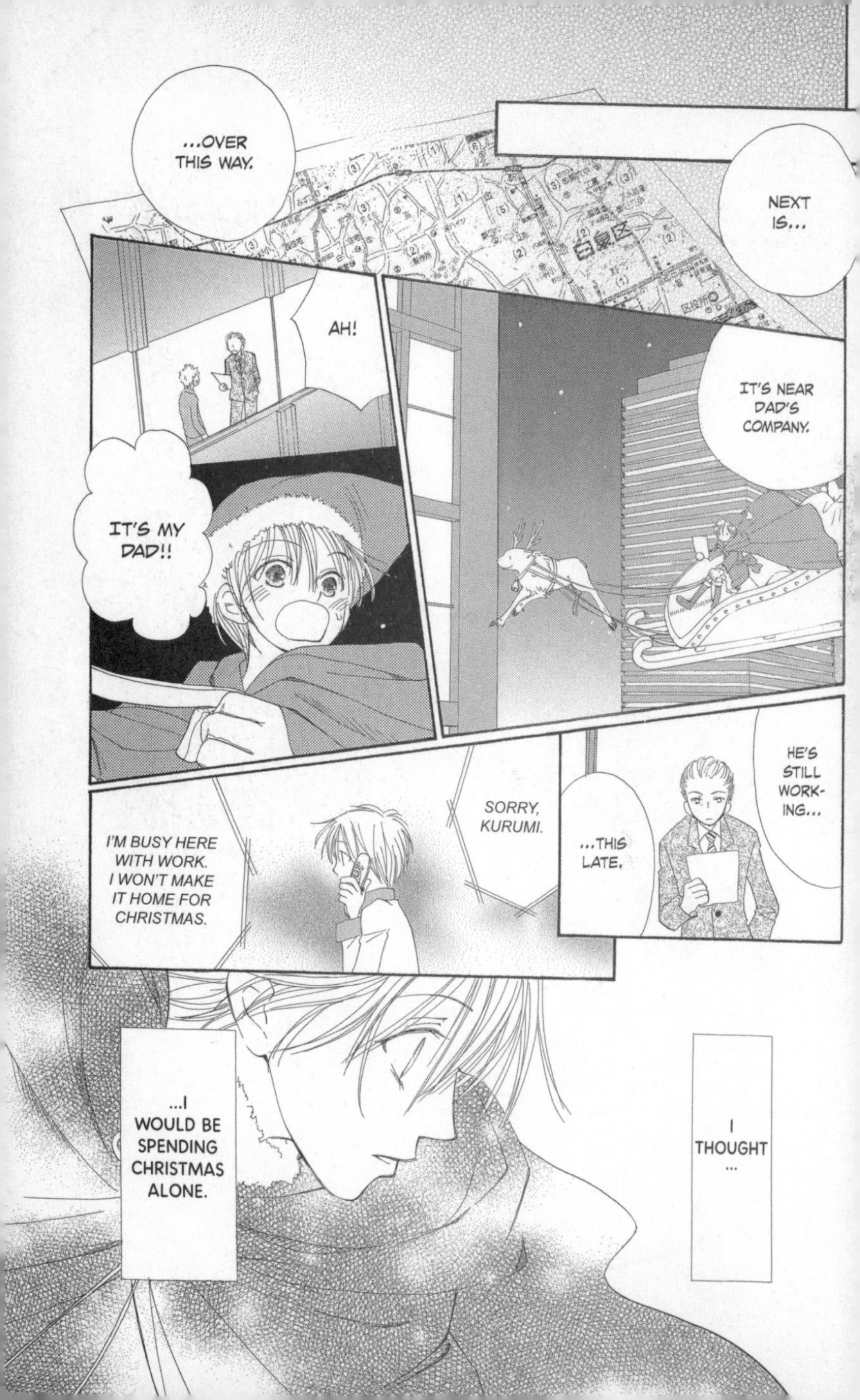
NEXT IS...
...OVER THIS WAY.
白泉区
IT'S NEAR DAD'S COMPANY.
AH!
IT'S MY DAD!!
HE'S STILL WORKING...
...THIS LATE.
SORRY, KURUMI.
I'M BUSY HERE WITH WORK. I WON'T MAKE IT HOME FOR CHRISTMAS.
I THOUGHT...
...I WOULD BE SPENDING CHRISTMAS ALONE.

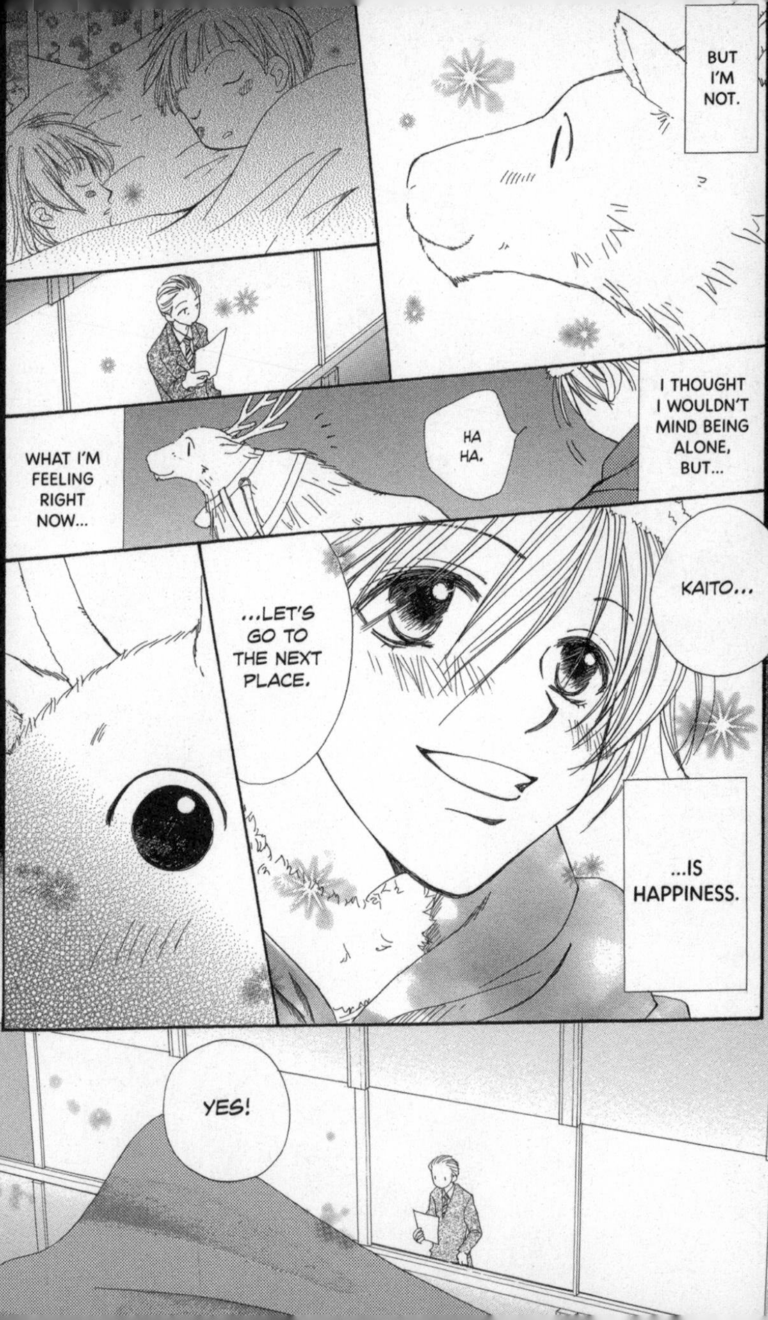
BUT I'M NOT.
I THOUGHT I WOULDN'T MIND BEING ALONE, BUT...
HA HA.
WHAT I'M FEELING RIGHT NOW...
KAITO...
...IS HAPPINESS.
...LET'S GO TO THE NEXT PLACE.
YES!

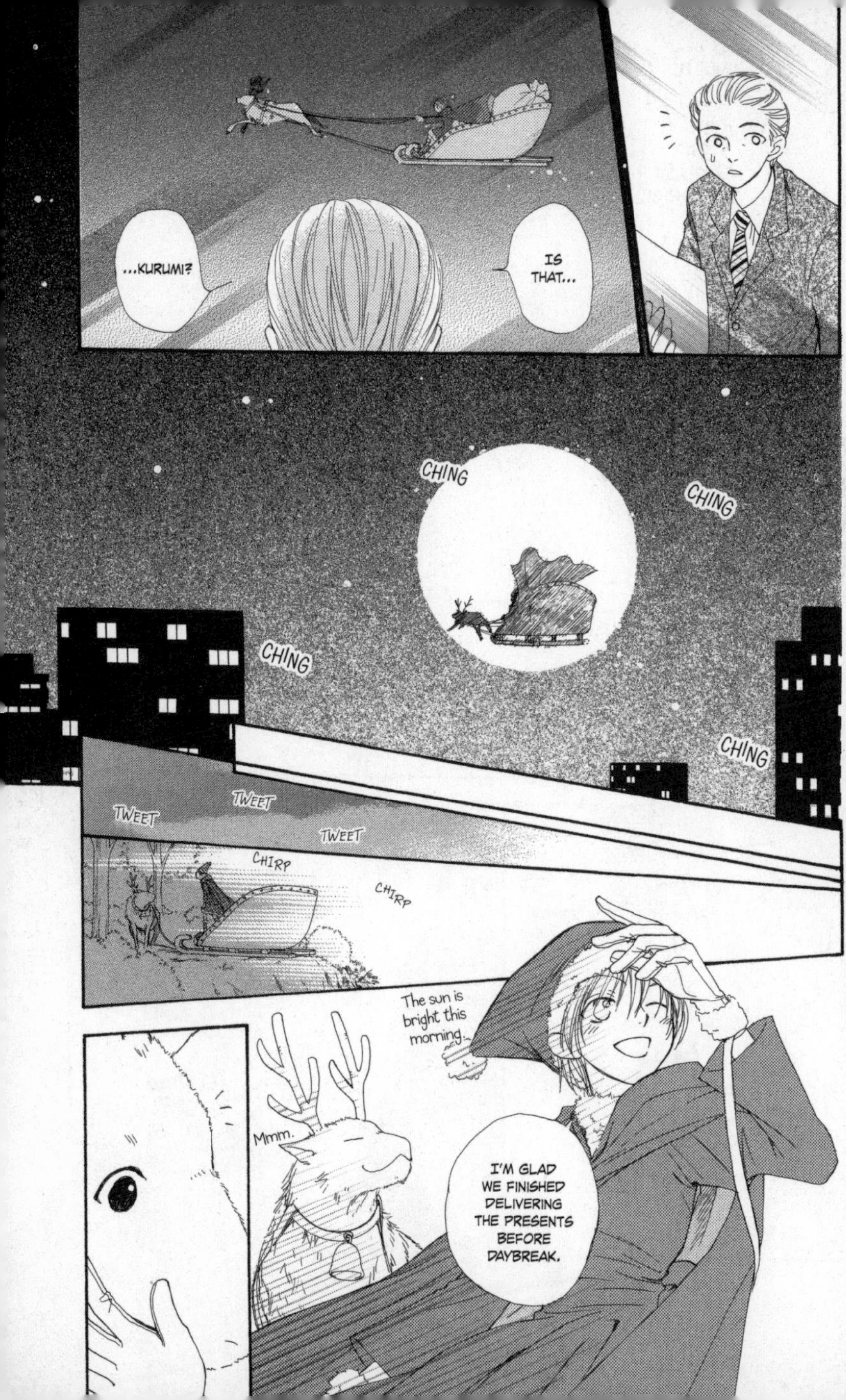
IS THAT...
...KURUMI?
CHING
CHING
CHING
CHING
TWEET
TWEET
TWEET
CHIRP
CHIRP
The sun is bright this morning.
I'M GLAD WE FINISHED DELIVERING THE PRESENTS BEFORE DAYBREAK.
Mmm.

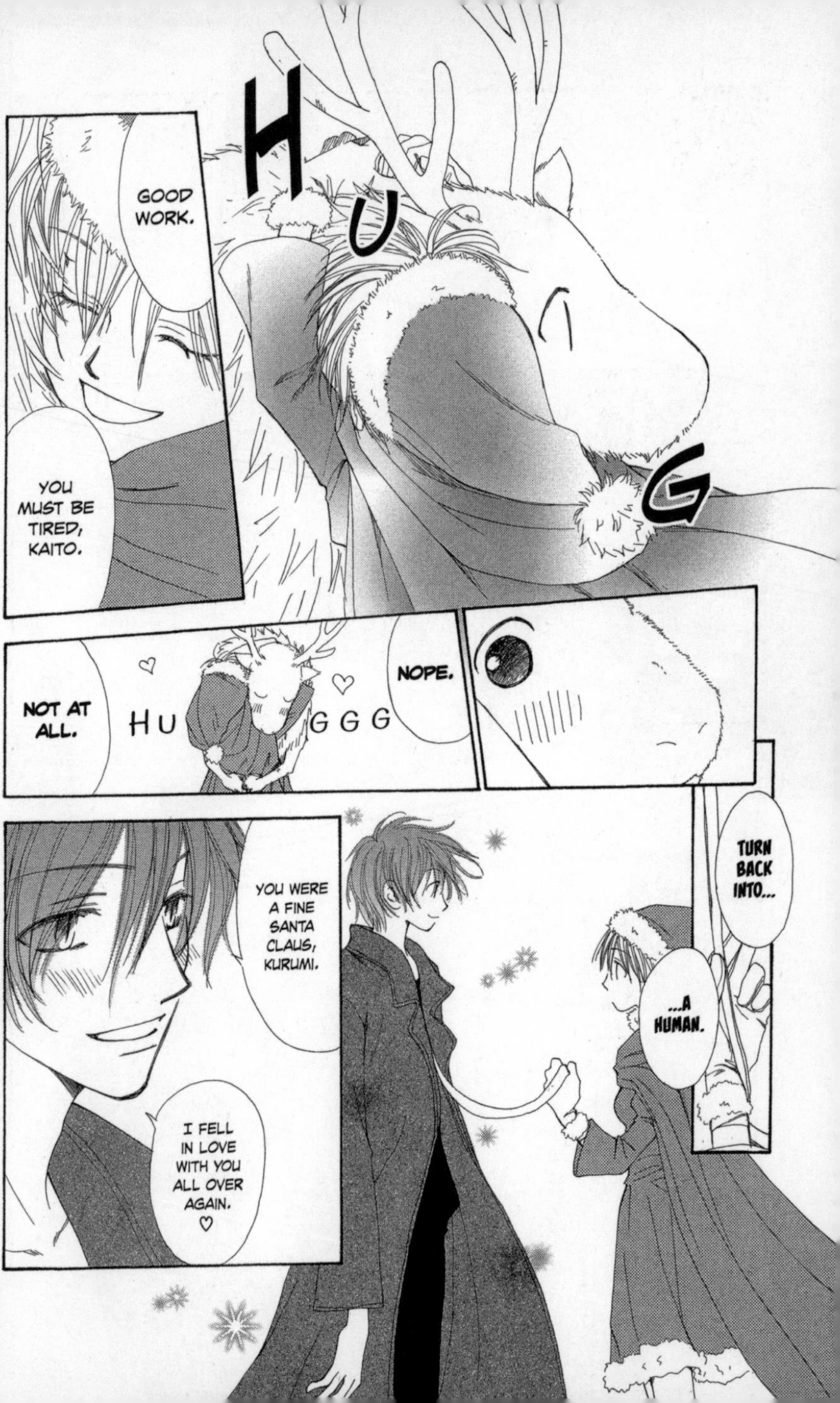
HUG
GOOD WORK.
YOU MUST BE TIRED, KAITO.
NOPE.
HUGGG
NOT AT ALL.
TURN BACK INTO...
...A HUMAN.
YOU WERE A FINE SANTA CLAUS, KURUMI.
I FELL IN LOVE WITH YOU ALL OVER AGAIN. ♡

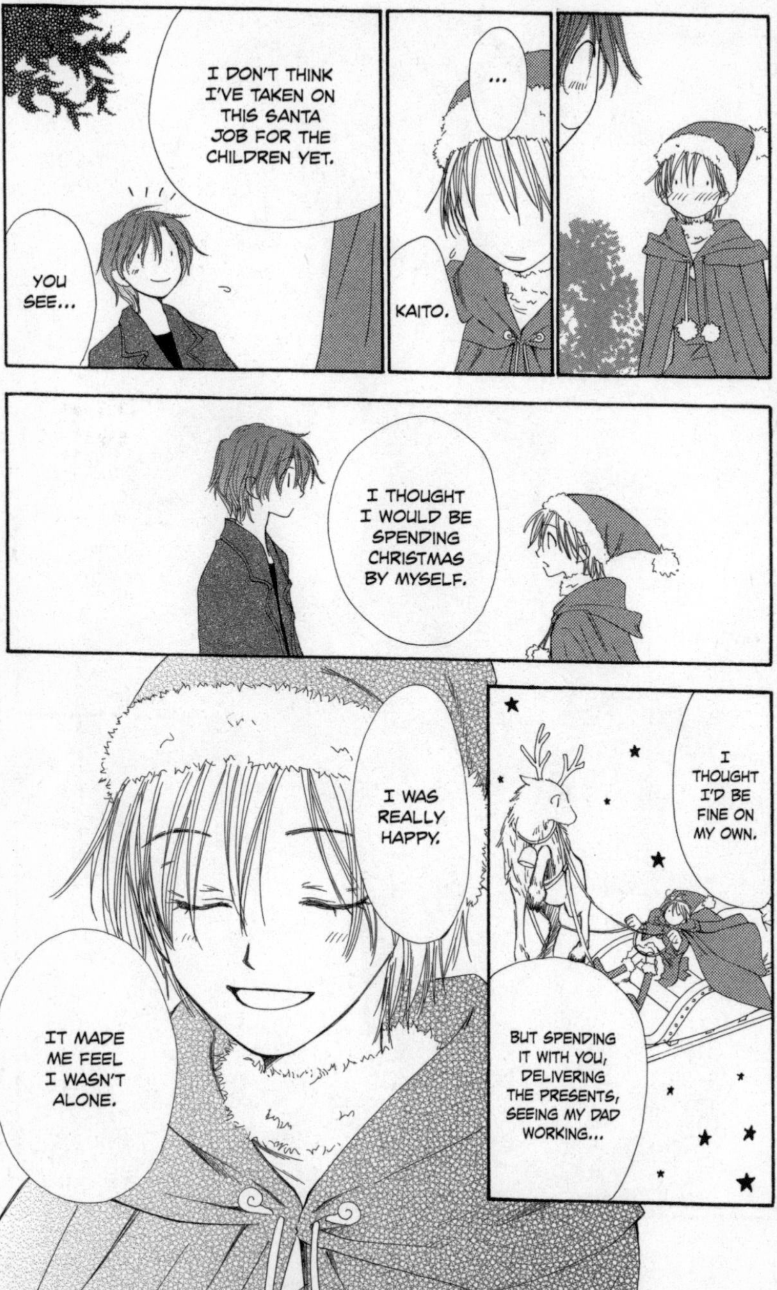
...
KAITO.
I DON'T THINK I'VE TAKEN ON THIS SANTA JOB FOR THE CHILDREN YET.
YOU SEE...
I THOUGHT I WOULD BE SPENDING CHRISTMAS BY MYSELF.
I THOUGHT I'D BE FINE ON MY OWN.
BUT SPENDING IT WITH YOU, DELIVERING THE PRESENTS, SEEING MY DAD WORKING...
I WAS REALLY HAPPY.
IT MADE ME FEEL I WASN'T ALONE.

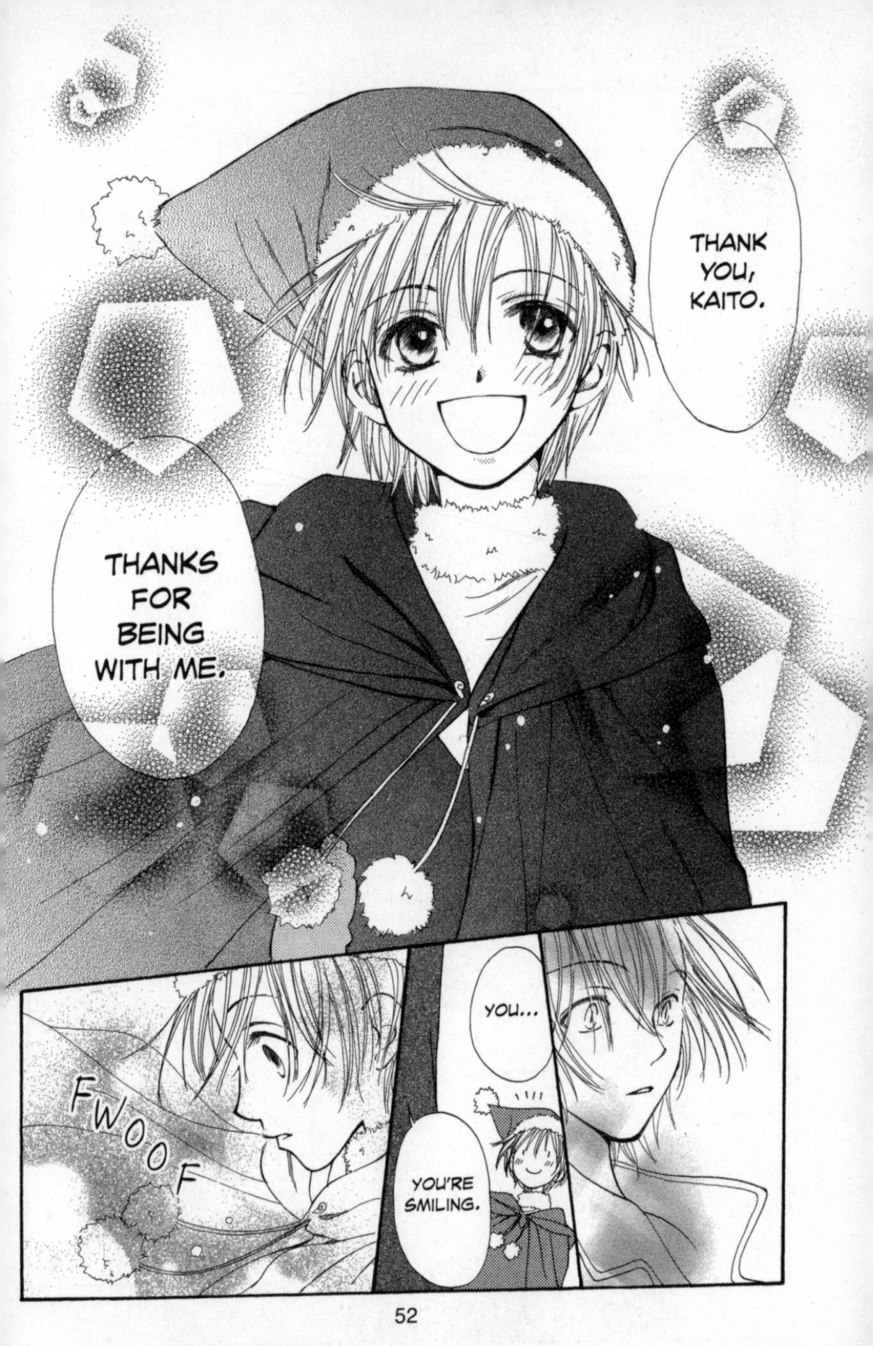
THANK YOU, KAITO.
THANKS FOR BEING WITH ME.
YOU...
YOU'RE SMILING.
FWOOF

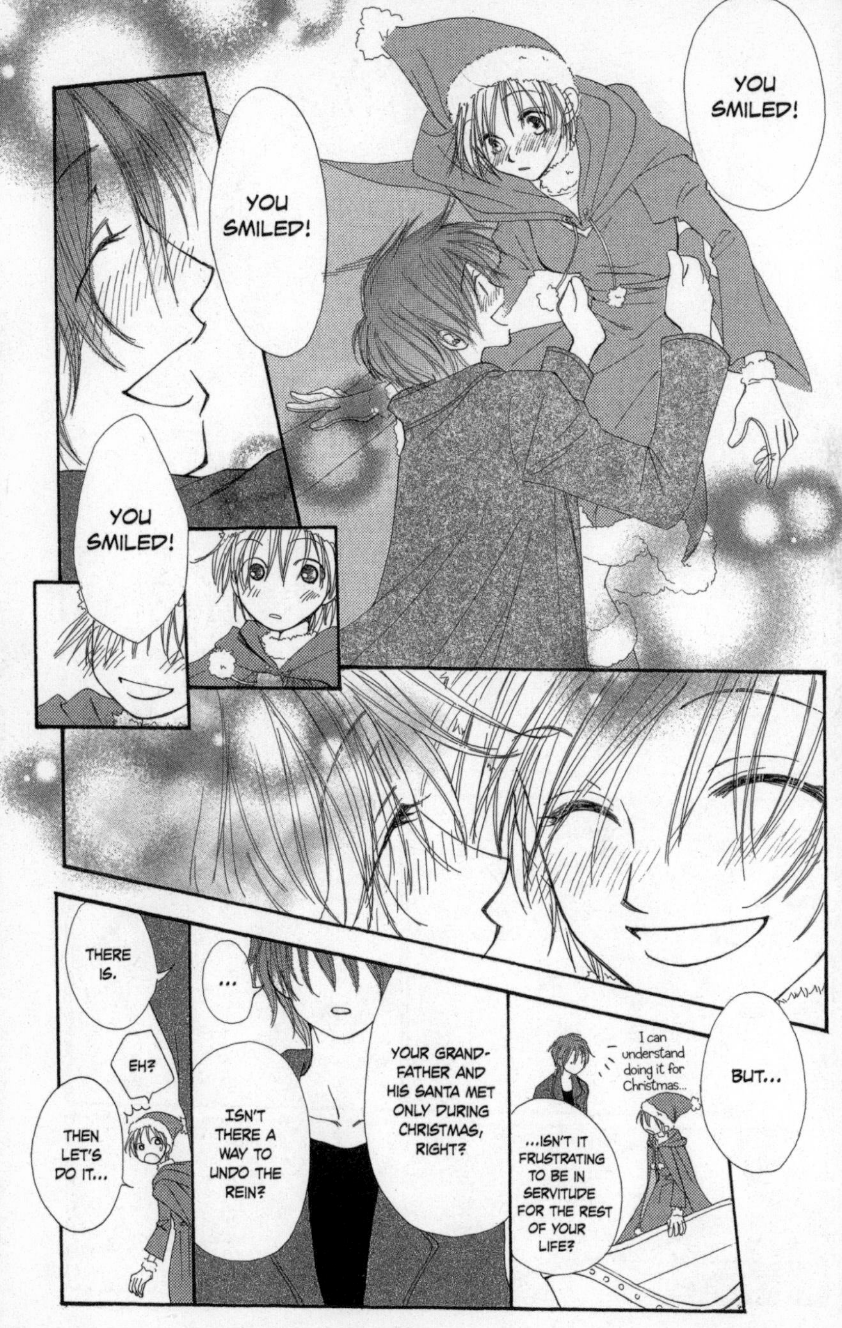
YOU SMILED!
YOU SMILED!
YOU SMILED!
BUT...
I can understand doing it for Christmas...
...ISN'T IT FRUSTRATING TO BE IN SERVITUDE FOR THE REST OF YOUR LIFE?
...
YOUR GRAND-FATHER AND HIS SANTA MET ONLY DURING CHRISTMAS, RIGHT?
ISN'T THERE A WAY TO UNDO THE REIN?
THERE IS.
EH?
THEN LET'S DO IT...

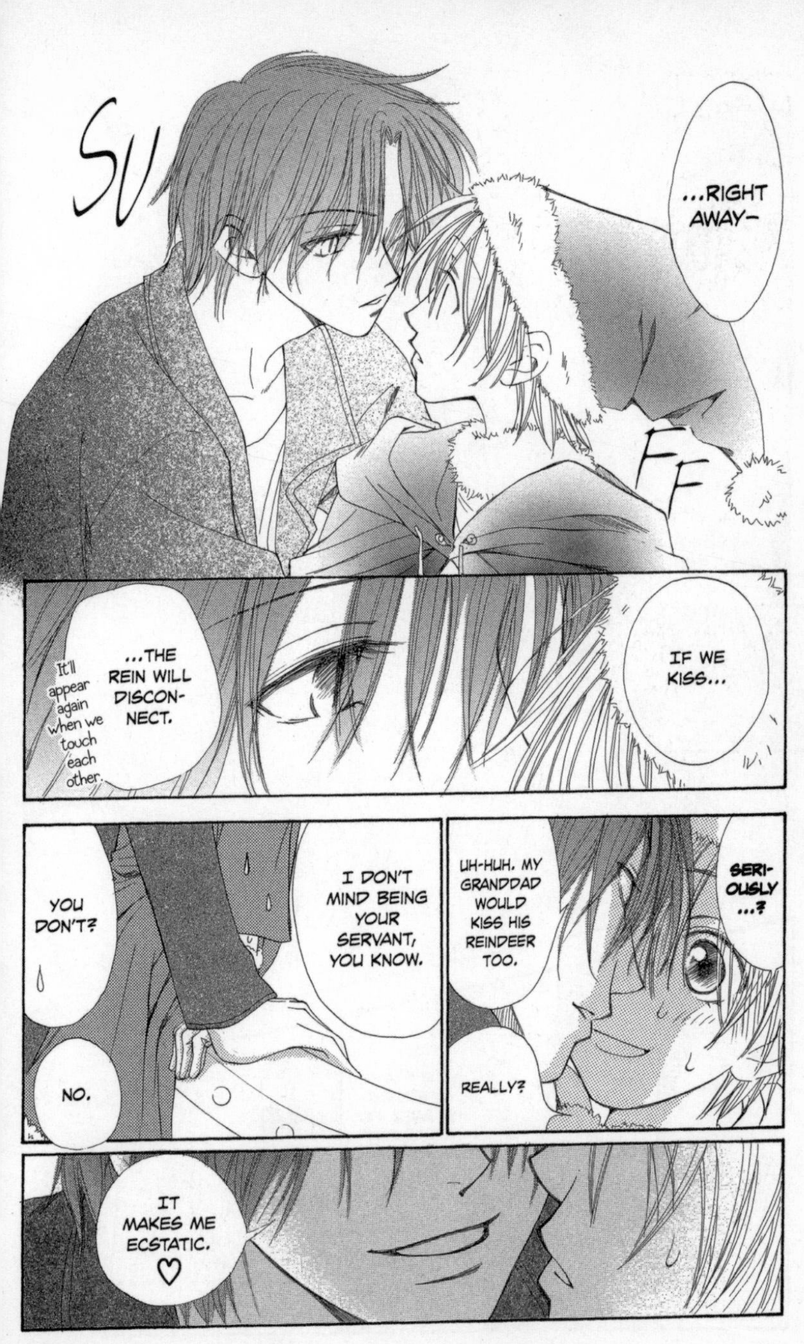
...RIGHT AWAY—
SU
FF
IF WE KISS...
...THE REIN WILL DISCONNECT.
It'll appear again when we touch each other.
SERIOUSLY...?
UH-HUH. MY GRANDDAD WOULD KISS HIS REINDEER TOO.
REALLY?
I DON'T MIND BEING YOUR SERVANT, YOU KNOW.
YOU DON'T?
NO.
IT MAKES ME ECSTATIC. ♡

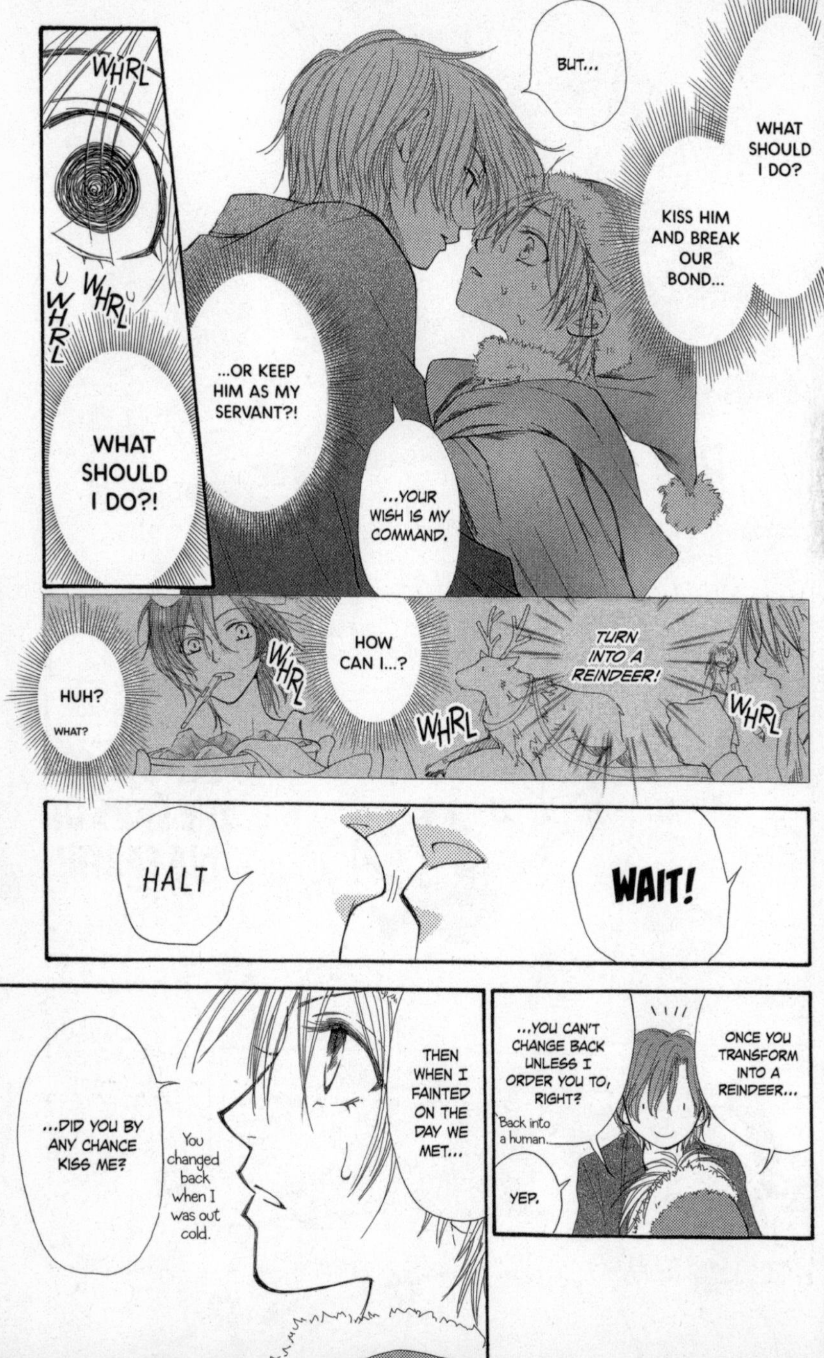
BUT...
WHAT SHOULD I DO?
KISS HIM AND BREAK OUR BOND...
...OR KEEP HIM AS MY SERVANT?!
...YOUR WISH IS MY COMMAND.
WHRL
WHRL
WHRL
WHAT SHOULD I DO?!
WHRL
TURN INTO A REINDEER!
WHRL
HOW CAN I...?
WHRL
HUH?
WHAT?
WAIT!
HALT
ONCE YOU TRANSFORM INTO A REINDEER...
...YOU CAN'T CHANGE BACK UNLESS I ORDER YOU TO, RIGHT?
Back into a human.
YEP.
THEN WHEN I FAINTED ON THE DAY WE MET...
You changed back when I was out cold.
...DID YOU BY ANY CHANCE KISS ME?

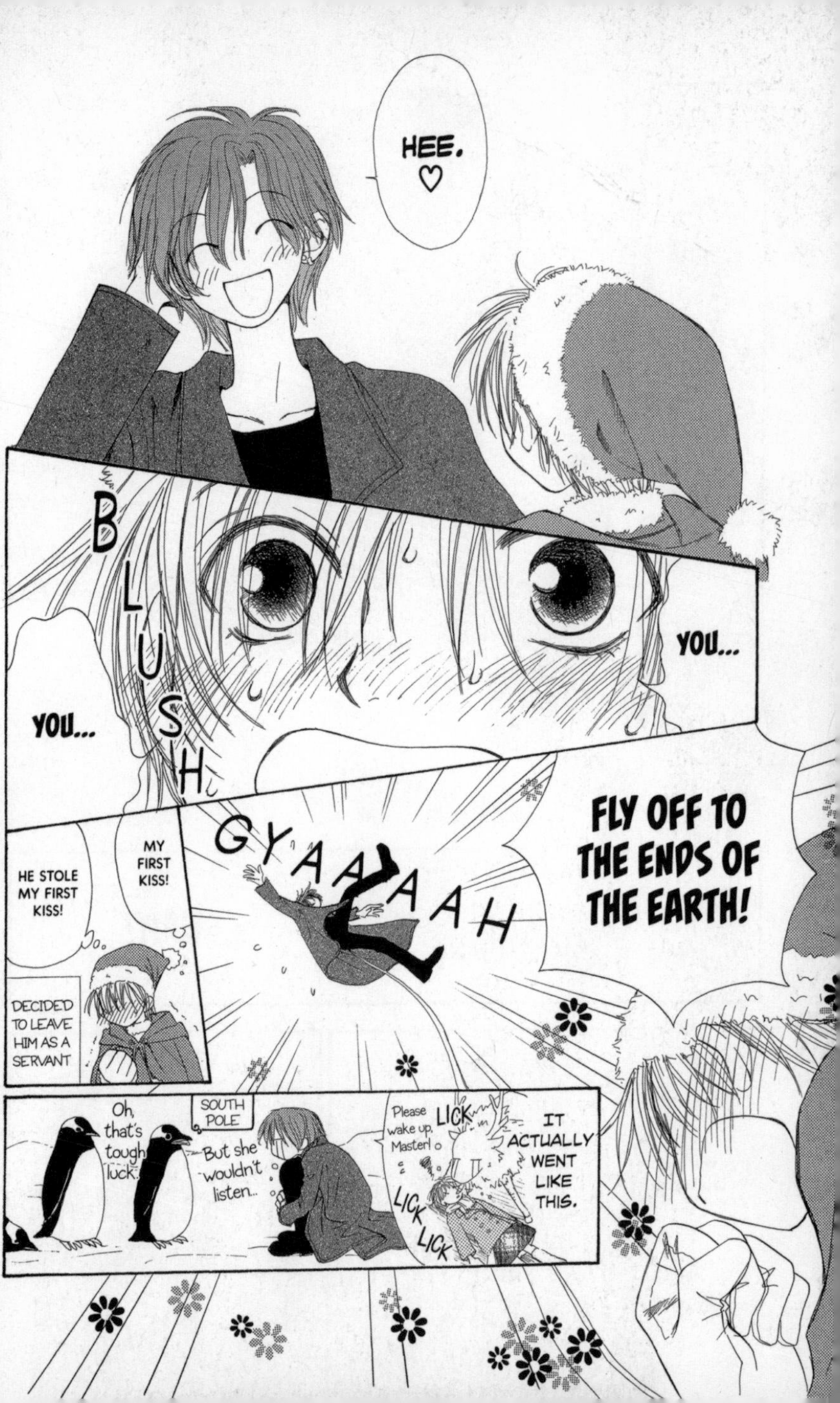
HEE. ♡
YOU...
BLUSH
YOU...
FLY OFF TO THE ENDS OF THE EARTH!
GYAAAAAH
MY FIRST KISS!
HE STOLE MY FIRST KISS!
DECIDED TO LEAVE HIM AS A SERVANT
IT ACTUALLY WENT LIKE THIS.
LICK
Please wake up, Master!
LICK LICK
SOUTH POLE
But she wouldn't listen...
Oh, that's tough luck.

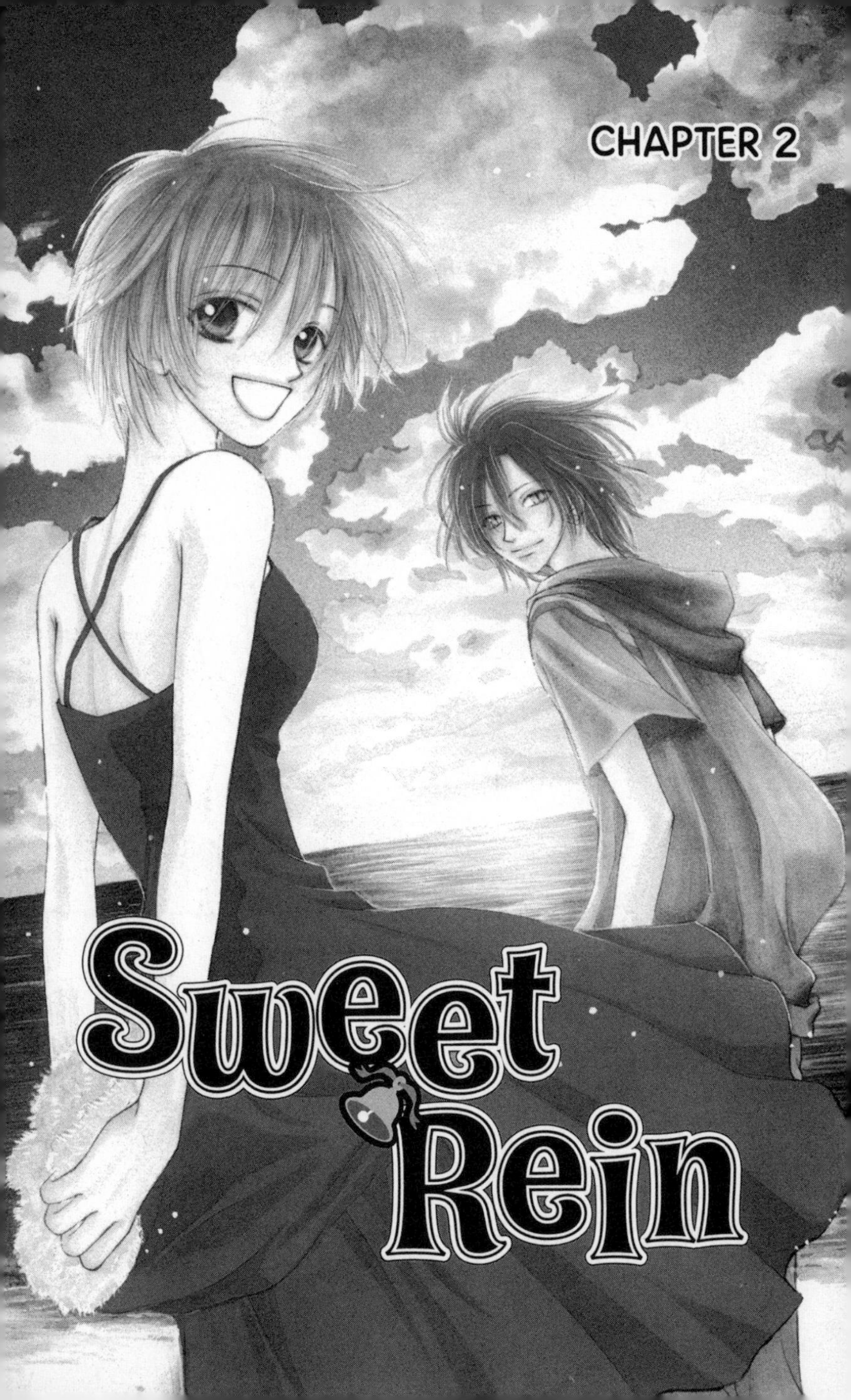
CHAPTER 2
Sweet Rein

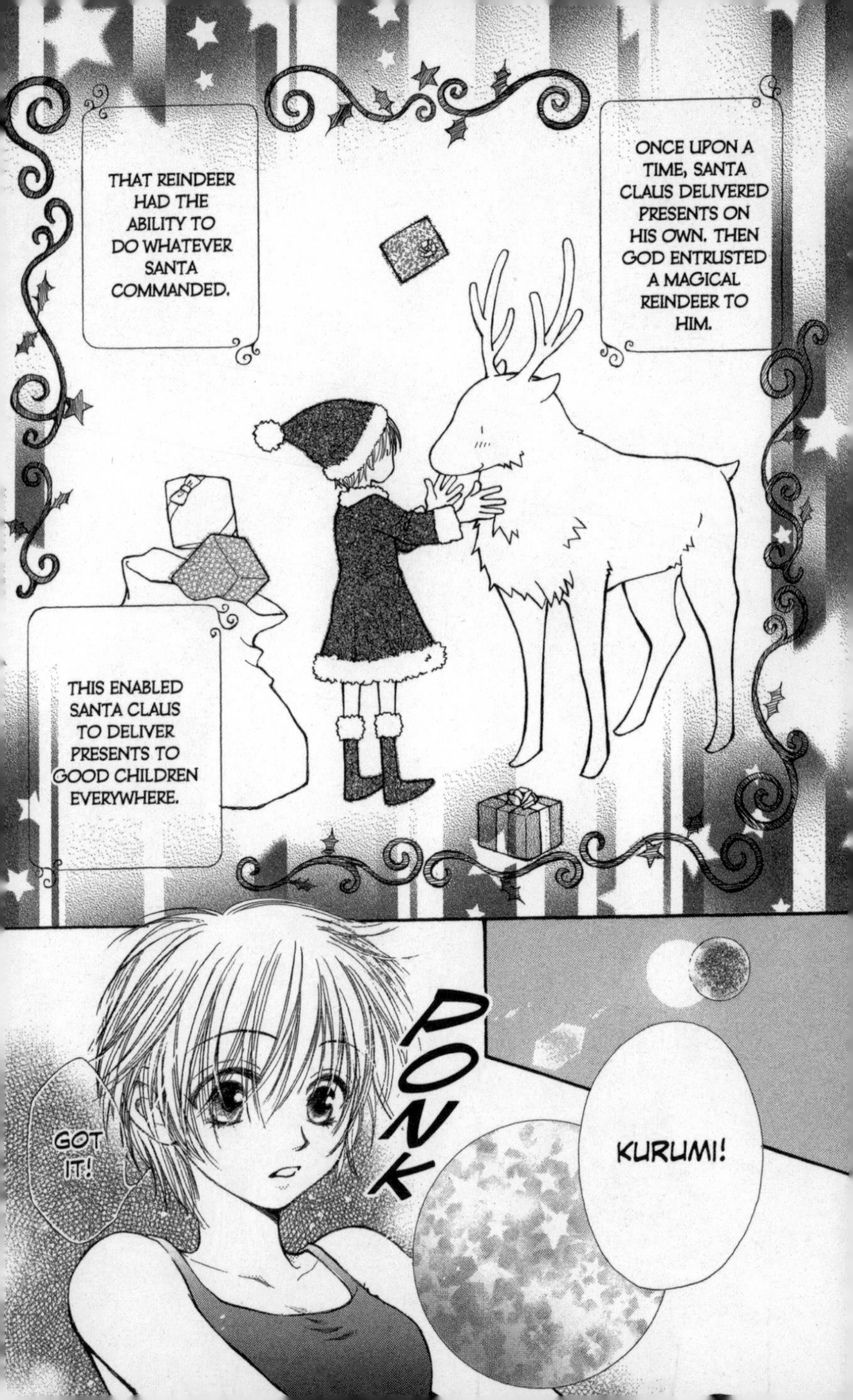
ONCE UPON A TIME, SANTA CLAUS DELIVERED PRESENTS ON HIS OWN. THEN GOD ENTRUSTED A MAGICAL REINDEER TO HIM.
THAT REINDEER HAD THE ABILITY TO DO WHATEVER SANTA COMMANDED.
THIS ENABLED SANTA CLAUS TO DELIVER PRESENTS TO GOOD CHILDREN EVERYWHERE.
KURUMI!
PONK
GOT IT!

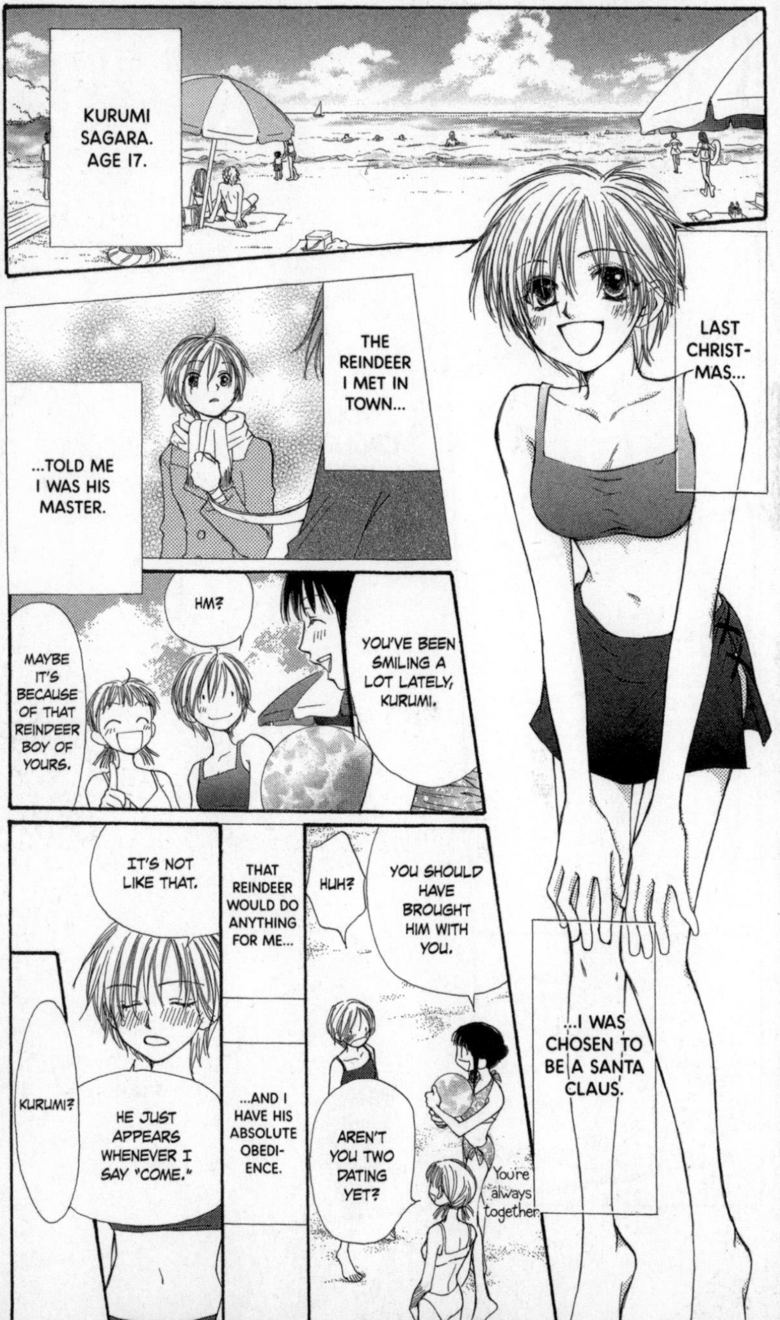
KURUMI SAGARA. AGE 17.
LAST CHRIST-MAS...
...I WAS CHOSEN TO BE A SANTA CLAUS.
THE REINDEER I MET IN TOWN...
...TOLD ME I WAS HIS MASTER.
YOU'VE BEEN SMILING A LOT LATELY, KURUMI.
HM?
MAYBE IT'S BECAUSE OF THAT REINDEER BOY OF YOURS.
YOU SHOULD HAVE BROUGHT HIM WITH YOU.
HUH?
AREN'T YOU TWO DATING YET?
You're always together.
THAT REINDEER WOULD DO ANYTHING FOR ME...
IT'S NOT LIKE THAT.
...AND I HAVE HIS ABSOLUTE OBEDI-ENCE.
HE JUST APPEARS WHENEVER I SAY "COME."
KURUMI?

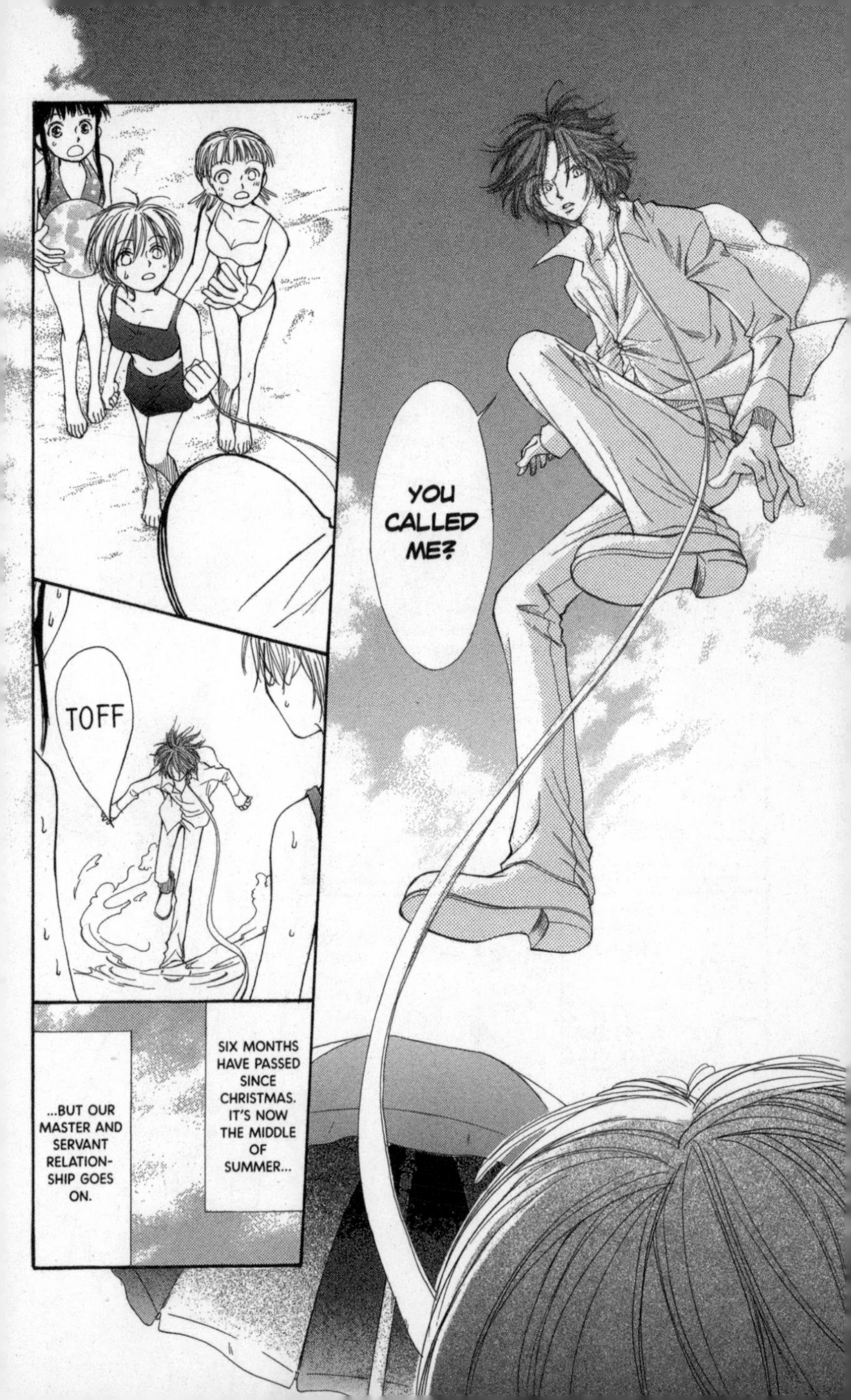
YOU CALLED ME?
TOFF
SIX MONTHS HAVE PASSED SINCE CHRISTMAS. IT'S NOW THE MIDDLE OF SUMMER...
...BUT OUR MASTER AND SERVANT RELATION-SHIP GOES ON.

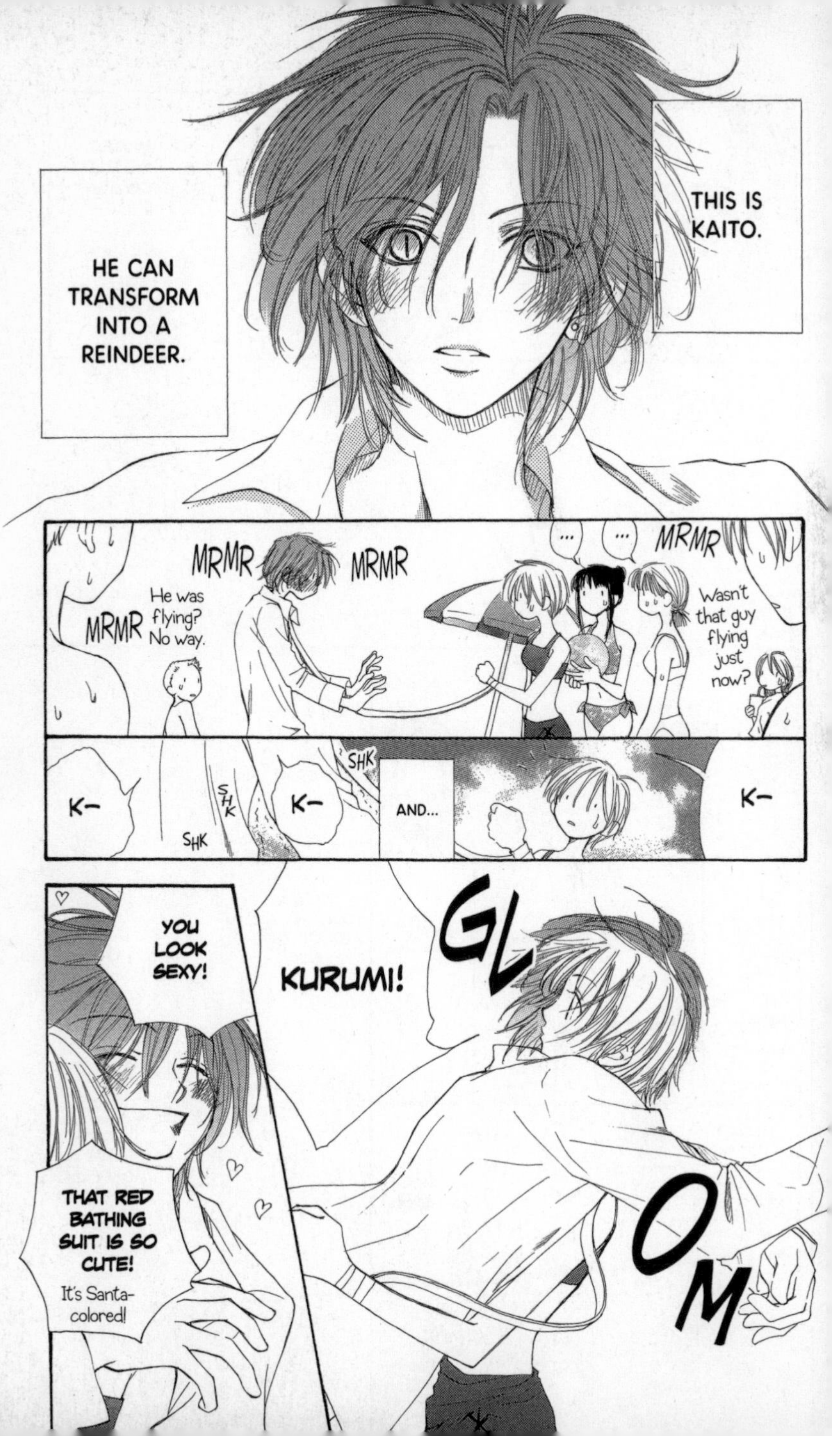
THIS IS KAITO.
HE CAN TRANSFORM INTO A REINDEER.
MRMR
...
...
Wasn't that guy flying just now?
MRMR
MRMR
He was flying? No way.
MRMR
K–
AND...
SHK
K–
SHK
SHK
K–
GL
OM
KURUMI!
YOU LOOK SEXY!
THAT RED BATHING SUIT IS SO CUTE!
It's Santa-colored!

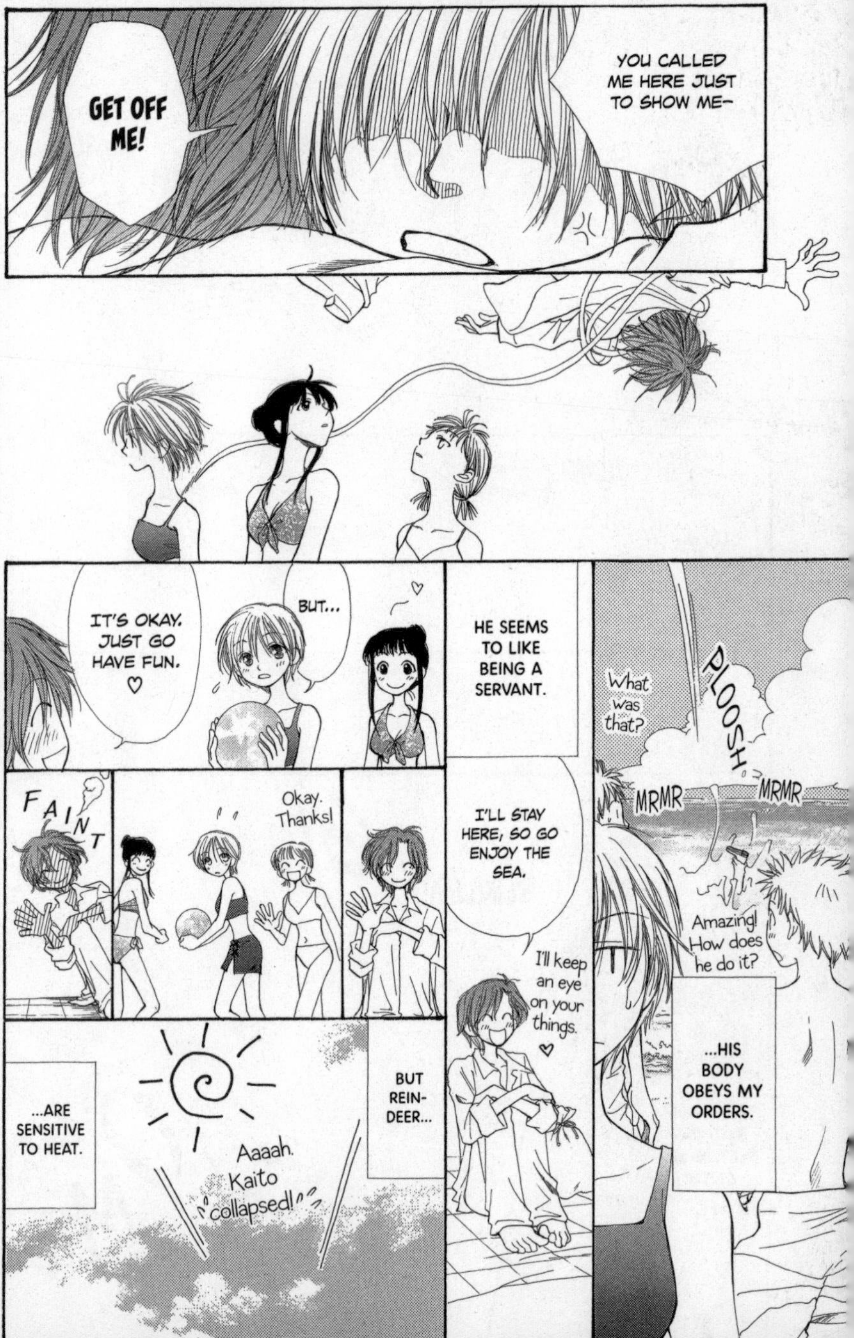
YOU CALLED ME HERE JUST TO SHOW ME—
GET OFF ME!
What was that?
PLOOSH
MRMR
MRMR
Amazing! How does he do it?
...HIS BODY OBEYS MY ORDERS.
HE SEEMS TO LIKE BEING A SERVANT.
BUT...
IT'S OKAY. JUST GO HAVE FUN. ♡
I'LL STAY HERE, SO GO ENJOY THE SEA.
I'll keep an eye on your things. ♡
Okay. Thanks!
FAINT
BUT REIN-DEER...
Aaaah. Kaito collapsed!
...ARE SENSITIVE TO HEAT.

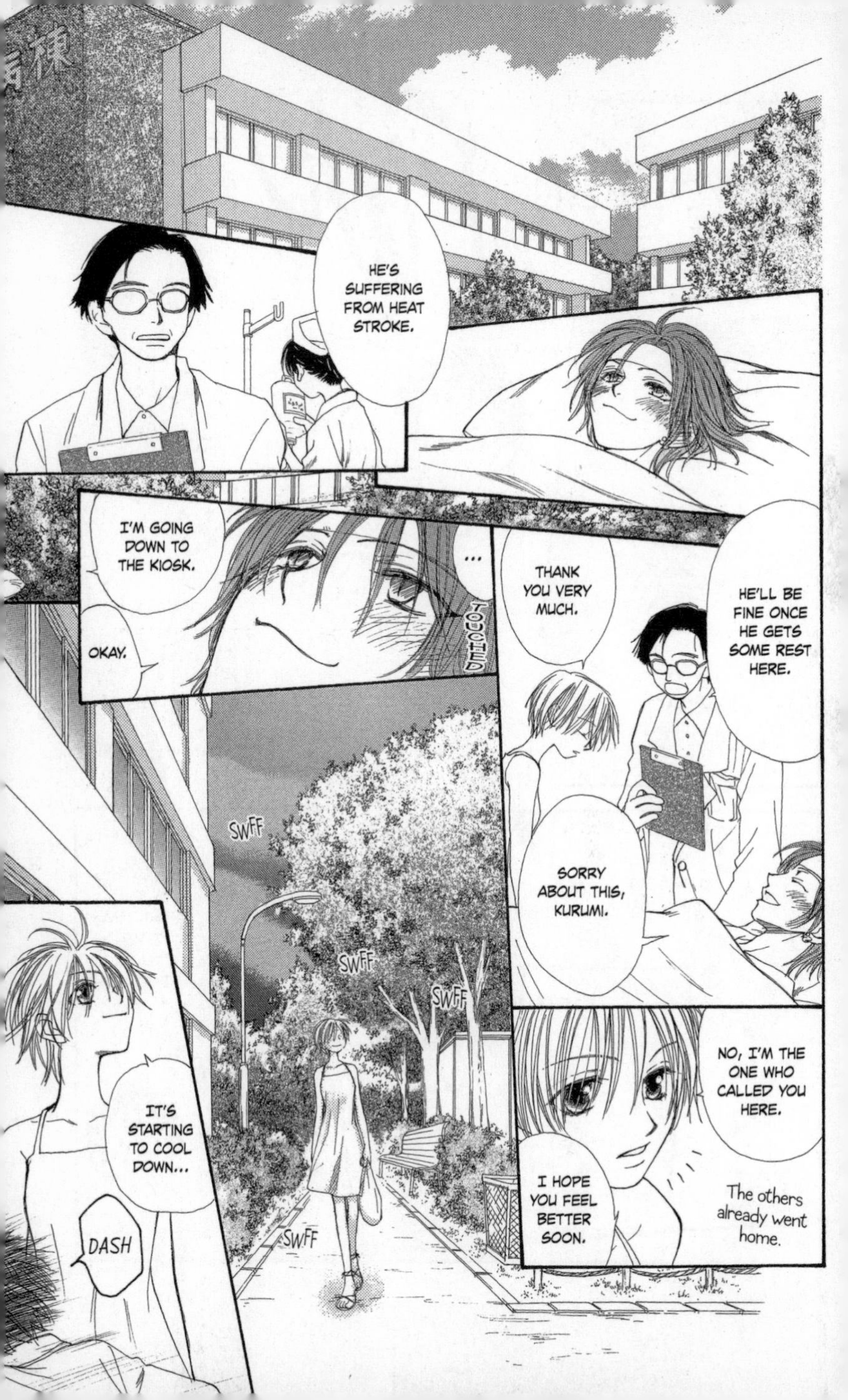
HE'S SUFFERING FROM HEAT STROKE.
HE'LL BE FINE ONCE HE GETS SOME REST HERE.
THANK YOU VERY MUCH.
SORRY ABOUT THIS, KURUMI.
NO, I'M THE ONE WHO CALLED YOU HERE.
The others already went home.
I HOPE YOU FEEL BETTER SOON.
...
TOUCHED
I'M GOING DOWN TO THE KIOSK.
OKAY.
SWFF
SWFF
SWFF
SWFF
IT'S STARTING TO COOL DOWN...
DASH

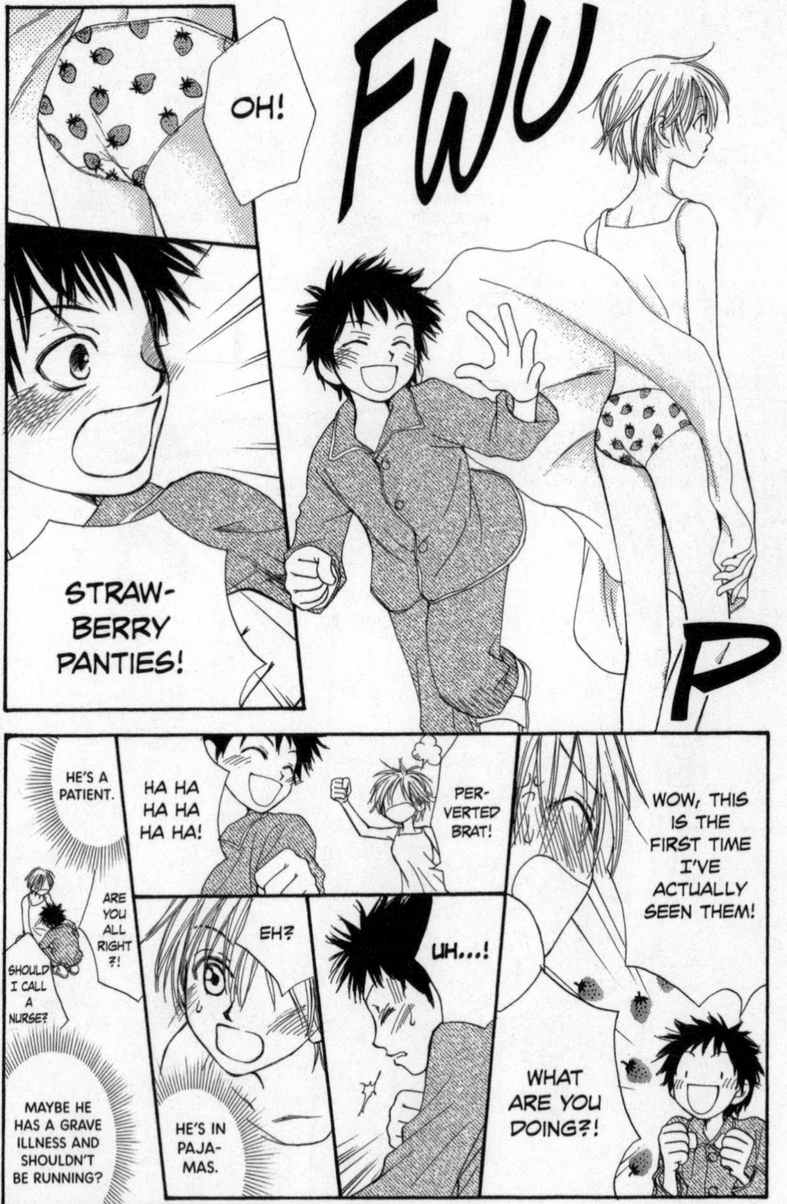
FWU
P
OH!
STRAW-BERRY PANTIES!
WOW, THIS IS THE FIRST TIME I'VE ACTUALLY SEEN THEM!
WHAT ARE YOU DOING?!
PER-VERTED BRAT!
HA HA HA HA HA HA!
HE'S A PATIENT.
UH...!
EH?
HE'S IN PAJA-MAS.
ARE YOU ALL RIGHT?!
SHOULD I CALL A NURSE?
MAYBE HE HAS A GRAVE ILLNESS AND SHOULDN'T BE RUNNING?

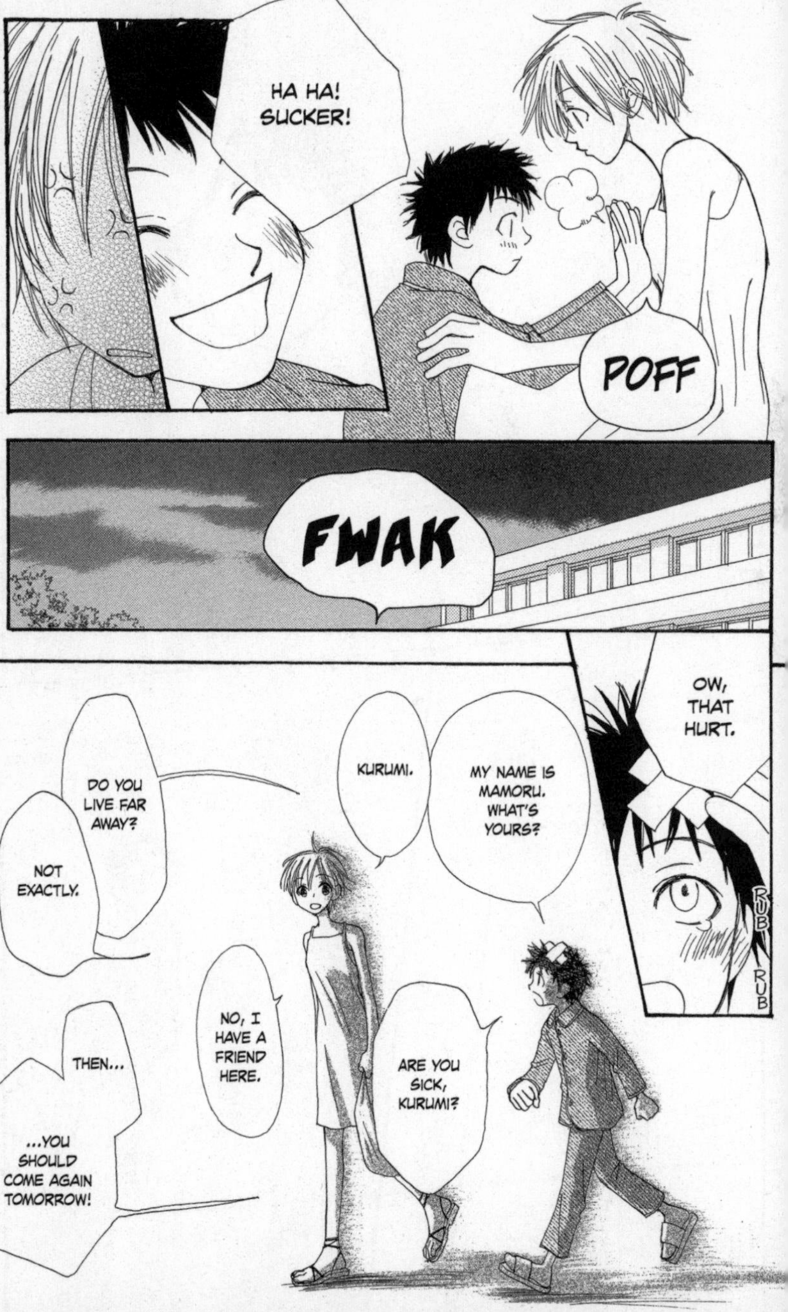
POFF
HA HA! SUCKER!
FWAK
OW, THAT HURT.
RUB RUB
MY NAME IS MAMORU. WHAT'S YOURS?
KURUMI.
ARE YOU SICK, KURUMI?
NO, I HAVE A FRIEND HERE.
DO YOU LIVE FAR AWAY?
NOT EXACTLY.
THEN...
...YOU SHOULD COME AGAIN TOMORROW!

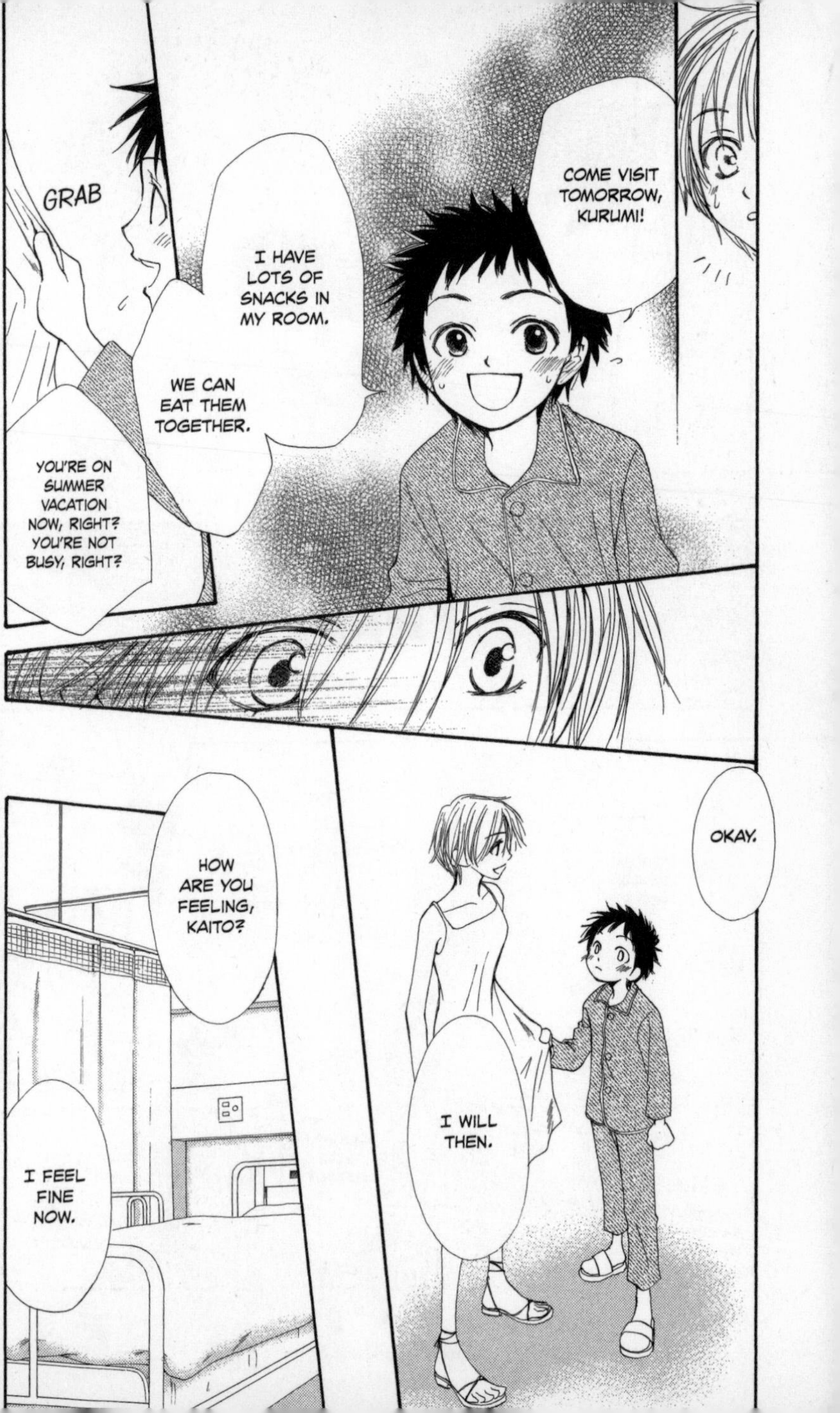

COME VISIT TOMORROW, KURUMI!
I HAVE LOTS OF SNACKS IN MY ROOM.
WE CAN EAT THEM TOGETHER.
GRAB
YOU'RE ON SUMMER VACATION NOW, RIGHT? YOU'RE NOT BUSY, RIGHT?
OKAY.
I WILL THEN.
HOW ARE YOU FEELING, KAITO?
I FEEL FINE NOW.

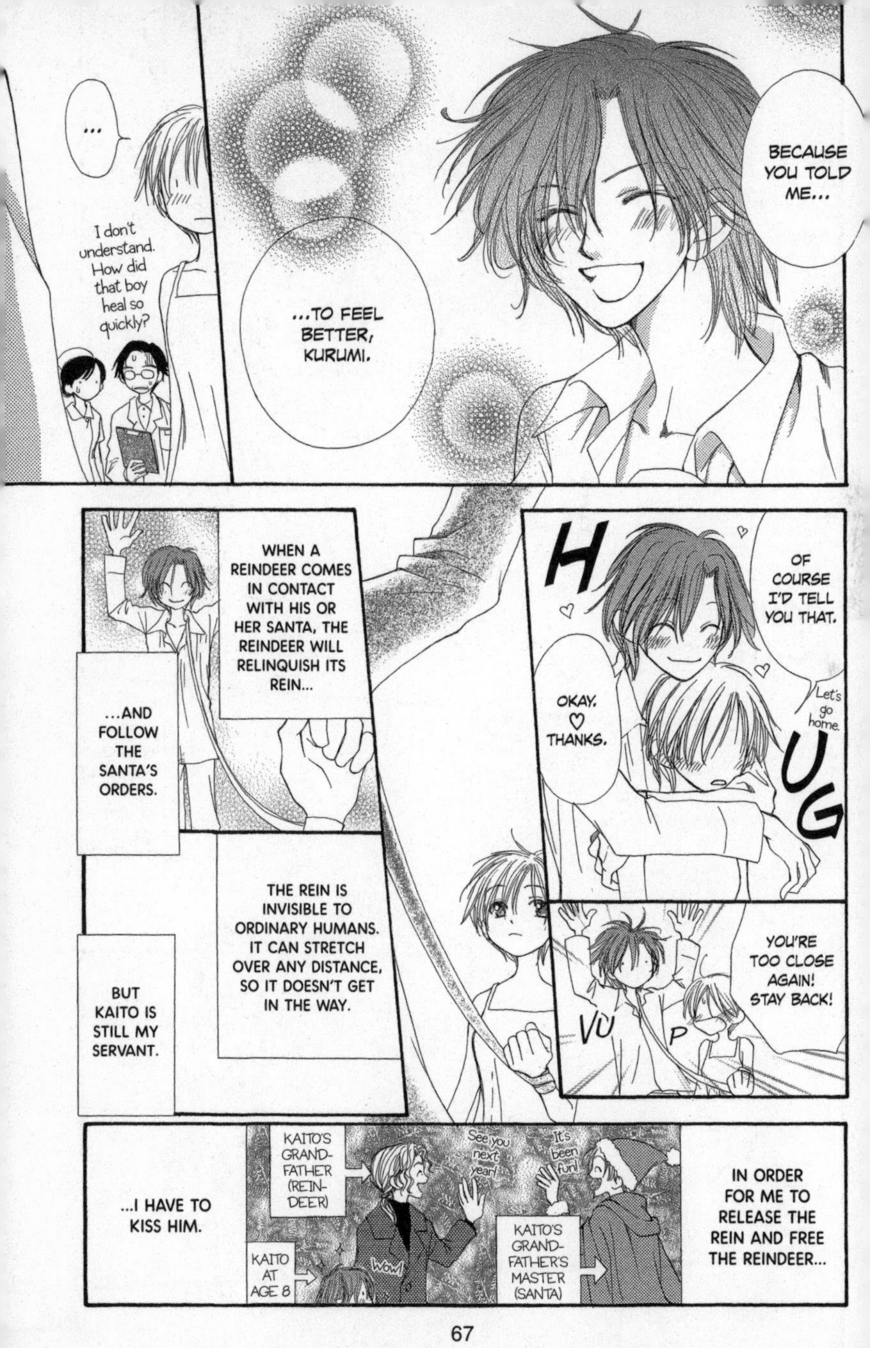

BECAUSE YOU TOLD ME...
...TO FEEL BETTER, KURUMI.
...
I don't understand. How did that boy heal so quickly?
H
OF COURSE I'D TELL YOU THAT.
OKAY. ♡ THANKS.
Let's go home.
UG
YOU'RE TOO CLOSE AGAIN! STAY BACK!
VU
P
WHEN A REINDEER COMES IN CONTACT WITH HIS OR HER SANTA, THE REINDEER WILL RELINQUISH ITS REIN...
...AND FOLLOW THE SANTA'S ORDERS.
THE REIN IS INVISIBLE TO ORDINARY HUMANS. IT CAN STRETCH OVER ANY DISTANCE, SO IT DOESN'T GET IN THE WAY.
BUT KAITO IS STILL MY SERVANT.
IN ORDER FOR ME TO RELEASE THE REIN AND FREE THE REINDEER...
It's been fun!
KAITO'S GRANDFATHER'S MASTER (SANTA)
See you next year!
KAITO'S GRANDFATHER (REINDEER)
Wow!
KAITO AT AGE 8
...I HAVE TO KISS HIM.

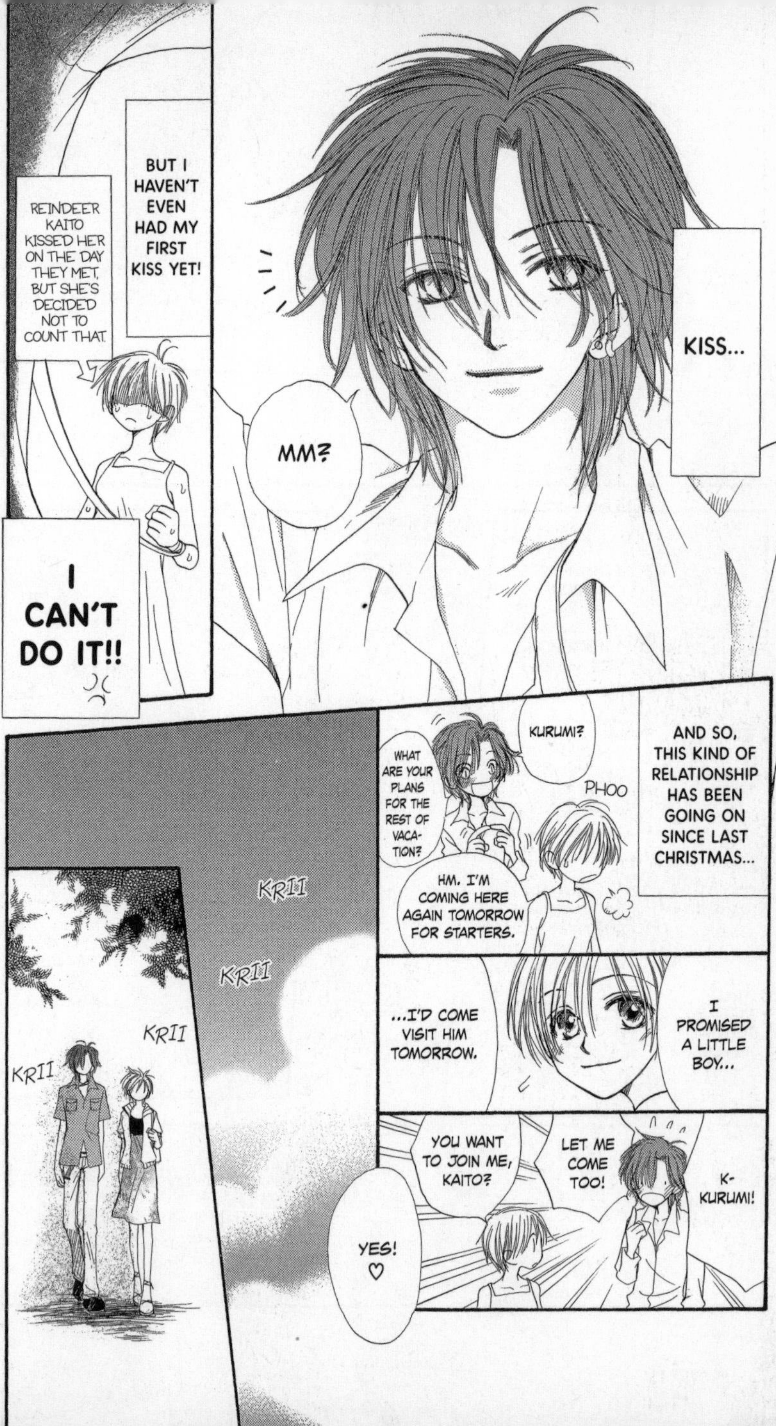
KISS...
MM?
BUT I HAVEN'T EVEN HAD MY FIRST KISS YET!
REINDEER KAITO KISSED HER ON THE DAY THEY MET, BUT SHE'S DECIDED NOT TO COUNT THAT.
I CAN'T DO IT!!
AND SO, THIS KIND OF RELATIONSHIP HAS BEEN GOING ON SINCE LAST CHRISTMAS...
KURUMI?
WHAT ARE YOUR PLANS FOR THE REST OF VACA-TION?
PHOO
HM. I'M COMING HERE AGAIN TOMORROW FOR STARTERS.
I PROMISED A LITTLE BOY...
...I'D COME VISIT HIM TOMORROW.
K-KURUMI!
LET ME COME TOO!
YOU WANT TO JOIN ME, KAITO?
YES! ♡
KRII
KRII
KRII
KRII

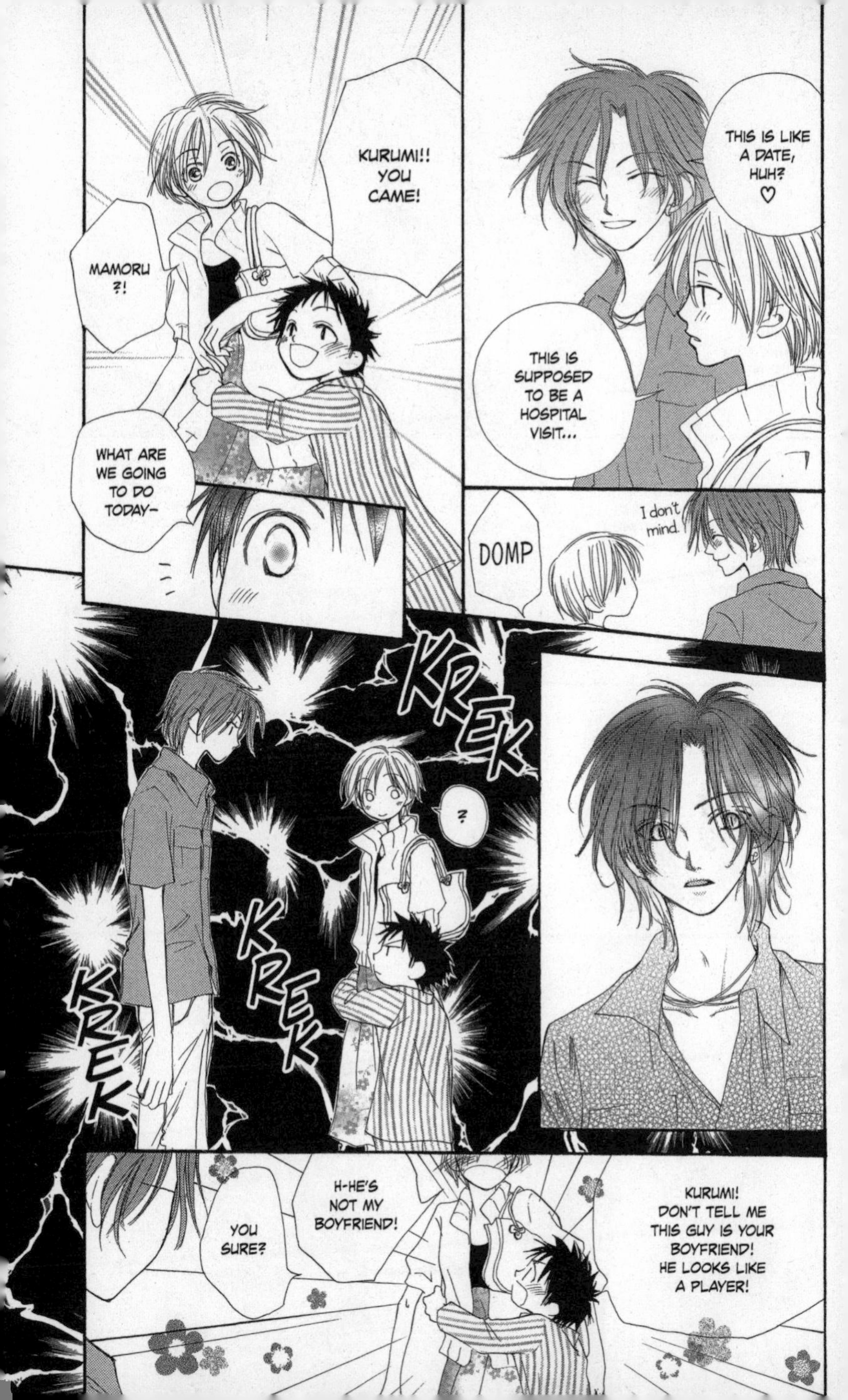
THIS IS LIKE A DATE, HUH? ♡
THIS IS SUPPOSED TO BE A HOSPITAL VISIT...
DOMP
I don't mind.
KURUMI!! YOU CAME!
MAMORU ?!
WHAT ARE WE GOING TO DO TODAY—
KREK
?
KREK
KREK
KURUMI! DON'T TELL ME THIS GUY IS YOUR BOYFRIEND! HE LOOKS LIKE A PLAYER!
H-HE'S NOT MY BOYFRIEND!
YOU SURE?

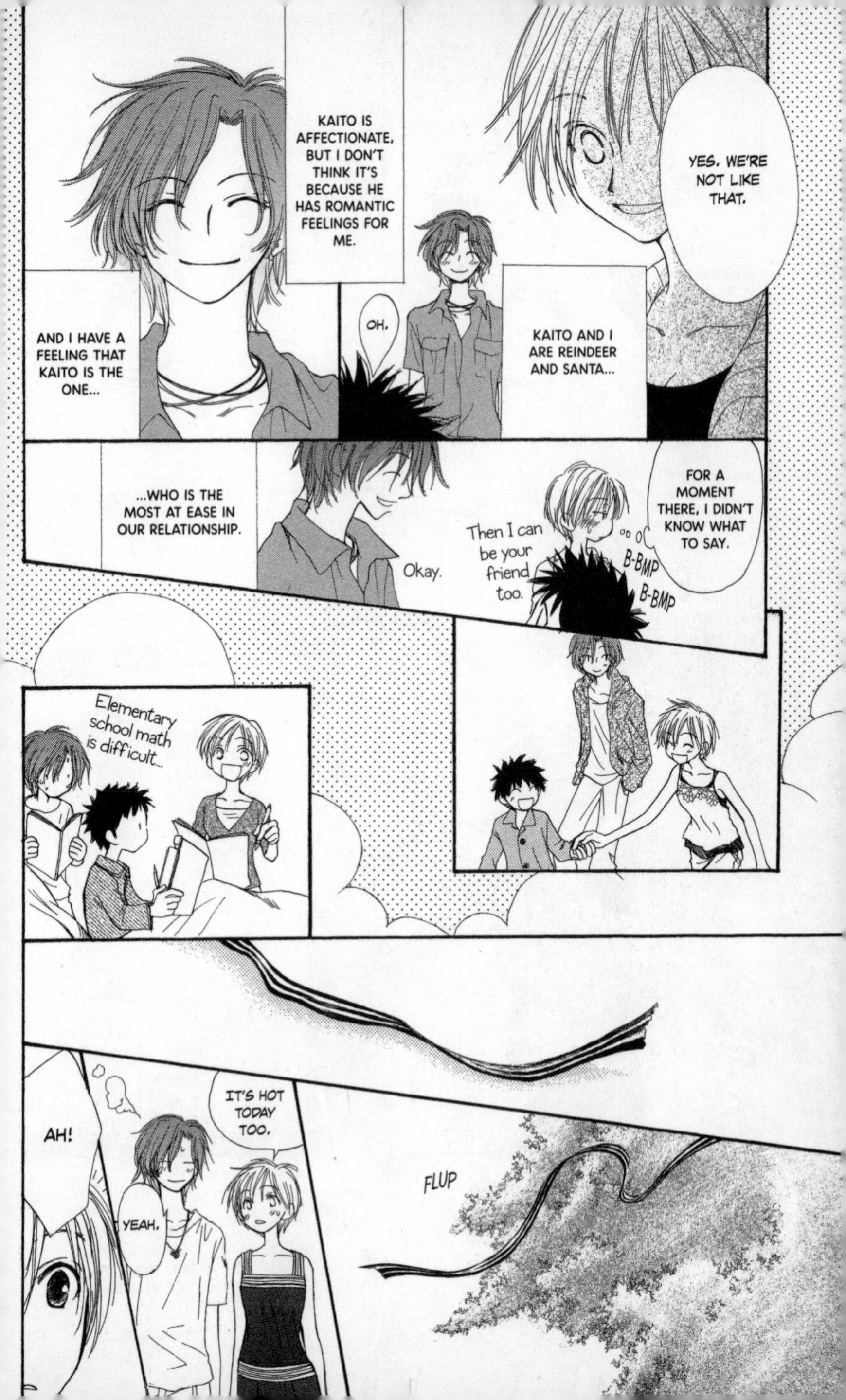
YES. WE'RE NOT LIKE THAT.
KAITO AND I ARE REINDEER AND SANTA...
OH.
KAITO IS AFFECTIONATE, BUT I DON'T THINK IT'S BECAUSE HE HAS ROMANTIC FEELINGS FOR ME.
AND I HAVE A FEELING THAT KAITO IS THE ONE...
FOR A MOMENT THERE, I DIDN'T KNOW WHAT TO SAY.
B-BMP
B-BMP
Then I can be your friend too.
Okay.
...WHO IS THE MOST AT EASE IN OUR RELATIONSHIP.
Elementary school math is difficult...
FLUP
IT'S HOT TODAY TOO.
YEAH.
AH!

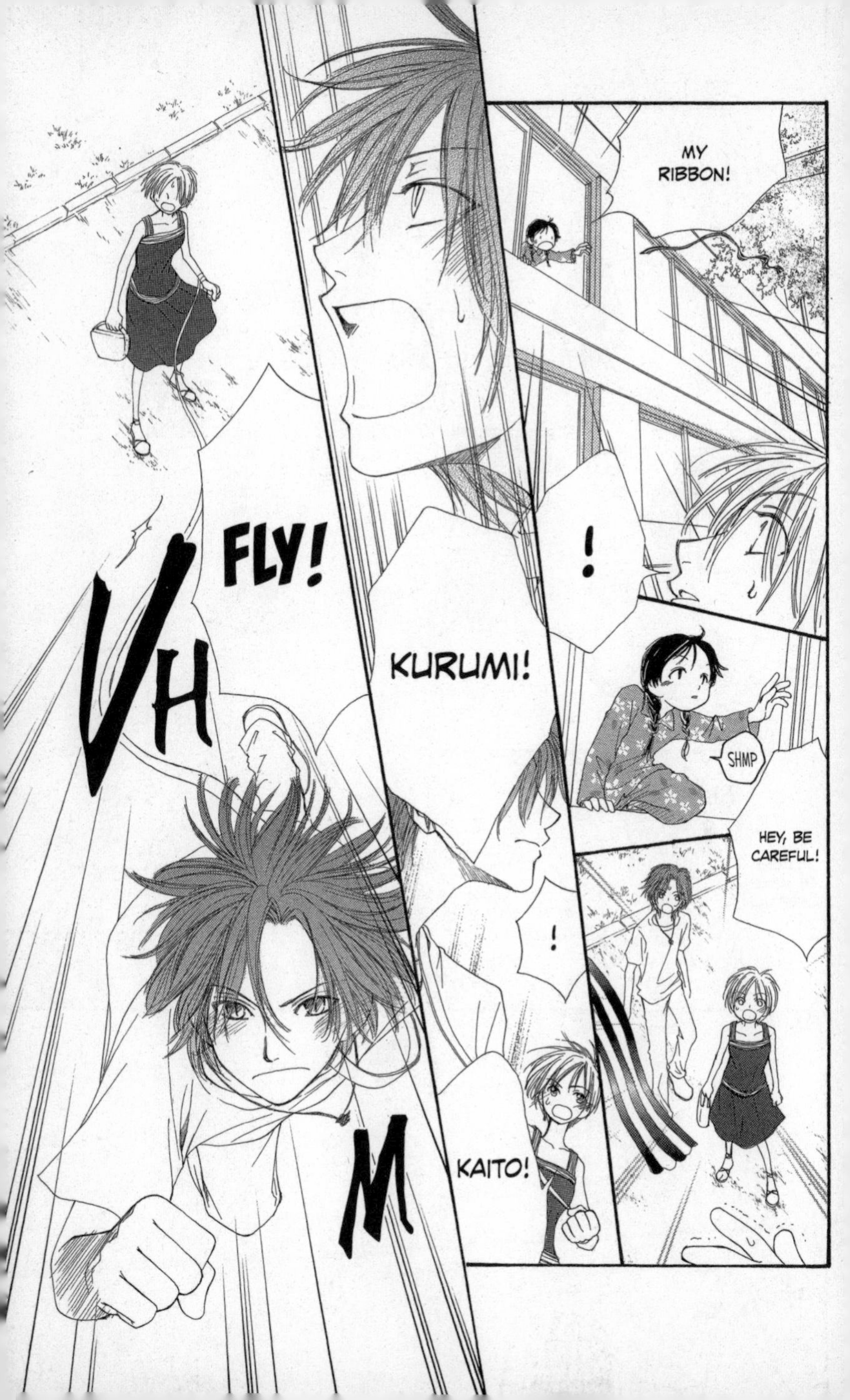
MY RIBBON!
!
SHMP
HEY, BE CAREFUL!
KURUMI!
!
KAITO!
FLY!
VHM

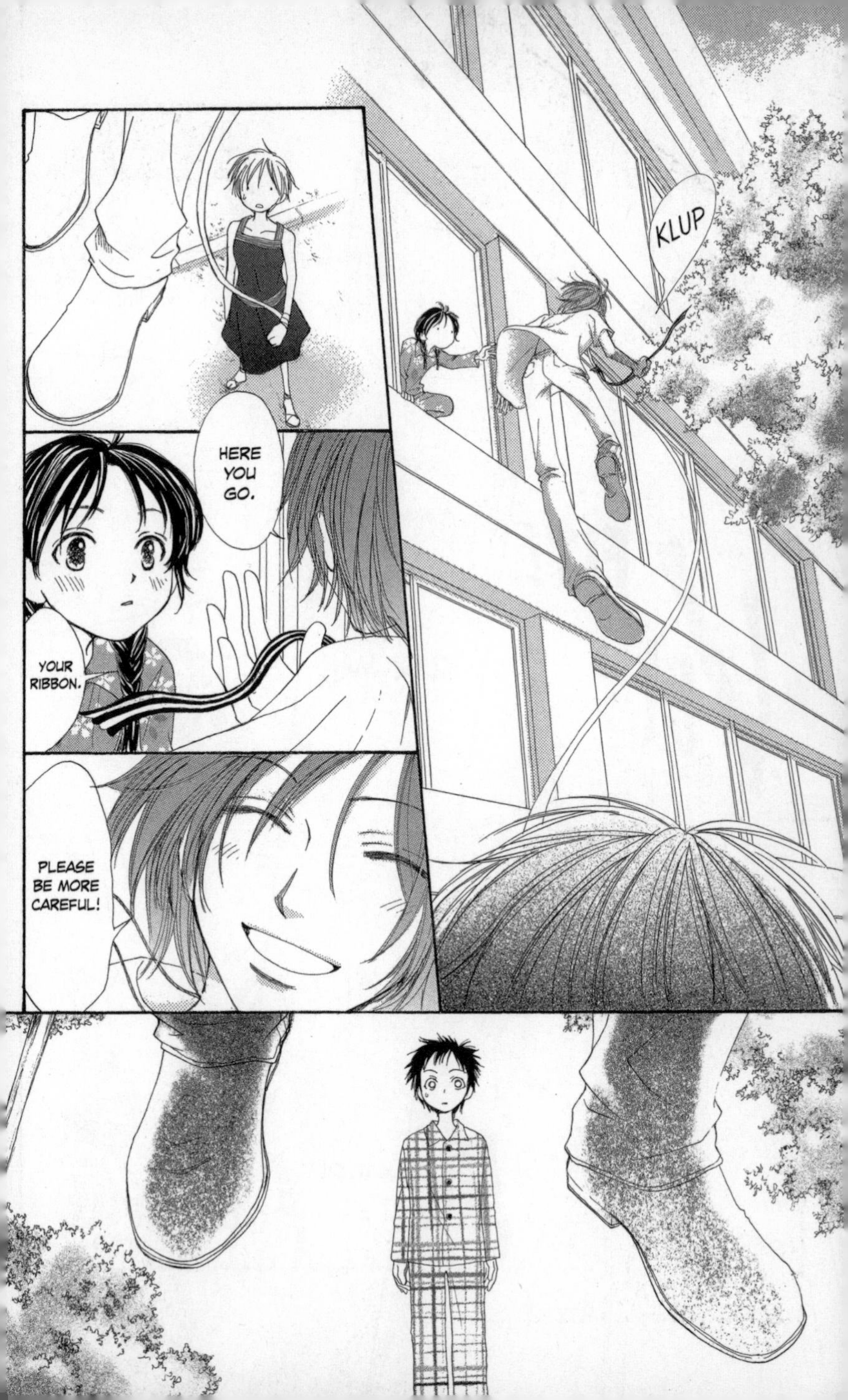
KLUP
HERE YOU GO.
YOUR RIBBON.
PLEASE BE MORE CAREFUL!

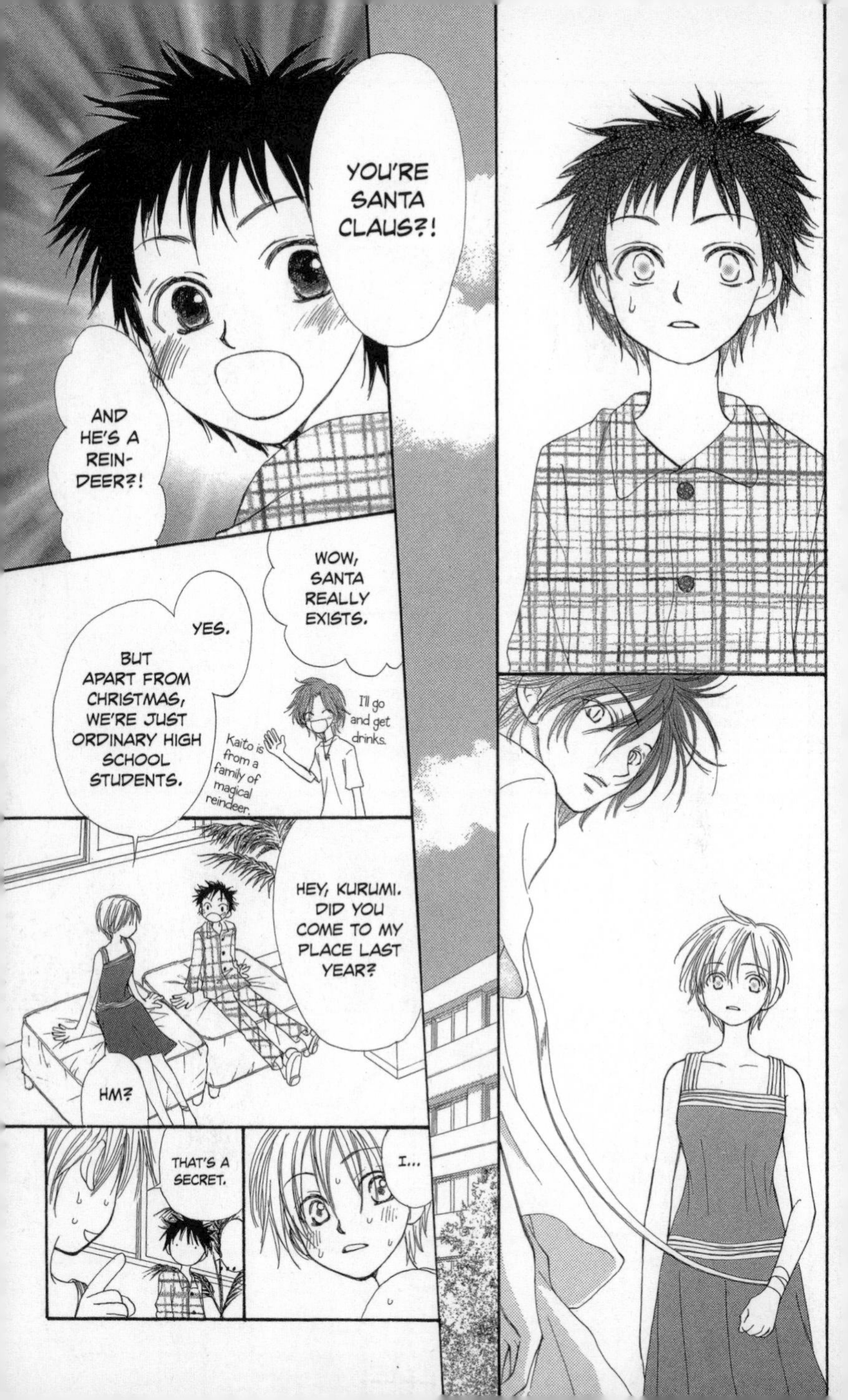
YOU'RE SANTA CLAUS?!
AND HE'S A REIN-DEER?!
WOW, SANTA REALLY EXISTS.
YES.
BUT APART FROM CHRISTMAS, WE'RE JUST ORDINARY HIGH SCHOOL STUDENTS.
I'll go and get drinks.
Kaito is from a family of magical reindeer.
HEY, KURUMI. DID YOU COME TO MY PLACE LAST YEAR?
HM?
I...
THAT'S A SECRET.

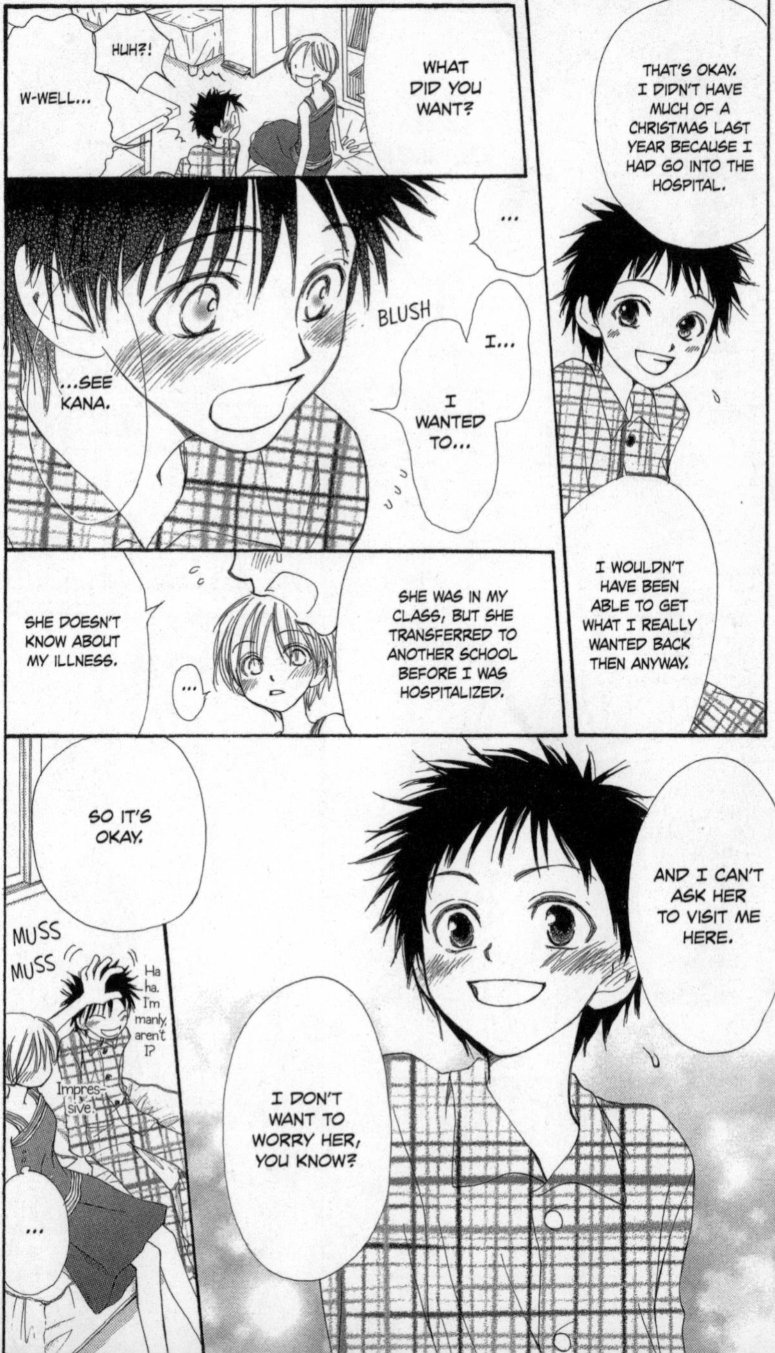
THAT'S OKAY. I DIDN'T HAVE MUCH OF A CHRISTMAS LAST YEAR BECAUSE I HAD GO INTO THE HOSPITAL.
I WOULDN'T HAVE BEEN ABLE TO GET WHAT I REALLY WANTED BACK THEN ANYWAY.
WHAT DID YOU WANT?
HUH?!
W-WELL...
...
BLUSH
I...
I WANTED TO...
...SEE KANA.
SHE WAS IN MY CLASS, BUT SHE TRANSFERRED TO ANOTHER SCHOOL BEFORE I WAS HOSPITALIZED.
...
SHE DOESN'T KNOW ABOUT MY ILLNESS.
AND I CAN'T ASK HER TO VISIT ME HERE.
I DON'T WANT TO WORRY HER, YOU KNOW?
SO IT'S OKAY.
MUSS MUSS
Ha ha. I'm manly, aren't I?
Impres-sive.
...

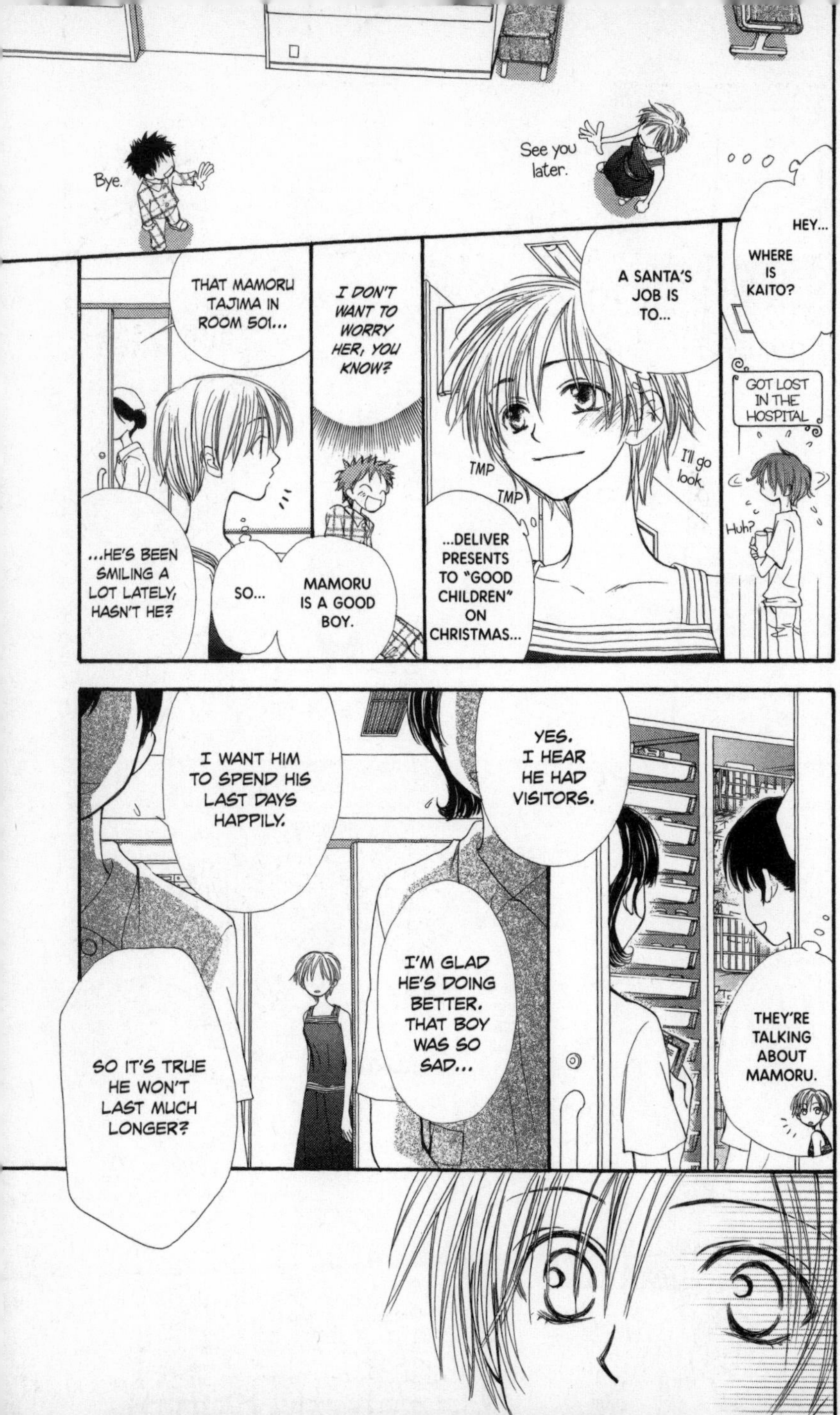
See you later.
Bye.
HEY... WHERE IS KAITO?
GOT LOST IN THE HOSPITAL
Huh?
A SANTA'S JOB IS TO...
I'll go look.
TMP
TMP
...DELIVER PRESENTS TO "GOOD CHILDREN" ON CHRISTMAS...
I DON'T WANT TO WORRY HER, YOU KNOW?
MAMORU IS A GOOD BOY.
SO...
THAT MAMORU TAJIMA IN ROOM 501...
...HE'S BEEN SMILING A LOT LATELY, HASN'T HE?
YES. I HEAR HE HAD VISITORS.
THEY'RE TALKING ABOUT MAMORU.
I WANT HIM TO SPEND HIS LAST DAYS HAPPILY.
I'M GLAD HE'S DOING BETTER. THAT BOY WAS SO SAD...
SO IT'S TRUE HE WON'T LAST MUCH LONGER?

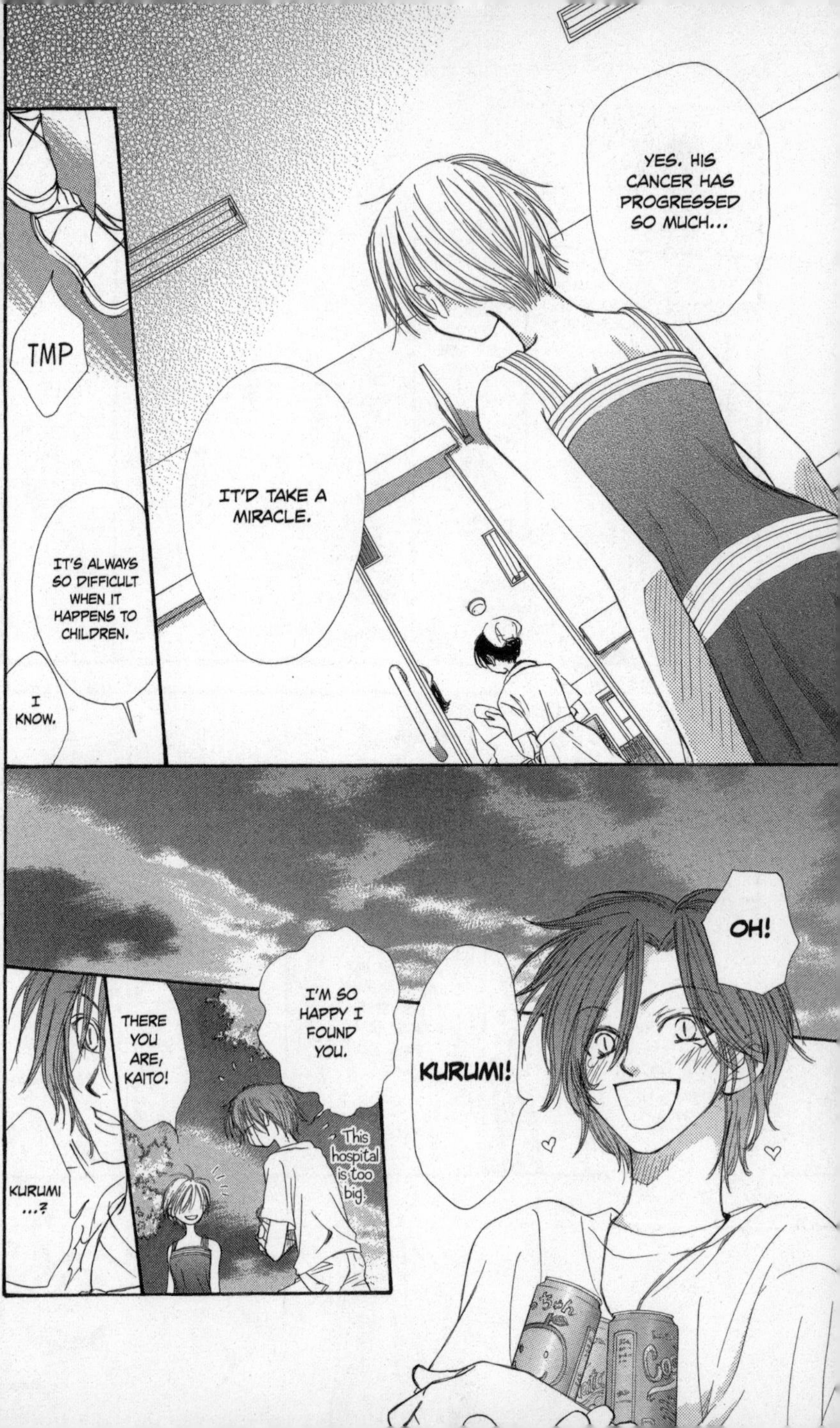
YES. HIS CANCER HAS PROGRESSED SO MUCH...
IT'D TAKE A MIRACLE.
TMP
IT'S ALWAYS SO DIFFICULT WHEN IT HAPPENS TO CHILDREN.
I KNOW.
OH!
KURUMI!
I'M SO HAPPY I FOUND YOU.
THERE YOU ARE, KAITO!
This hospital is too big.
KURUMI ...?

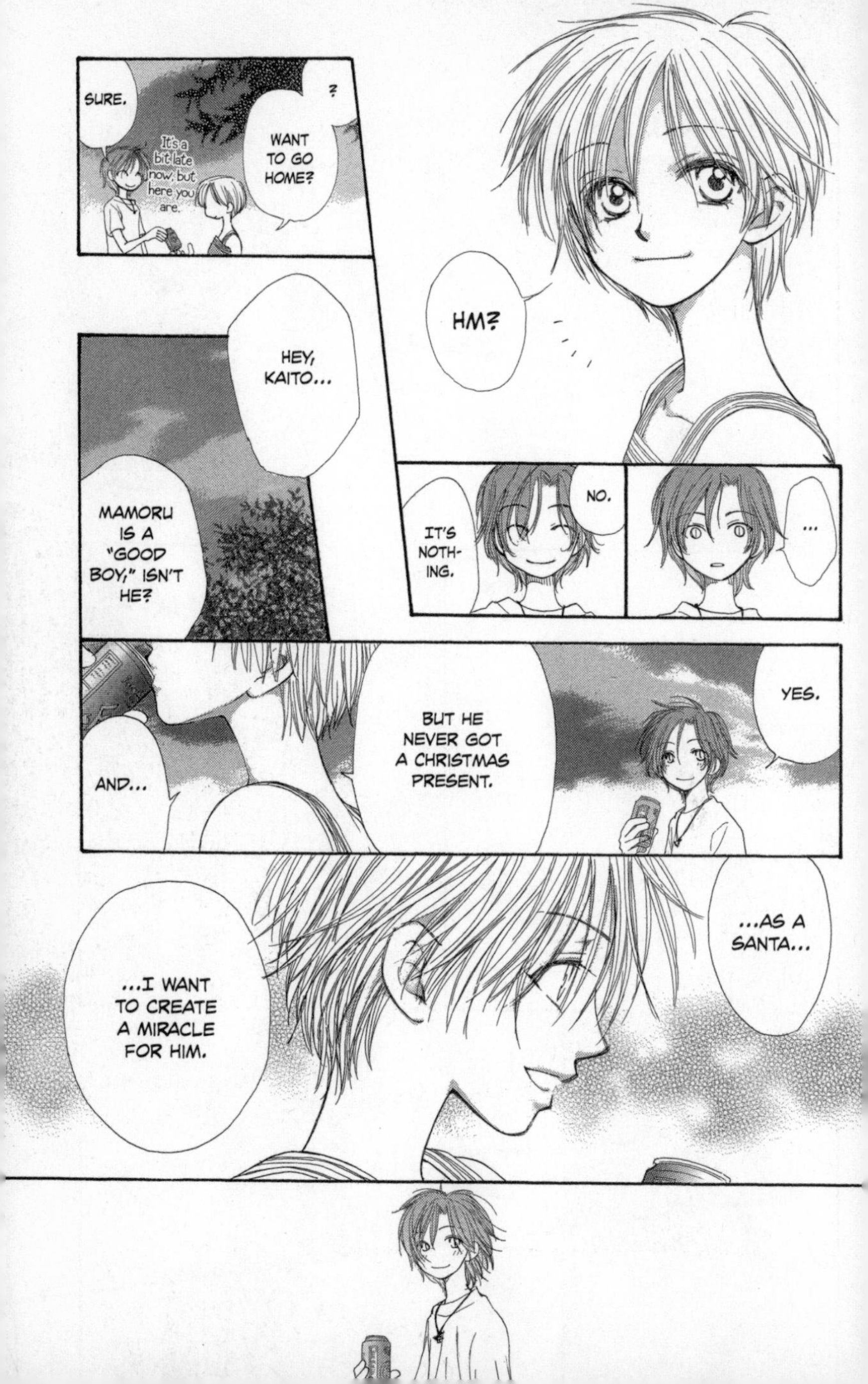
?
WANT TO GO HOME?
SURE.
It's a bit late now, but here you are.
HEY, KAITO...
HM?
...
NO.
IT'S NOTHING.
MAMORU IS A "GOOD BOY," ISN'T HE?
YES.
BUT HE NEVER GOT A CHRISTMAS PRESENT.
AND...
...AS A SANTA...
...I WANT TO CREATE A MIRACLE FOR HIM.

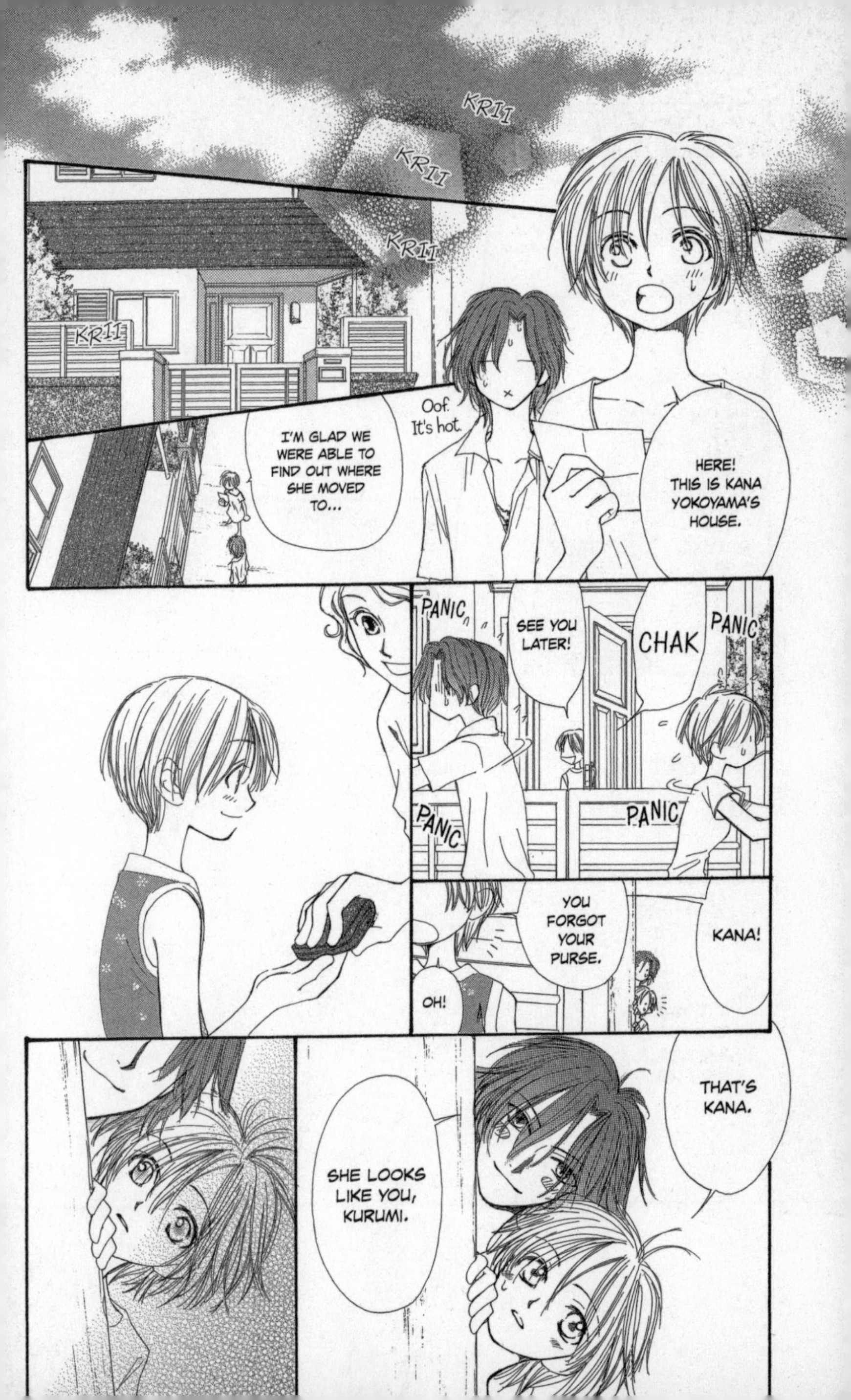
KRII
KRII
KRII
KRII
HERE! THIS IS KANA YOKOYAMA'S HOUSE.
Oof. It's hot.
I'M GLAD WE WERE ABLE TO FIND OUT WHERE SHE MOVED TO...
PANIC
CHAK
SEE YOU LATER!
PANIC
PANIC
PANIC
KANA!
YOU FORGOT YOUR PURSE.
OH!
THAT'S KANA.
SHE LOOKS LIKE YOU, KURUMI.

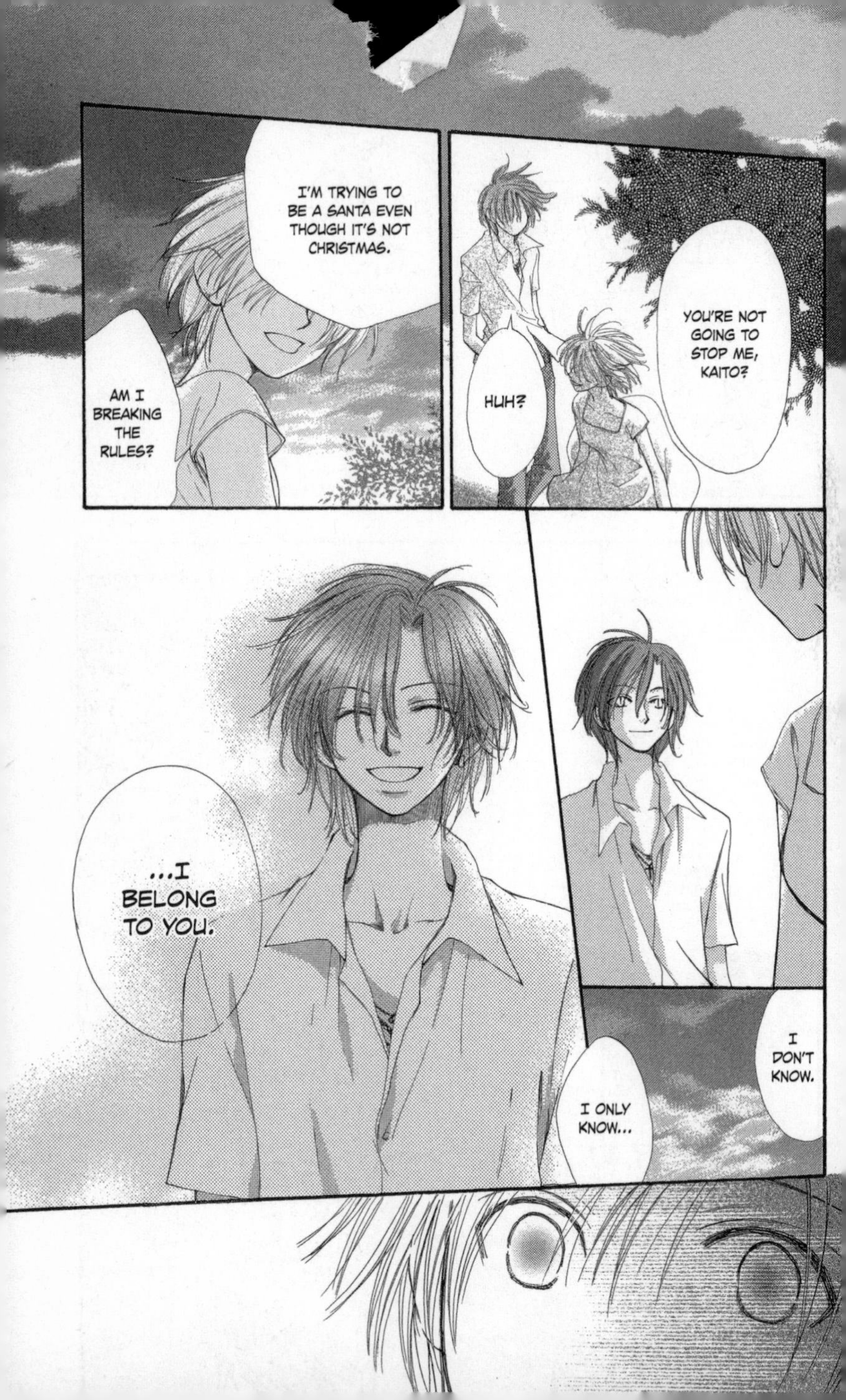
YOU'RE NOT GOING TO STOP ME, KAITO?
HUH?
I'M TRYING TO BE A SANTA EVEN THOUGH IT'S NOT CHRISTMAS.
AM I BREAKING THE RULES?
I DON'T KNOW.
I ONLY KNOW...
...I BELONG TO YOU.

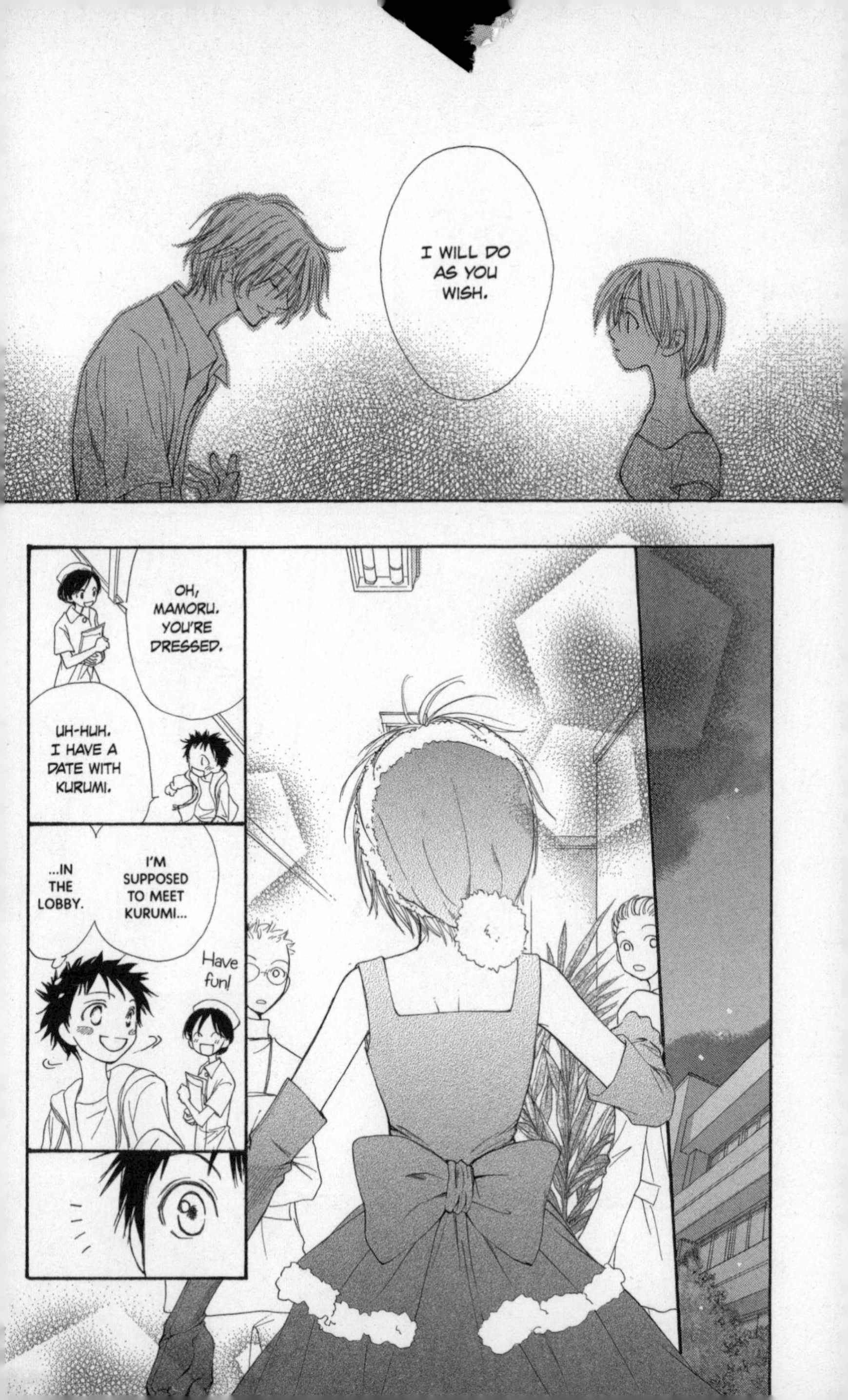
I WILL DO AS YOU WISH.
OH, MAMORU. YOU'RE DRESSED.
UH-HUH. I HAVE A DATE WITH KURUMI.
I'M SUPPOSED TO MEET KURUMI...
...IN THE LOBBY.
Have fun!

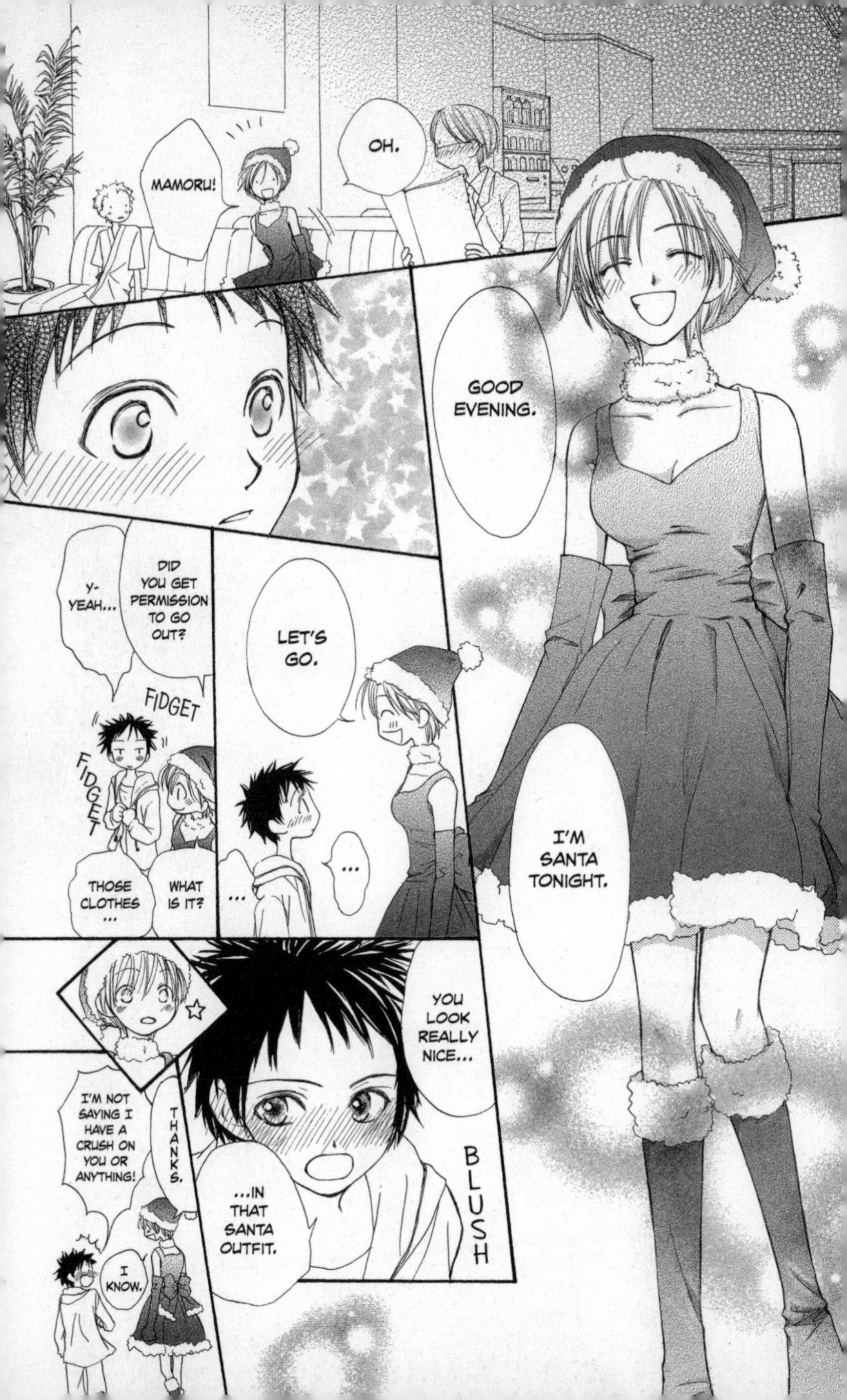
OH.
MAMORU!
GOOD EVENING.
I'M SANTA TONIGHT.
LET'S GO.
...
...
DID YOU GET PERMISSION TO GO OUT?
Y-YEAH...
FIDGET
FIDGET
WHAT IS IT?
THOSE CLOTHES...
YOU LOOK REALLY NICE...
...IN THAT SANTA OUTFIT.
BLUSH
THANKS.
I'M NOT SAYING I HAVE A CRUSH ON YOU OR ANYTHING!
Y-
I KNOW.

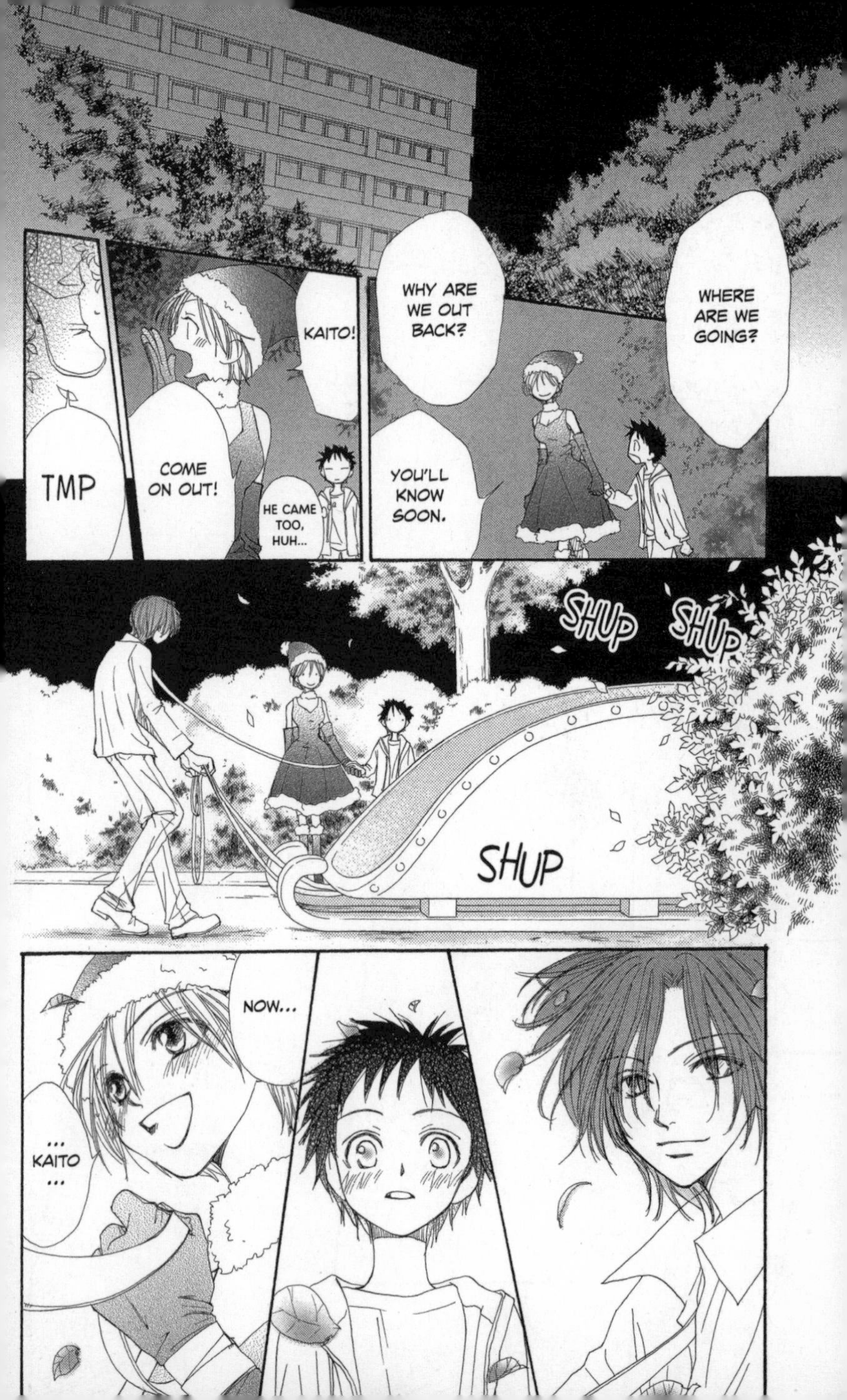
WHERE ARE WE GOING?
WHY ARE WE OUT BACK?
YOU'LL KNOW SOON.
KAITO!
COME ON OUT!
HE CAME TOO, HUH...
TMP
SHUP SHUP
SHUP
NOW...
...KAITO...

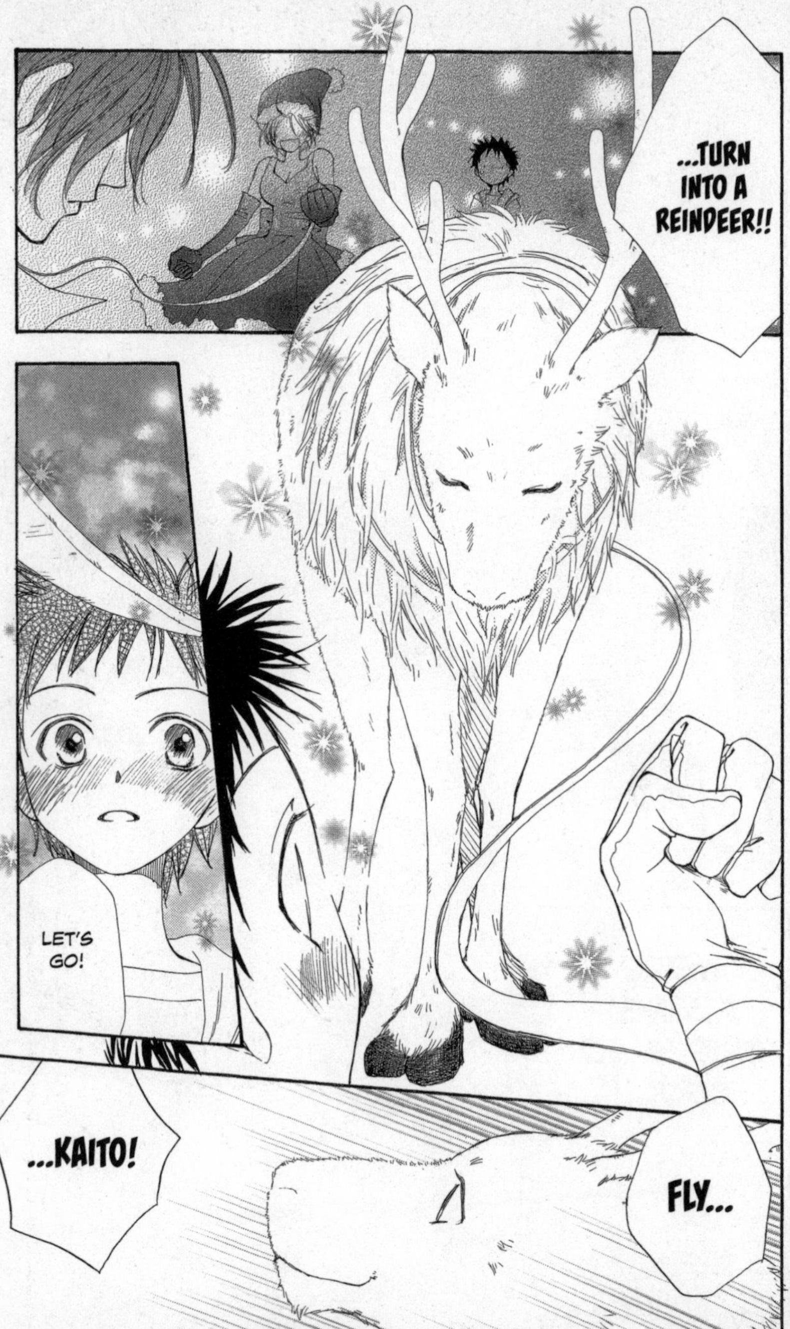
...TURN INTO A REINDEER!!
LET'S GO!
FLY...
...KAITO!

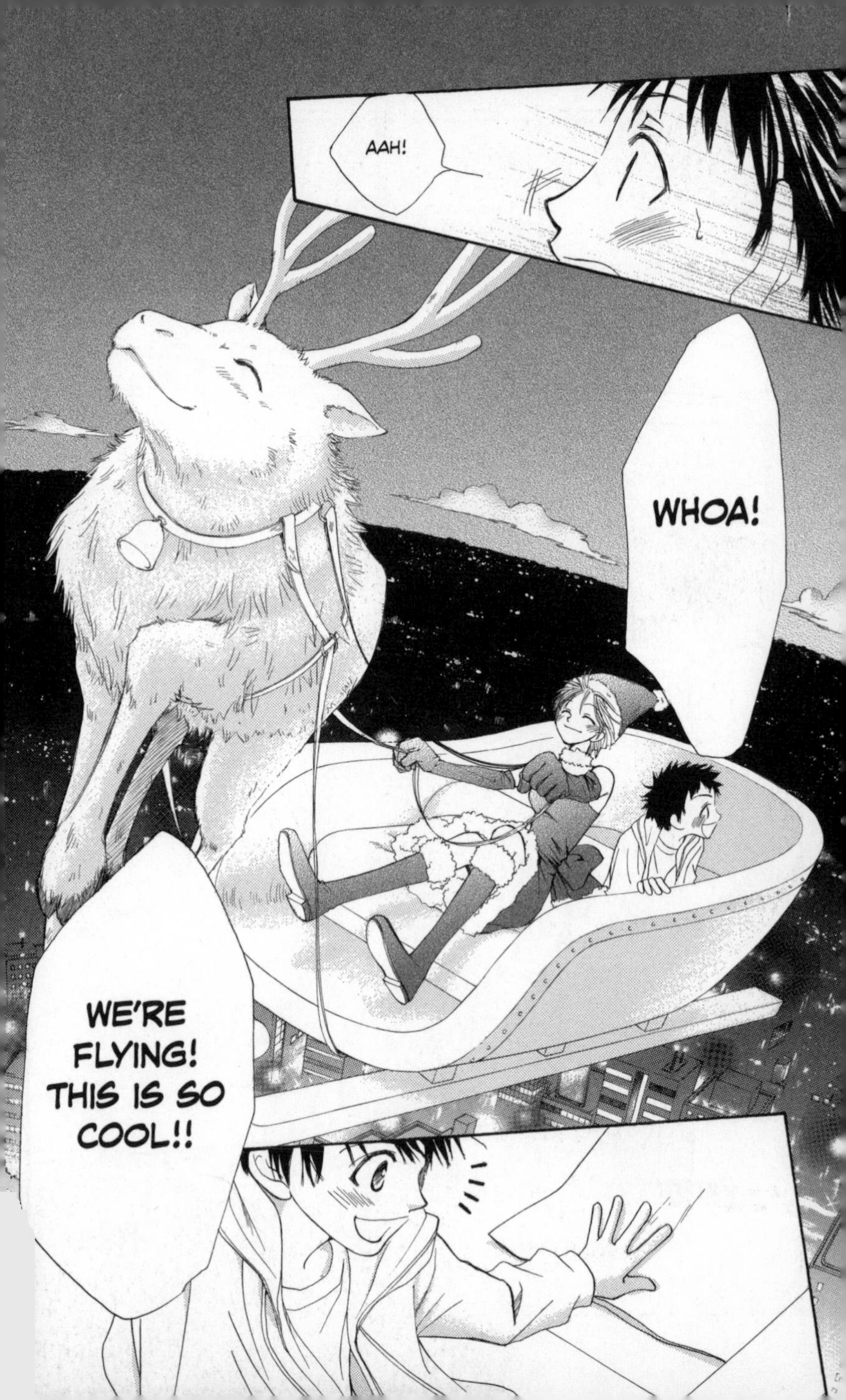
AAH!
WHOA!
WE'RE FLYING! THIS IS SO COOL!!

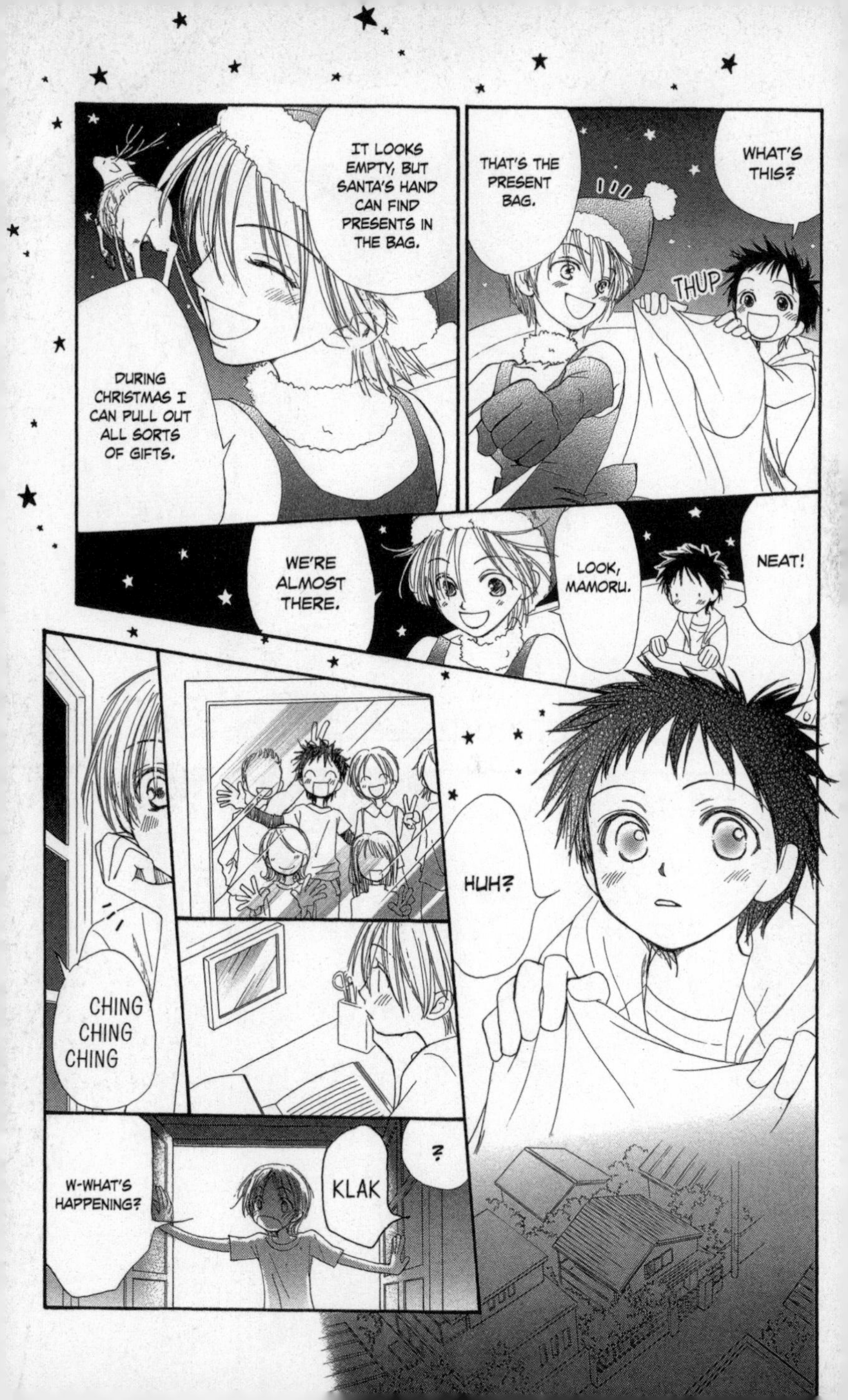
WHAT'S THIS?
THUP
THAT'S THE PRESENT BAG.
IT LOOKS EMPTY, BUT SANTA'S HAND CAN FIND PRESENTS IN THE BAG.
DURING CHRISTMAS I CAN PULL OUT ALL SORTS OF GIFTS.
NEAT!
LOOK, MAMORU.
WE'RE ALMOST THERE.
HUH?
CHING CHING CHING
?
KLAK
W-WHAT'S HAPPENING?

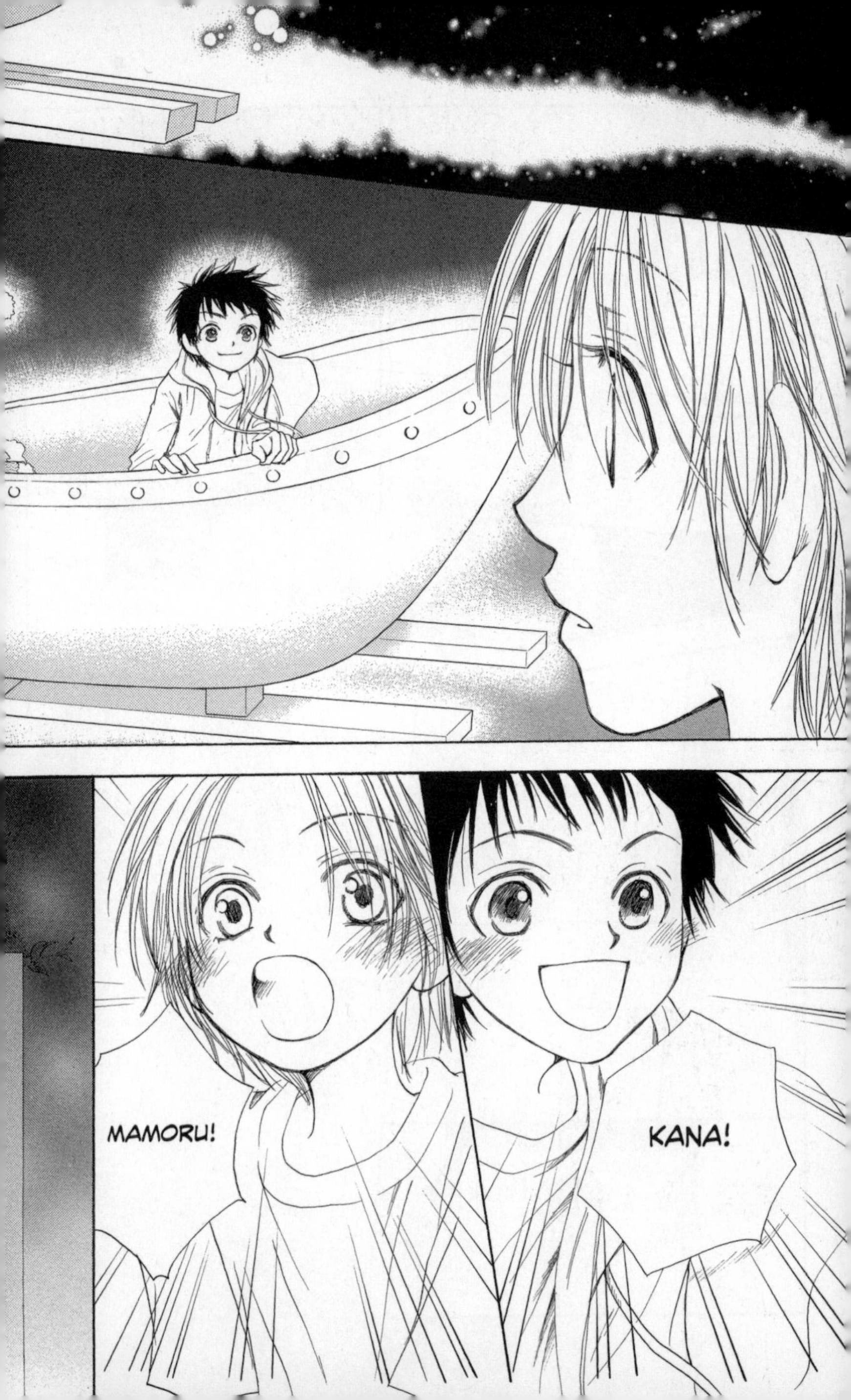
KANA!
MAMORU!

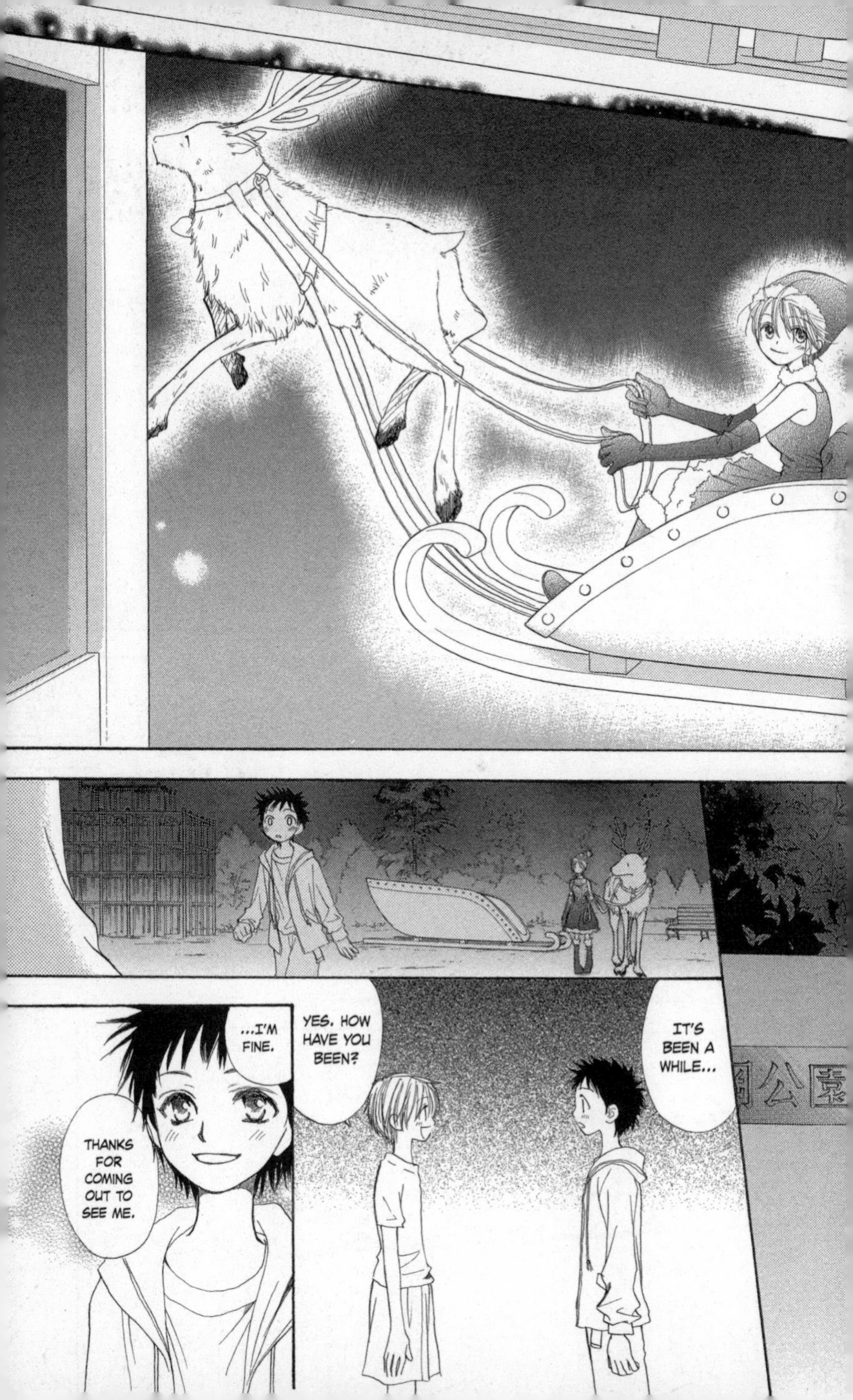
IT'S BEEN A WHILE...
公園
YES. HOW HAVE YOU BEEN?
...I'M FINE.
THANKS FOR COMING OUT TO SEE ME.

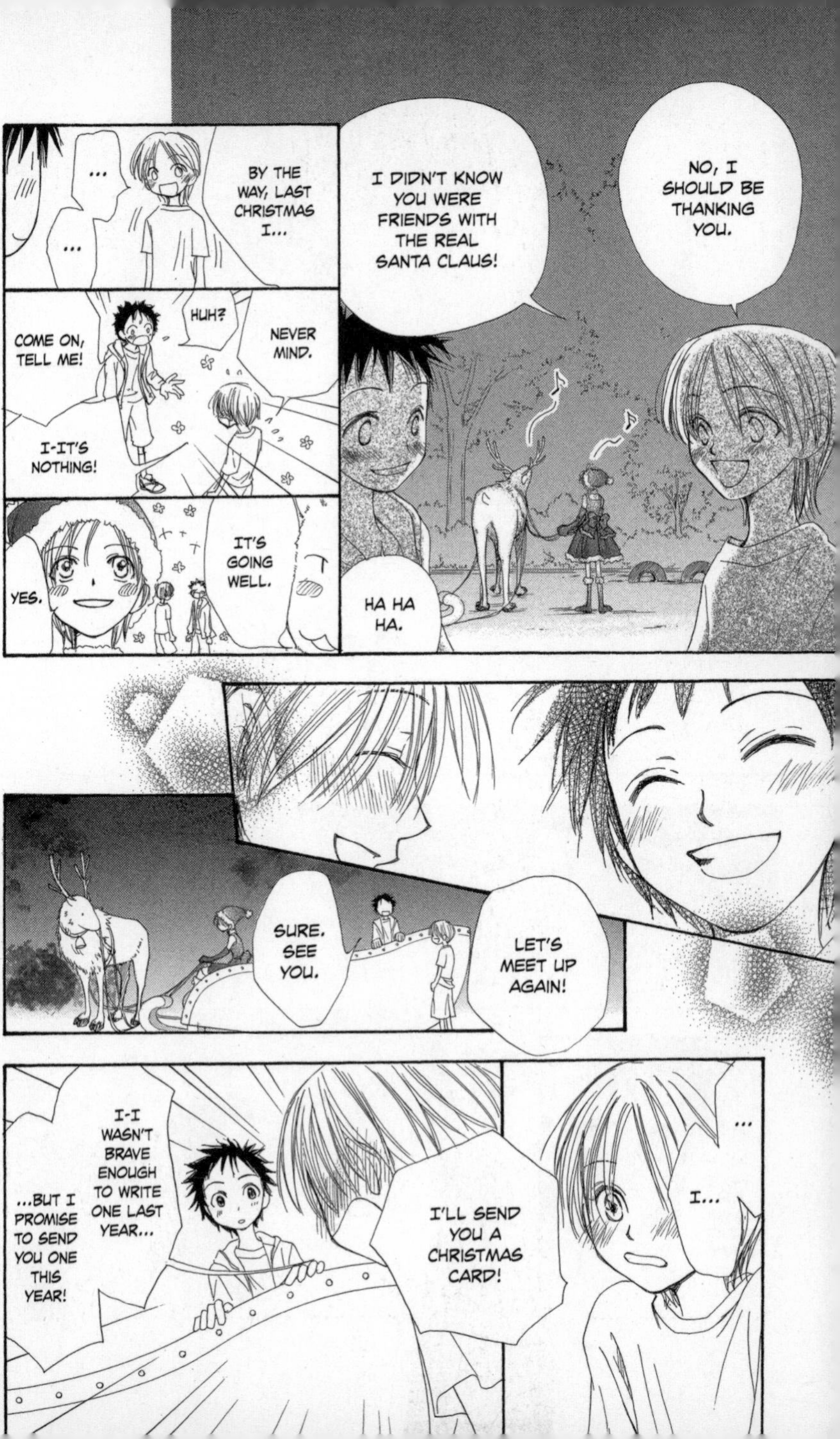
NO, I SHOULD BE THANKING YOU.
I DIDN'T KNOW YOU WERE FRIENDS WITH THE REAL SANTA CLAUS!
HA HA HA.
BY THE WAY, LAST CHRISTMAS I...
...
...
NEVER MIND.
HUH?
COME ON, TELL ME!
I-IT'S NOTHING!
IT'S GOING WELL.
YES.
LET'S MEET UP AGAIN!
SURE. SEE YOU.
...
I...
I'LL SEND YOU A CHRISTMAS CARD!
I-I WASN'T BRAVE ENOUGH TO WRITE ONE LAST YEAR...
...BUT I PROMISE TO SEND YOU ONE THIS YEAR!

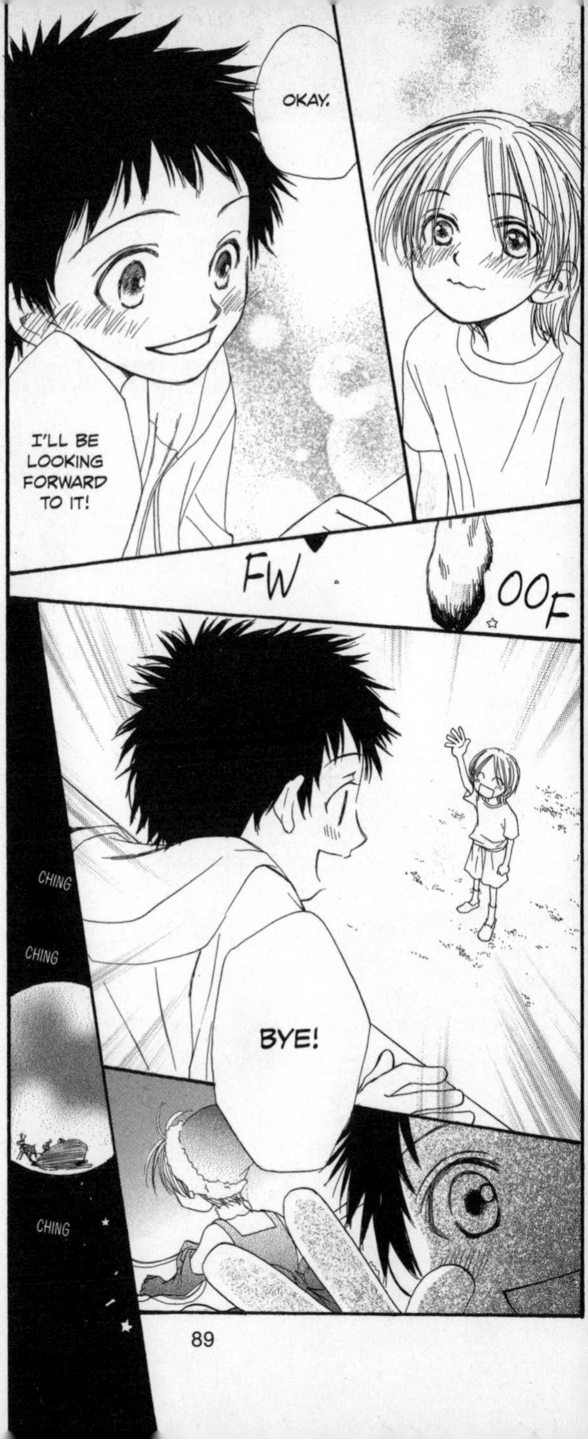
OKAY.
I'LL BE LOOKING FORWARD TO IT!
FWOOF
BYE!
CHING
CHING
CHING

1/4 Sakura Mail

Part 3

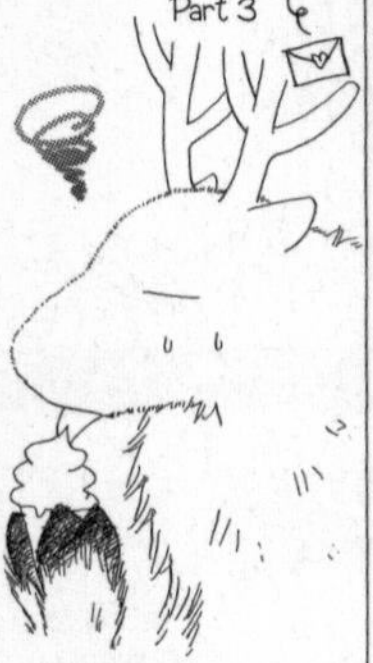

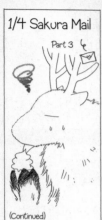

(Continued)

If the manga is about a Santa and a reindeer, then there should be cute Santa outfits! That's why I made a female Santa, so it followed that the servant would be a boy. I had a lot of trouble deciding on the setting for the story. Kaito's background was easy, but Kurumi started out as a completely different kind of character. It's probably because the image of a master and servant relationship in my mind was too strong.

(Continues)

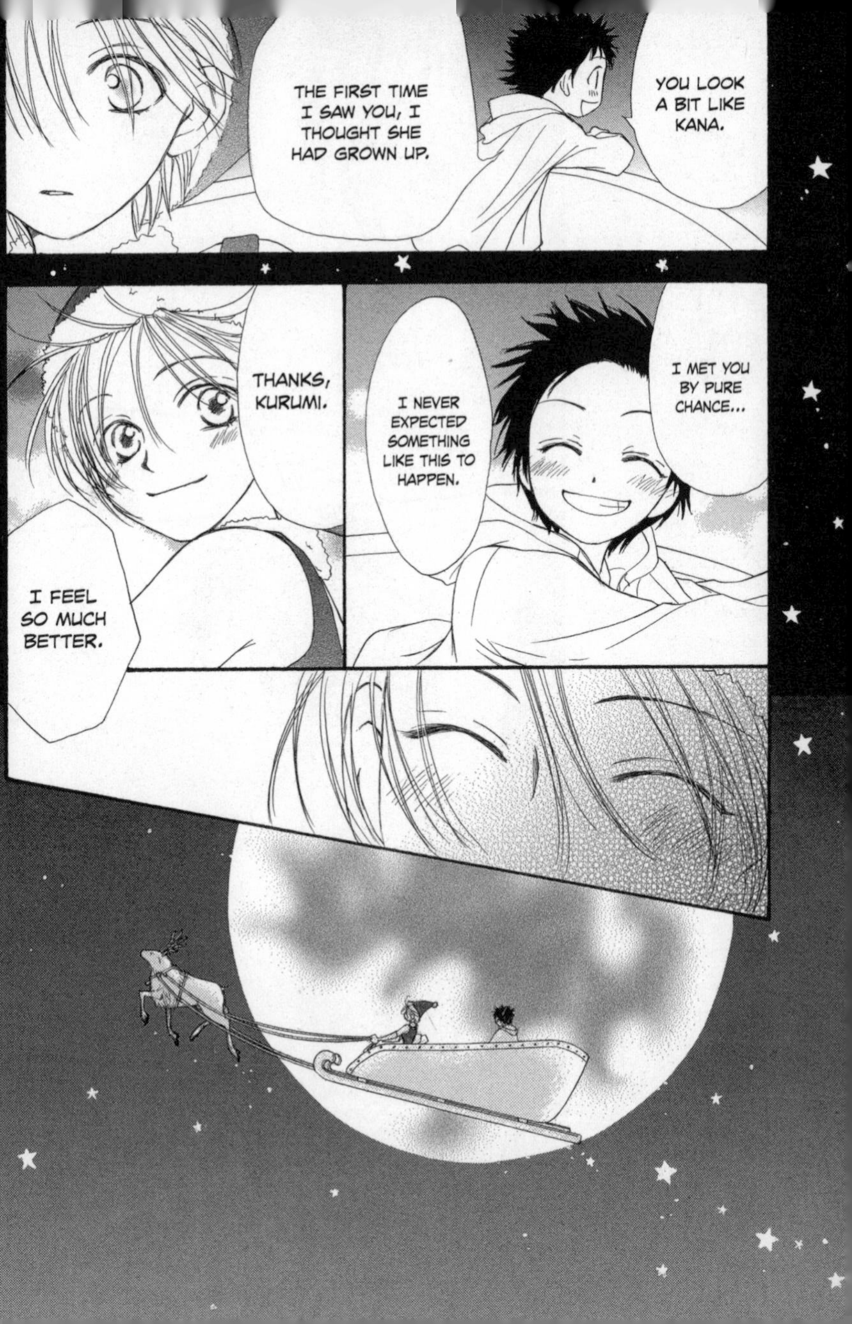
YOU LOOK A BIT LIKE KANA.
THE FIRST TIME I SAW YOU, I THOUGHT SHE HAD GROWN UP.
I MET YOU BY PURE CHANCE...
I NEVER EXPECTED SOMETHING LIKE THIS TO HAPPEN.
THANKS, KURUMI.
I FEEL SO MUCH BETTER.

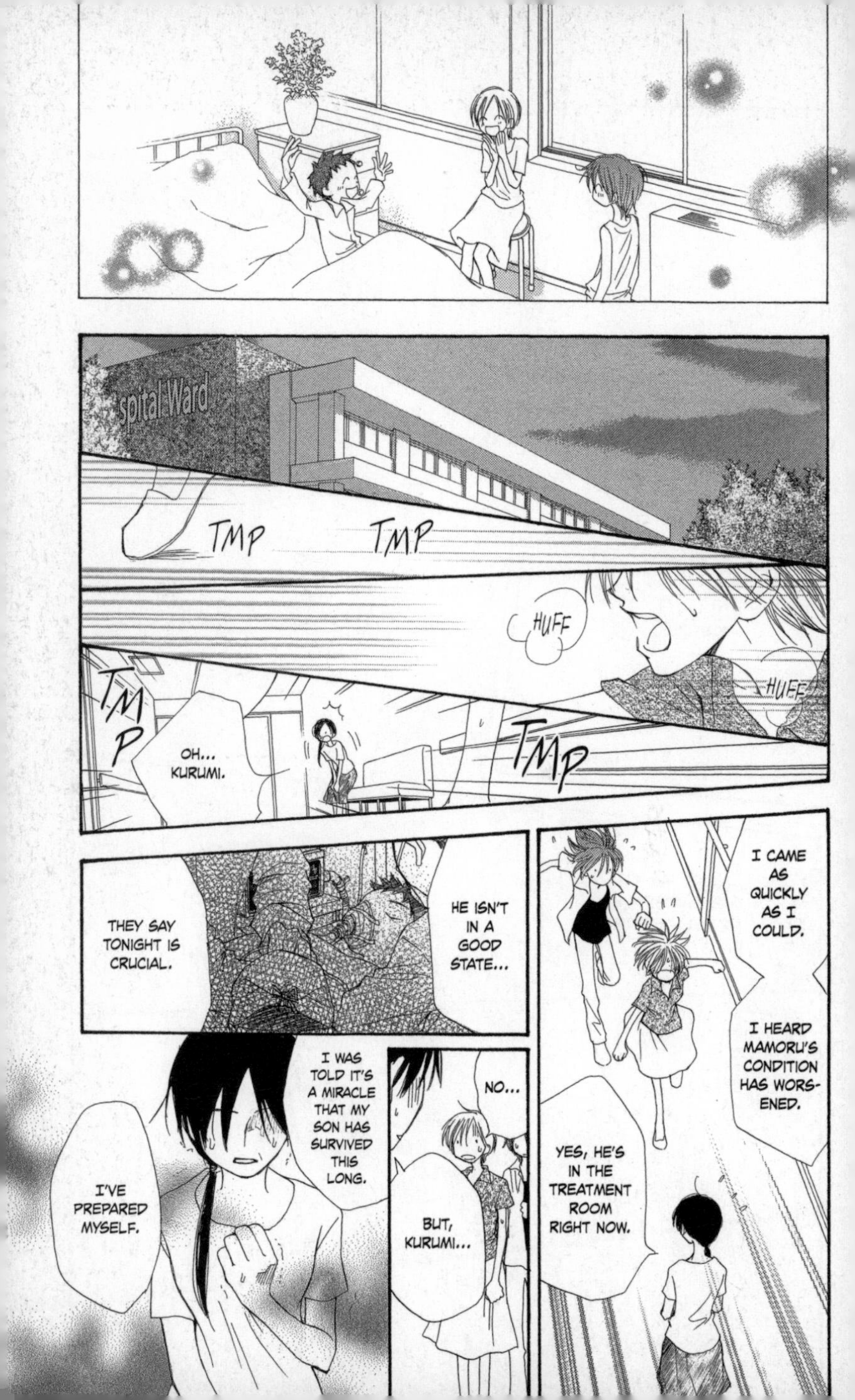
spital Ward
TMP
TMP
HUFF
HUFF
TMP
TMP
OH... KURUMI.
I CAME AS QUICKLY AS I COULD.
I HEARD MAMORU'S CONDITION HAS WORSENED.
YES, HE'S IN THE TREATMENT ROOM RIGHT NOW.
HE ISN'T IN A GOOD STATE...
THEY SAY TONIGHT IS CRUCIAL.
NO...
BUT, KURUMI...
I WAS TOLD IT'S A MIRACLE THAT MY SON HAS SURVIVED THIS LONG.
I'VE PREPARED MYSELF.

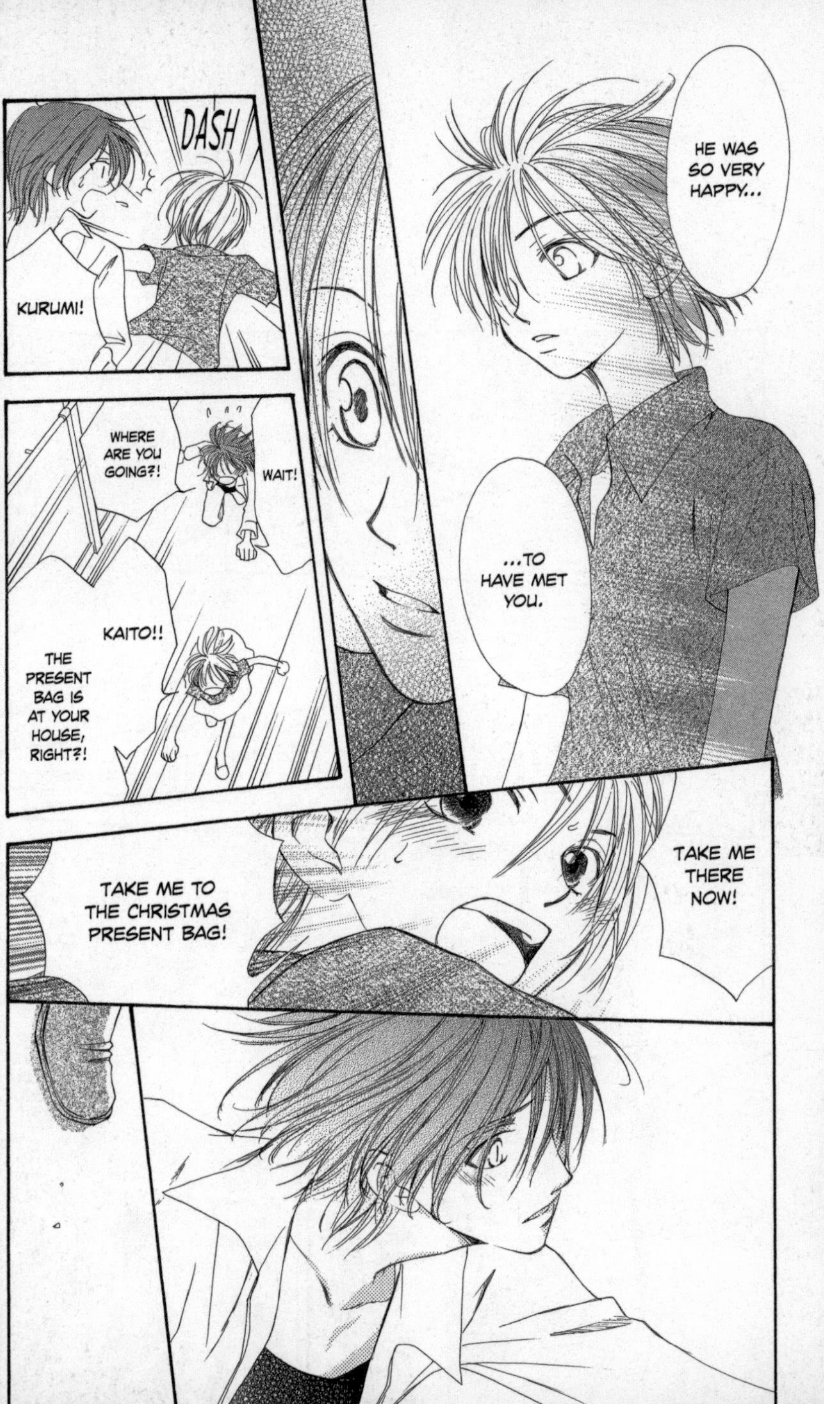
HE WAS SO VERY HAPPY...
...TO HAVE MET YOU.
DASH
KURUMI!
WHERE ARE YOU GOING?!
WAIT!
KAITO!!
THE PRESENT BAG IS AT YOUR HOUSE, RIGHT?!
TAKE ME THERE NOW!
TAKE ME TO THE CHRISTMAS PRESENT BAG!

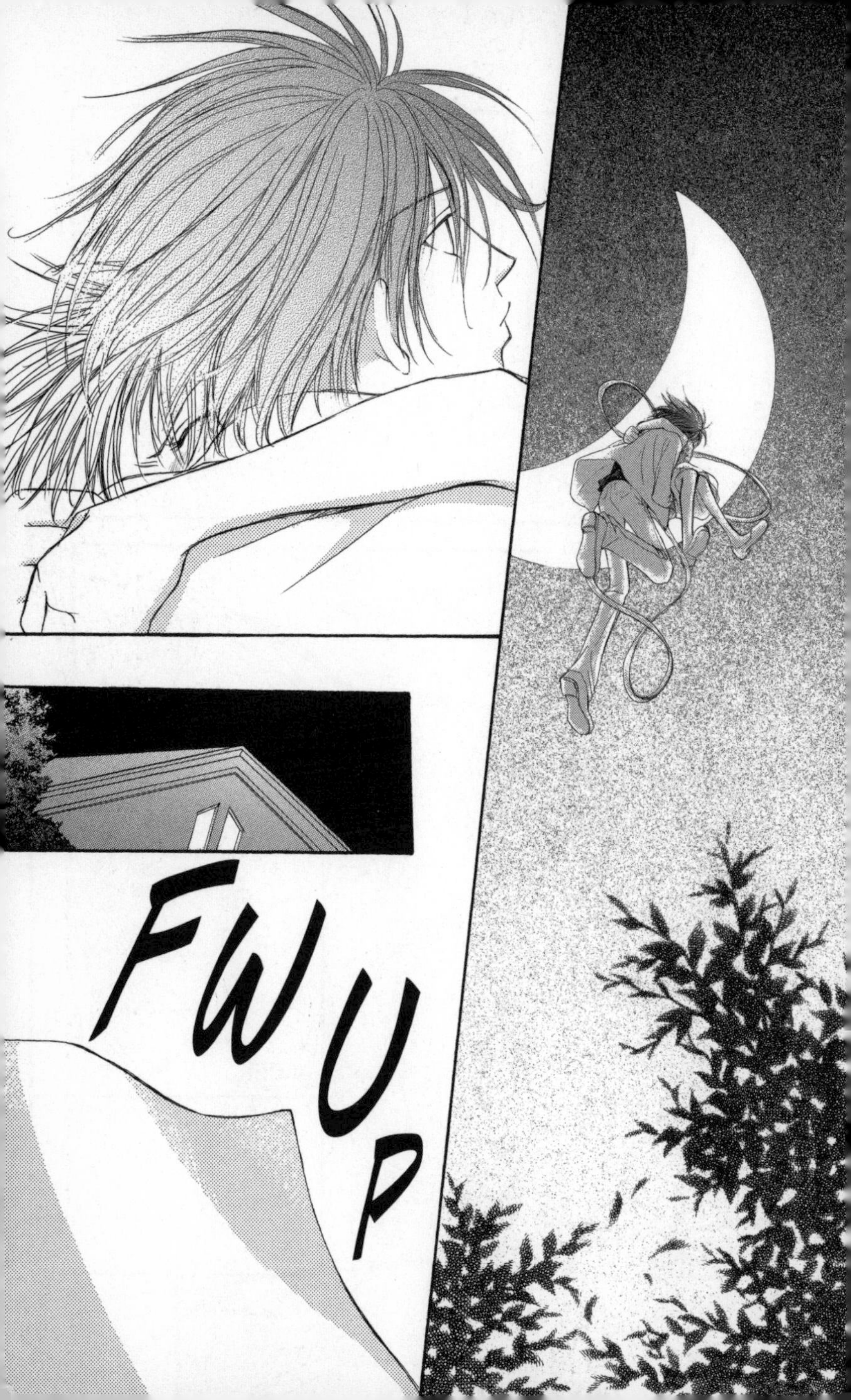
FWUP

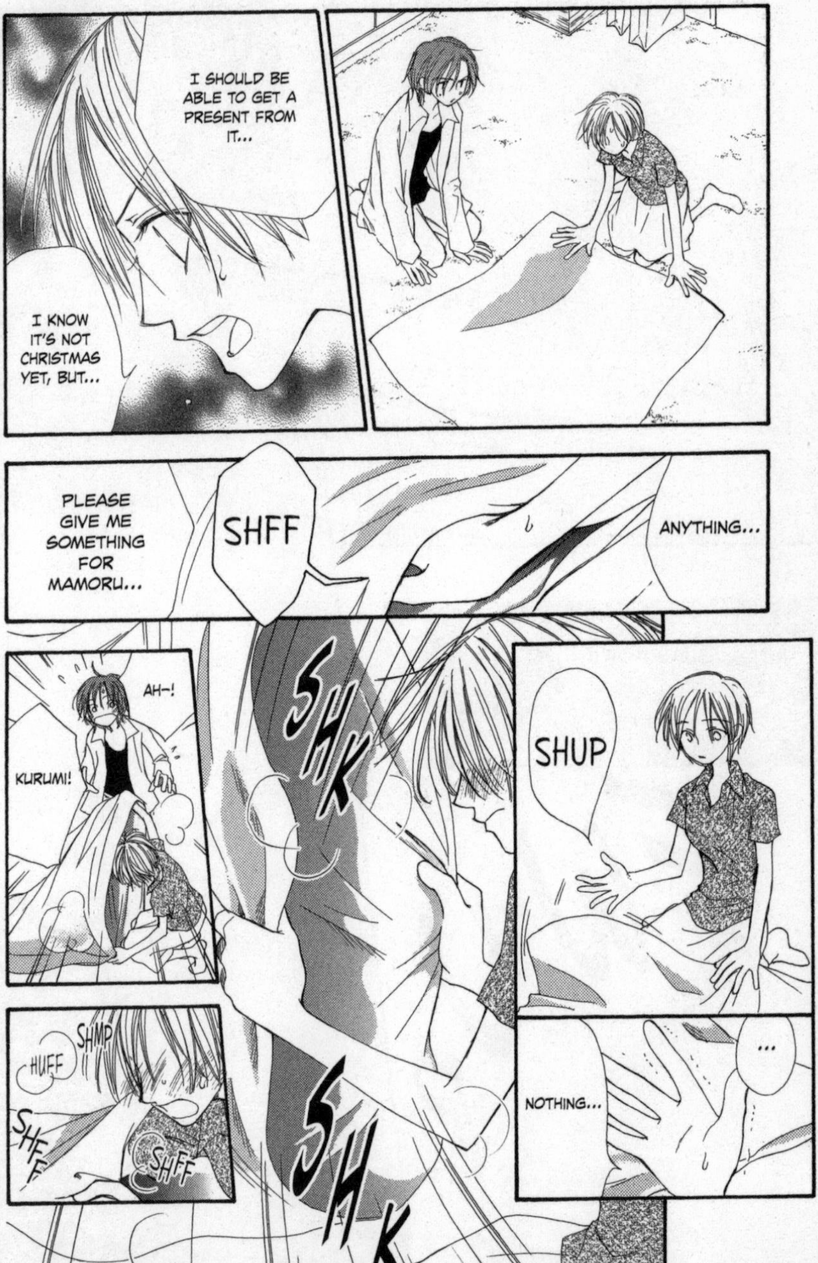
I SHOULD BE ABLE TO GET A PRESENT FROM IT...
I KNOW IT'S NOT CHRISTMAS YET, BUT...
ANYTHING...
SHFF
PLEASE GIVE ME SOMETHING FOR MAMORU...
SHUP
SHK
AH-!
KURUMI!
...
NOTHING...
SHK
SHMP
HUFF
SHFF
SHFF

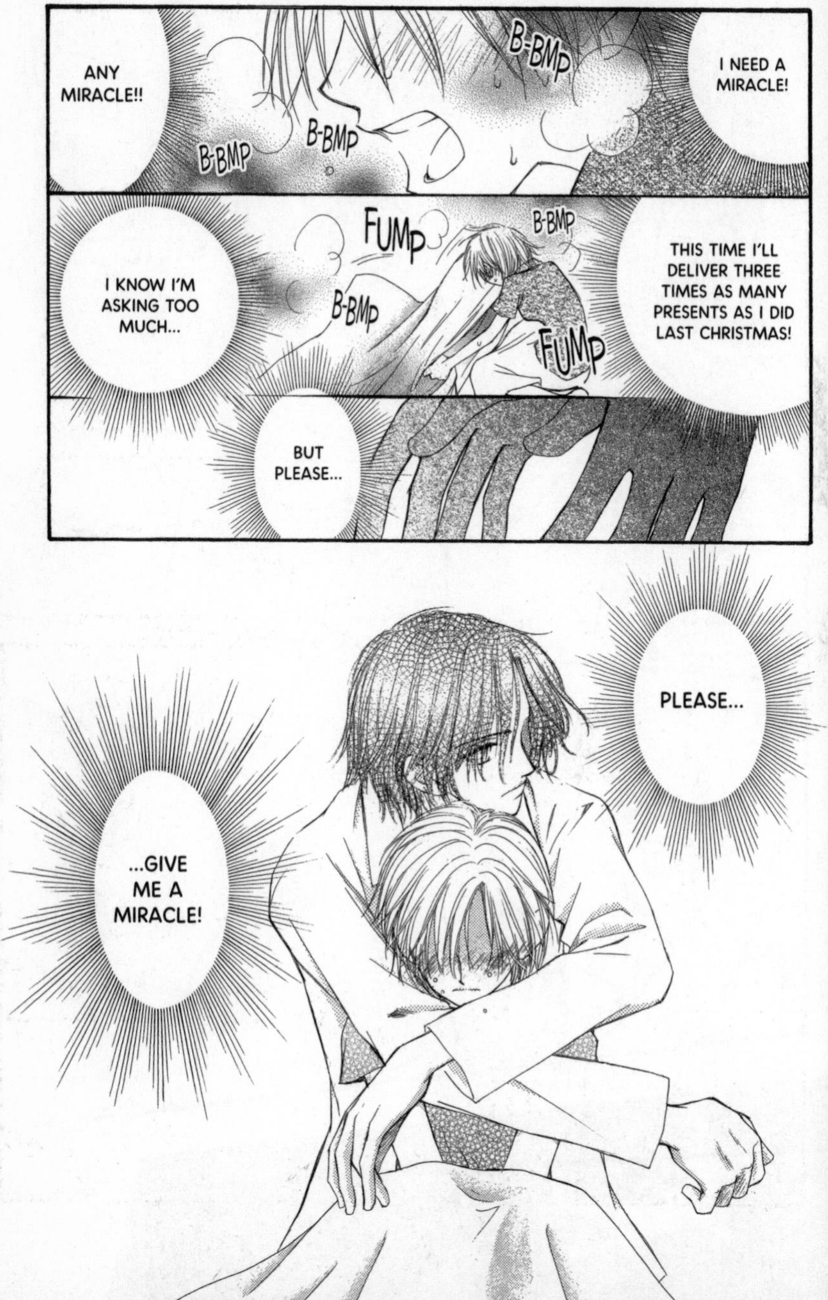
I NEED A MIRACLE!
B-BMP
B-BMP
B-BMP
ANY MIRACLE!!
THIS TIME I'LL DELIVER THREE TIMES AS MANY PRESENTS AS I DID LAST CHRISTMAS!
B-BMP
FUMP
FUMP
B-BMP
I KNOW I'M ASKING TOO MUCH...
BUT PLEASE...
PLEASE...
...GIVE ME A MIRACLE!

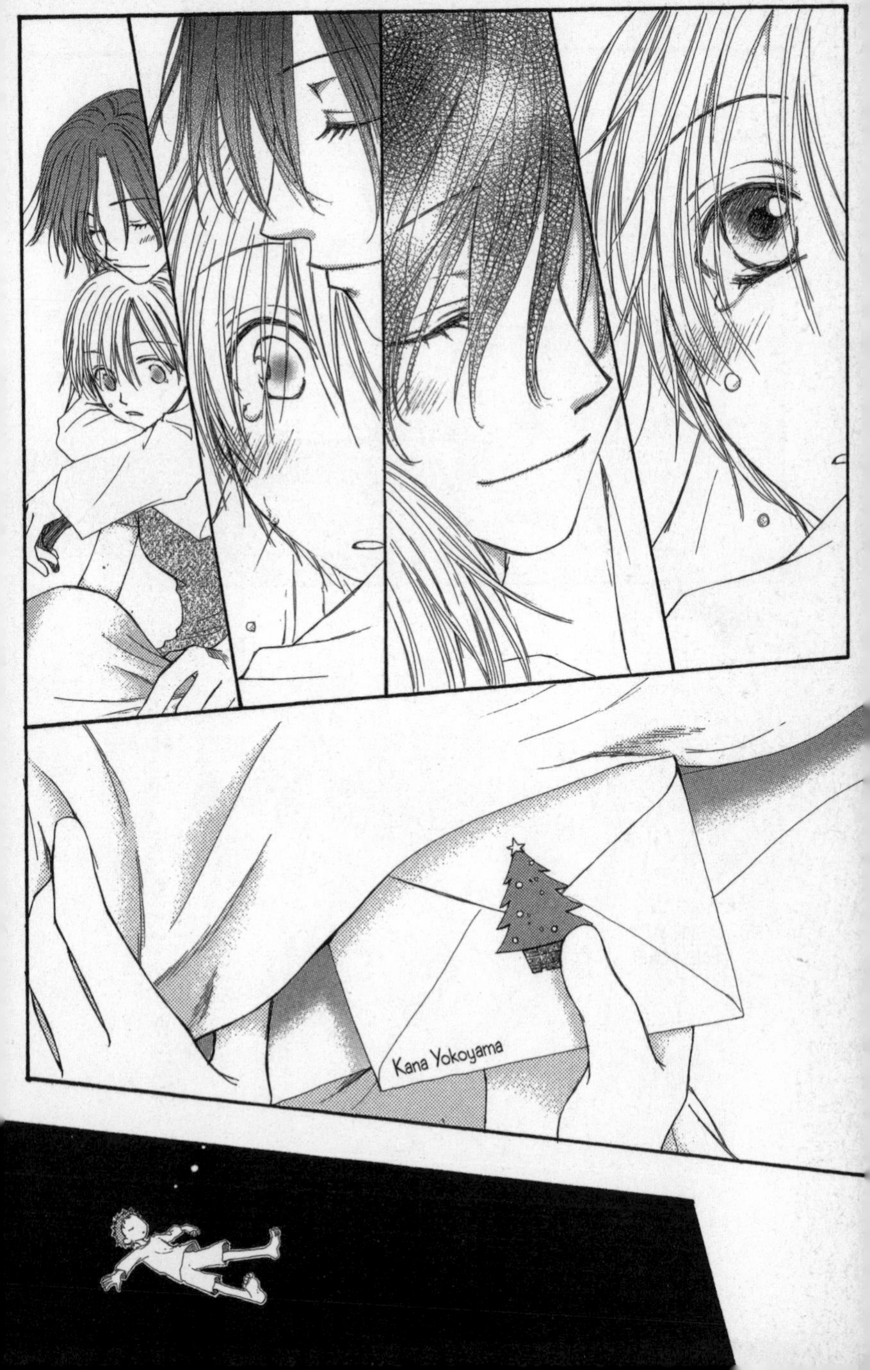
Kana Yokoyama

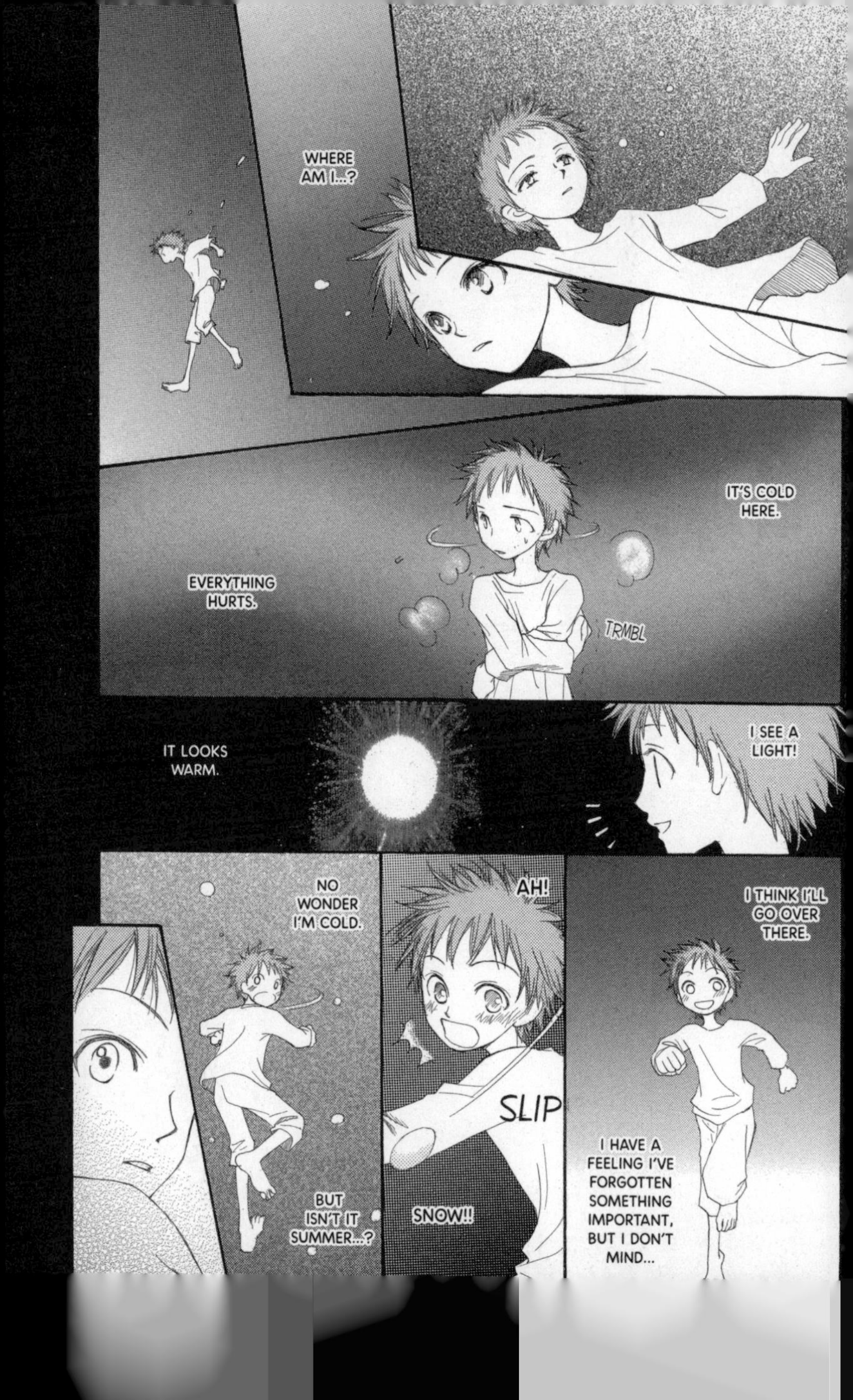
WHERE AM I...?
IT'S COLD HERE.
EVERYTHING HURTS.
TRMBL
I SEE A LIGHT!
IT LOOKS WARM.
I THINK I'LL GO OVER THERE.
I HAVE A FEELING I'VE FORGOTTEN SOMETHING IMPORTANT, BUT I DON'T MIND...
AH!
SLIP
SNOW!!
NO WONDER I'M COLD.
BUT ISN'T IT SUMMER...?

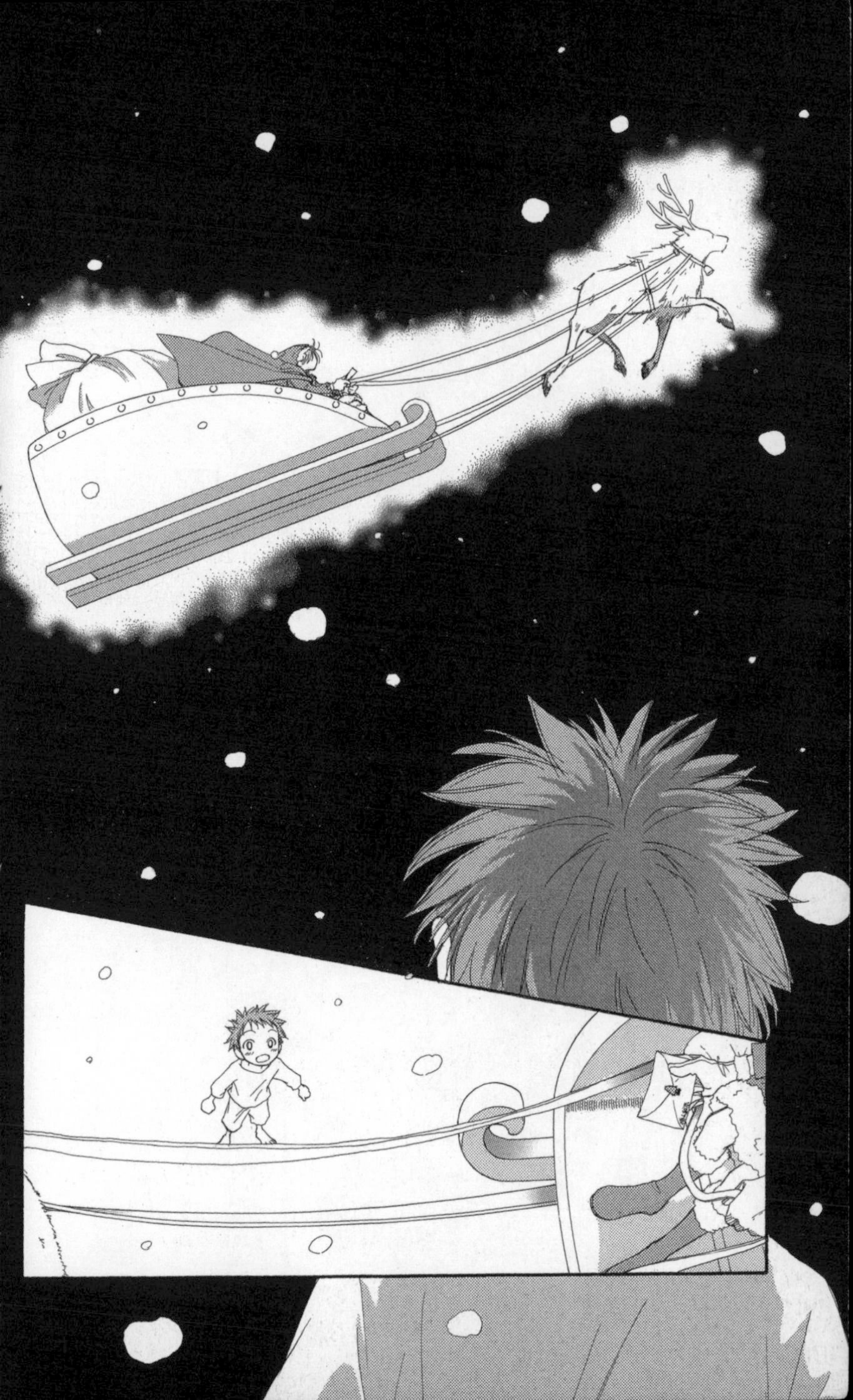

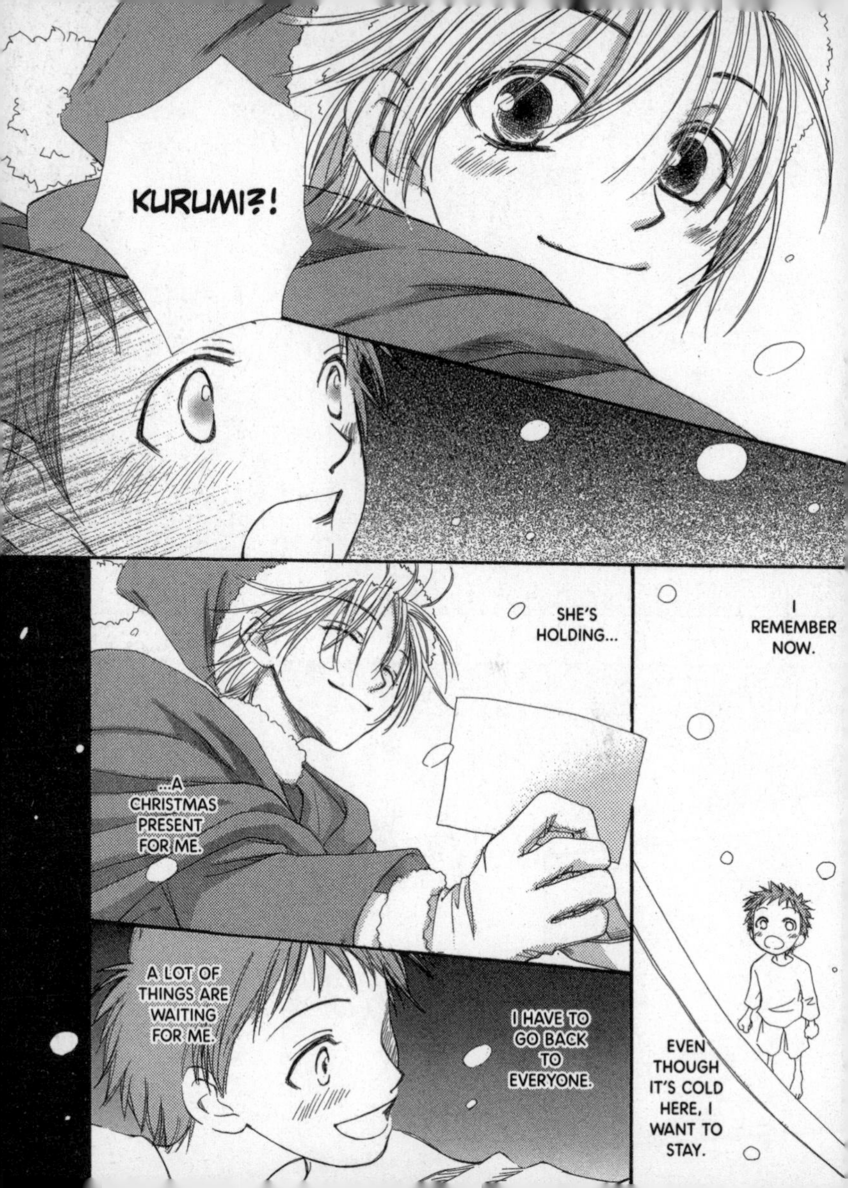
KURUMI?!
I REMEMBER NOW.
EVEN THOUGH IT'S COLD HERE, I WANT TO STAY.
SHE'S HOLDING...
...A CHRISTMAS PRESENT FOR ME.
I HAVE TO GO BACK TO EVERYONE.
A LOT OF THINGS ARE WAITING FOR ME.

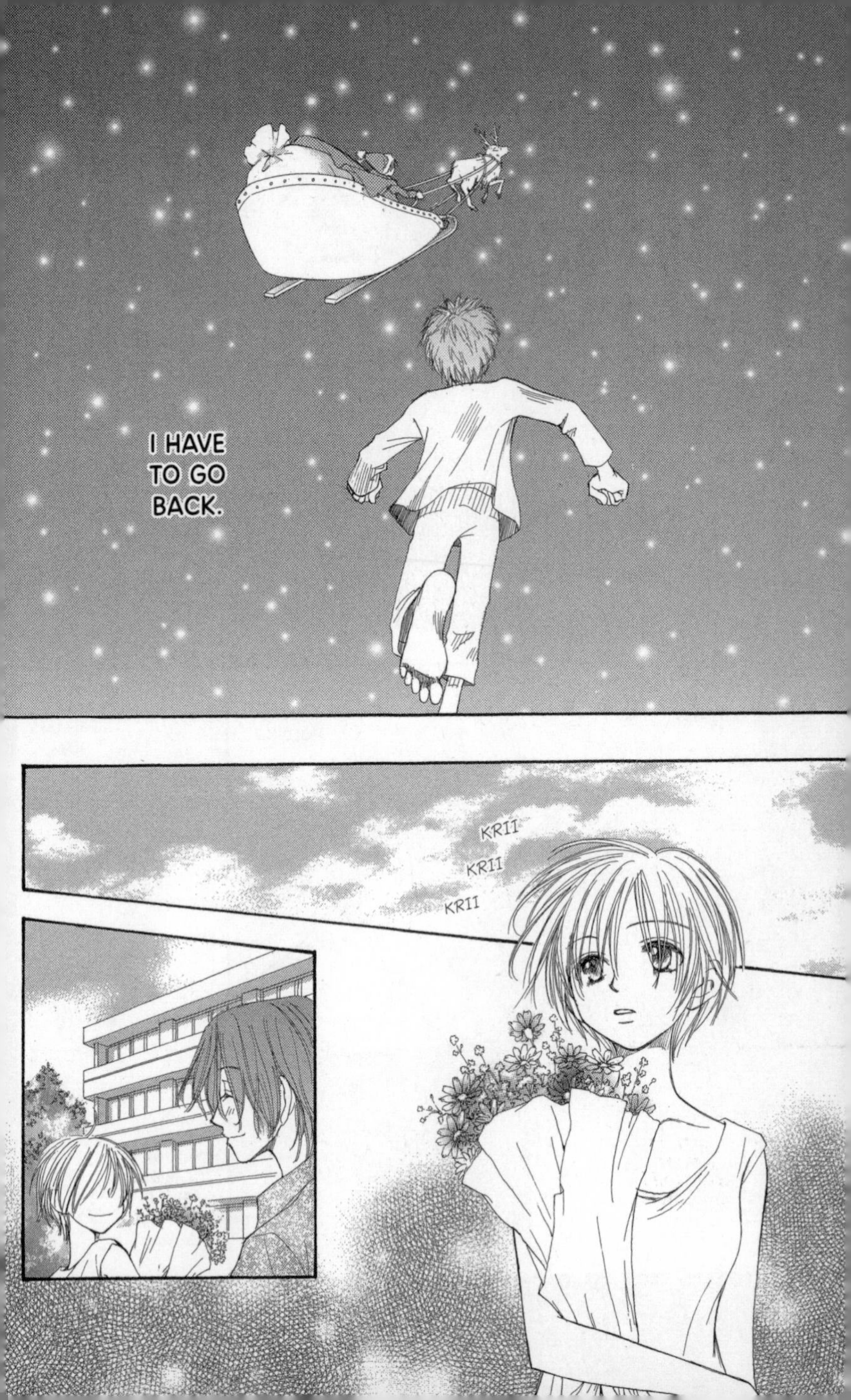
I HAVE TO GO BACK.
KRII
KRII
KRII

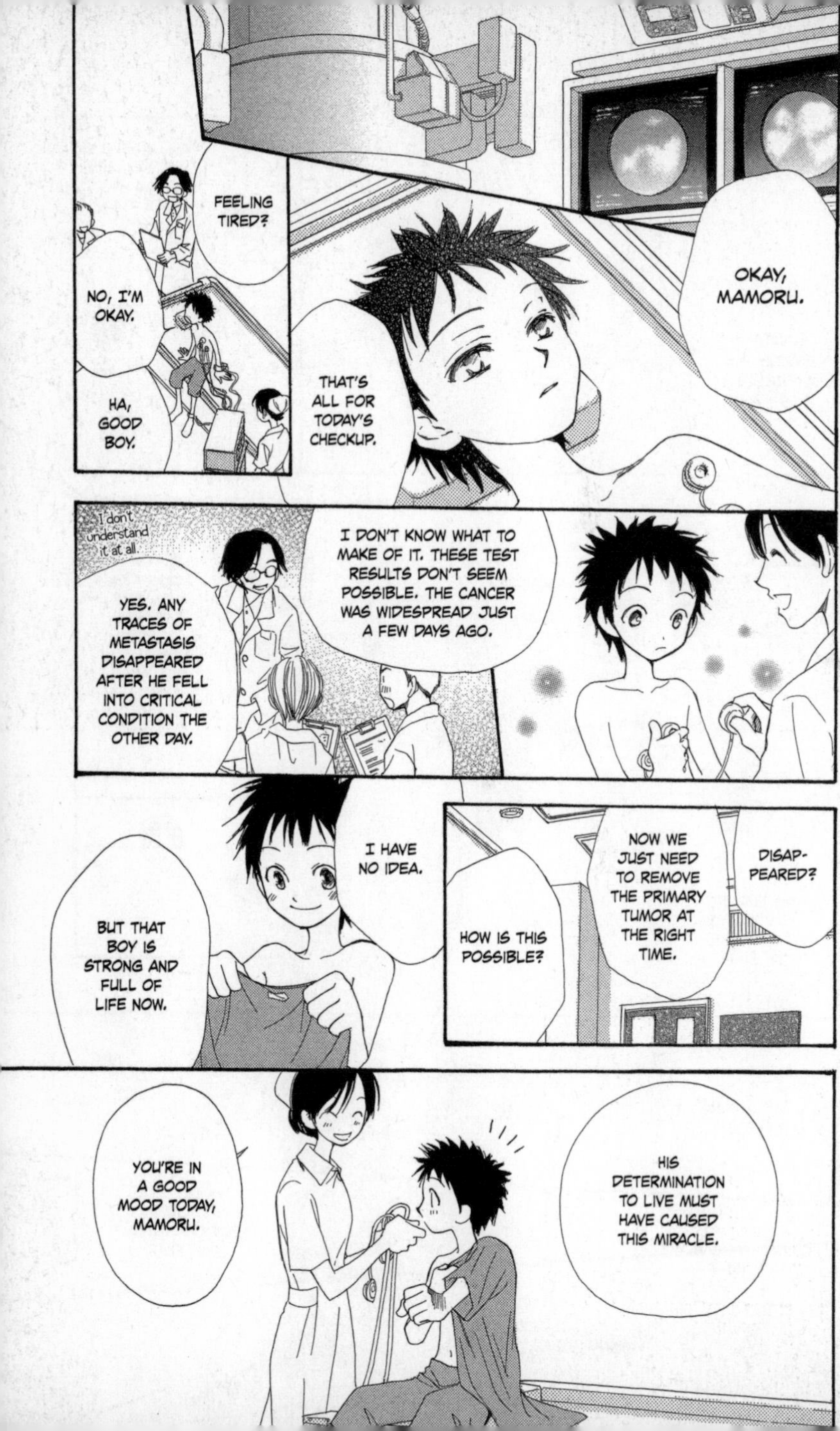
OKAY, MAMORU.
THAT'S ALL FOR TODAY'S CHECKUP.
FEELING TIRED?
NO, I'M OKAY.
HA, GOOD BOY.
I DON'T KNOW WHAT TO MAKE OF IT. THESE TEST RESULTS DON'T SEEM POSSIBLE. THE CANCER WAS WIDESPREAD JUST A FEW DAYS AGO.
I don't understand it at all.
YES. ANY TRACES OF METASTASIS DISAPPEARED AFTER HE FELL INTO CRITICAL CONDITION THE OTHER DAY.
DISAP-PEARED?
NOW WE JUST NEED TO REMOVE THE PRIMARY TUMOR AT THE RIGHT TIME.
HOW IS THIS POSSIBLE?
I HAVE NO IDEA.
BUT THAT BOY IS STRONG AND FULL OF LIFE NOW.
HIS DETERMINATION TO LIVE MUST HAVE CAUSED THIS MIRACLE.
YOU'RE IN A GOOD MOOD TODAY, MAMORU.

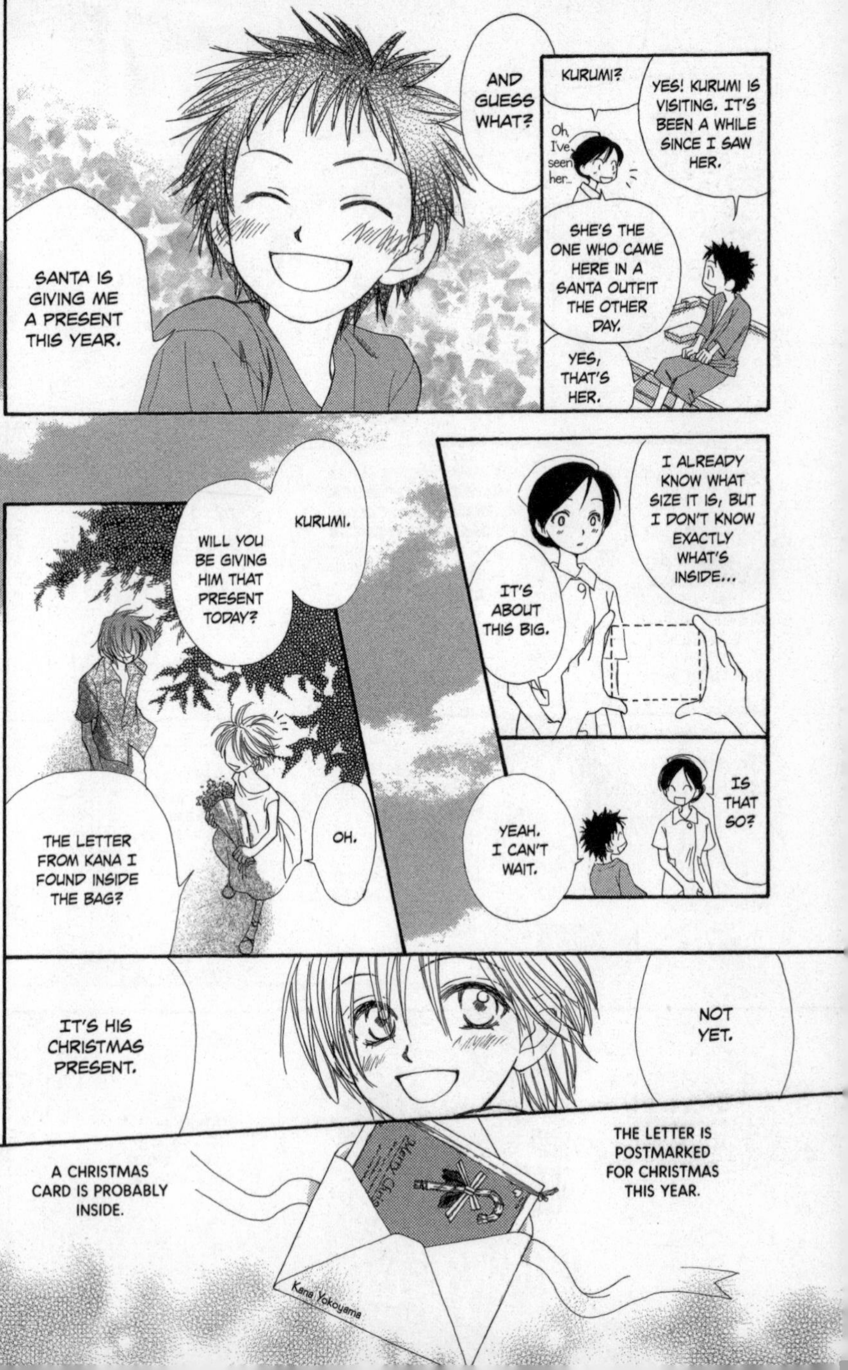
YES! KURUMI IS VISITING. IT'S BEEN A WHILE SINCE I SAW HER.
KURUMI?
Oh, I've seen her...
SHE'S THE ONE WHO CAME HERE IN A SANTA OUTFIT THE OTHER DAY.
YES, THAT'S HER.
AND GUESS WHAT?
SANTA IS GIVING ME A PRESENT THIS YEAR.
I ALREADY KNOW WHAT SIZE IT IS, BUT I DON'T KNOW EXACTLY WHAT'S INSIDE...
IT'S ABOUT THIS BIG.
IS THAT SO?
YEAH. I CAN'T WAIT.
KURUMI.
WILL YOU BE GIVING HIM THAT PRESENT TODAY?
OH.
THE LETTER FROM KANA I FOUND INSIDE THE BAG?
NOT YET.
IT'S HIS CHRISTMAS PRESENT.
THE LETTER IS POSTMARKED FOR CHRISTMAS THIS YEAR.
A CHRISTMAS CARD IS PROBABLY INSIDE.
Kana Yokoyama

1/4 Sakura Mail

Part 4

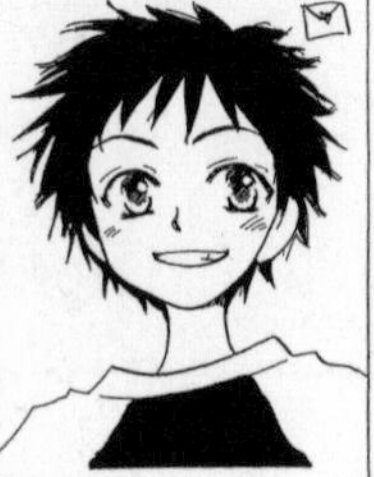

(Continued)

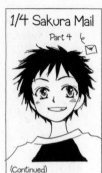

It took me a very long time to create the stories for *Sweet Rein*. I spent a lot of time on the first three chapters. When I had the opportunity to create the second chapter, I thought it would be a piece of cake compared to the first, but I was wrong. It took an awfully long time. But I'm glad I managed in the end. Although it's set in summer, I wanted to create a story about Santa and a child! It's funny to see how Kurumi is starting to get used to wearing her Santa outfit.

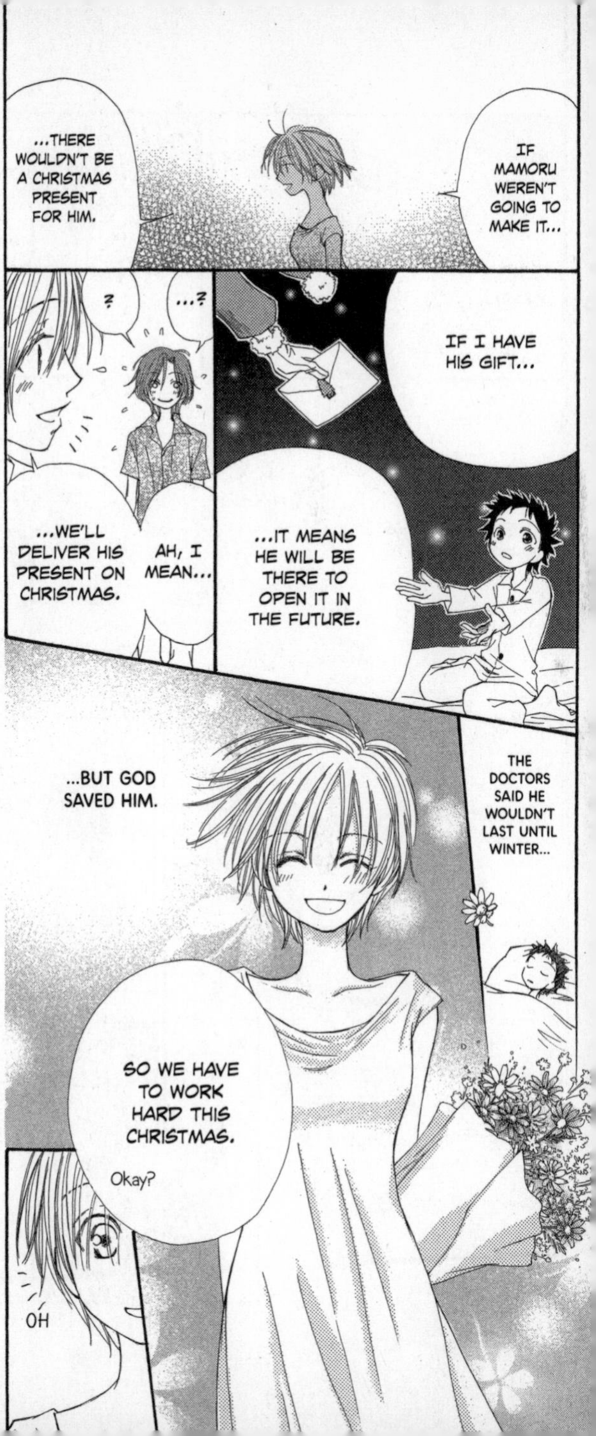
IF MAMORU WEREN'T GOING TO MAKE IT...
...THERE WOULDN'T BE A CHRISTMAS PRESENT FOR HIM.
IF I HAVE HIS GIFT...
...IT MEANS HE WILL BE THERE TO OPEN IT IN THE FUTURE.
...?
?
AH, I MEAN...
...WE'LL DELIVER HIS PRESENT ON CHRISTMAS.
THE DOCTORS SAID HE WOULDN'T LAST UNTIL WINTER...
...BUT GOD SAVED HIM.
SO WE HAVE TO WORK HARD THIS CHRISTMAS.
Okay?
OH

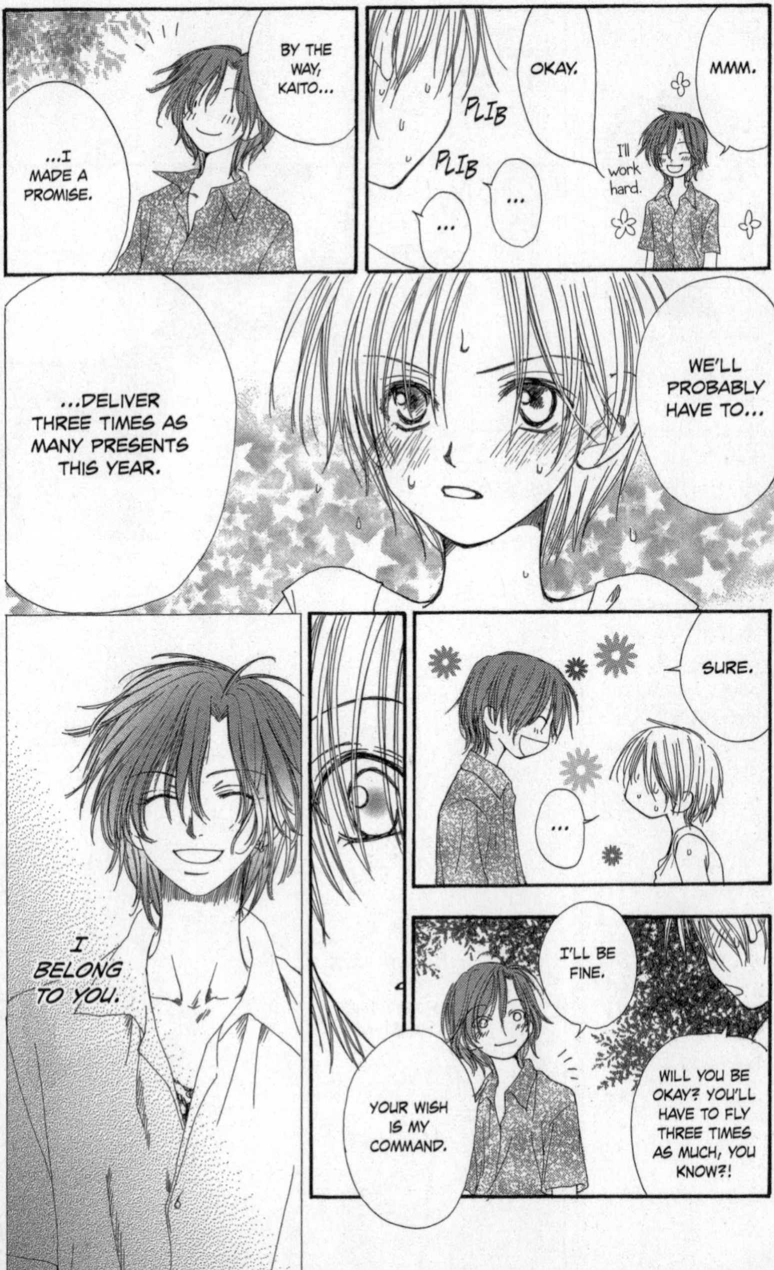
MMM.
I'll work hard.
OKAY.
PLIB
PLIB
...
...
BY THE WAY, KAITO...
...I MADE A PROMISE.
WE'LL PROBABLY HAVE TO...
...DELIVER THREE TIMES AS MANY PRESENTS THIS YEAR.
SURE.
...
WILL YOU BE OKAY? YOU'LL HAVE TO FLY THREE TIMES AS MUCH, YOU KNOW?!
I'LL BE FINE.
YOUR WISH IS MY COMMAND.
I BELONG TO YOU.

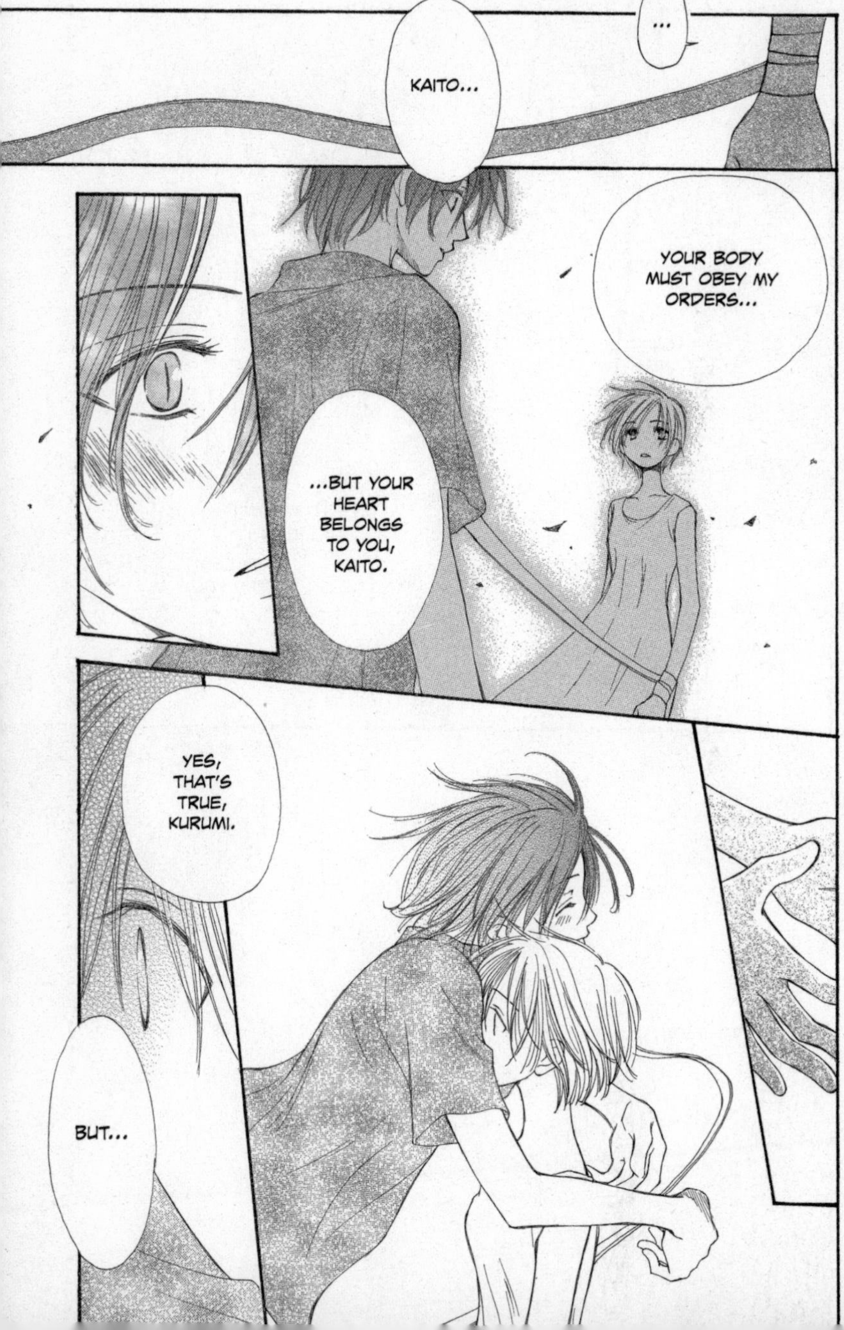
...
KAITO...
YOUR BODY MUST OBEY MY ORDERS...
...BUT YOUR HEART BELONGS TO YOU, KAITO.
YES, THAT'S TRUE, KURUMI.
BUT...

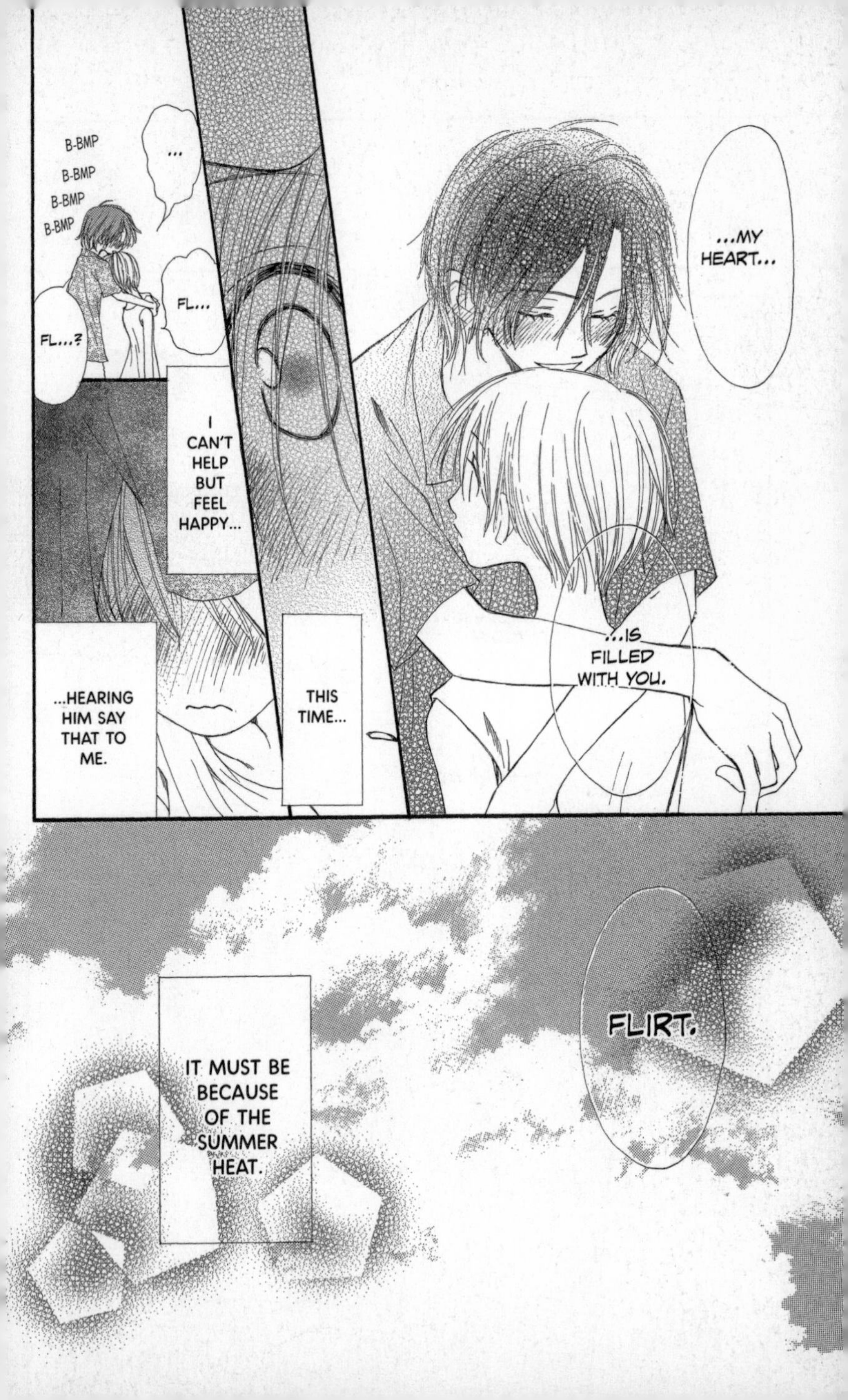
...MY HEART...
...IS FILLED WITH YOU.
THIS TIME...
I CAN'T HELP BUT FEEL HAPPY...
...
FL...
FL...?
B-BMP B-BMP B-BMP B-BMP
...HEARING HIM SAY THAT TO ME.
FLIRT.
IT MUST BE BECAUSE OF THE SUMMER HEAT.

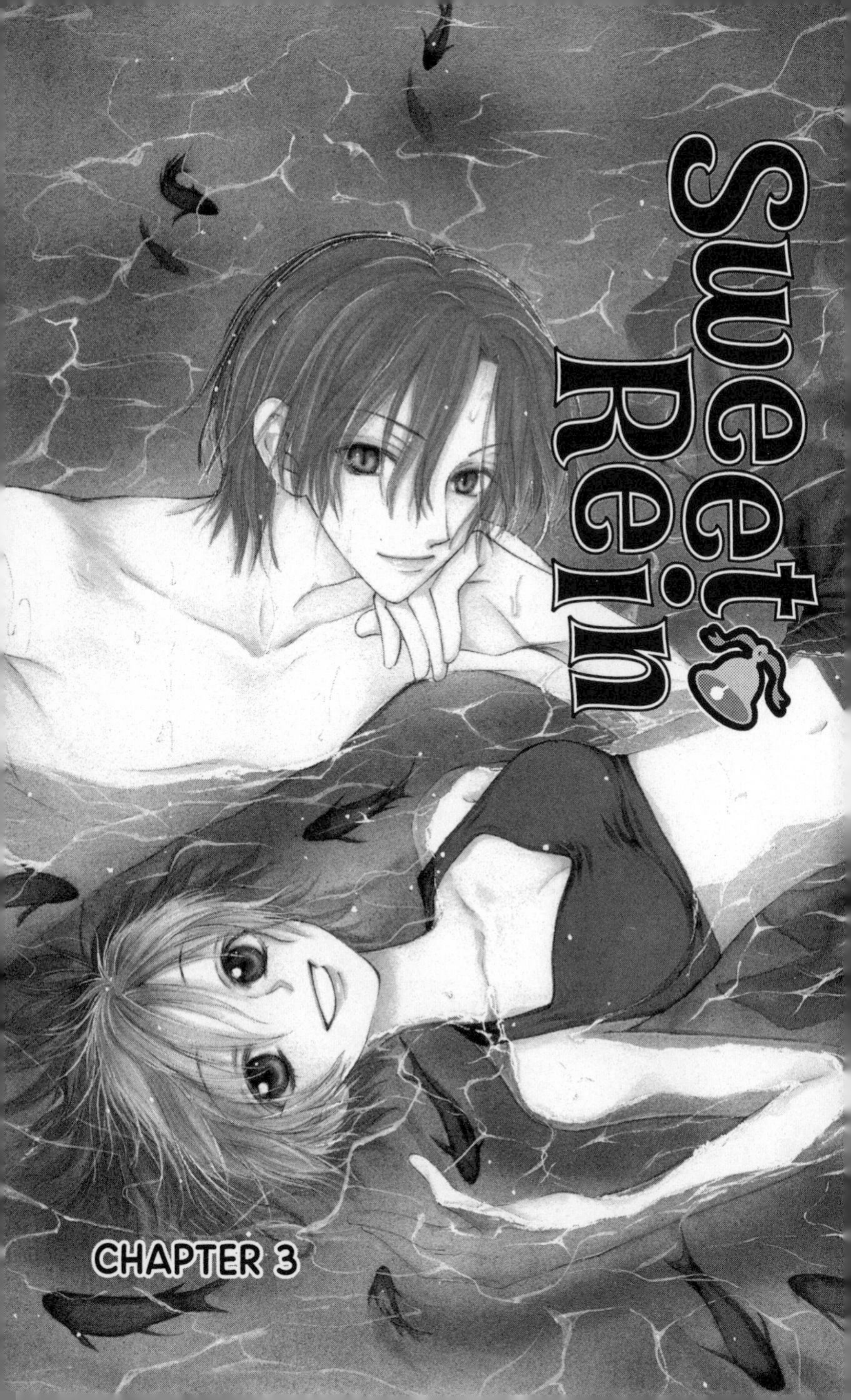
Sweet Rein
CHAPTER 3

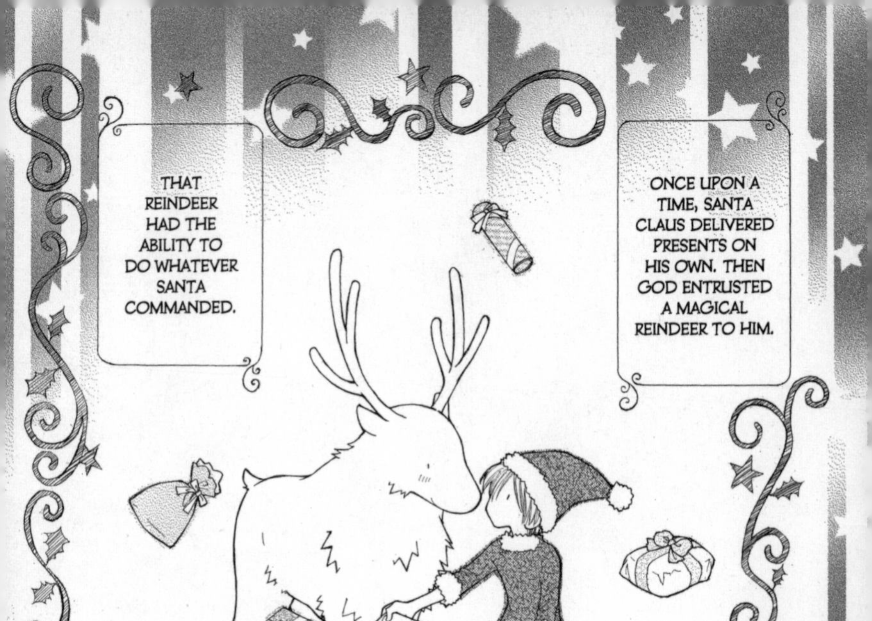
ONCE UPON A TIME, SANTA CLAUS DELIVERED PRESENTS ON HIS OWN. THEN GOD ENTRUSTED A MAGICAL REINDEER TO HIM.
THAT REINDEER HAD THE ABILITY TO DO WHATEVER SANTA COMMANDED.
THIS ENABLED SANTA CLAUS TO DELIVER PRESENTS TO GOOD CHILDREN EVERYWHERE.

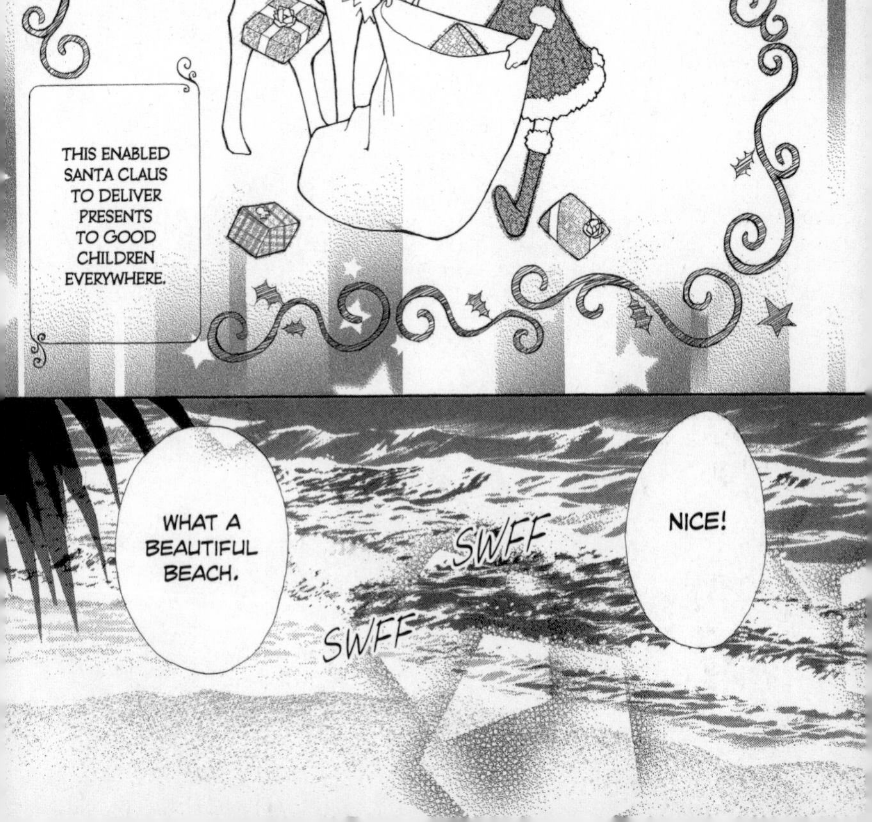
NICE!
SWFF
WHAT A BEAUTIFUL BEACH.
SWFF

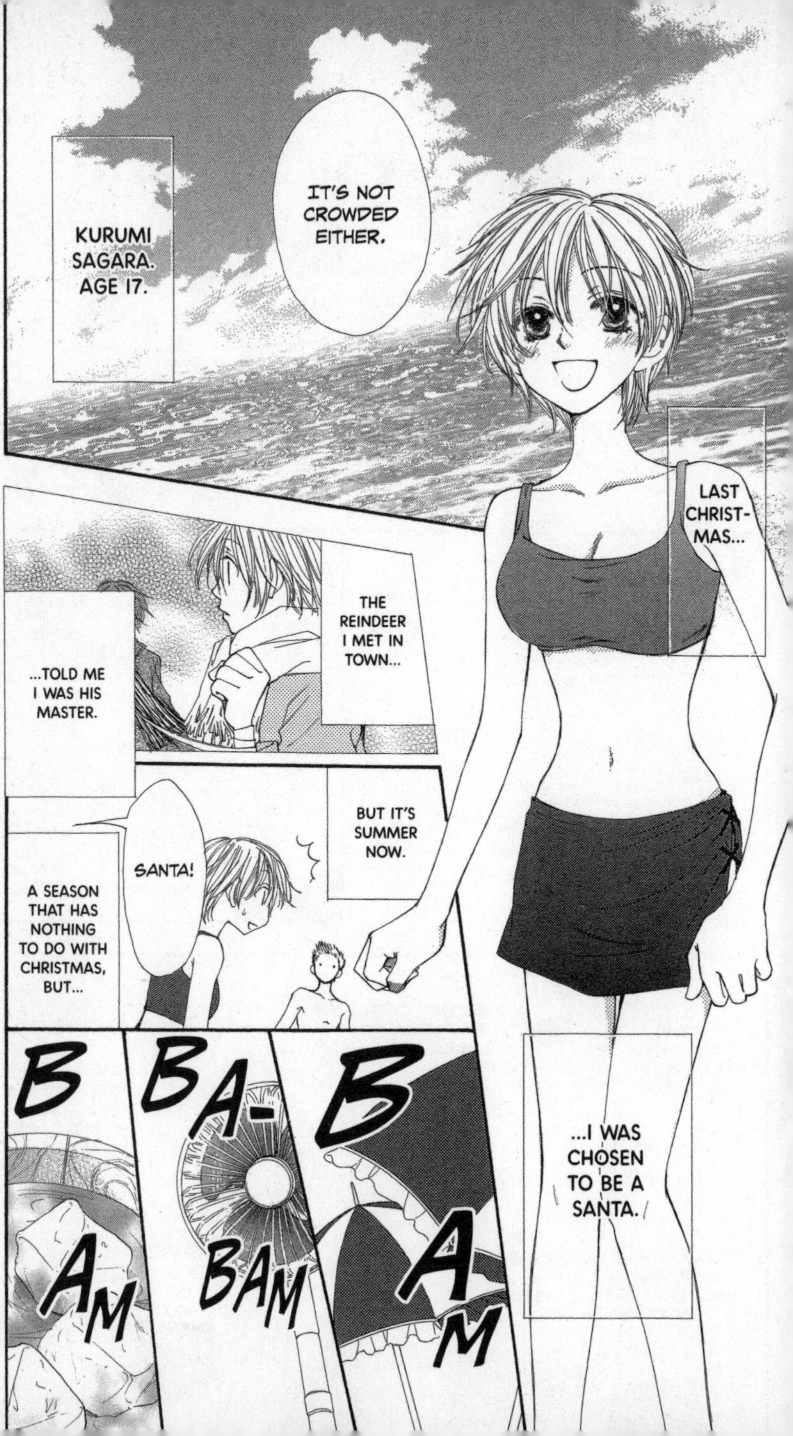
IT'S NOT CROWDED EITHER.
KURUMI SAGARA. AGE 17.
LAST CHRIST-MAS...
THE REINDEER I MET IN TOWN...
...TOLD ME I WAS HIS MASTER.
BUT IT'S SUMMER NOW.
SANTA!
A SEASON THAT HAS NOTHING TO DO WITH CHRISTMAS, BUT...
...I WAS CHOSEN TO BE A SANTA.
BAM
BA-BAM
BAM

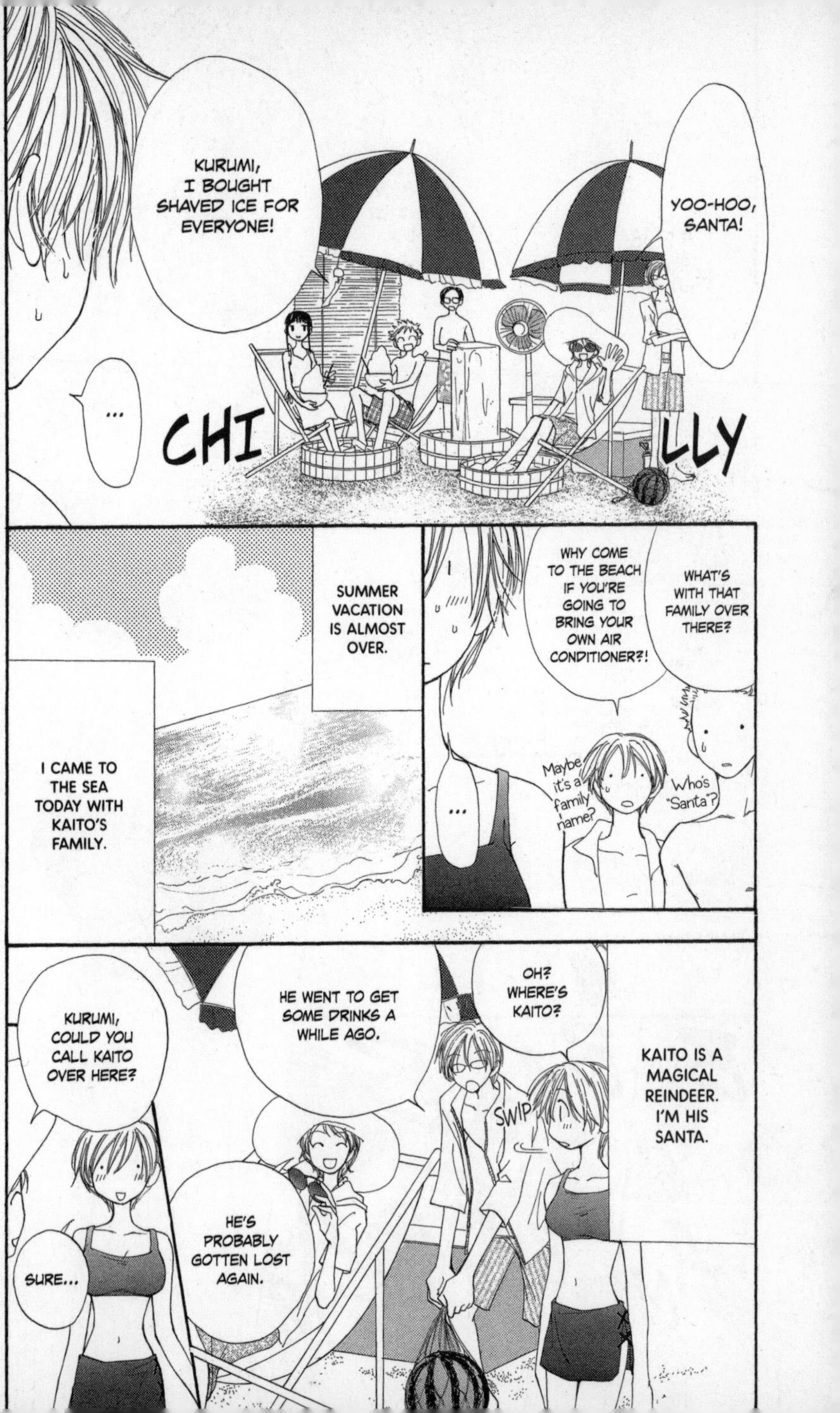
YOO-HOO, SANTA!
KURUMI, I BOUGHT SHAVED ICE FOR EVERYONE!
...
CHI LLY
WHAT'S WITH THAT FAMILY OVER THERE?
WHY COME TO THE BEACH IF YOU'RE GOING TO BRING YOUR OWN AIR CONDITIONER?!
Who's "Santa"?
Maybe it's a family name?
...
SUMMER VACATION IS ALMOST OVER.
I CAME TO THE SEA TODAY WITH KAITO'S FAMILY.
KAITO IS A MAGICAL REINDEER. I'M HIS SANTA.
OH? WHERE'S KAITO?
SWIP
HE WENT TO GET SOME DRINKS A WHILE AGO.
HE'S PROBABLY GOTTEN LOST AGAIN.
KURUMI, COULD YOU CALL KAITO OVER HERE?
SURE...

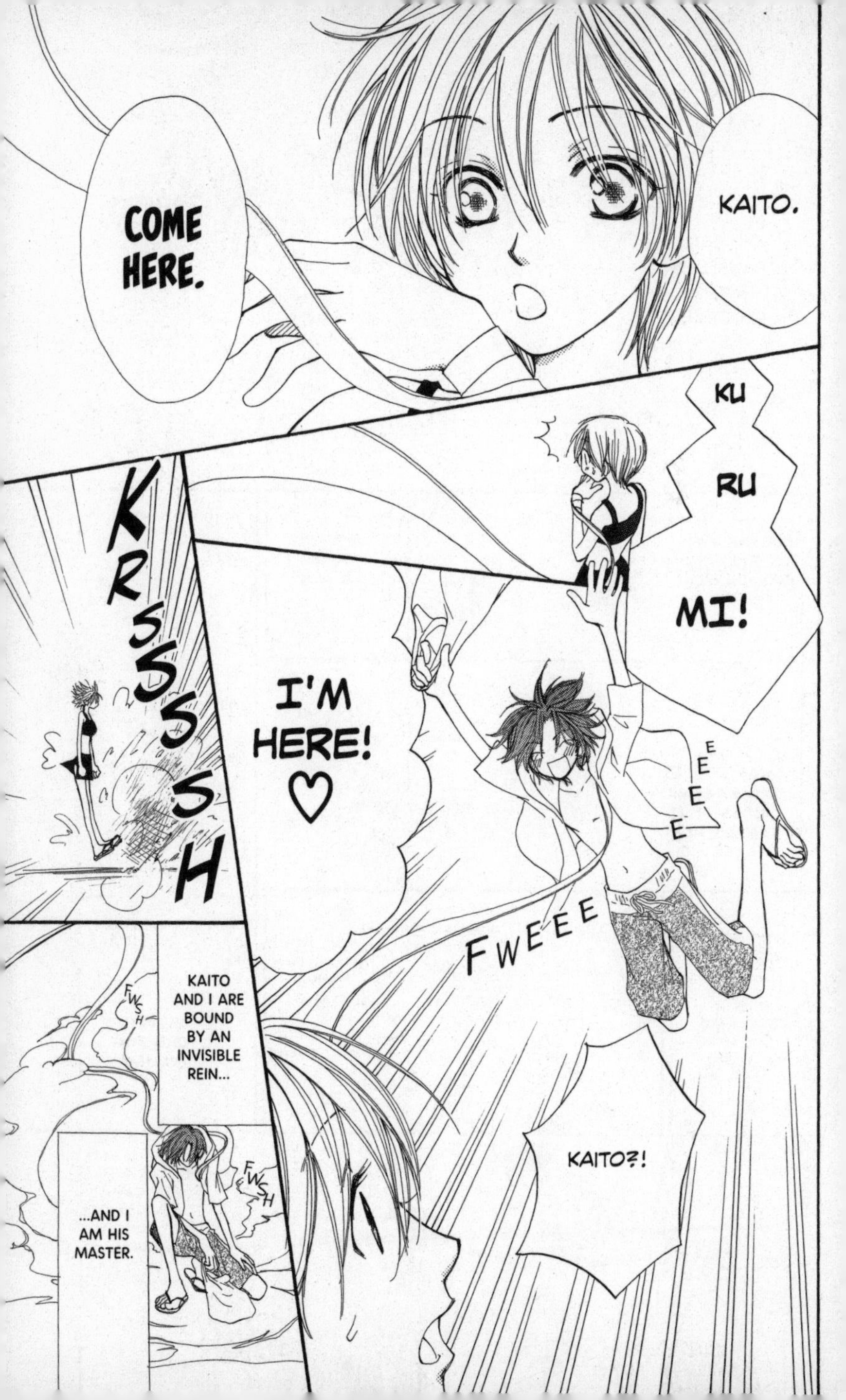
KAITO.
COME HERE.
KU RU MI!
I'M HERE! ♡
EEEE
FWEEE
KRSSSSH
KAITO?!
KAITO AND I ARE BOUND BY AN INVISIBLE REIN...
FWSH
FWSH
...AND I AM HIS MASTER.

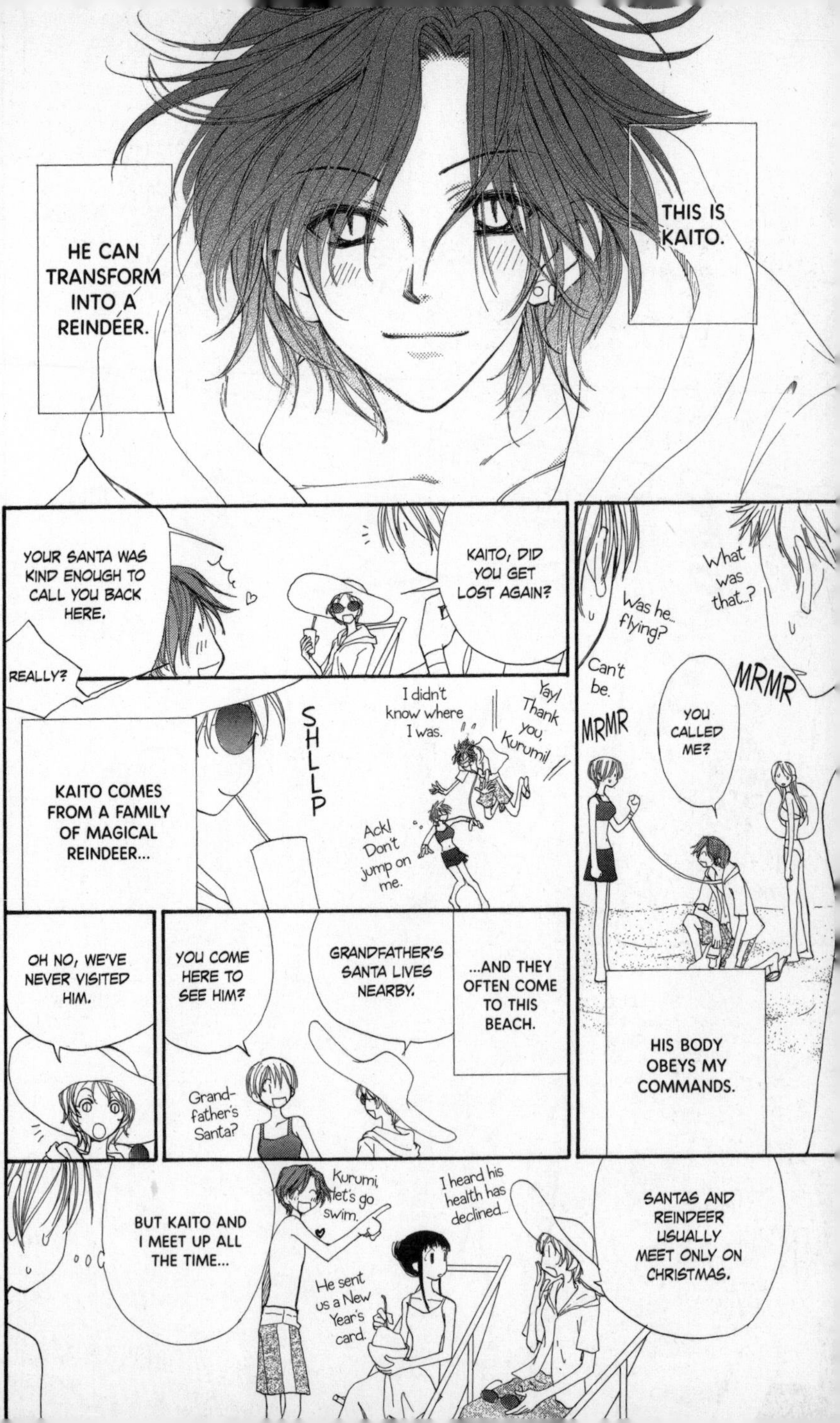

THIS IS KAITO.
HE CAN TRANSFORM INTO A REINDEER.
What was that...?
Was he... flying?
Can't be.
MRMR
YOU CALLED ME?
MRMR
HIS BODY OBEYS MY COMMANDS.
KAITO, DID YOU GET LOST AGAIN?
YOUR SANTA WAS KIND ENOUGH TO CALL YOU BACK HERE.
REALLY?
Yay! Thank you, Kurumi!
I didn't know where I was.
SHLLP
Ack! Don't jump on me.
KAITO COMES FROM A FAMILY OF MAGICAL REINDEER...
...AND THEY OFTEN COME TO THIS BEACH.
GRANDFATHER'S SANTA LIVES NEARBY.
YOU COME HERE TO SEE HIM?
Grand-father's Santa?
OH NO, WE'VE NEVER VISITED HIM.
SANTAS AND REINDEER USUALLY MEET ONLY ON CHRISTMAS.
I heard his health has declined...
Kurumi, let's go swim.
He sent us a New Year's card.
BUT KAITO AND I MEET UP ALL THE TIME...

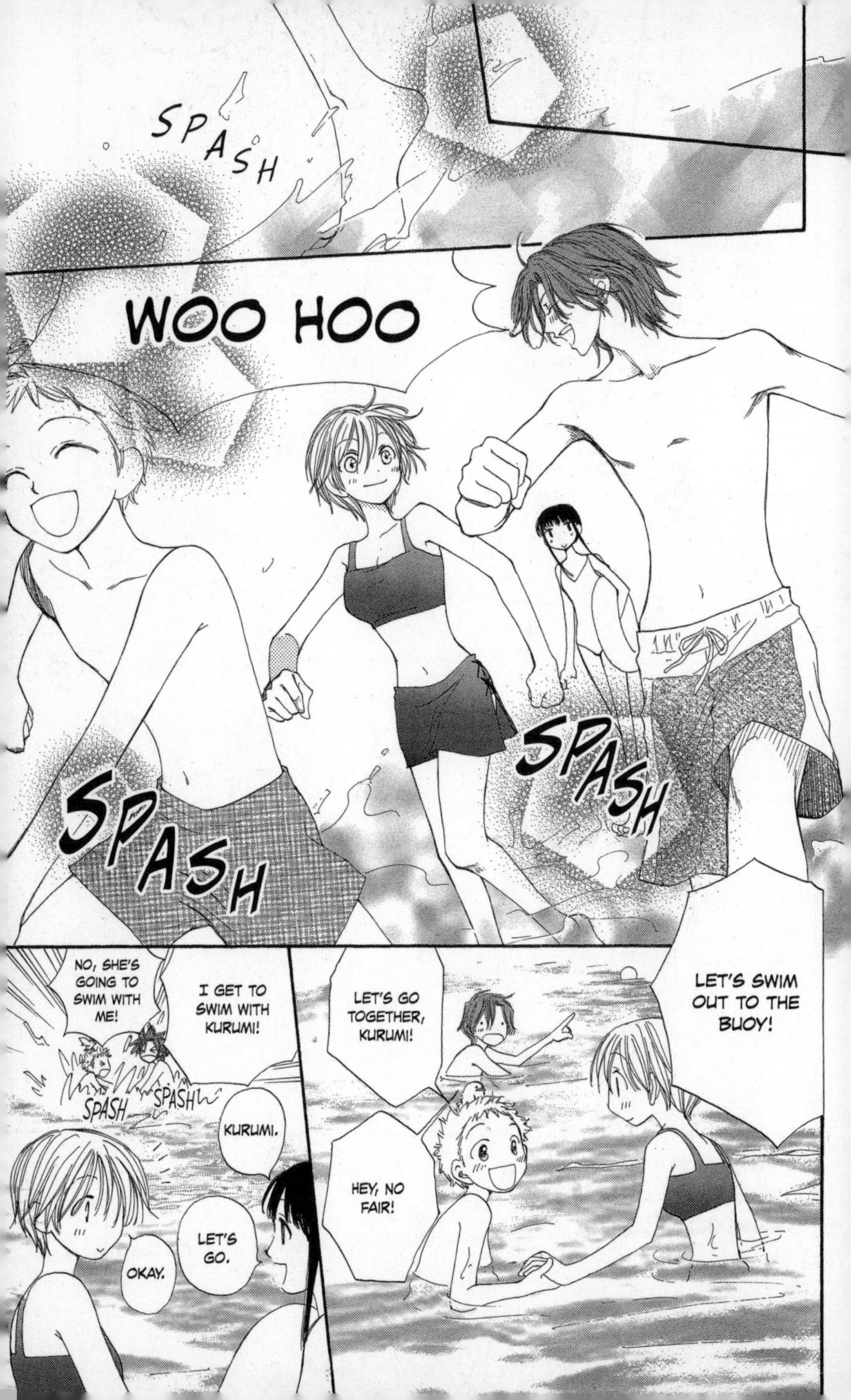
SPASH
WOO HOO
SPASH
SPASH
LET'S SWIM OUT TO THE BUOY!
LET'S GO TOGETHER, KURUMI!
HEY, NO FAIR!
I GET TO SWIM WITH KURUMI!
NO, SHE'S GOING TO SWIM WITH ME!
SPASH
SPASH
KURUMI.
LET'S GO.
OKAY.

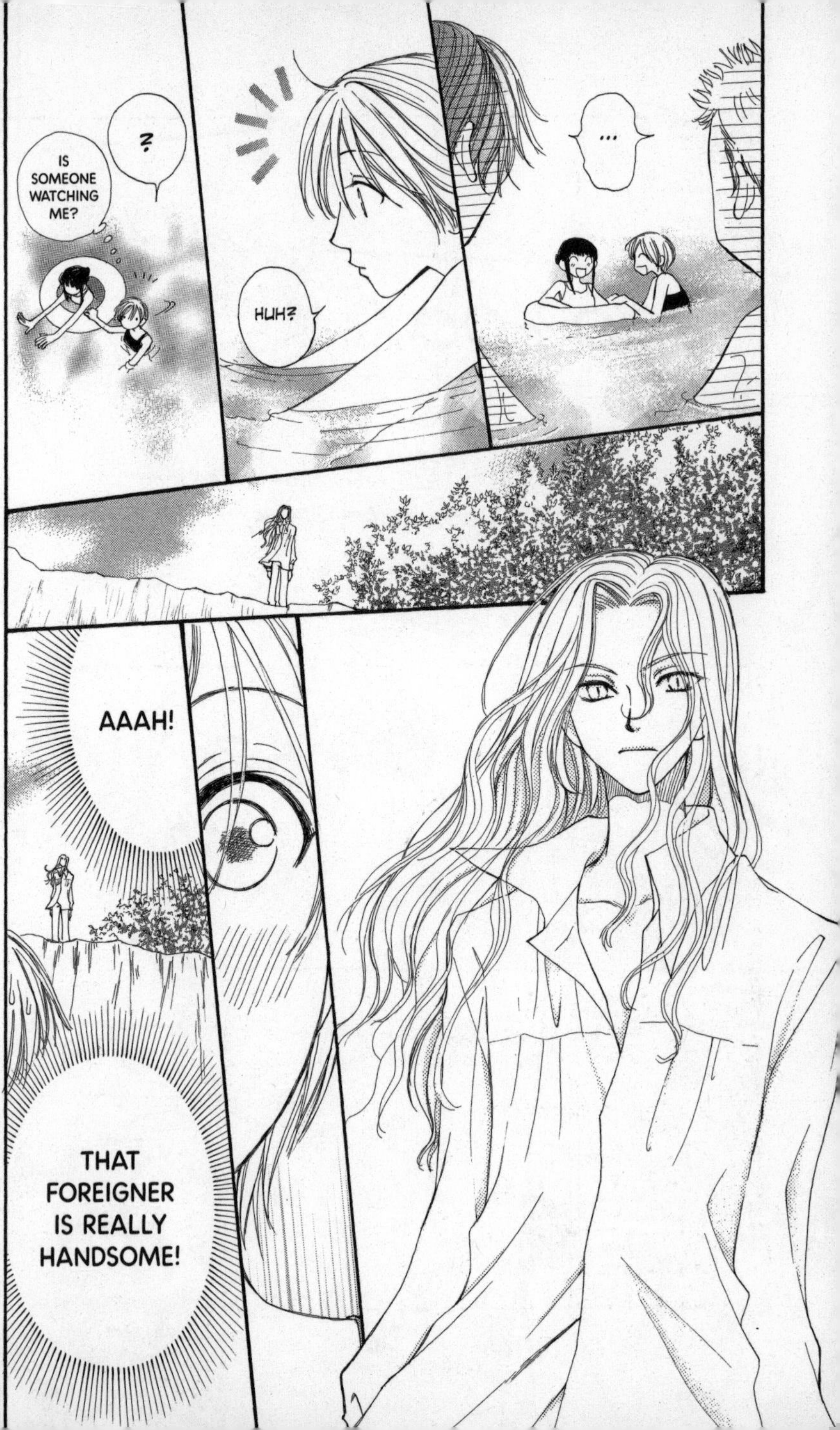
...
HUH?
?
IS SOMEONE WATCHING ME?
AAAH!
THAT FOREIGNER IS REALLY HANDSOME!

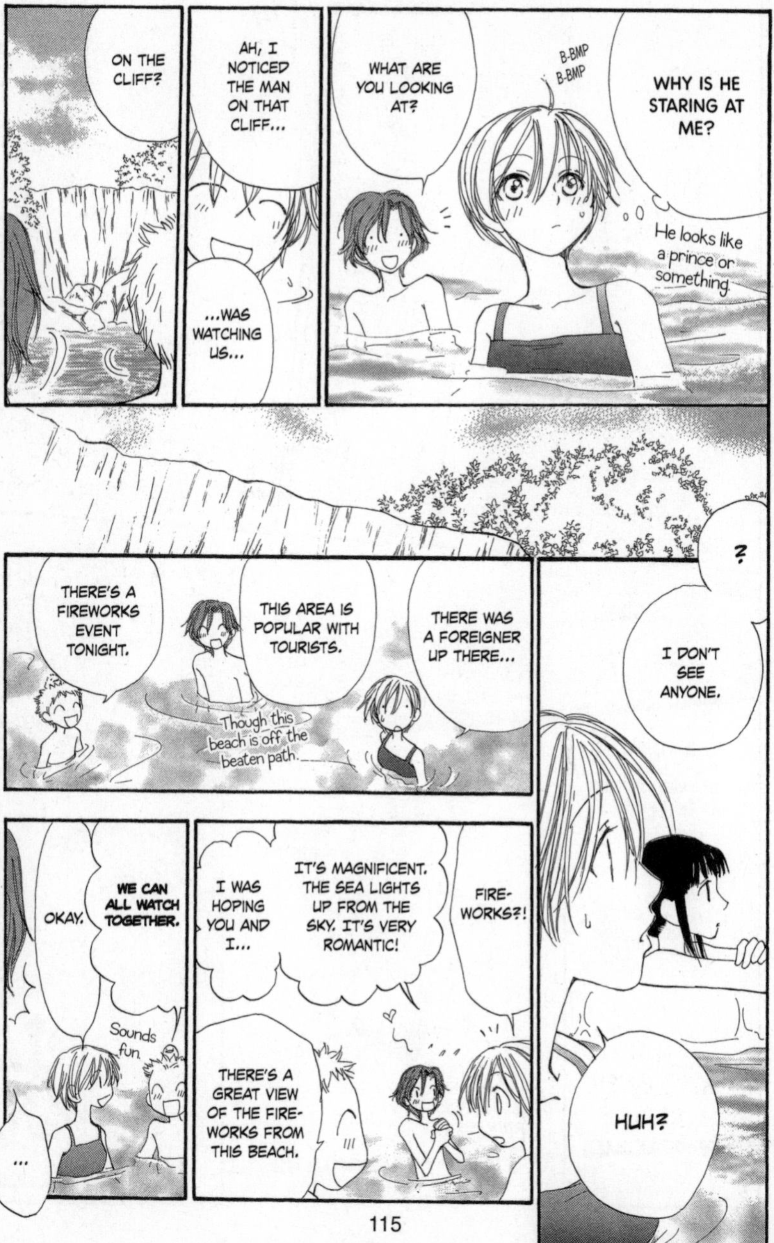
WHY IS HE STARING AT ME?
B-BMP B-BMP
WHAT ARE YOU LOOKING AT?
He looks like a prince or something.
AH, I NOTICED THE MAN ON THAT CLIFF...
...WAS WATCHING US...
ON THE CLIFF?
?
I DON'T SEE ANYONE.
HUH?
THERE WAS A FOREIGNER UP THERE...
THIS AREA IS POPULAR WITH TOURISTS.
Though this beach is off the beaten path.
THERE'S A FIREWORKS EVENT TONIGHT.
FIRE-WORKS?!
IT'S MAGNIFICENT. THE SEA LIGHTS UP FROM THE SKY. IT'S VERY ROMANTIC!
I WAS HOPING YOU AND I...
THERE'S A GREAT VIEW OF THE FIRE-WORKS FROM THIS BEACH.
WE CAN ALL WATCH TOGETHER.
OKAY.
Sounds fun.
...

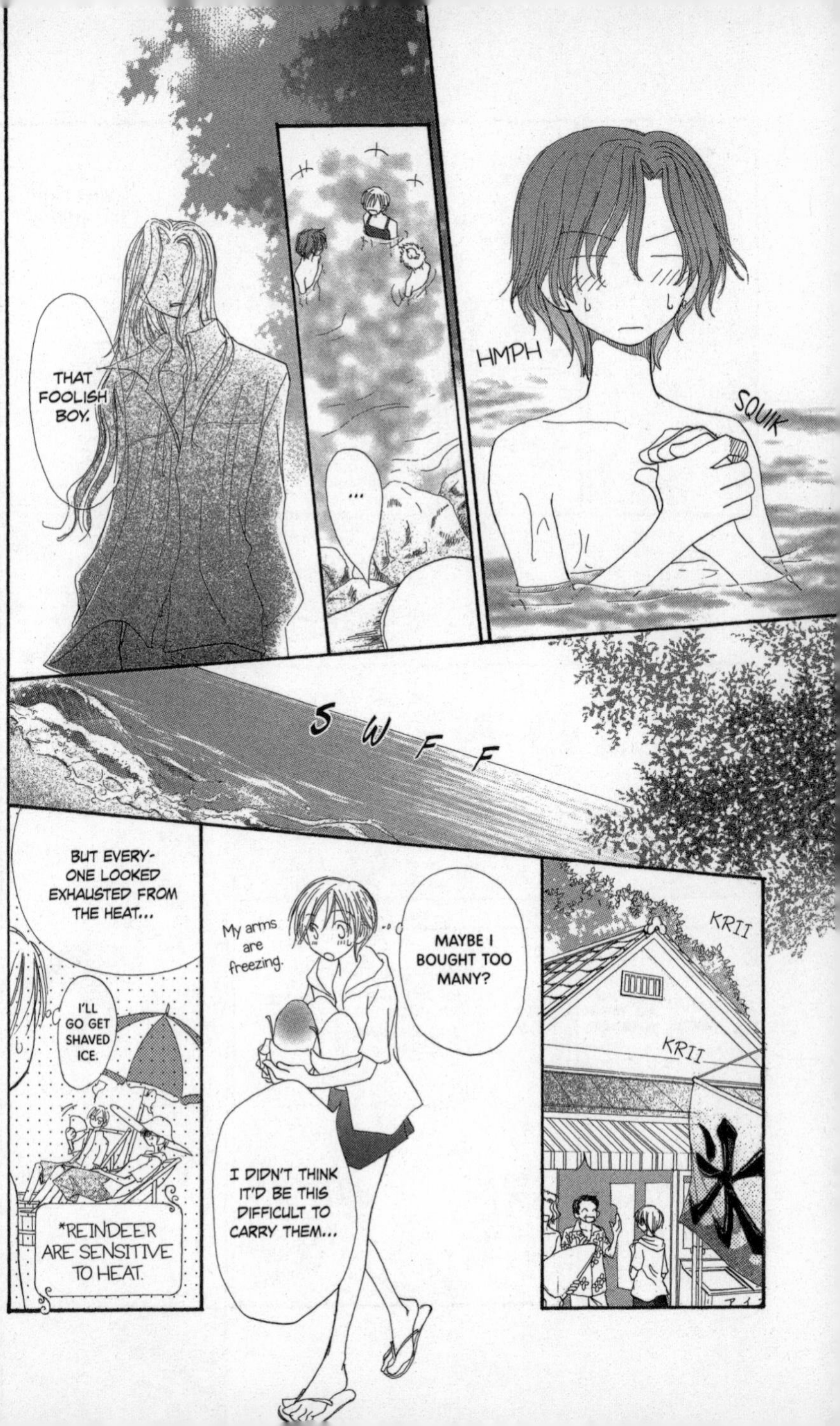
HMPH
SQUIK
...
THAT FOOLISH BOY.
S W F F
KRII
KRII
氷
MAYBE I BOUGHT TOO MANY?
My arms are freezing.
I DIDN'T THINK IT'D BE THIS DIFFICULT TO CARRY THEM...
BUT EVERY-ONE LOOKED EXHAUSTED FROM THE HEAT...
I'LL GO GET SHAVED ICE.
*REINDEER ARE SENSITIVE TO HEAT.

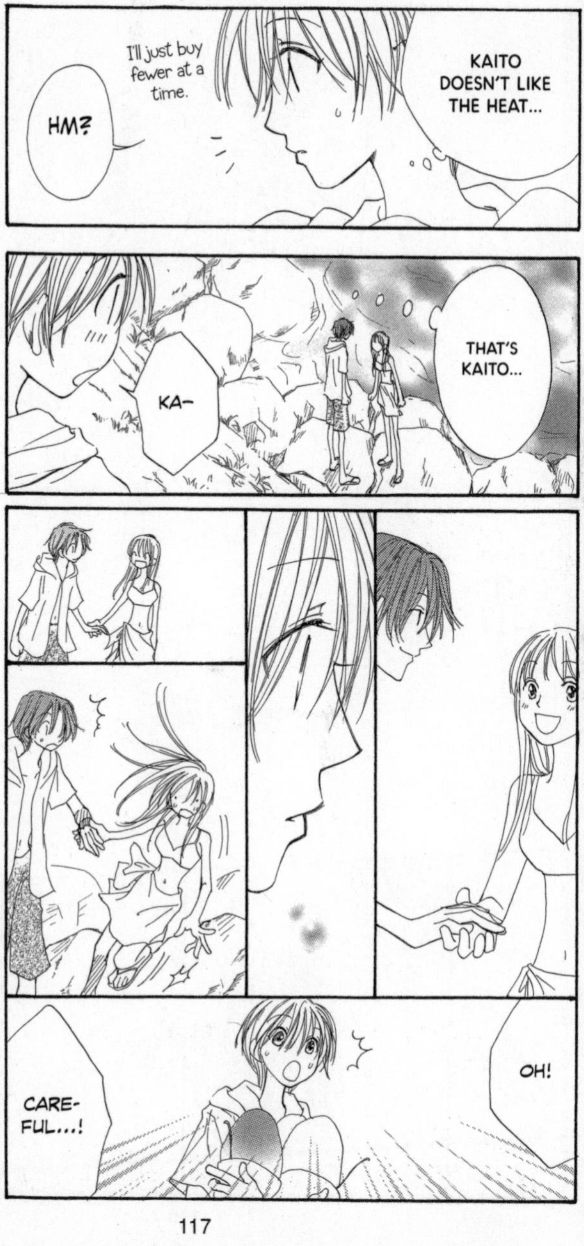
KAITO DOESN'T LIKE THE HEAT...
I'll just buy fewer at a time.
HM?
THAT'S KAITO...
KA-
OH!
CARE-FUL...!

1/4 Sakura Mail

Part 5

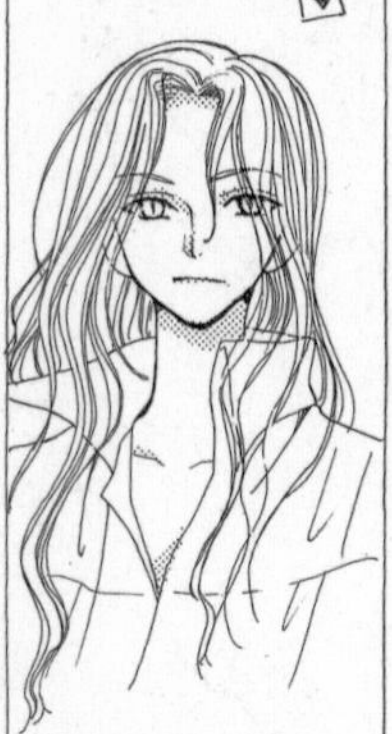

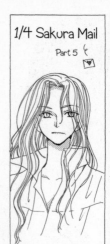

And here is chapter 3. Once again it's set in summer, even though the story is about a Santa Claus. The story in chapter 2 occurred in the beginning of summer, and this occurs around the end of the summer. I didn't draw very many summery things in the last chapter, so I put them in this one. Kaito's family members are magical reindeer and usually avoid the heat, but they like celebrating seasonal events so they come to the sea every year.

(Continues)

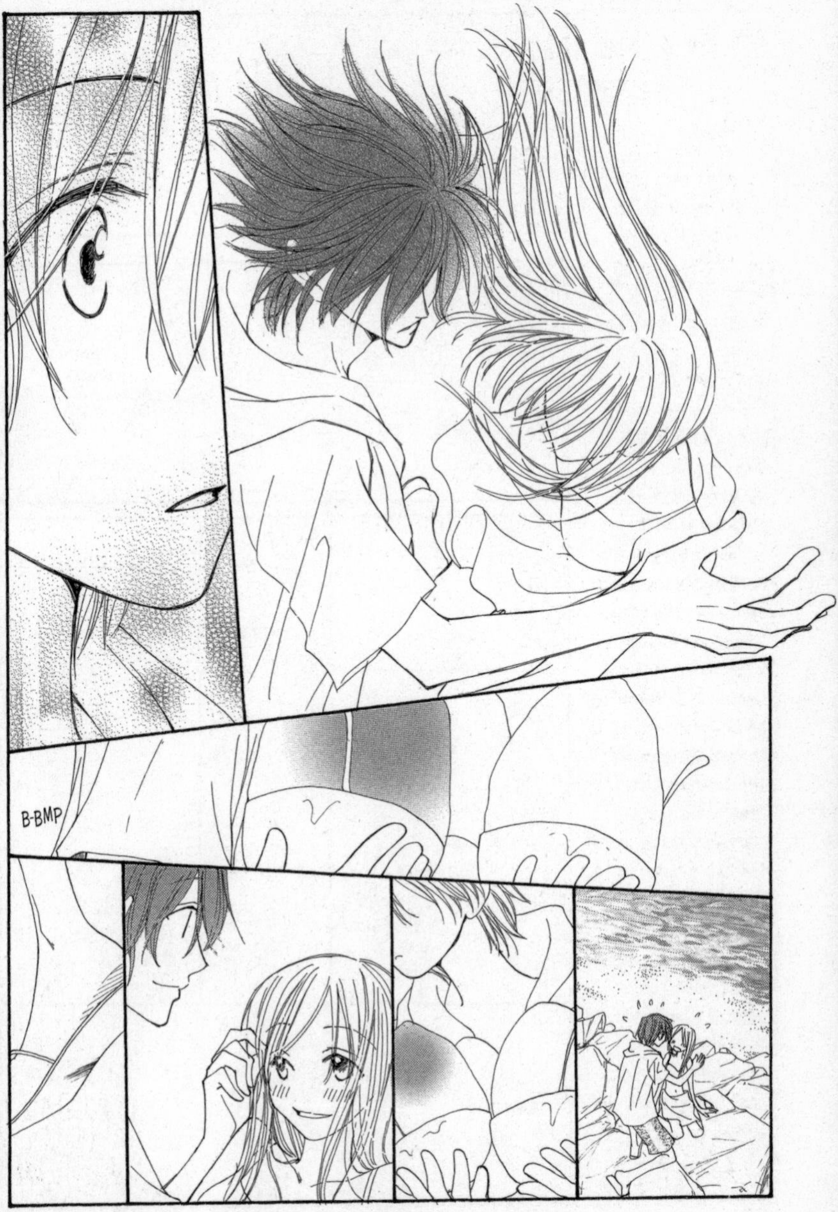
B-BMP

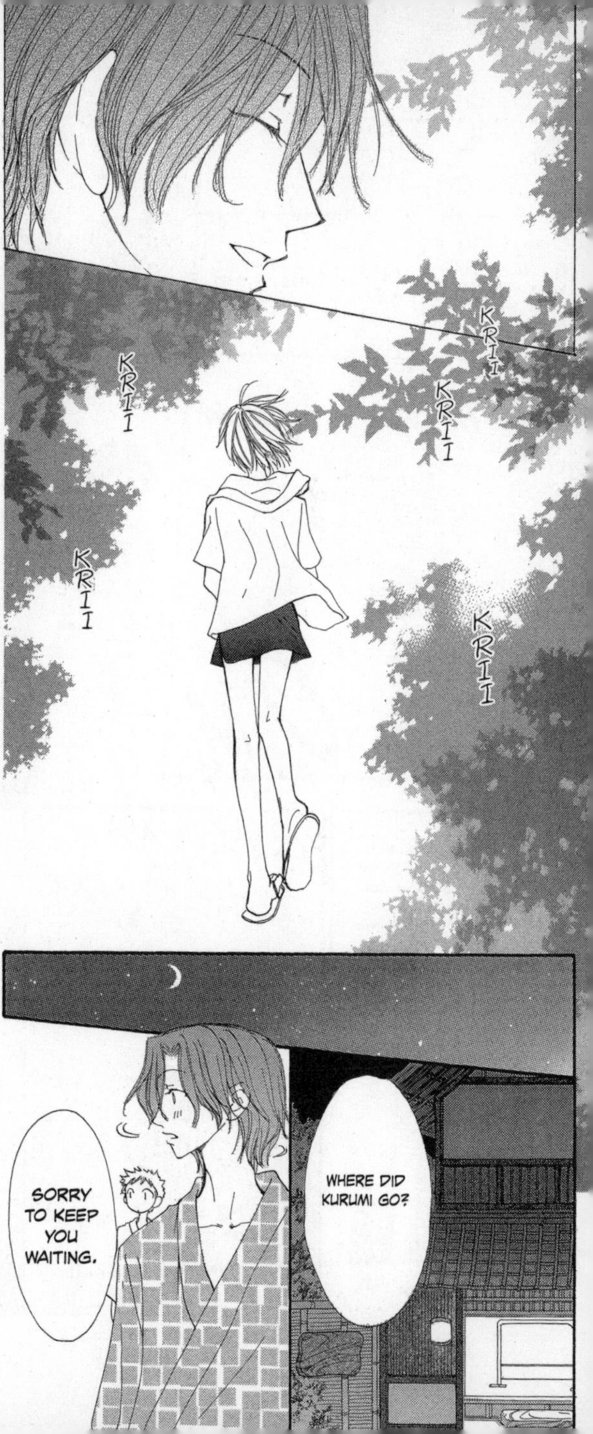
KRII
KRII
KRII
KRII
KRII
WHERE DID KURUMI GO?
SORRY TO KEEP YOU WAITING.

1/4 Sakura Mail

Part 6

(Continued)

Kurumi has hardly ever been on a family trip before because her father is always working. I had her accompany Kaito's family on their trip. Kaito seems to become more foolish in every chapter, but please be forgiving in regards to him. He's just overly excited. By the way, Kurumi is wearing the same red swimwear she was wearing in the previous chapter. Since *Sweet* 🔔 *Rein* has a Christmas theme, I've done my illustrations using holiday colors. Red, green, gold... Just using these colors brightens up the atmosphere, so I'm really enjoying coloring.

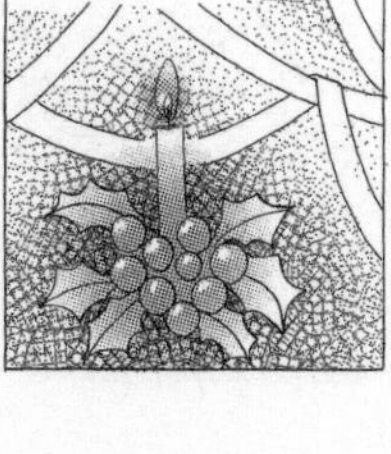

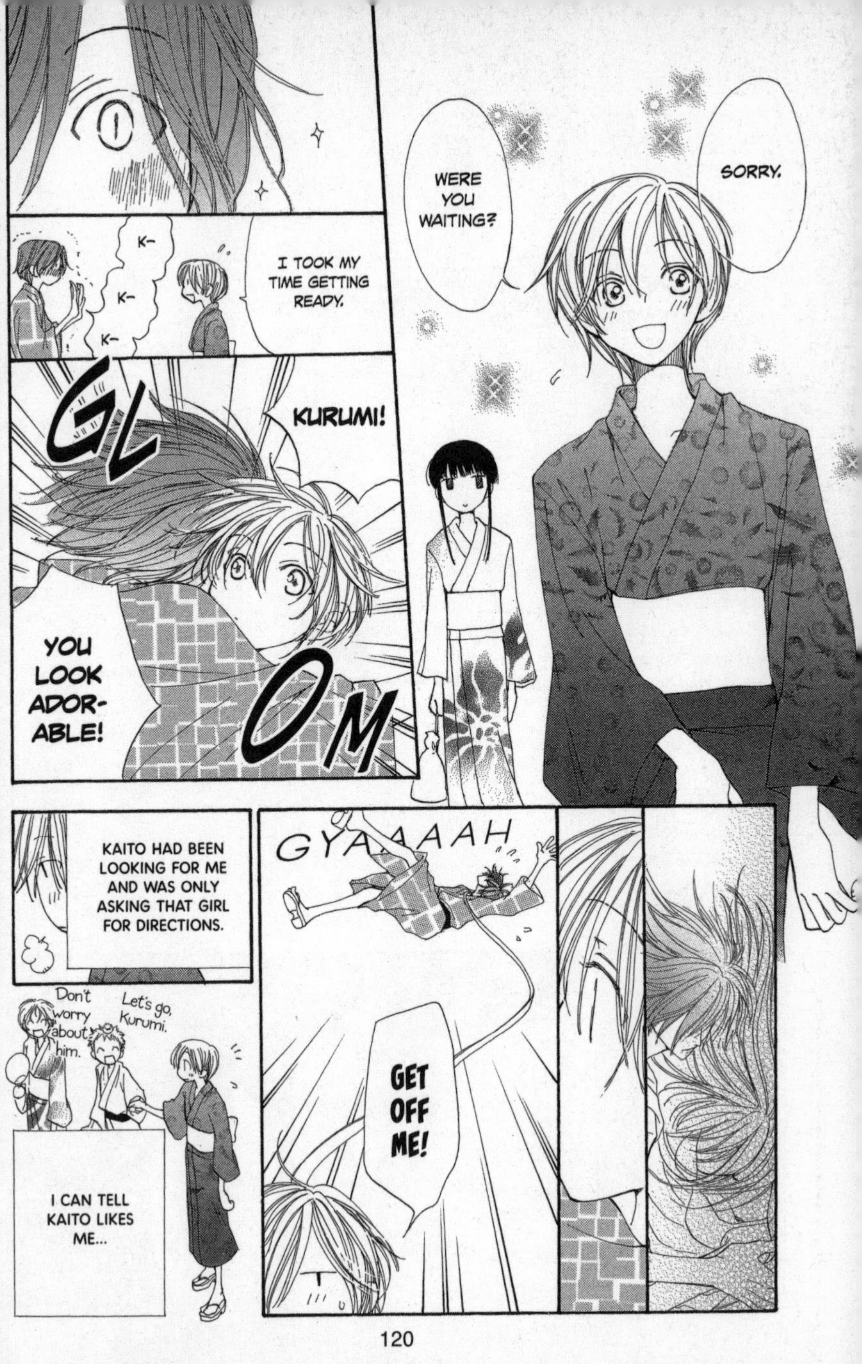
SORRY.
WERE YOU WAITING?
I TOOK MY TIME GETTING READY.
K–
K–
K–
KURUMI!
GL
OM
YOU LOOK ADORABLE!
GYAAAAH
GET OFF ME!
KAITO HAD BEEN LOOKING FOR ME AND WAS ONLY ASKING THAT GIRL FOR DIRECTIONS.
Let's go, Kurumi.
Don't worry about him.
I CAN TELL KAITO LIKES ME...

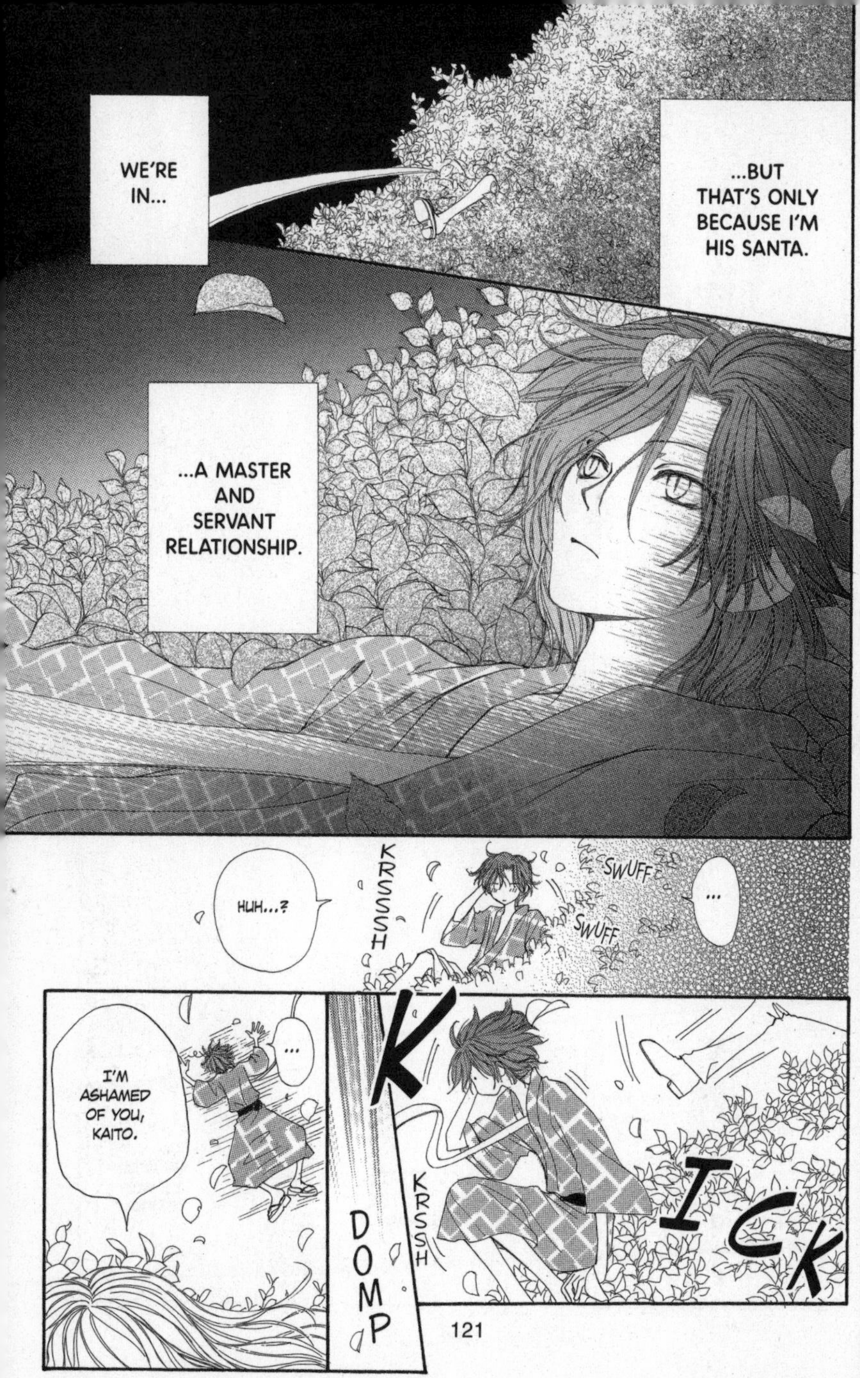

...BUT THAT'S ONLY BECAUSE I'M HIS SANTA.
WE'RE IN...
...A MASTER AND SERVANT RELATIONSHIP.
...
SWUFF
SWUFF
KRSSSH
HUH...?
K
ICK
KRSSH
DOMP
...
I'M ASHAMED OF YOU, KAITO.

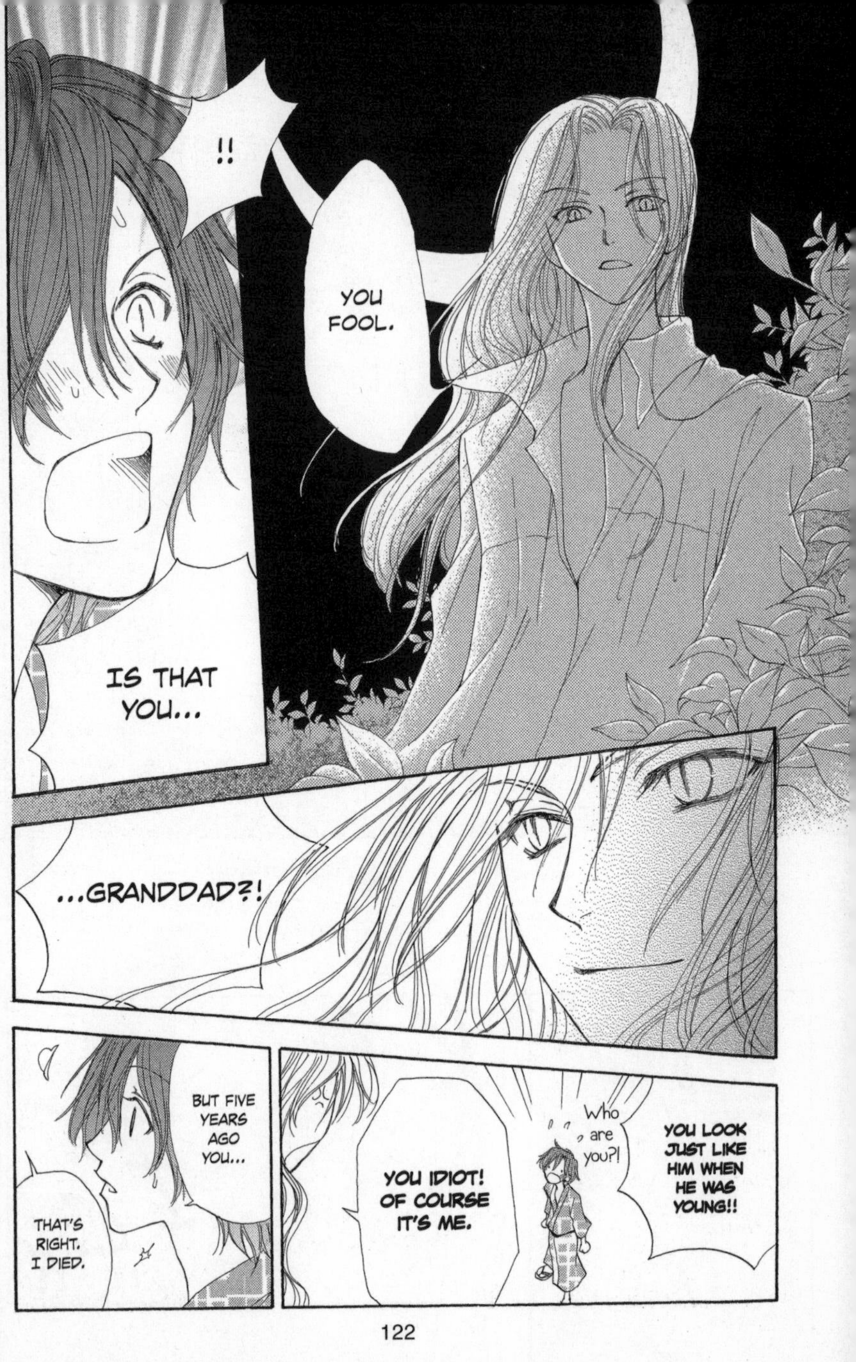
YOU FOOL.
!!
IS THAT YOU...
...GRANDDAD?!
YOU LOOK JUST LIKE HIM WHEN HE WAS YOUNG!!
Who are you?!
YOU IDIOT! OF COURSE IT'S ME.
BUT FIVE YEARS AGO YOU...
THAT'S RIGHT. I DIED.

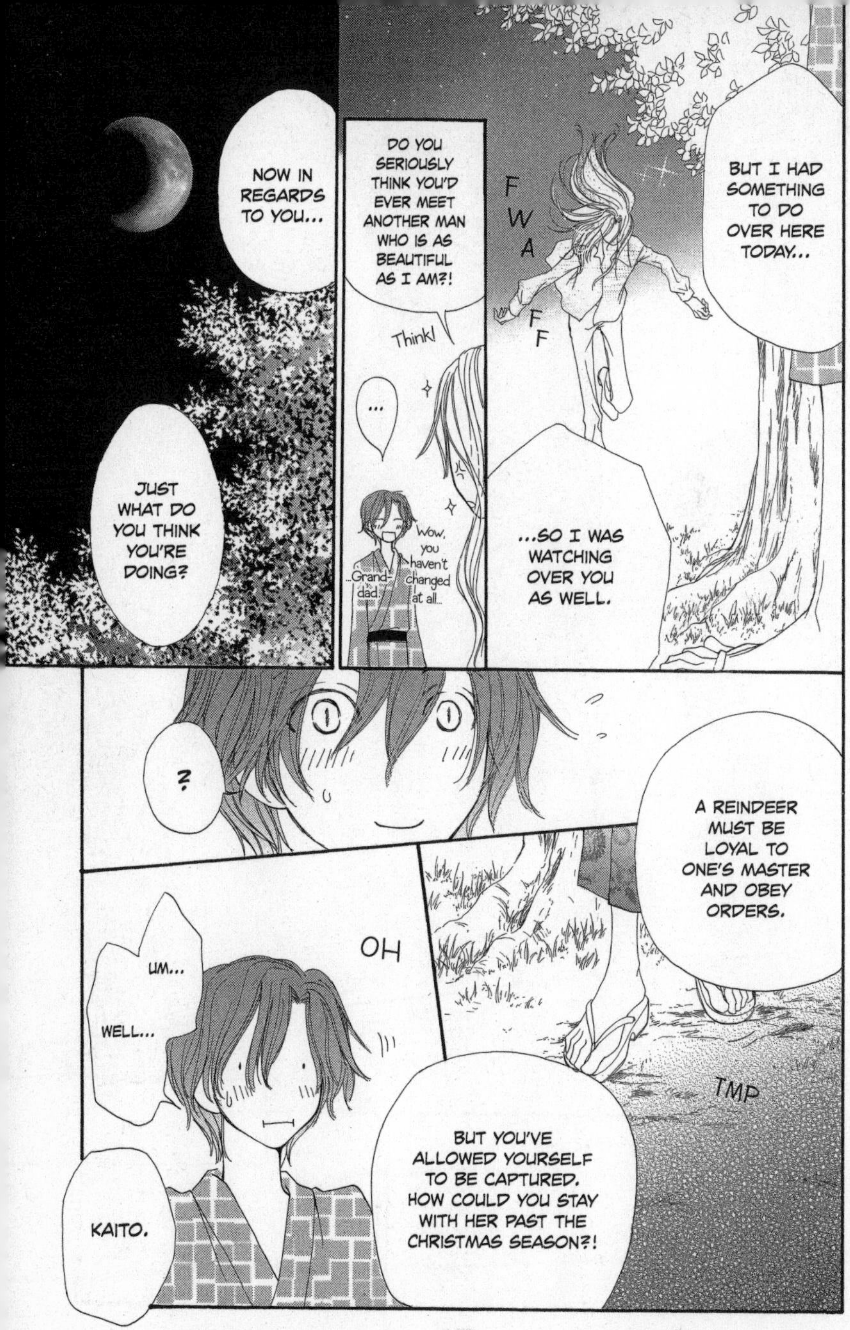
BUT I HAD SOMETHING TO DO OVER HERE TODAY...
FWAFF
...SO I WAS WATCHING OVER YOU AS WELL.
DO YOU SERIOUSLY THINK YOU'D EVER MEET ANOTHER MAN WHO IS AS BEAUTIFUL AS I AM?!
Think!
...
Wow, you haven't changed at all...
...Granddad.
NOW IN REGARDS TO YOU...
JUST WHAT DO YOU THINK YOU'RE DOING?
A REINDEER MUST BE LOYAL TO ONE'S MASTER AND OBEY ORDERS.
?
TMP
BUT YOU'VE ALLOWED YOURSELF TO BE CAPTURED. HOW COULD YOU STAY WITH HER PAST THE CHRISTMAS SEASON?!
OH
UM...
WELL...
KAITO.

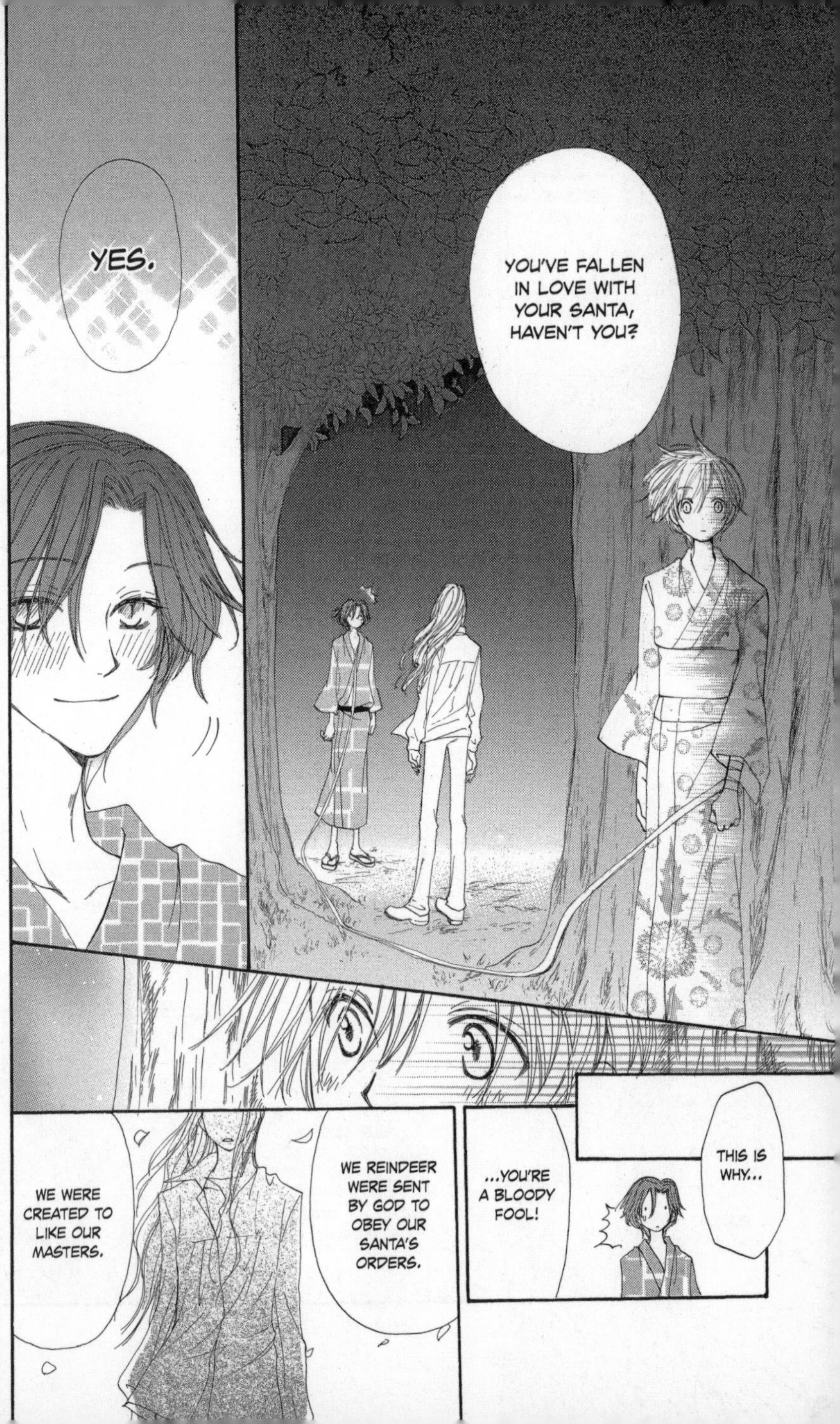
YOU'VE FALLEN IN LOVE WITH YOUR SANTA, HAVEN'T YOU?
YES.
THIS IS WHY...
...YOU'RE A BLOODY FOOL!
WE REINDEER WERE SENT BY GOD TO OBEY OUR SANTA'S ORDERS.
WE WERE CREATED TO LIKE OUR MASTERS.

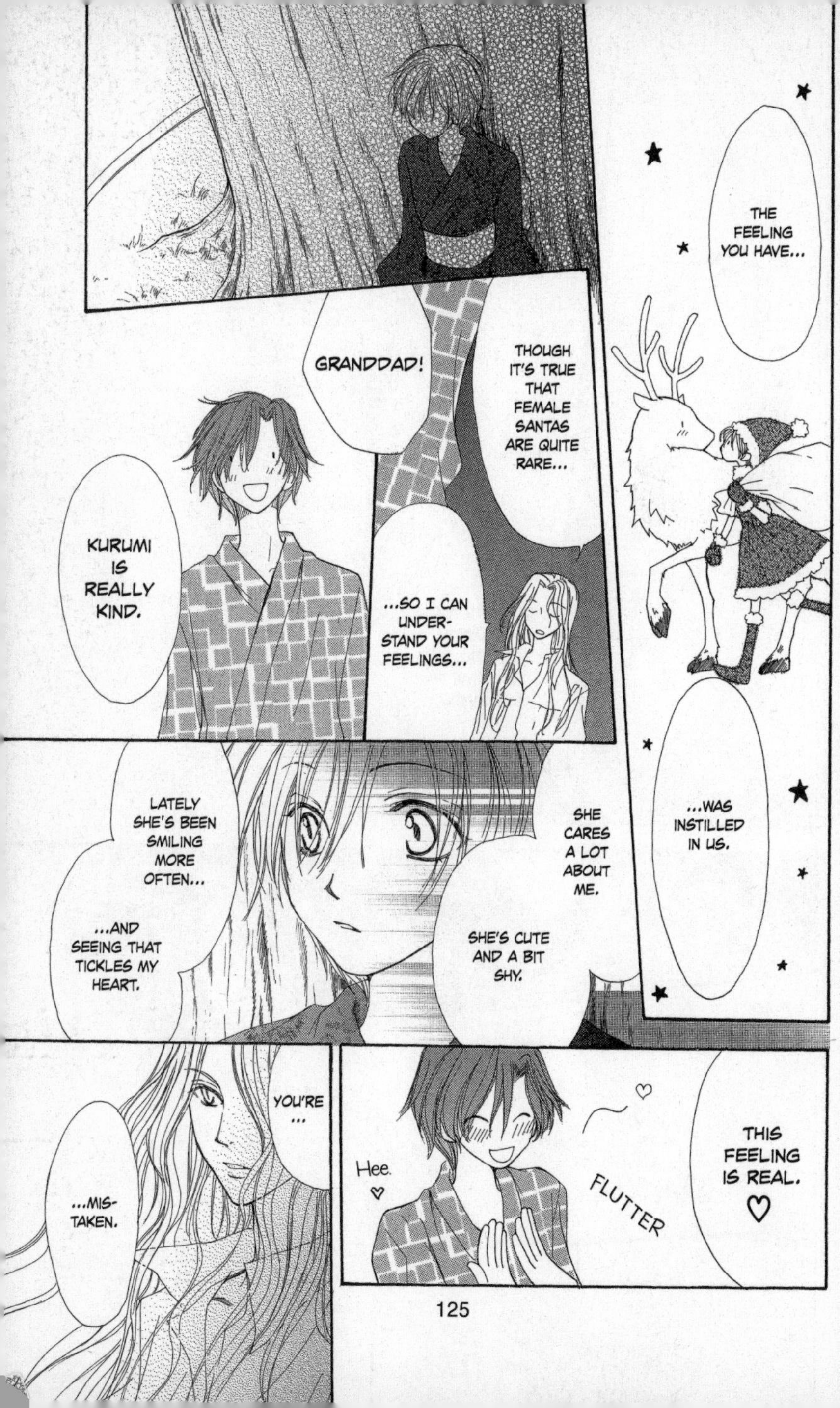
THE FEELING YOU HAVE...
...WAS INSTILLED IN US.
THOUGH IT'S TRUE THAT FEMALE SANTAS ARE QUITE RARE...
...SO I CAN UNDER-STAND YOUR FEELINGS...
GRANDDAD!
KURUMI IS REALLY KIND.
SHE CARES A LOT ABOUT ME.
SHE'S CUTE AND A BIT SHY.
LATELY SHE'S BEEN SMILING MORE OFTEN...
...AND SEEING THAT TICKLES MY HEART.
THIS FEELING IS REAL. ♡
FLUTTER
Hee. ♡
YOU'RE ...
...MIS-TAKEN.

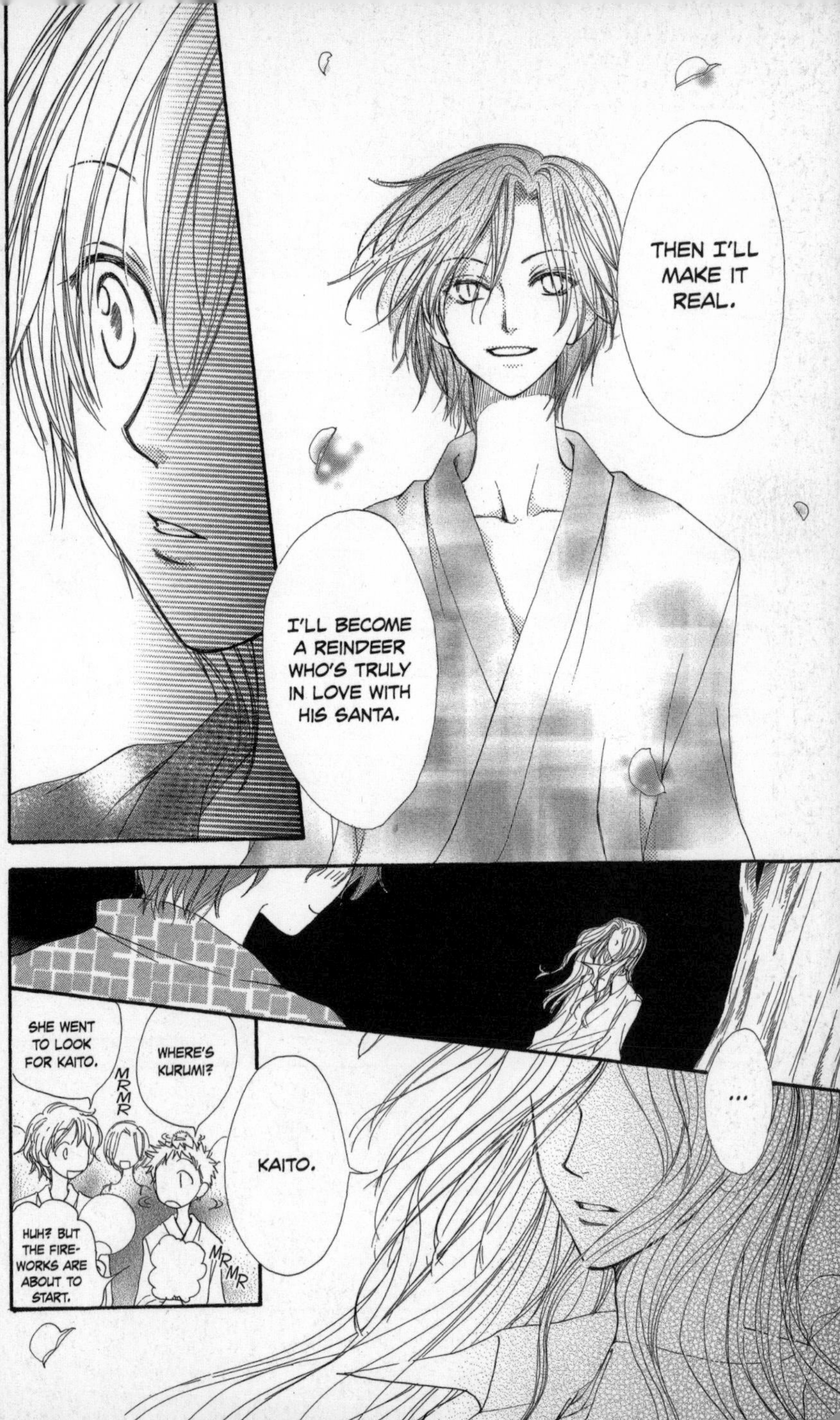
THEN I'LL MAKE IT REAL.
I'LL BECOME A REINDEER WHO'S TRULY IN LOVE WITH HIS SANTA.
...
KAITO.
WHERE'S KURUMI?
SHE WENT TO LOOK FOR KAITO.
MRMR
HUH? BUT THE FIRE-WORKS ARE ABOUT TO START.
MRMR

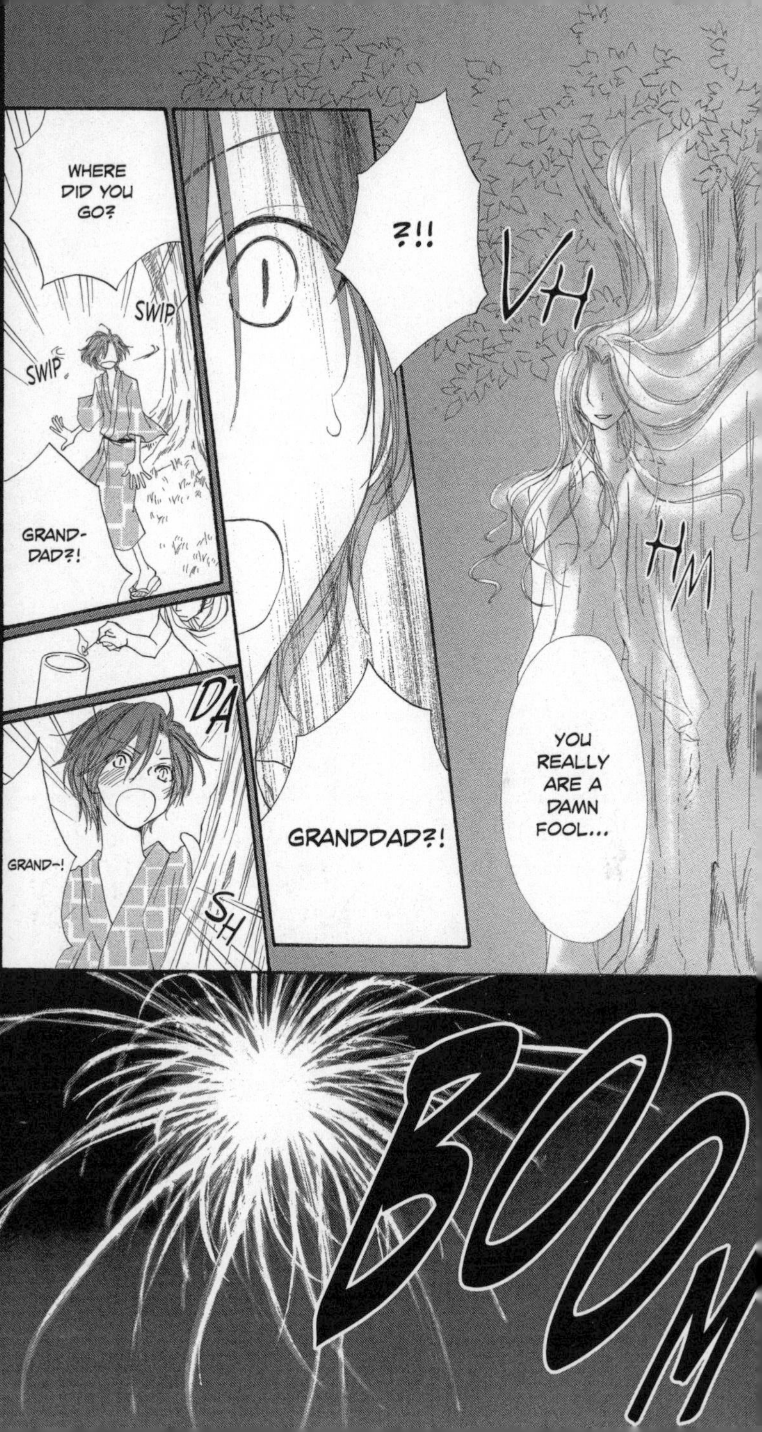
VH
HM
YOU REALLY ARE A DAMN FOOL...
?!!
GRANDDAD?!
WHERE DID YOU GO?
SWIP
SWIP
GRAND-DAD?!
DA
GRAND-!
SH
BOOM

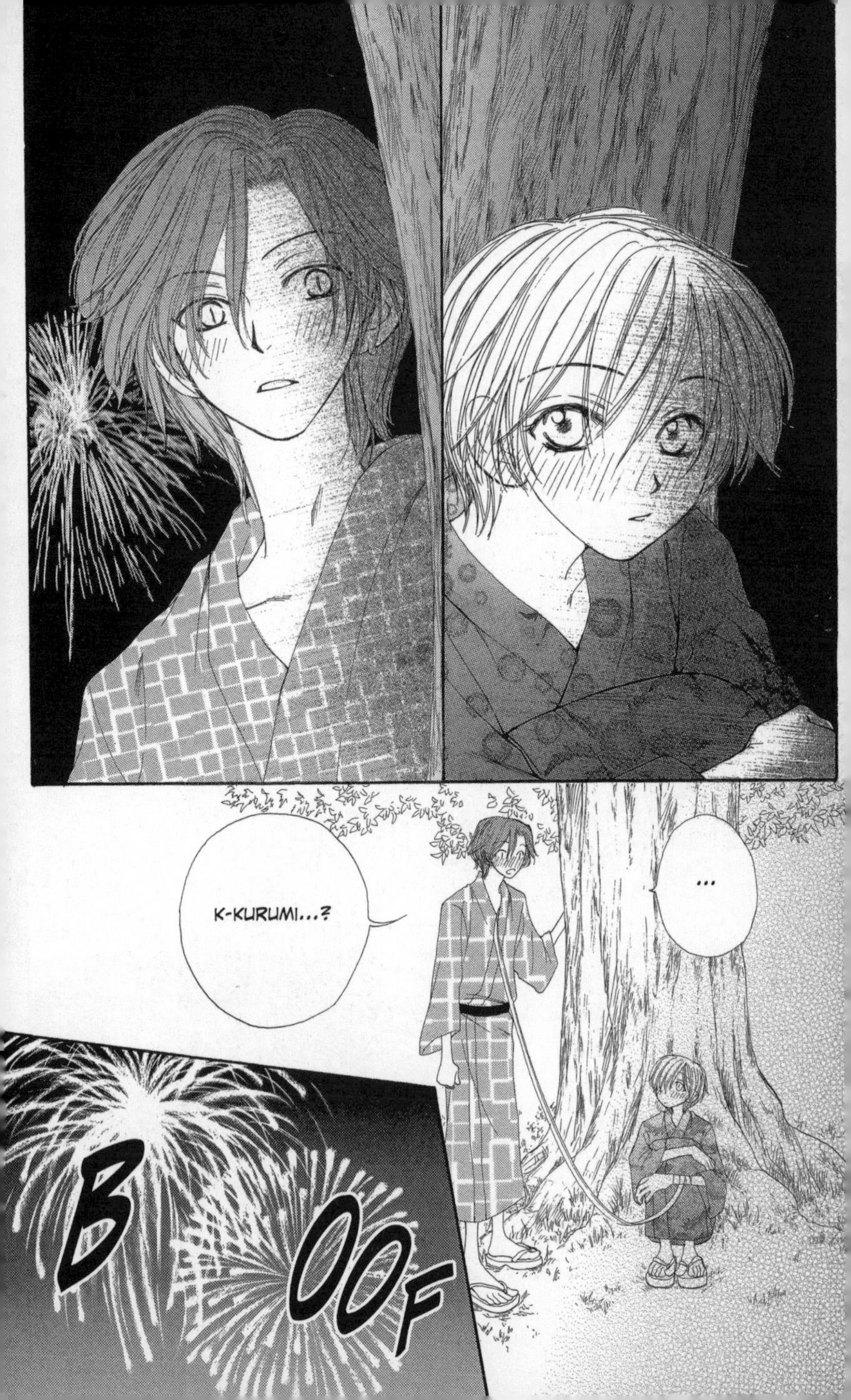
...
K-KURUMI...?
BOOF

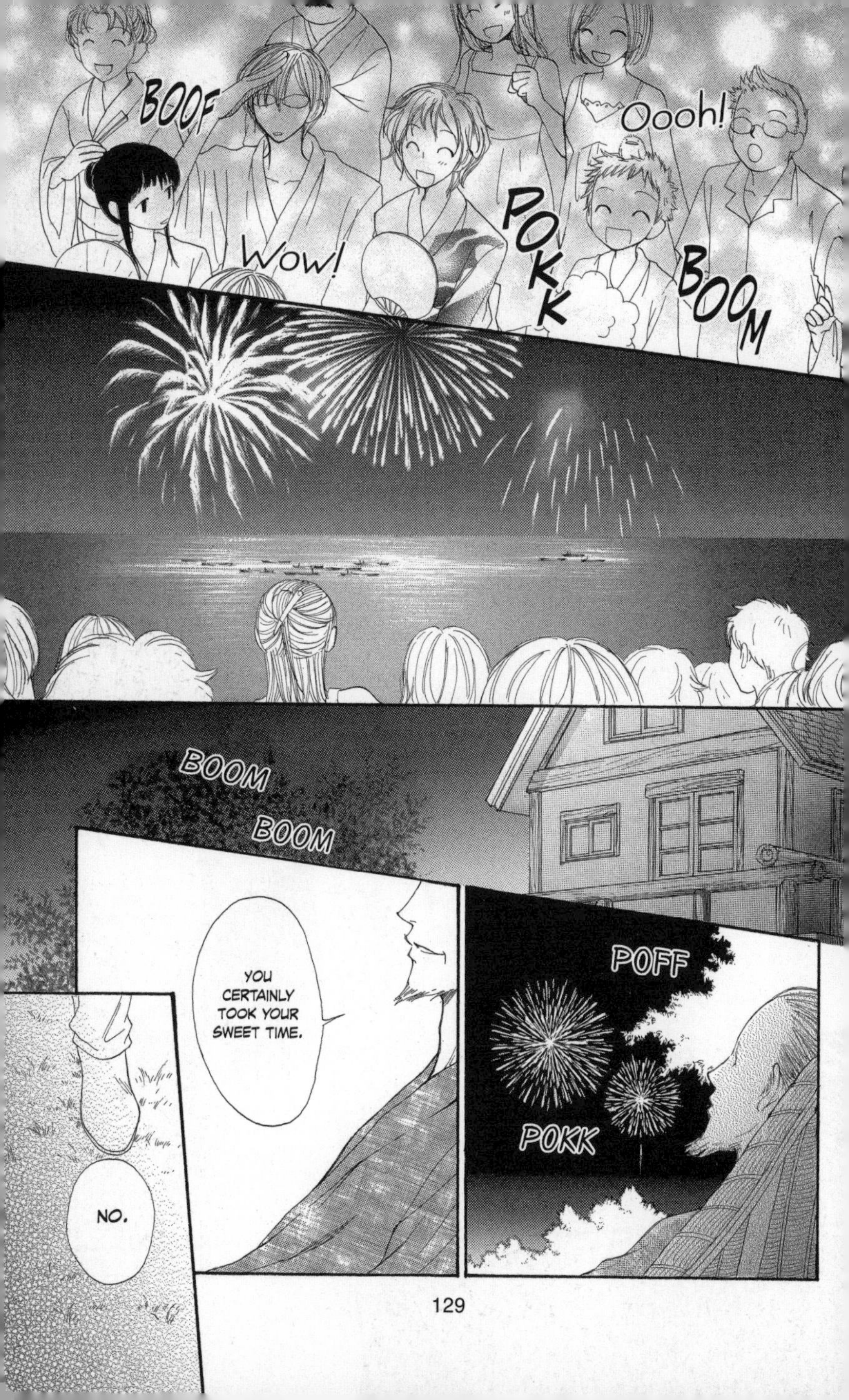

Oooh!
BOOM
POKK
BOOF
Wow!
BOOM
BOOM
POFF
POKK
YOU CERTAINLY TOOK YOUR SWEET TIME.
NO.

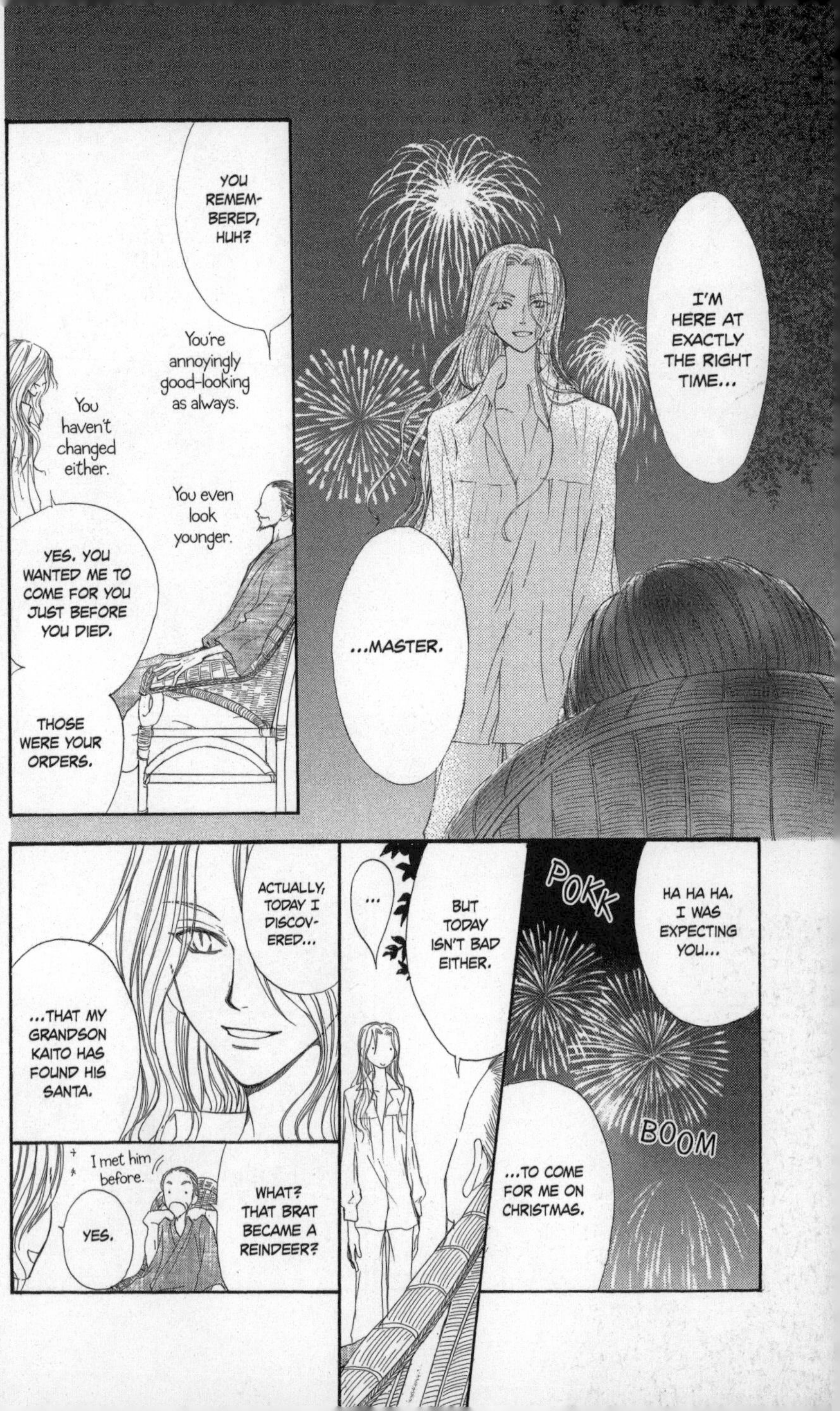
I'M HERE AT EXACTLY THE RIGHT TIME...
...MASTER.
YOU REMEMBERED, HUH?
You're annoyingly good-looking as always.
You haven't changed either.
You even look younger.
YES. YOU WANTED ME TO COME FOR YOU JUST BEFORE YOU DIED.
THOSE WERE YOUR ORDERS.
HA HA HA. I WAS EXPECTING YOU...
POKK
BOOM
...TO COME FOR ME ON CHRISTMAS.
BUT TODAY ISN'T BAD EITHER.
...
ACTUALLY, TODAY I DISCOVERED...
...THAT MY GRANDSON KAITO HAS FOUND HIS SANTA.
WHAT? THAT BRAT BECAME A REINDEER?
YES.
I met him before.

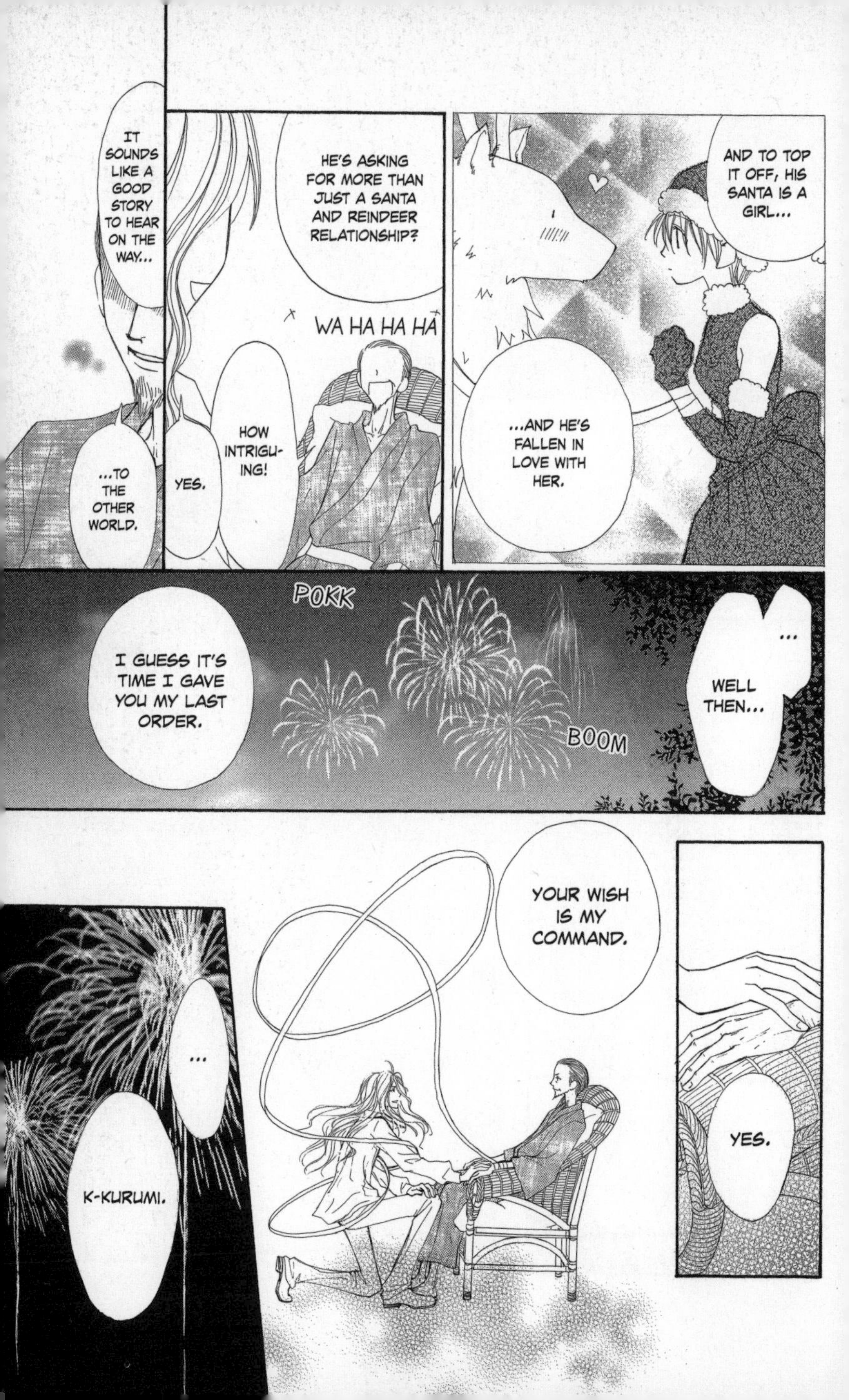
AND TO TOP IT OFF, HIS SANTA IS A GIRL...
...AND HE'S FALLEN IN LOVE WITH HER.
HE'S ASKING FOR MORE THAN JUST A SANTA AND REINDEER RELATIONSHIP?
WA HA HA HA
HOW INTRIGUING!
YES.
IT SOUNDS LIKE A GOOD STORY TO HEAR ON THE WAY...
...TO THE OTHER WORLD.
...
WELL THEN...
BOOM
POKK
I GUESS IT'S TIME I GAVE YOU MY LAST ORDER.
YES.
YOUR WISH IS MY COMMAND.
...
K-KURUMI.

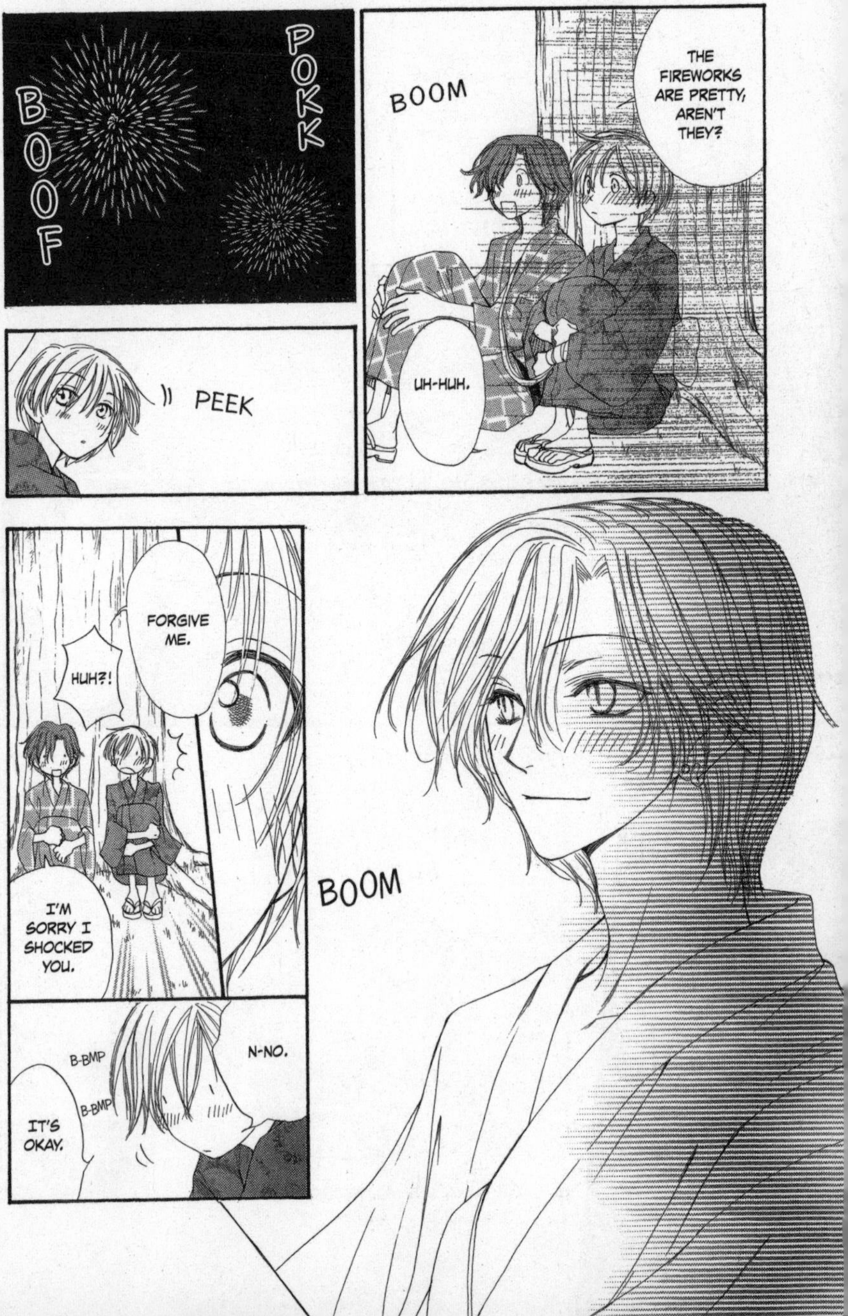
THE FIREWORKS ARE PRETTY, AREN'T THEY?
BOOM
UH-HUH.
POKK
BOOF
PEEK
BOOM
FORGIVE ME.
HUH?!
I'M SORRY I SHOCKED YOU.
N-NO.
B-BMP
B-BMP
IT'S OKAY.

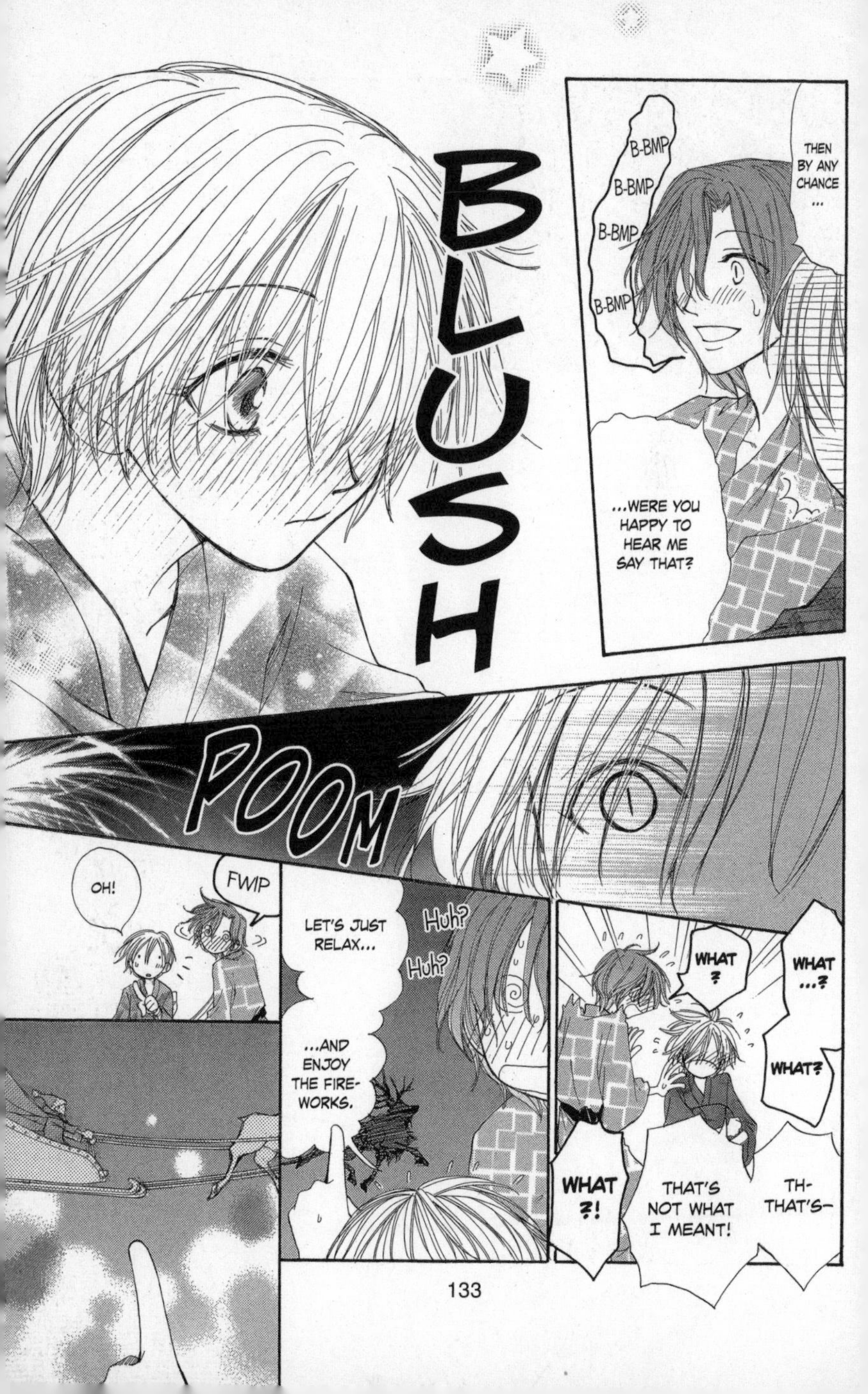
THEN BY ANY CHANCE...
B-BMP
B-BMP
B-BMP
B-BMP
...WERE YOU HAPPY TO HEAR ME SAY THAT?
BLUSH
POOM
WHAT...?
WHAT?
WHAT?
WHAT?
TH-THAT'S—
THAT'S NOT WHAT I MEANT!
WHAT?!
Huh?
Huh?
LET'S JUST RELAX...
...AND ENJOY THE FIRE-WORKS.
FWIP
OH!

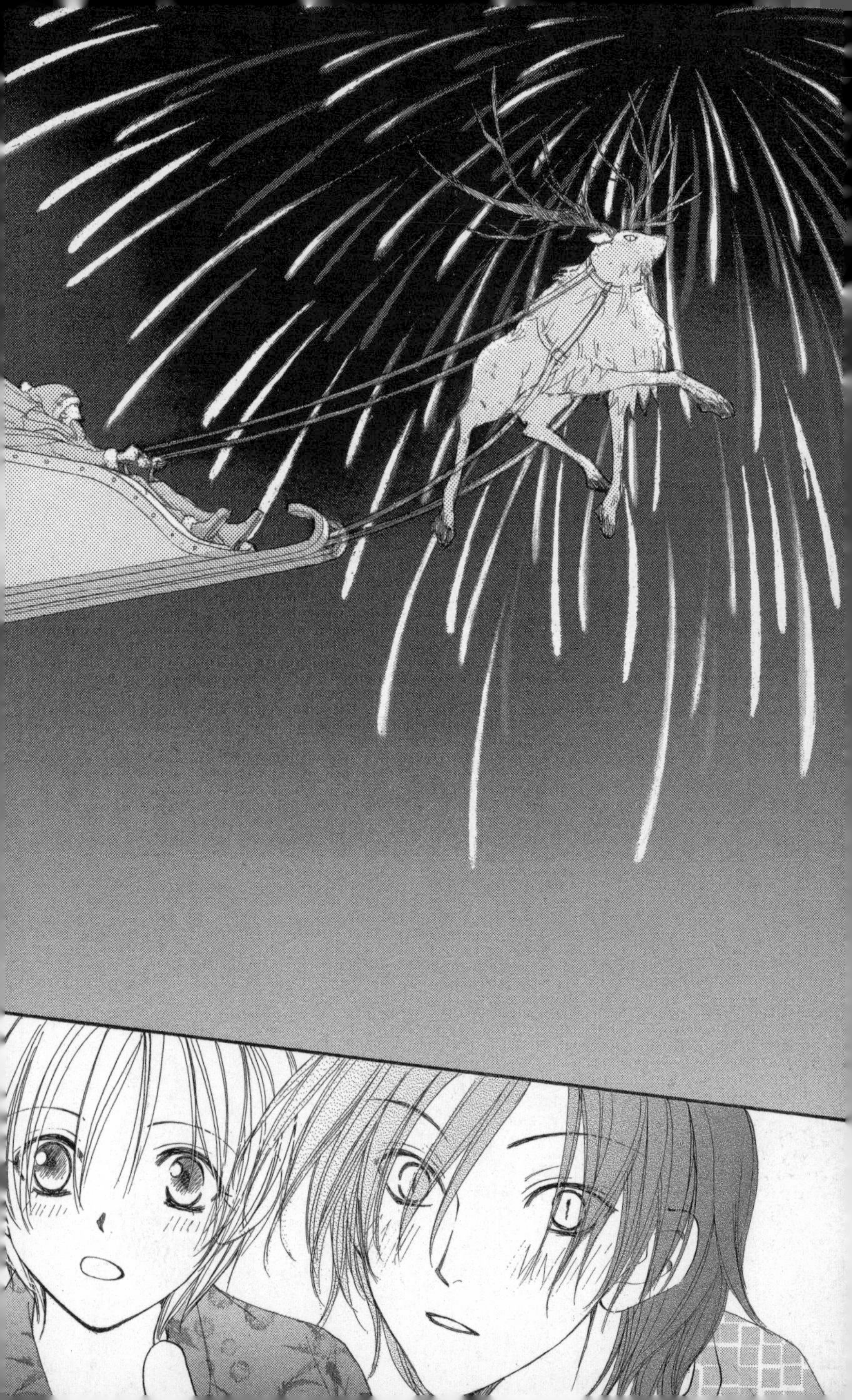

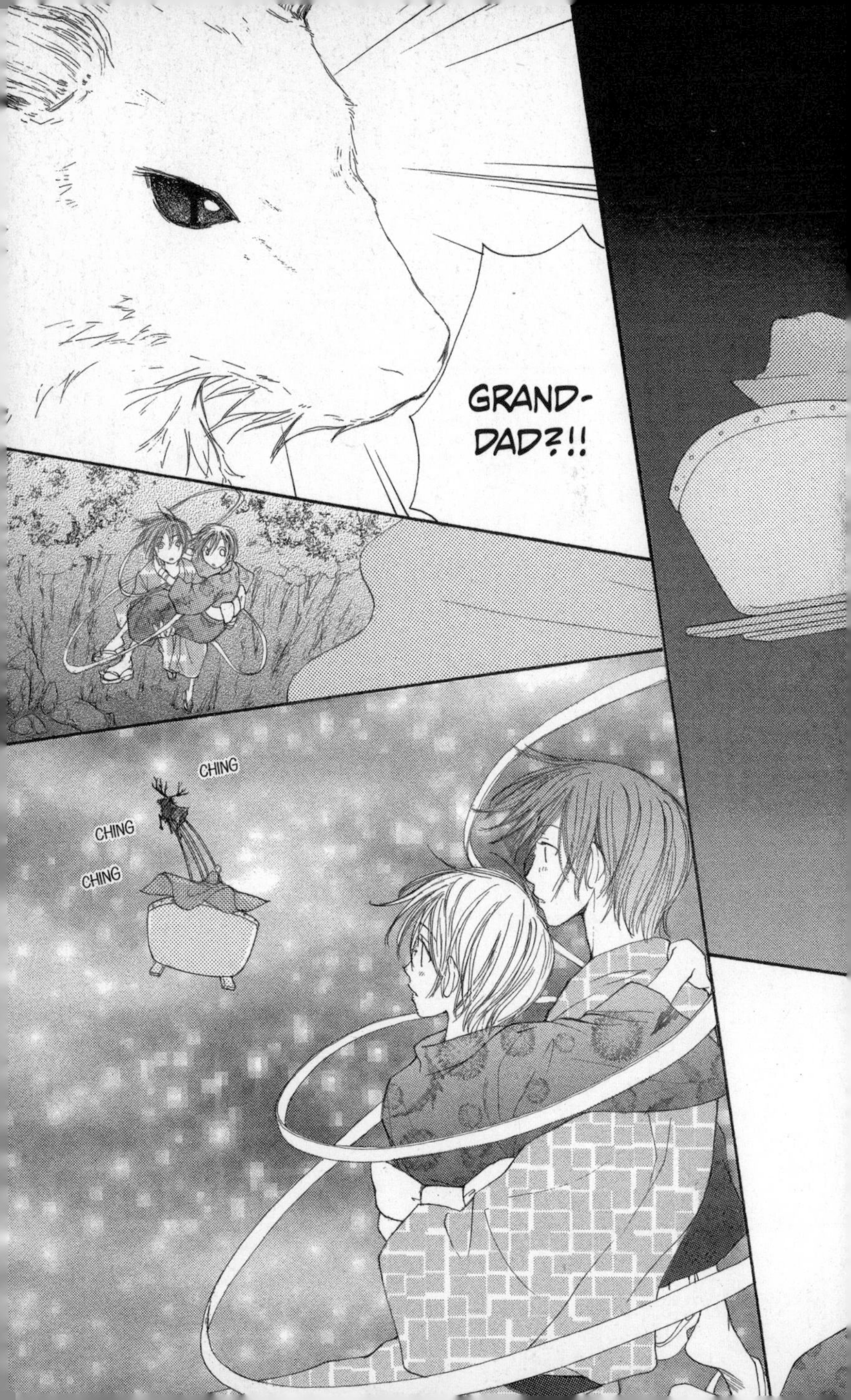
GRAND-
DAD?!!
CHING
CHING
CHING

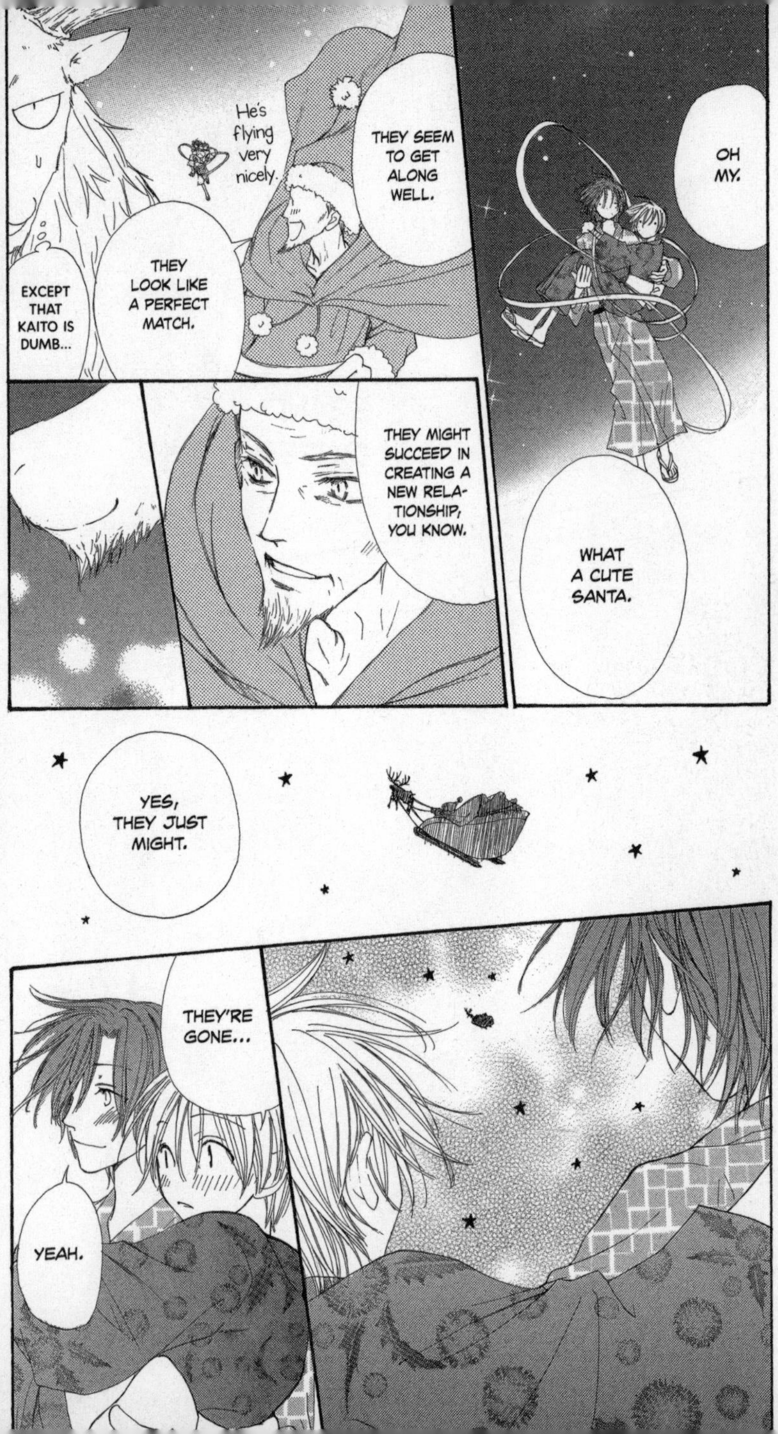
OH MY.
WHAT A CUTE SANTA.
THEY SEEM TO GET ALONG WELL.
He's flying very nicely.
THEY LOOK LIKE A PERFECT MATCH.
EXCEPT THAT KAITO IS DUMB...
THEY MIGHT SUCCEED IN CREATING A NEW RELA-TIONSHIP, YOU KNOW.
YES, THEY JUST MIGHT.
THEY'RE GONE...
YEAH.

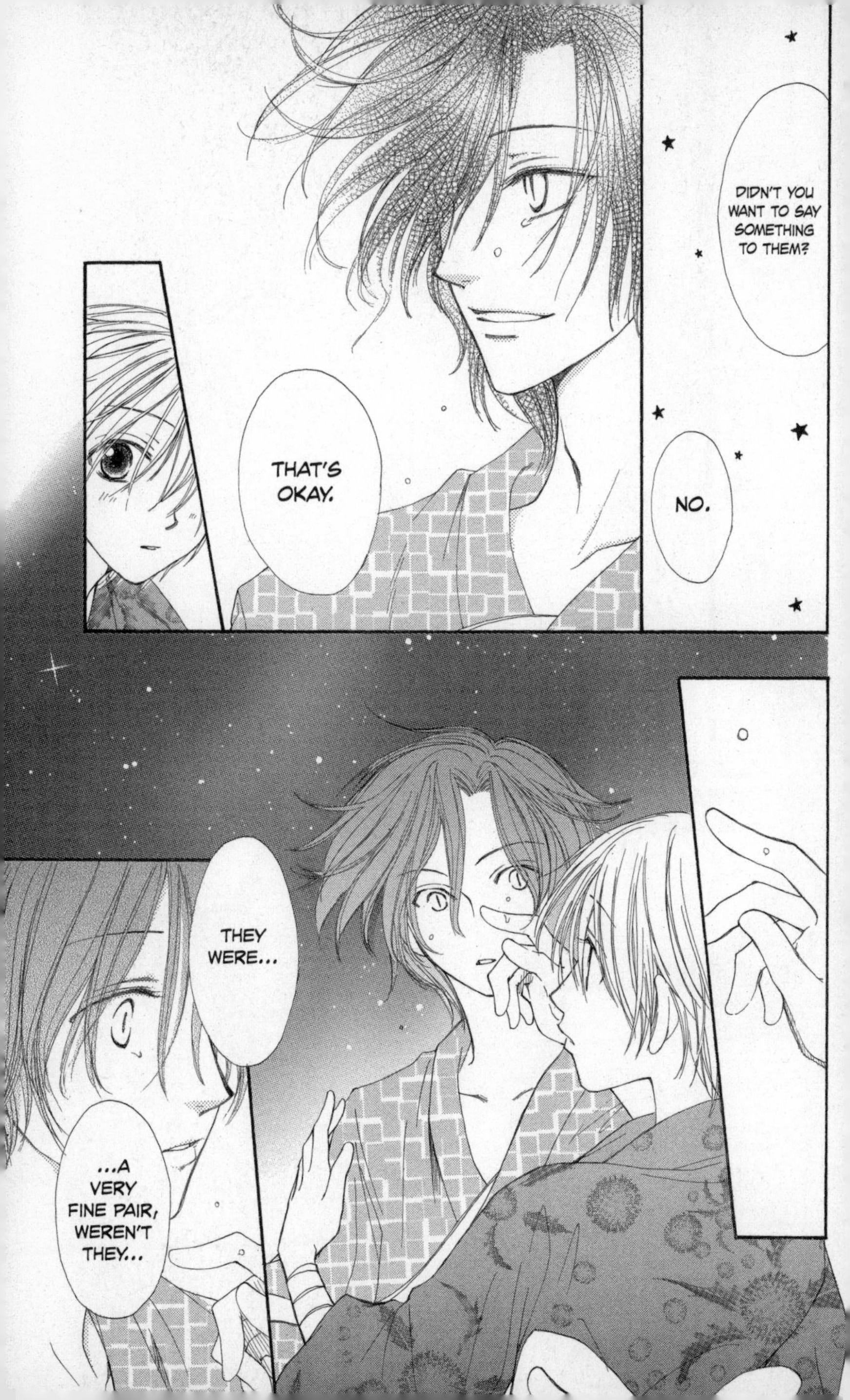
DIDN'T YOU WANT TO SAY SOMETHING TO THEM?
NO.
THAT'S OKAY.
THEY WERE...
...A VERY FINE PAIR, WEREN'T THEY...

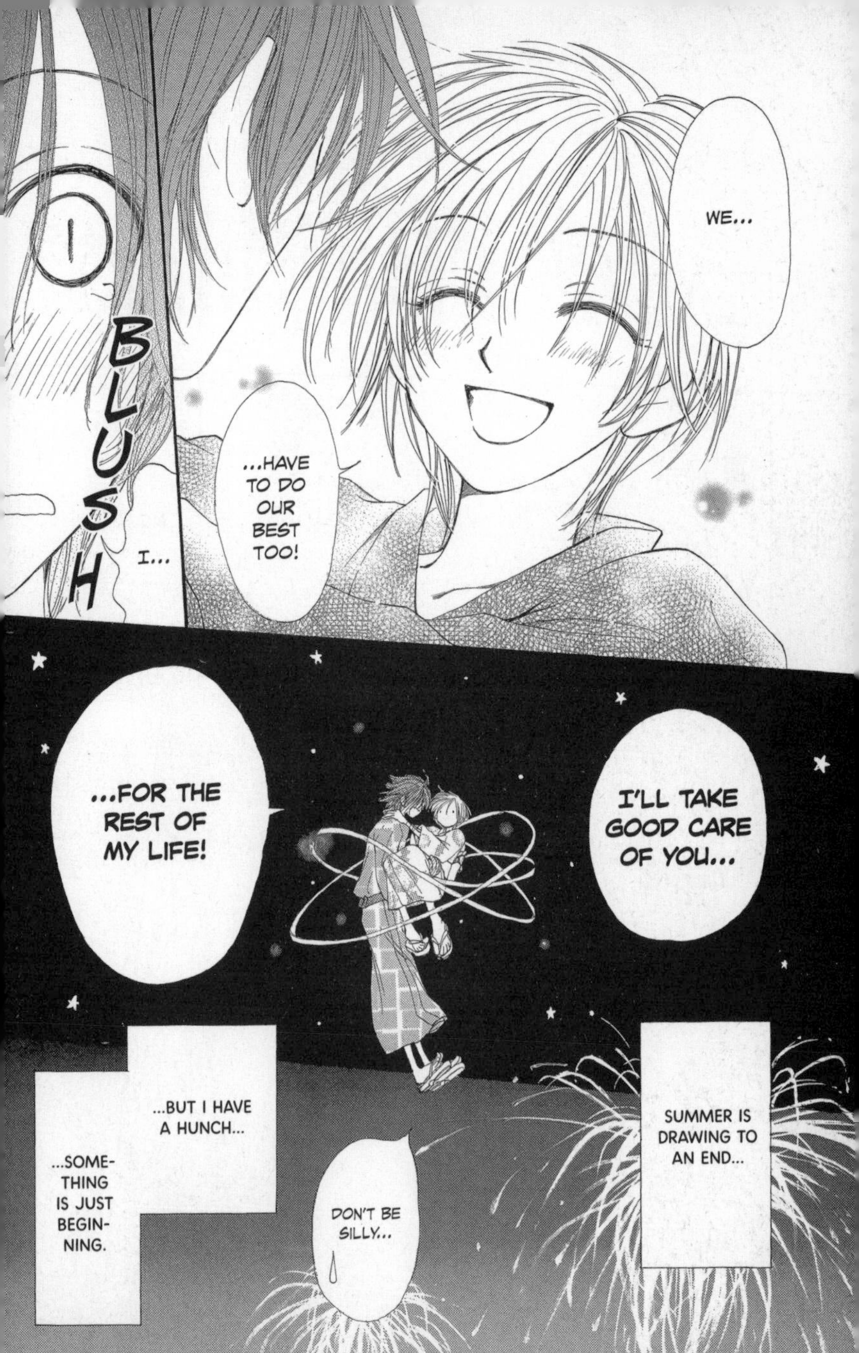
WE...
...HAVE TO DO OUR BEST TOO!
BLUSH
I...
I'LL TAKE GOOD CARE OF YOU...
...FOR THE REST OF MY LIFE!
SUMMER IS DRAWING TO AN END...
DON'T BE SILLY...
...BUT I HAVE A HUNCH...
...SOME-THING IS JUST BEGIN-NING.

SWEET REIN VOL. 1/END

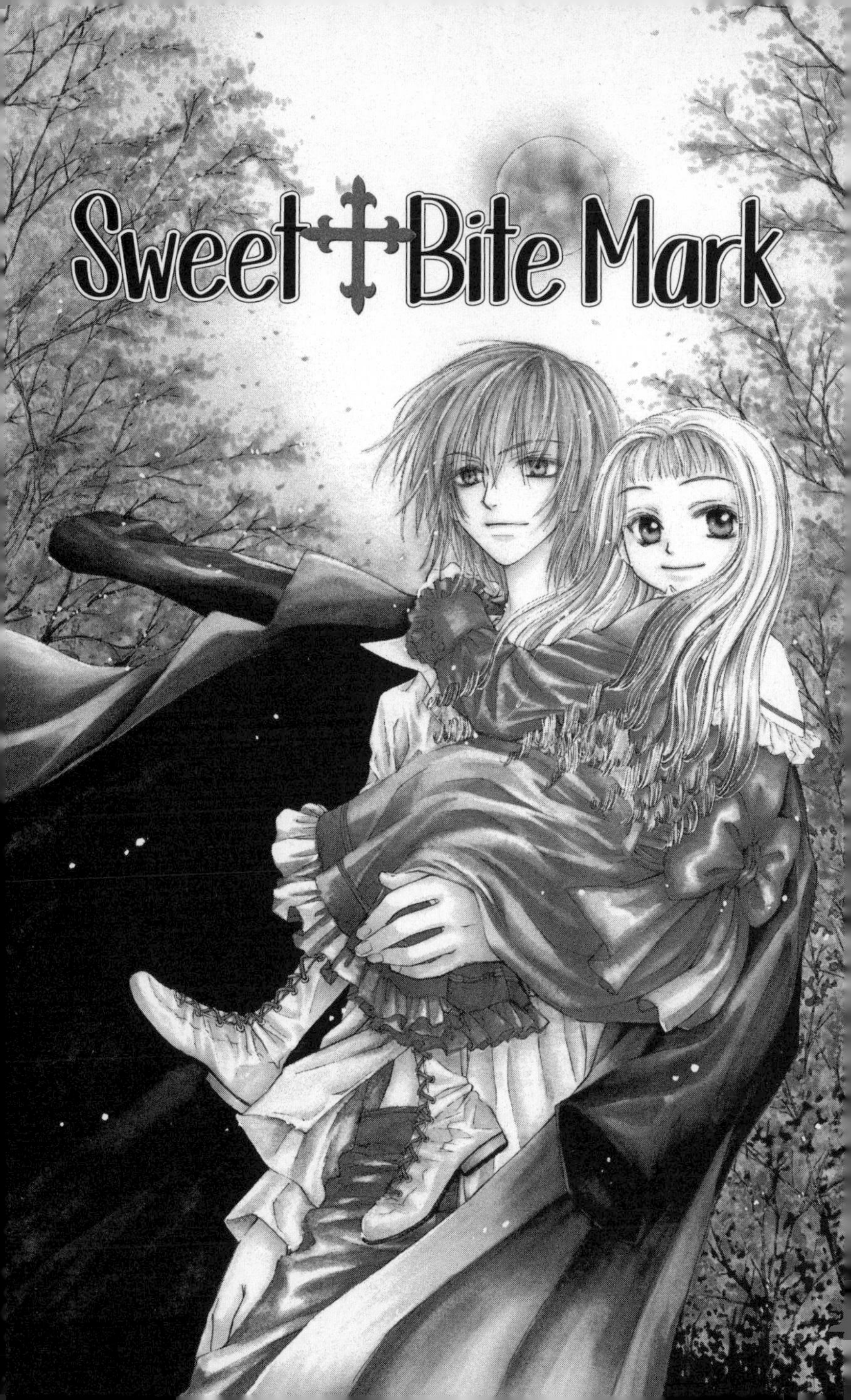
Sweet Bite Mark

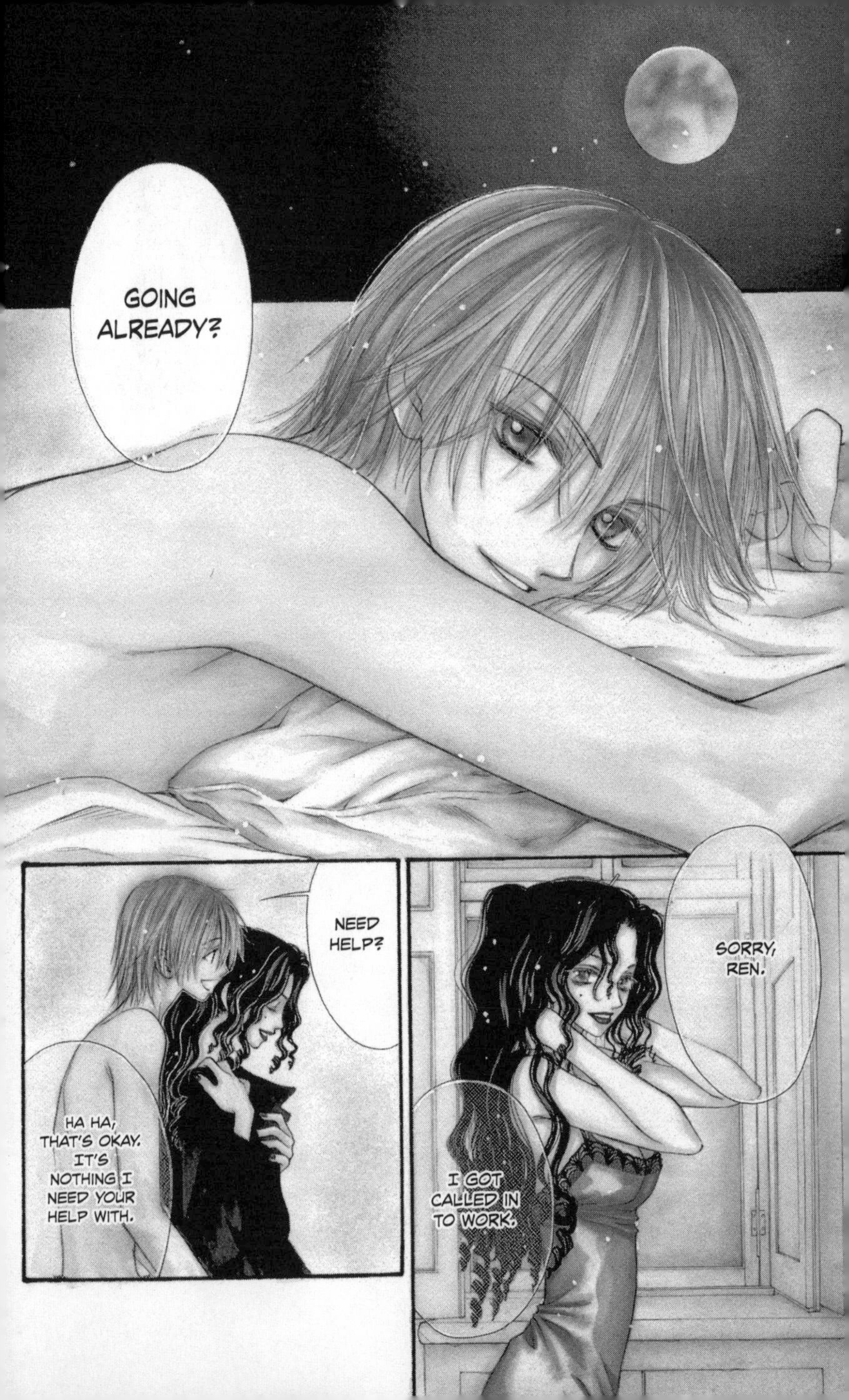
GOING ALREADY?
SORRY, REN.
I GOT CALLED IN TO WORK.
NEED HELP?
HA HA, THAT'S OKAY. IT'S NOTHING I NEED YOUR HELP WITH.

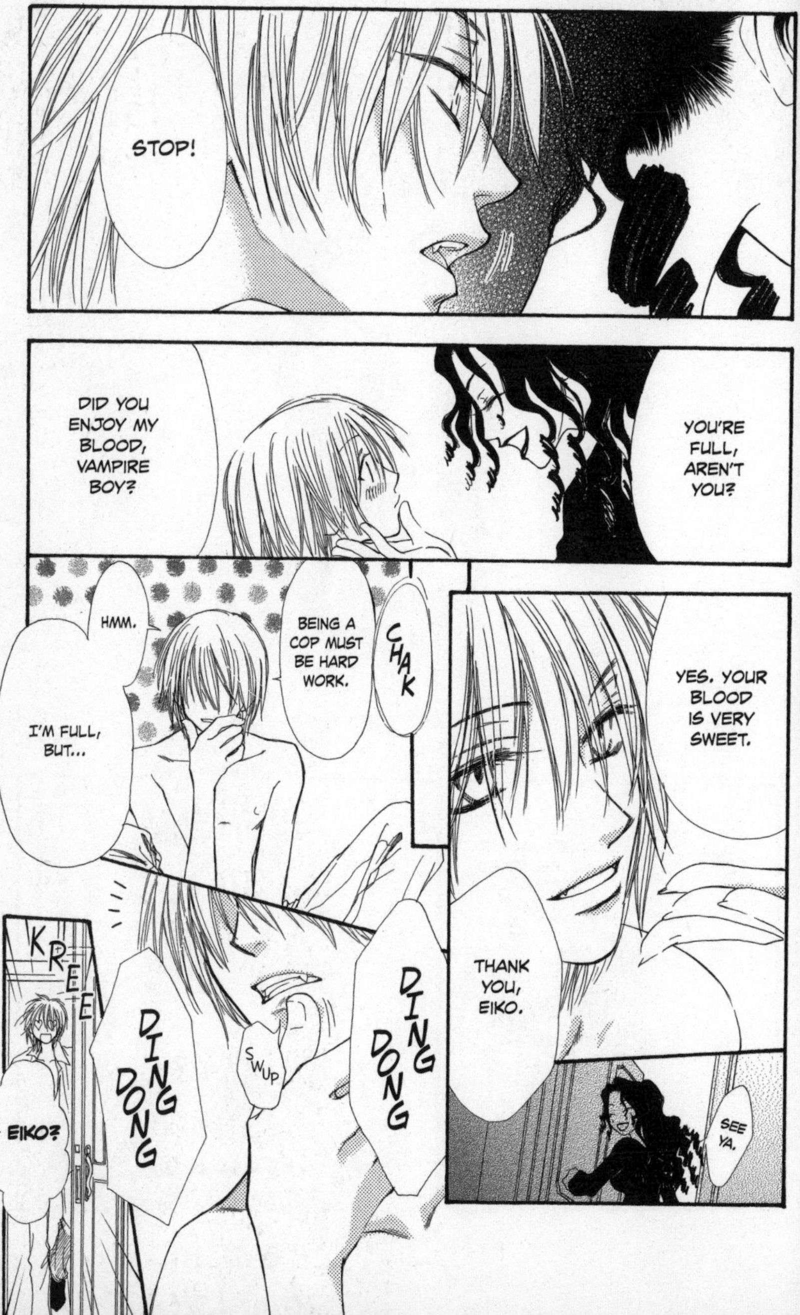
STOP!
YOU'RE FULL, AREN'T YOU?
DID YOU ENJOY MY BLOOD, VAMPIRE BOY?
YES. YOUR BLOOD IS VERY SWEET.
THANK YOU, EIKO.
SEE YA.
CHAK
BEING A COP MUST BE HARD WORK.
HMM.
I'M FULL, BUT...
DING DONG
SWUP
DING DONG
KREE
EIKO?

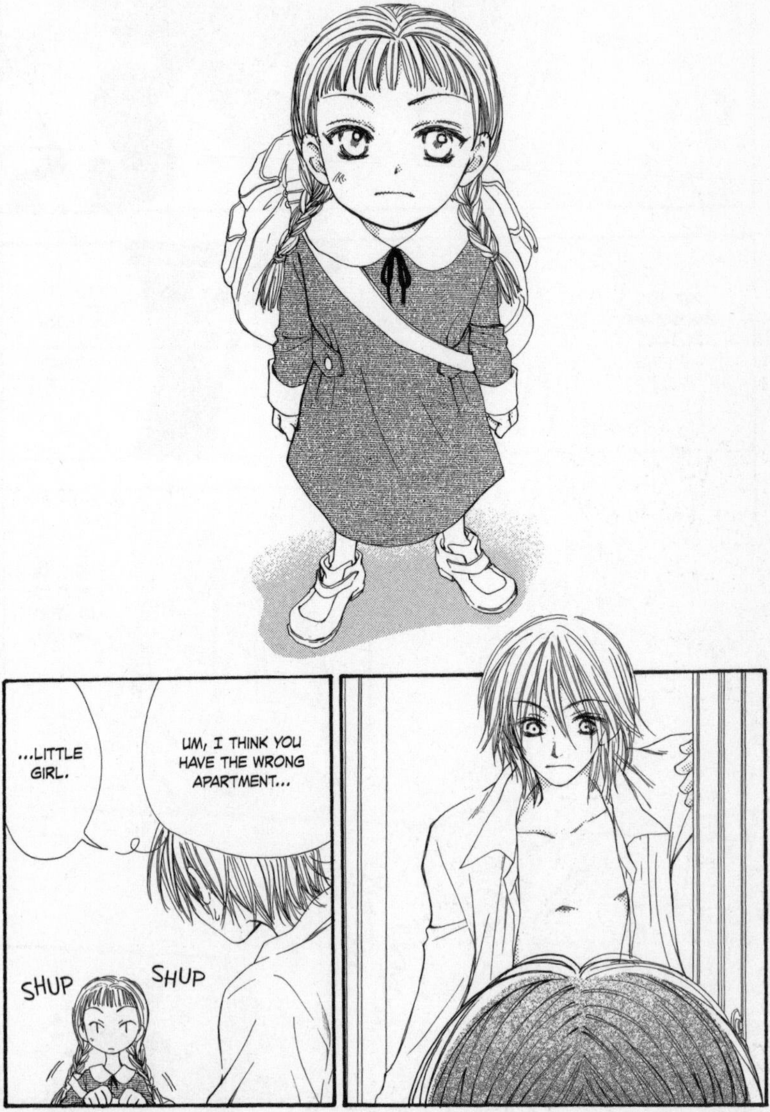
UM, I THINK YOU HAVE THE WRONG APARTMENT...
...LITTLE GIRL.
SHUP
SHUP

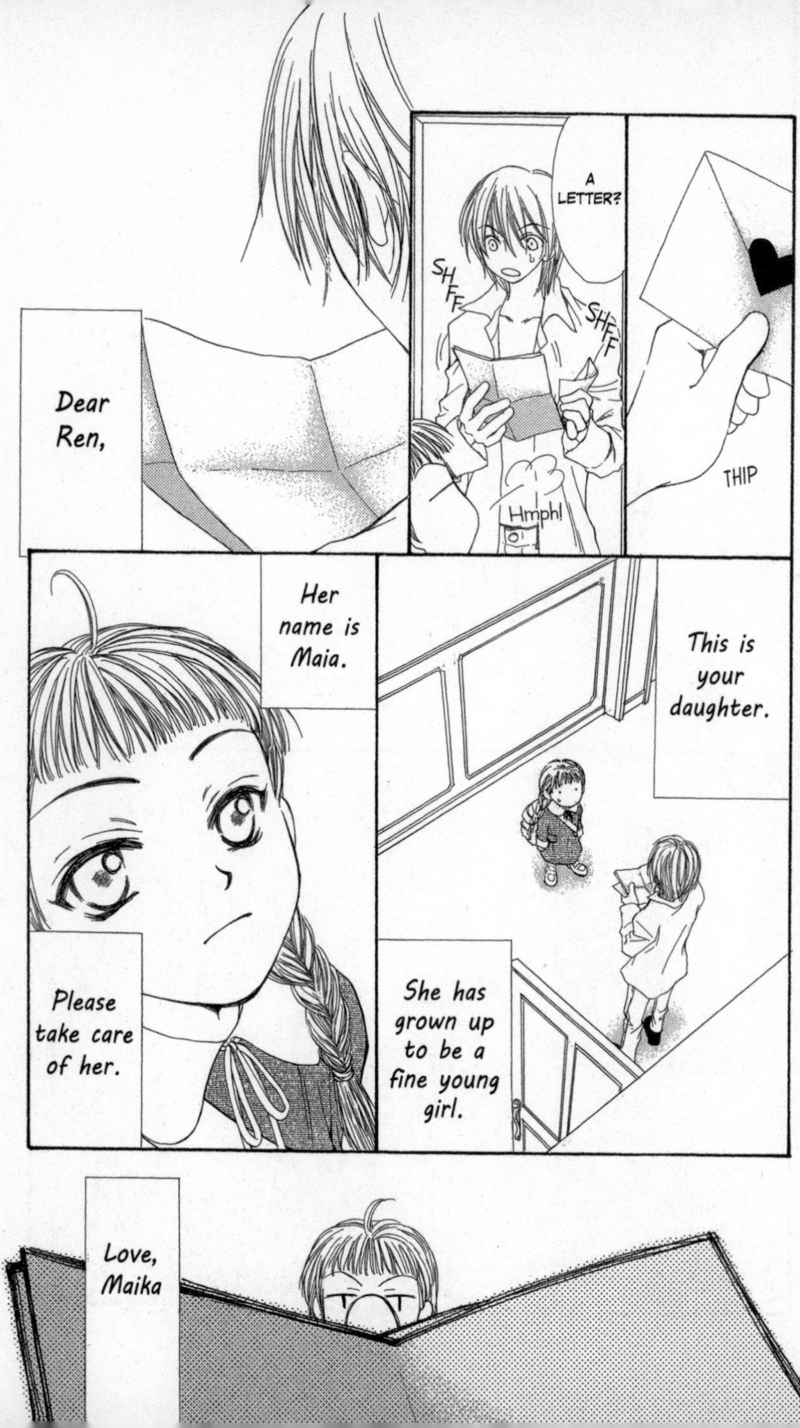
THIP
A LETTER?
SHFF
SHFF
Hmph!
Dear Ren,
This is your daughter.
She has grown up to be a fine young girl.
Her name is Maia.
Please take care of her.
Love, Maika

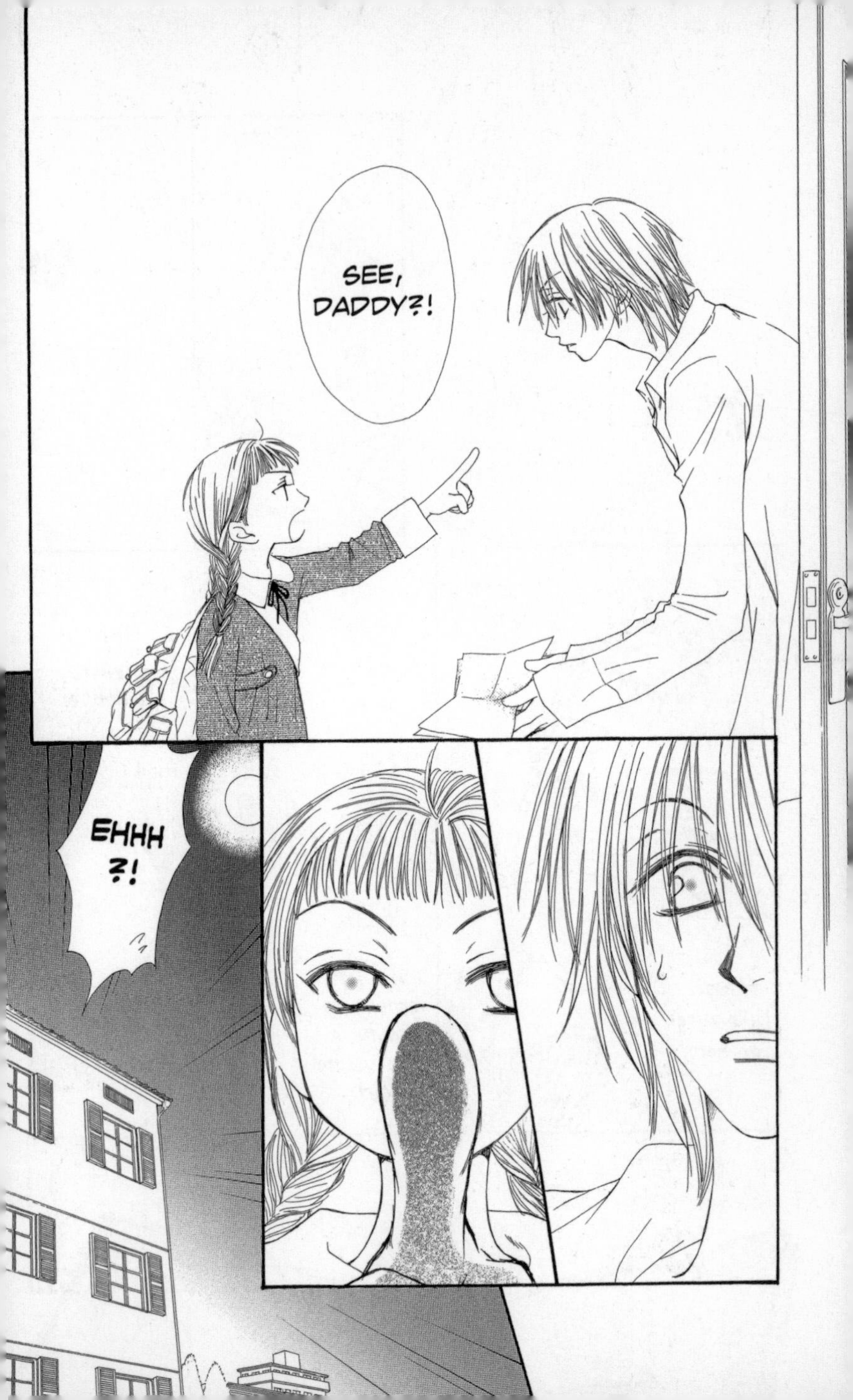
SEE, DADDY?!
EHHH ?!

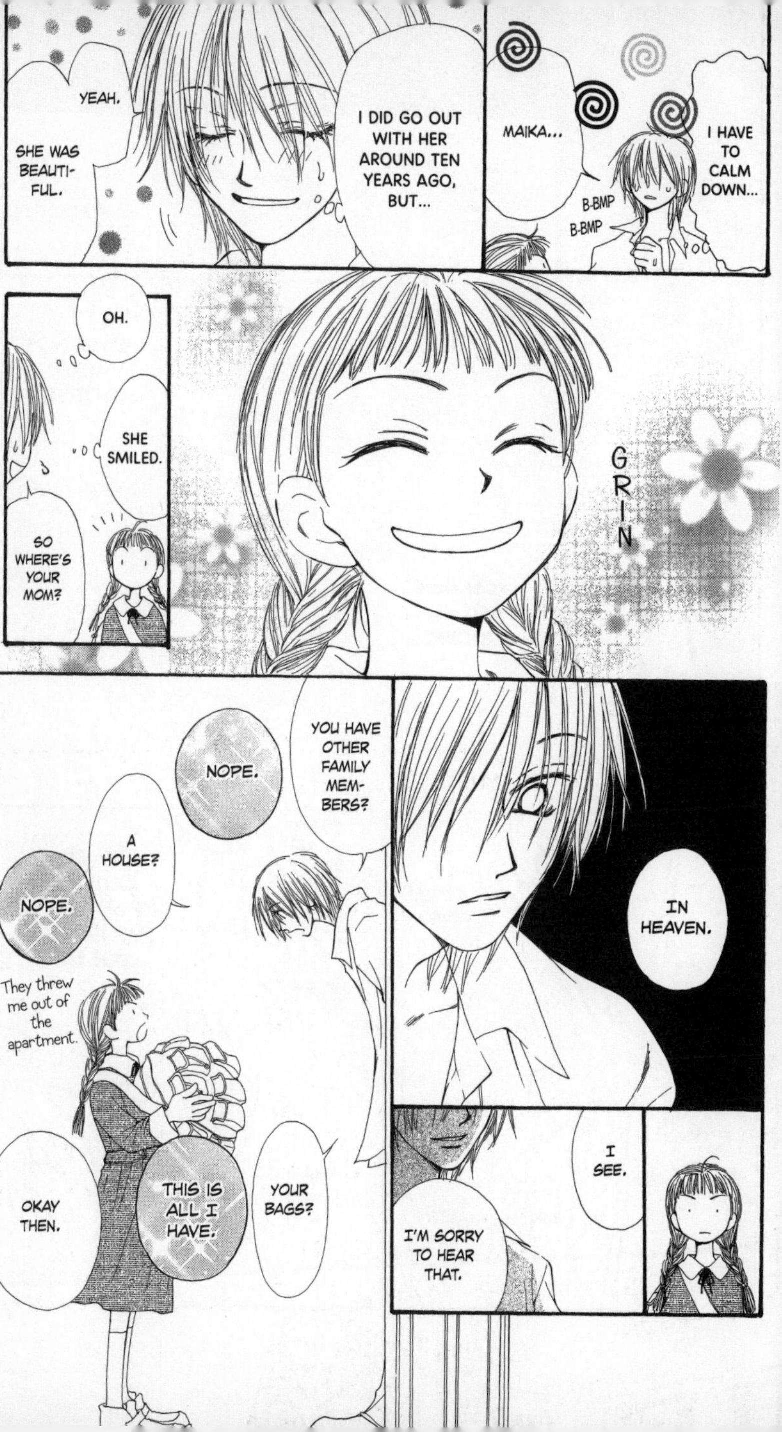
MAIKA...
I HAVE TO CALM DOWN...
B-BMP
B-BMP
I DID GO OUT WITH HER AROUND TEN YEARS AGO, BUT...
YEAH.
SHE WAS BEAUTI-FUL.
GRIN
OH.
SHE SMILED.
SO WHERE'S YOUR MOM?
IN HEAVEN.
I SEE.
I'M SORRY TO HEAR THAT.
YOU HAVE OTHER FAMILY MEM-BERS?
NOPE.
A HOUSE?
NOPE.
They threw me out of the apartment.
YOUR BAGS?
THIS IS ALL I HAVE.
OKAY THEN.

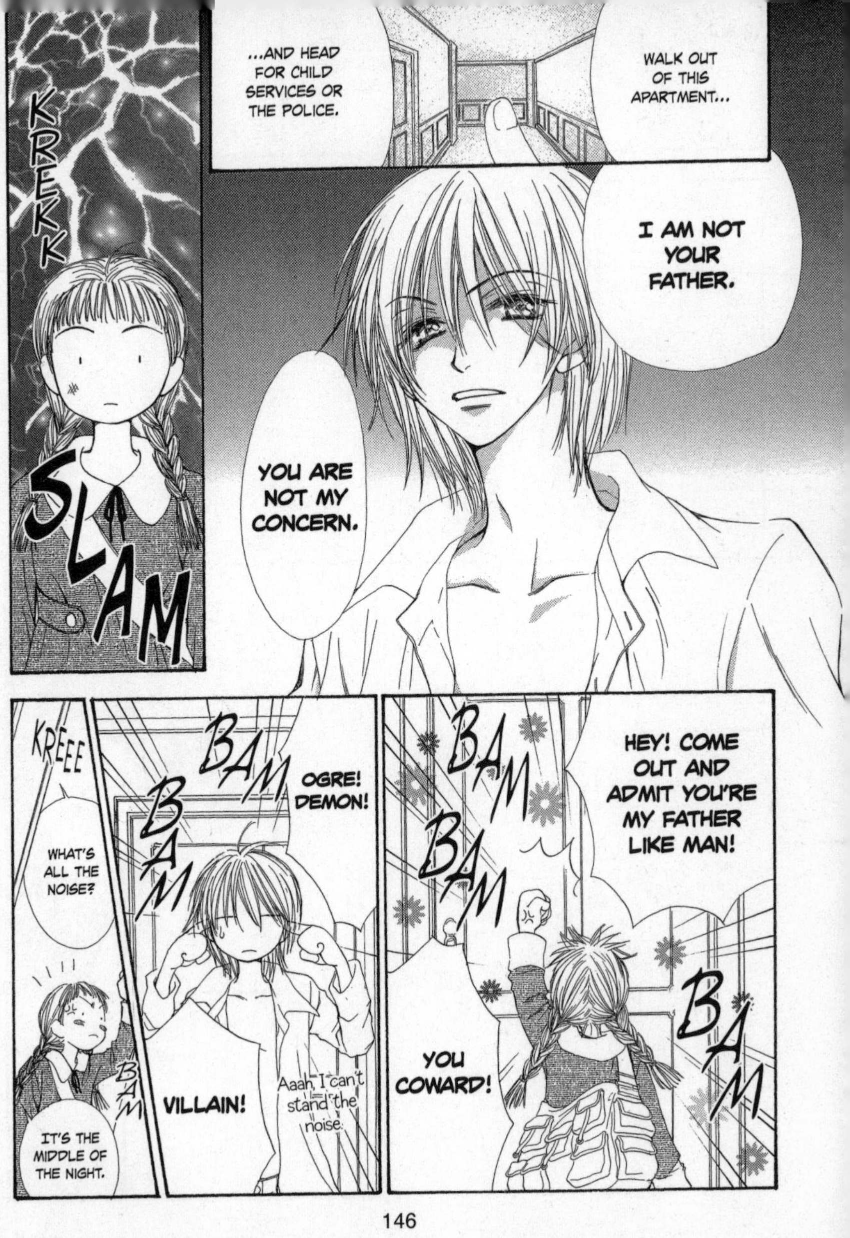
WALK OUT OF THIS APARTMENT...
...AND HEAD FOR CHILD SERVICES OR THE POLICE.
I AM NOT YOUR FATHER.
YOU ARE NOT MY CONCERN.
KREKK
SLAM
HEY! COME OUT AND ADMIT YOU'RE MY FATHER LIKE MAN!
BAM
BAM
BAM
YOU COWARD!
BAM
OGRE! DEMON!
BAM
VILLAIN!
Aaah, I can't stand the noise.
KREEE
WHAT'S ALL THE NOISE?
BAM
IT'S THE MIDDLE OF THE NIGHT.

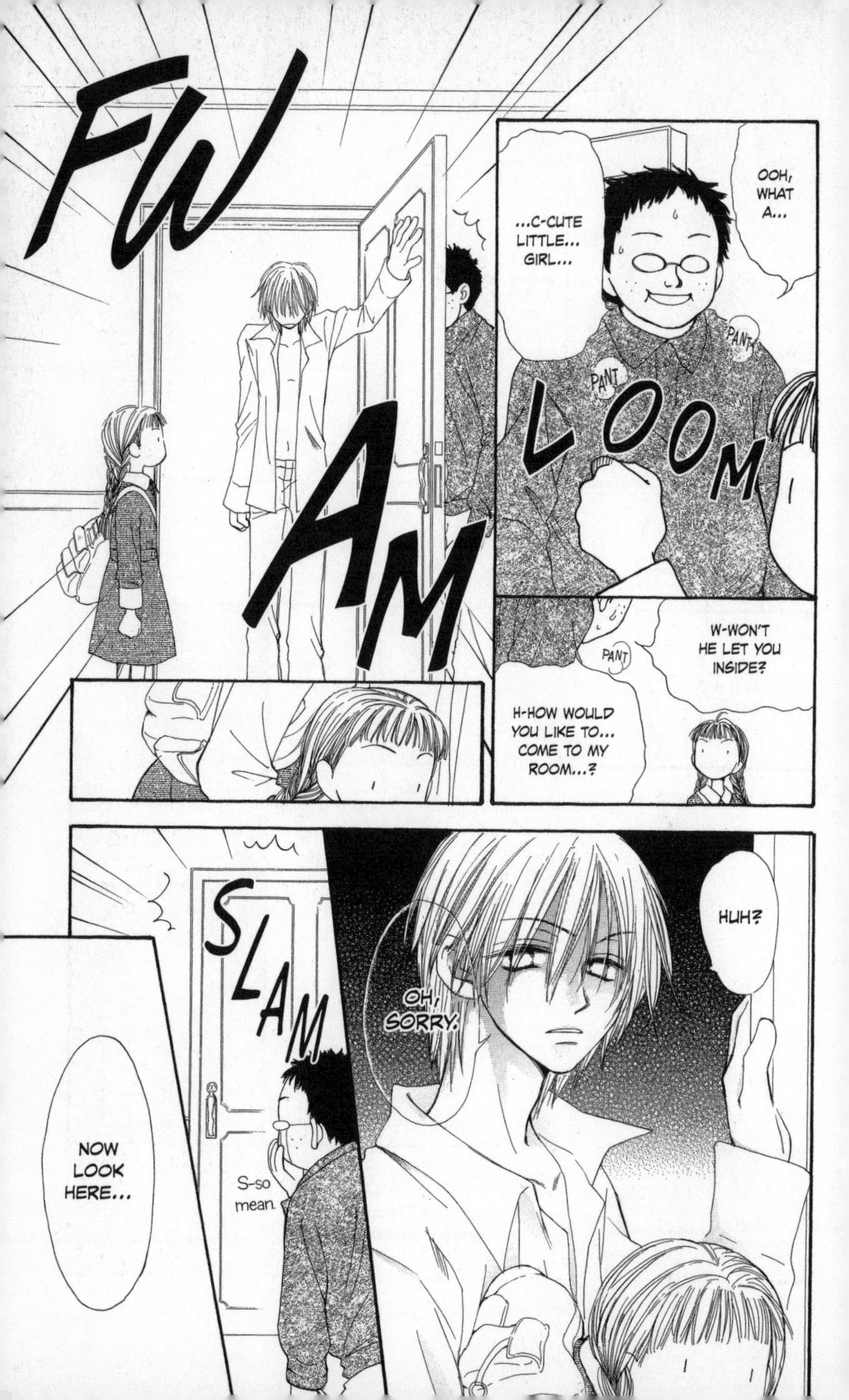

OOH, WHAT A...
...C-CUTE LITTLE... GIRL...
PANT
PANT
LOOM
PANT
W-WON'T HE LET YOU INSIDE?
H-HOW WOULD YOU LIKE TO... COME TO MY ROOM...?
FWAM
HUH?
OH, SORRY.
SLAM
S-so mean.
NOW LOOK HERE...

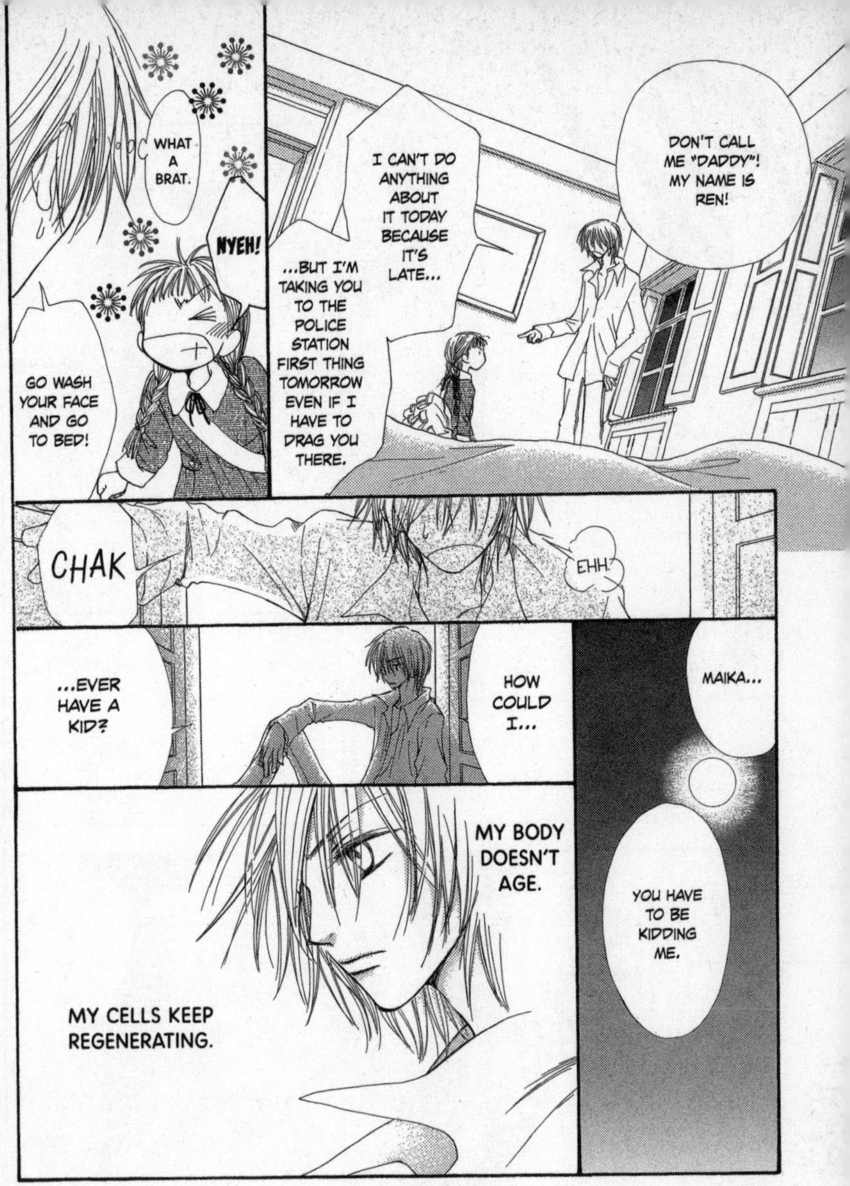
DON'T CALL ME "DADDY"! MY NAME IS REN!
I CAN'T DO ANYTHING ABOUT IT TODAY BECAUSE IT'S LATE...
...BUT I'M TAKING YOU TO THE POLICE STATION FIRST THING TOMORROW EVEN IF I HAVE TO DRAG YOU THERE.
NYEH!
WHAT A BRAT.
GO WASH YOUR FACE AND GO TO BED!
EHH?
CHAK
MAIKA...
YOU HAVE TO BE KIDDING ME.
HOW COULD I...
...EVER HAVE A KID?
MY BODY DOESN'T AGE.
MY CELLS KEEP REGENERATING.

I CAN'T LIVE OUT
MY LIFETIME
WITH OTHERS.

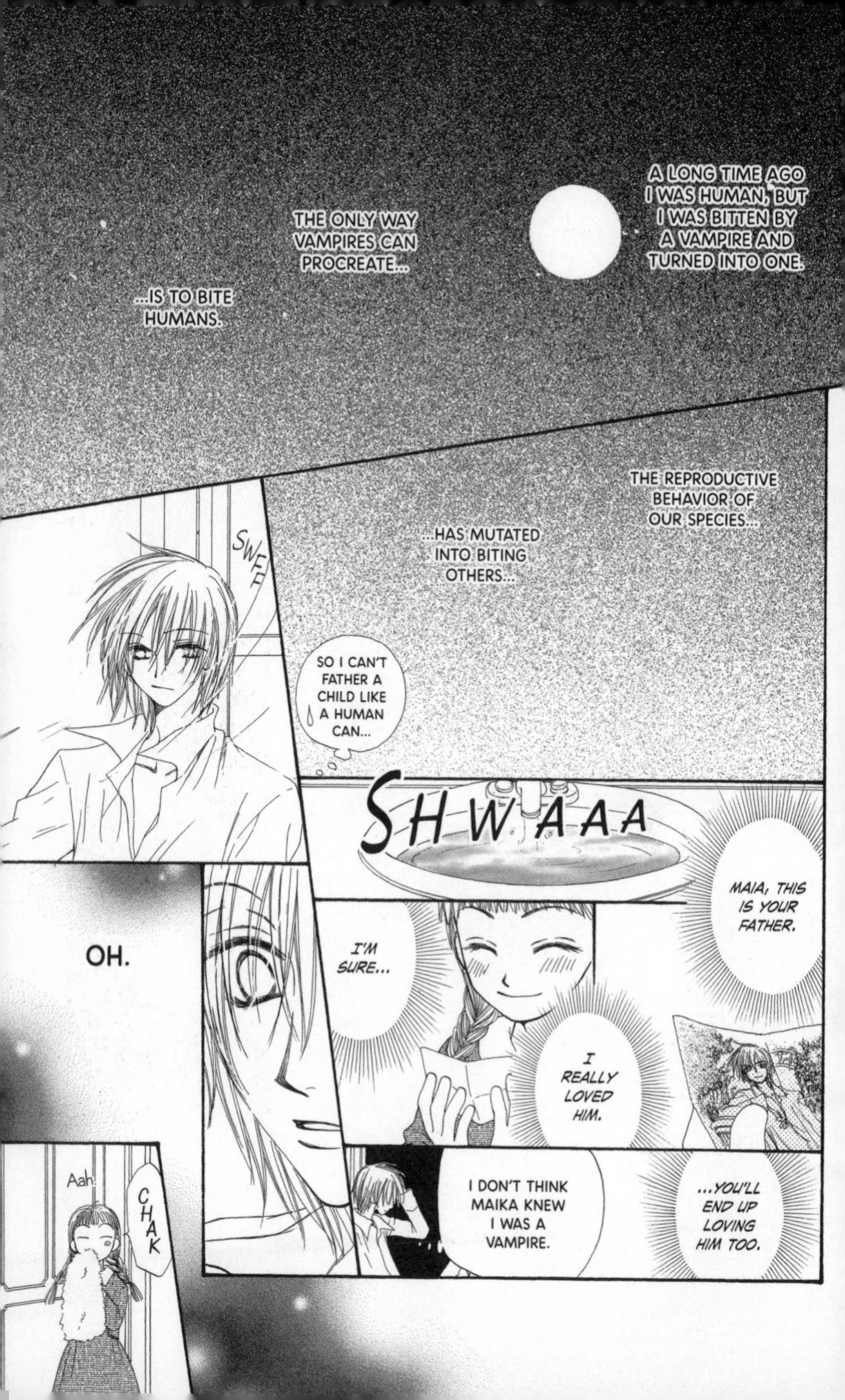
A LONG TIME AGO I WAS HUMAN, BUT I WAS BITTEN BY A VAMPIRE AND TURNED INTO ONE.
THE ONLY WAY VAMPIRES CAN PROCREATE...
...IS TO BITE HUMANS.
THE REPRODUCTIVE BEHAVIOR OF OUR SPECIES...
...HAS MUTATED INTO BITING OTHERS...
SO I CAN'T FATHER A CHILD LIKE A HUMAN CAN...
SWFF
SHWAAA
MAIA, THIS IS YOUR FATHER.
I'M SURE...
I REALLY LOVED HIM.
...YOU'LL END UP LOVING HIM TOO.
I DON'T THINK MAIKA KNEW I WAS A VAMPIRE.
OH.
CHAK
Aah!

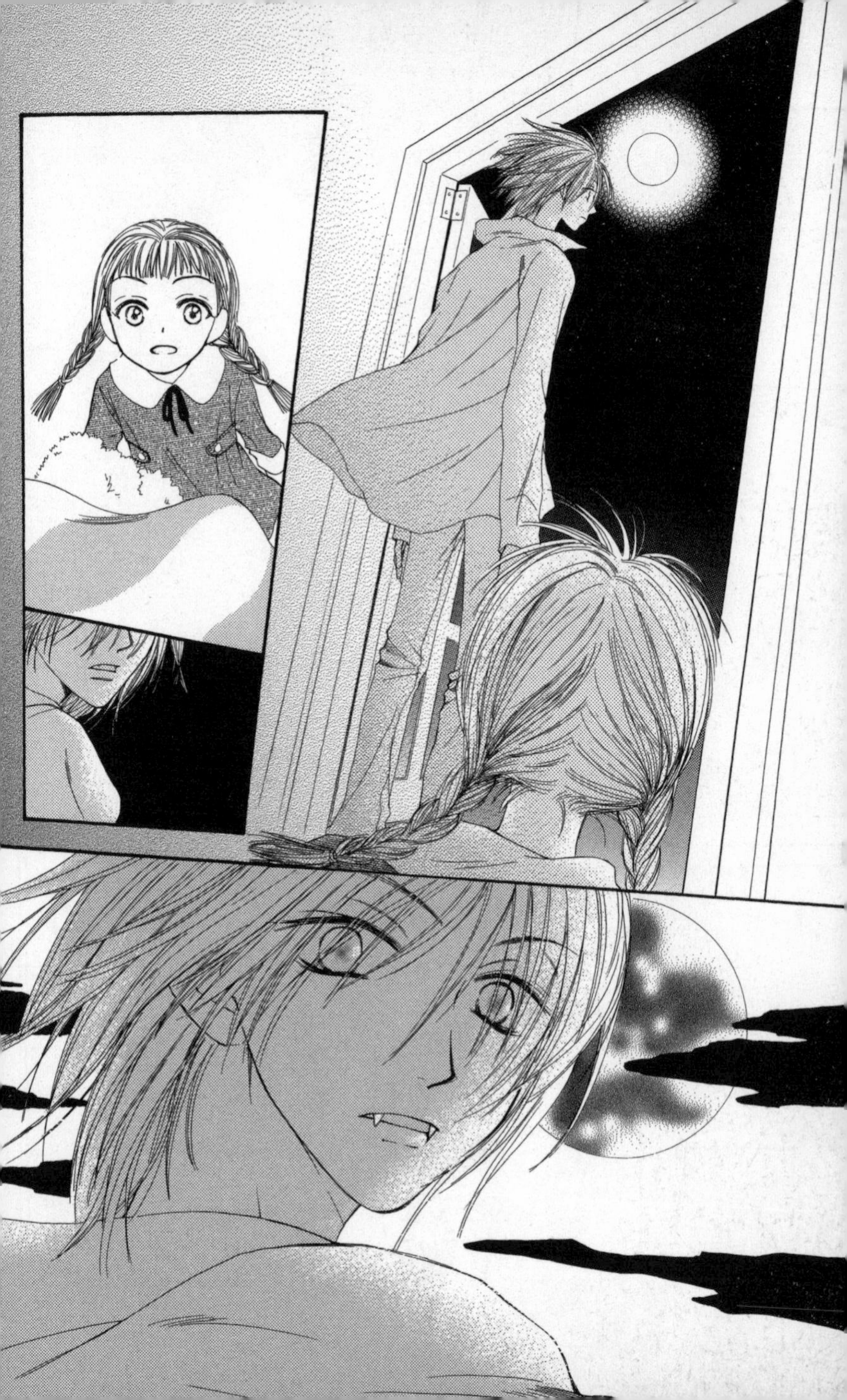

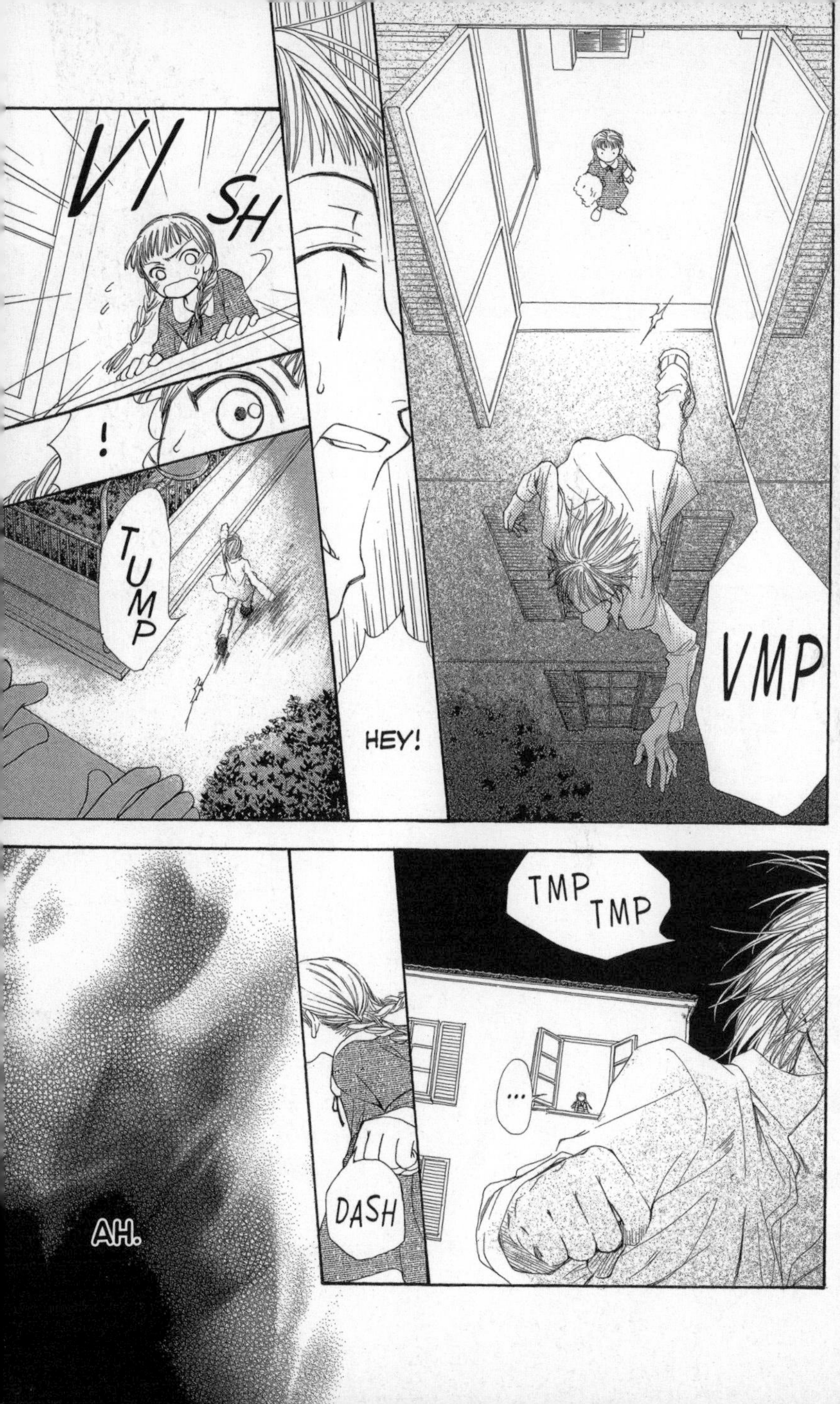
VMP
HEY!
VISH
!
TUMP
TMP TMP
...
DASH
AH.

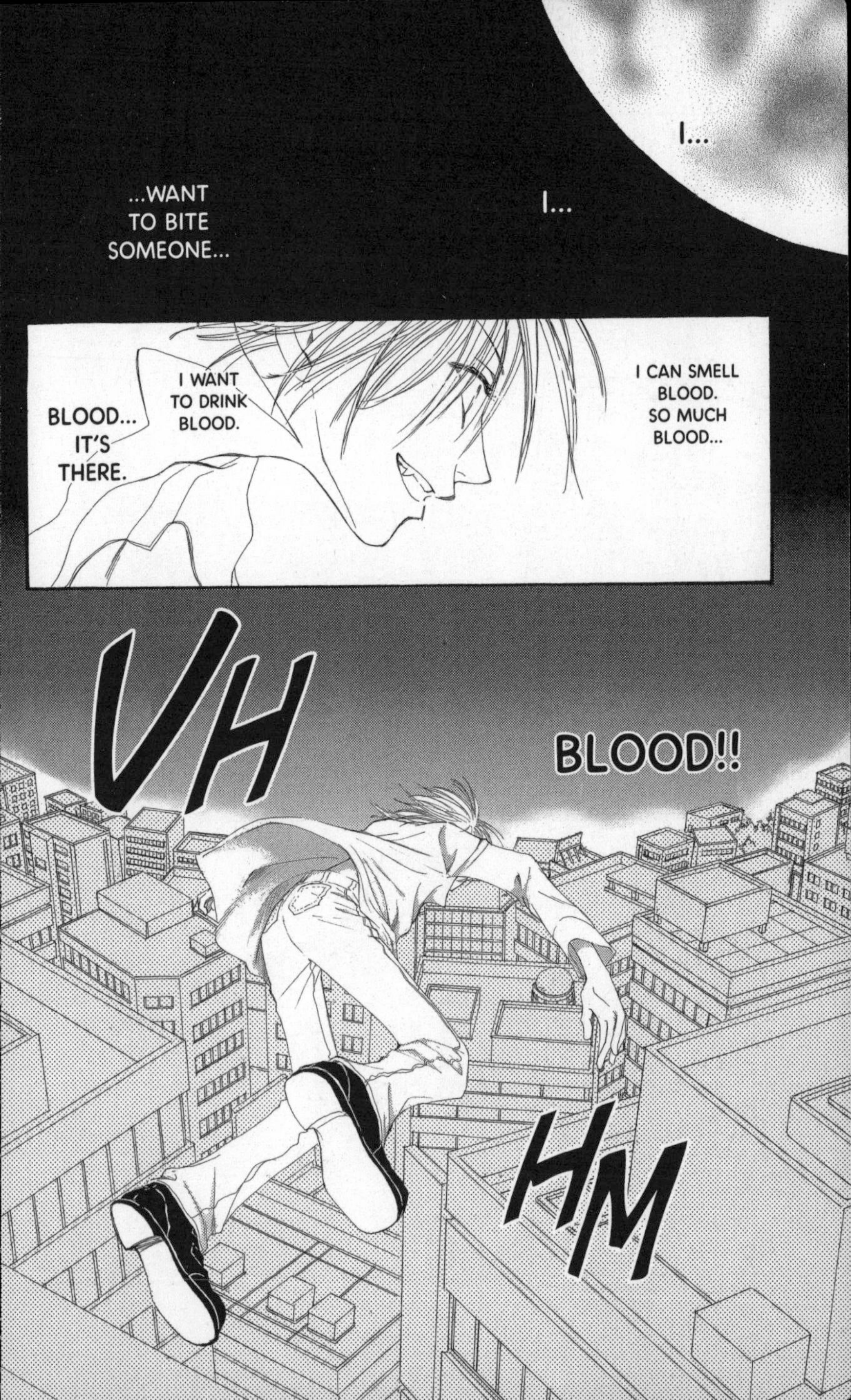
I...
I...
...WANT TO BITE SOMEONE...
I CAN SMELL BLOOD. SO MUCH BLOOD...
I WANT TO DRINK BLOOD.
BLOOD... IT'S THERE.
BLOOD!!
VH
HM

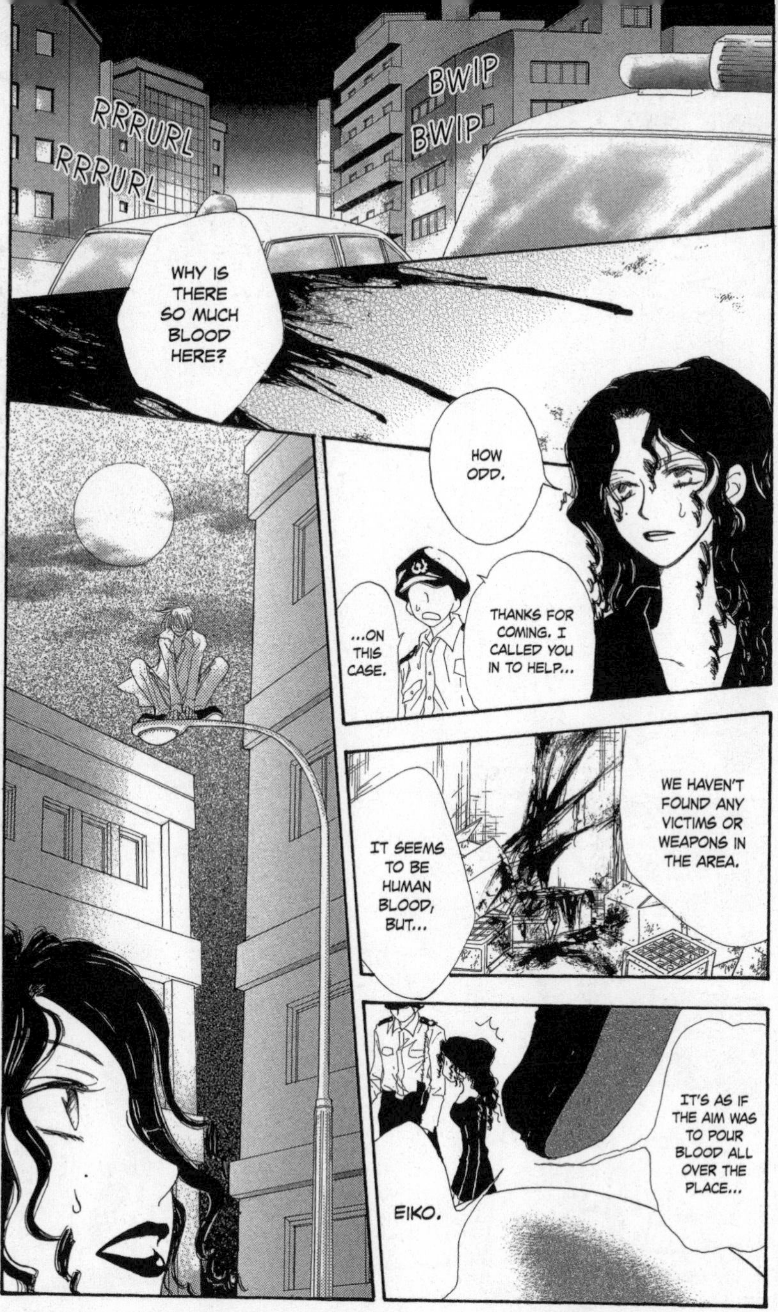
BWIP
BWIP
RRRURL
RRRURL
WHY IS THERE SO MUCH BLOOD HERE?
HOW ODD.
THANKS FOR COMING. I CALLED YOU IN TO HELP...
...ON THIS CASE.
WE HAVEN'T FOUND ANY VICTIMS OR WEAPONS IN THE AREA.
IT SEEMS TO BE HUMAN BLOOD, BUT...
IT'S AS IF THE AIM WAS TO POUR BLOOD ALL OVER THE PLACE...
EIKO.

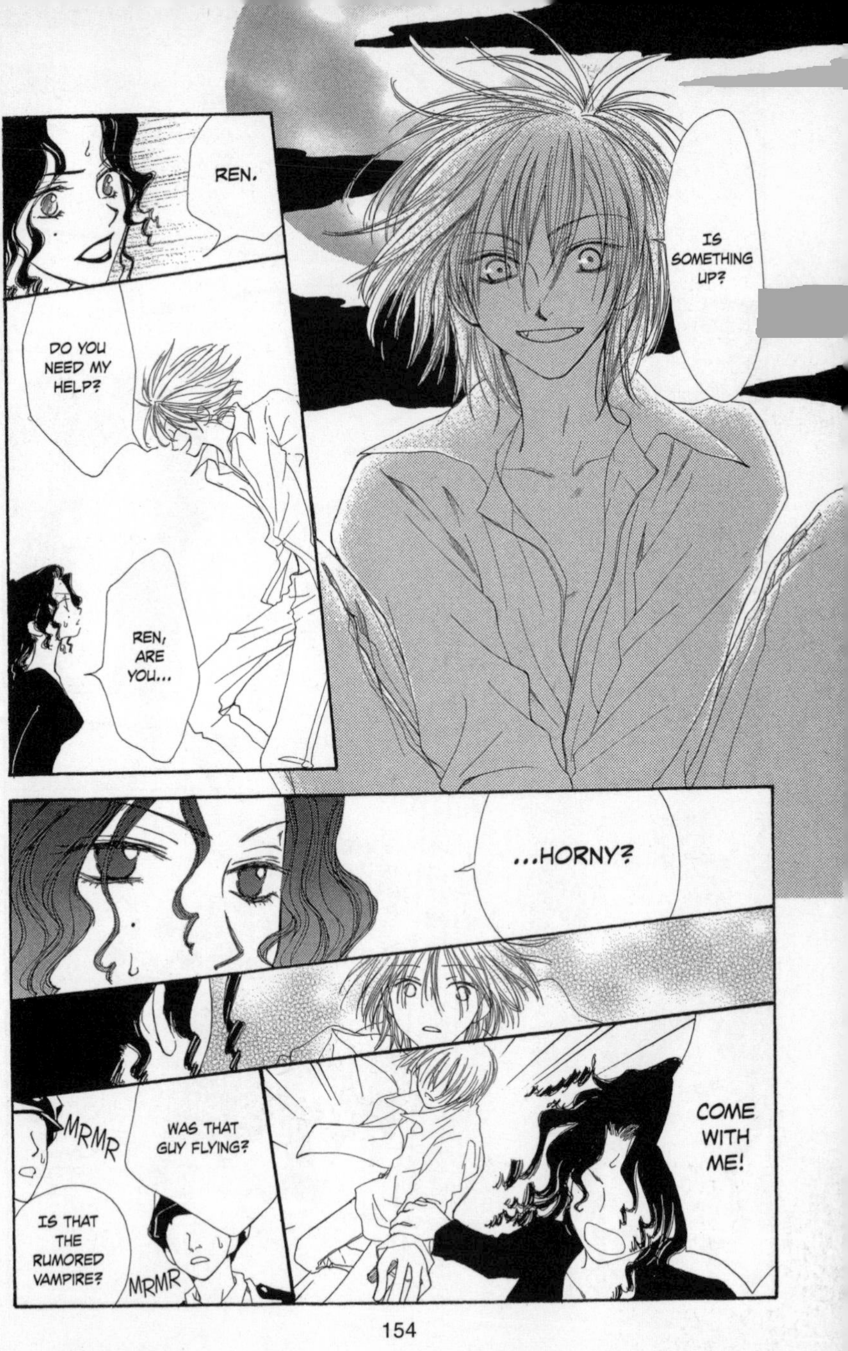
IS SOMETHING UP?
REN.
DO YOU NEED MY HELP?
REN, ARE YOU...
...HORNY?
COME WITH ME!
MRMR
WAS THAT GUY FLYING?
IS THAT THE RUMORED VAMPIRE?
MRMR

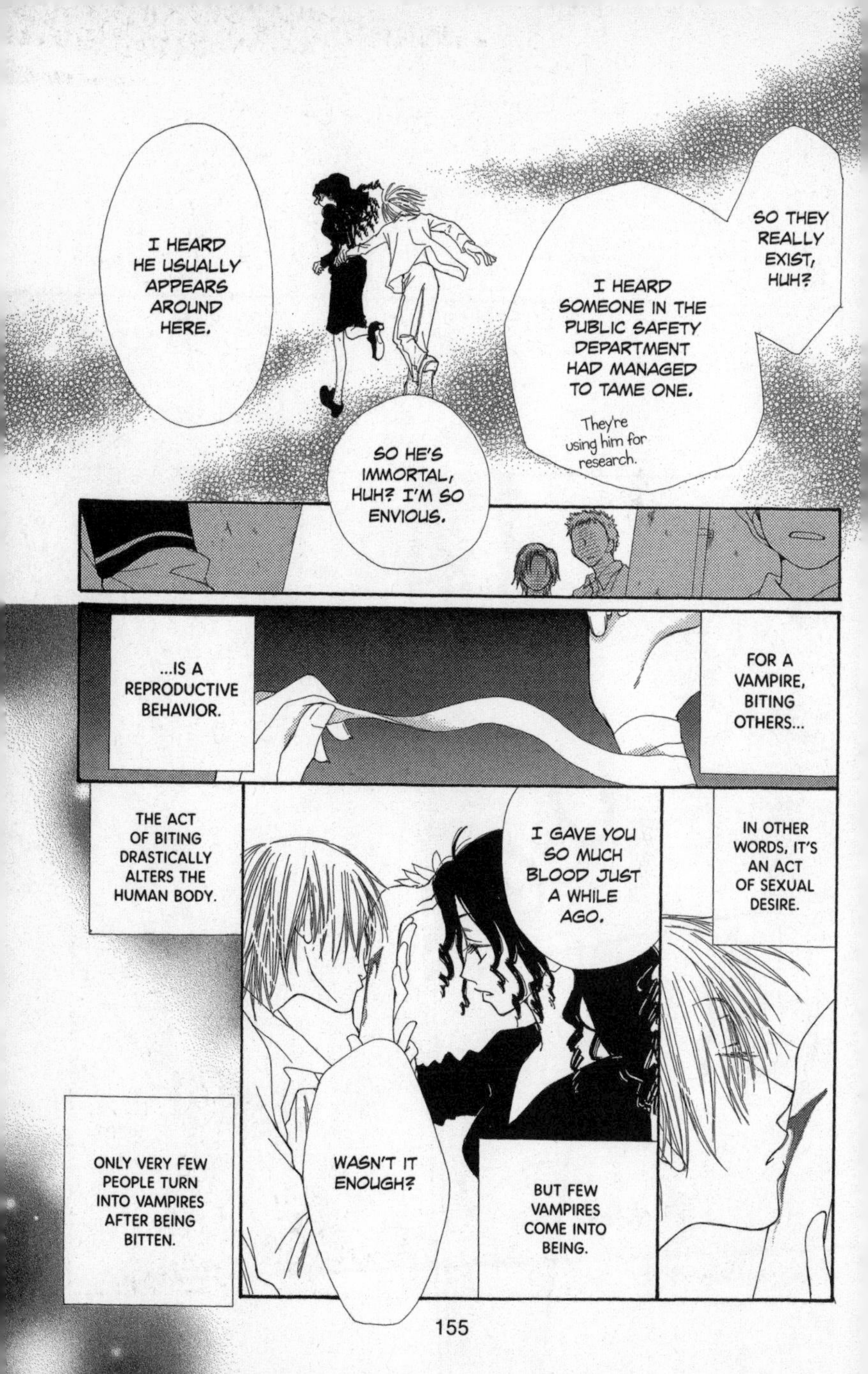
SO THEY REALLY EXIST, HUH?
I HEARD SOMEONE IN THE PUBLIC SAFETY DEPARTMENT HAD MANAGED TO TAME ONE.
They're using him for research.
I HEARD HE USUALLY APPEARS AROUND HERE.
SO HE'S IMMORTAL, HUH? I'M SO ENVIOUS.
FOR A VAMPIRE, BITING OTHERS...
...IS A REPRODUCTIVE BEHAVIOR.
IN OTHER WORDS, IT'S AN ACT OF SEXUAL DESIRE.
I GAVE YOU SO MUCH BLOOD JUST A WHILE AGO.
THE ACT OF BITING DRASTICALLY ALTERS THE HUMAN BODY.
BUT FEW VAMPIRES COME INTO BEING.
WASN'T IT ENOUGH?
ONLY VERY FEW PEOPLE TURN INTO VAMPIRES AFTER BEING BITTEN.

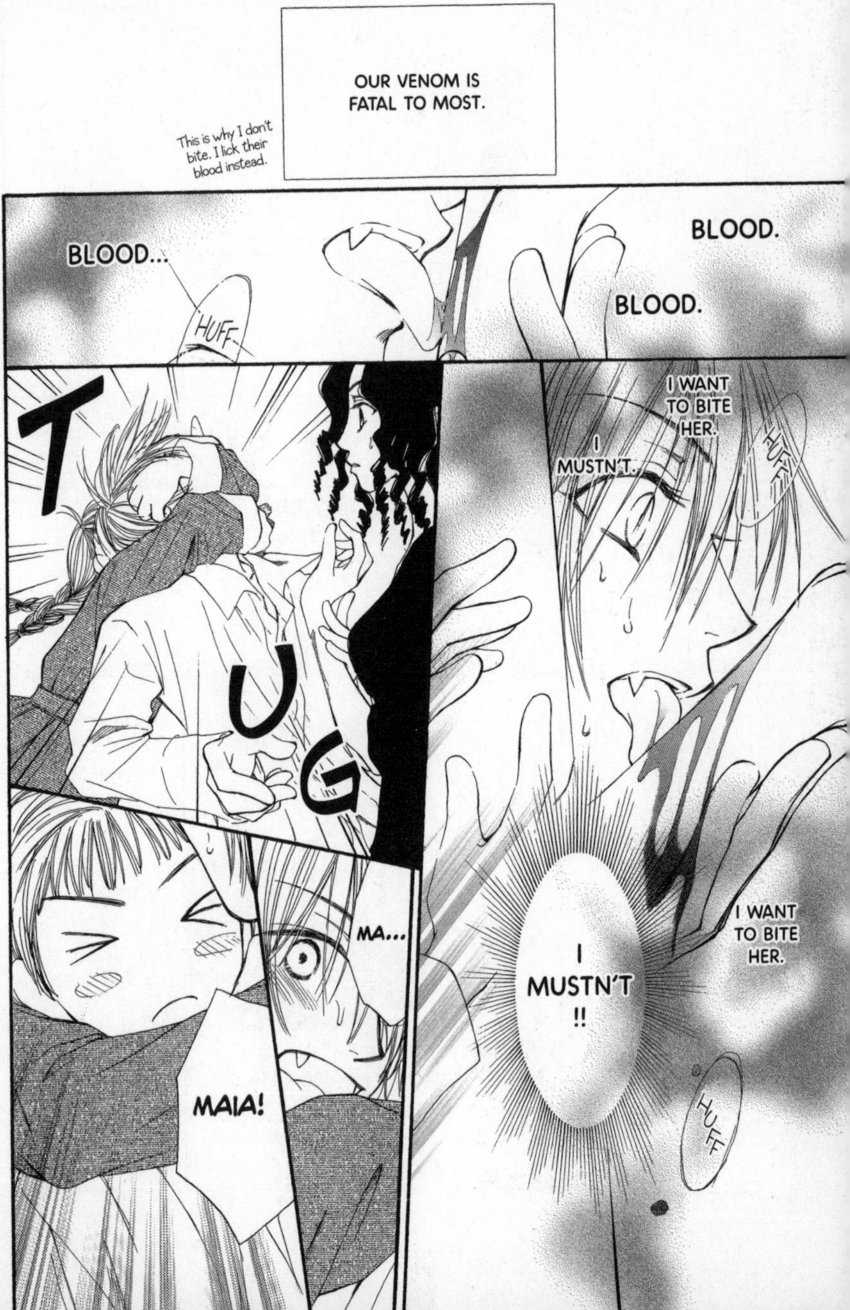
OUR VENOM IS FATAL TO MOST.
This is why I don't bite. I lick their blood instead.
BLOOD.
BLOOD.
BLOOD...
HUFF
HUFF
I WANT TO BITE HER.
I MUSTN'T.
I WANT TO BITE HER.
I MUSTN'T!!
HUFF
TUG
MA...
MAIA!

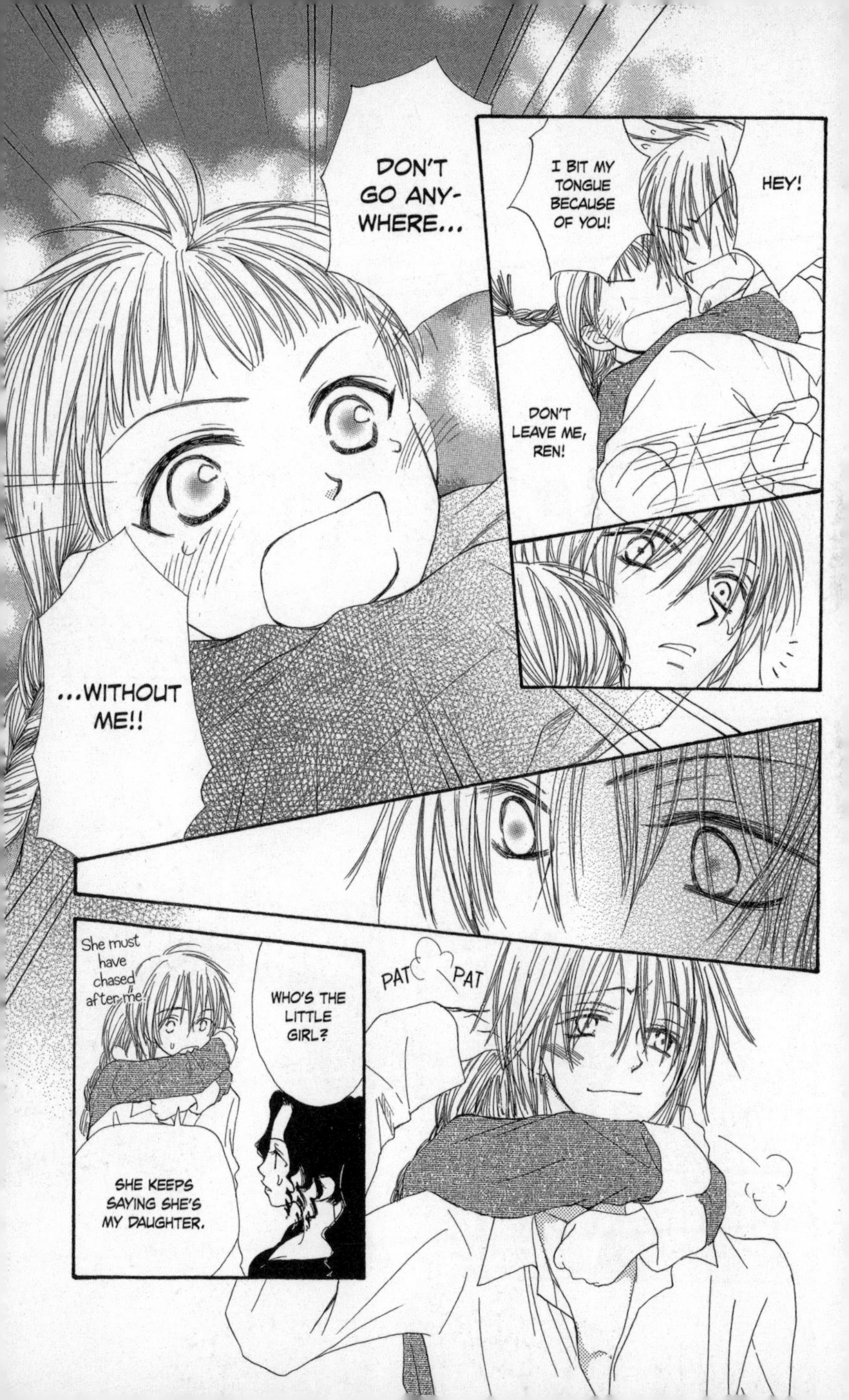
HEY!
I BIT MY TONGUE BECAUSE OF YOU!
DON'T LEAVE ME, REN!
DON'T GO ANY-WHERE...
...WITHOUT ME!!
PAT PAT
WHO'S THE LITTLE GIRL?
She must have chased after me.
SHE KEEPS SAYING SHE'S MY DAUGHTER.

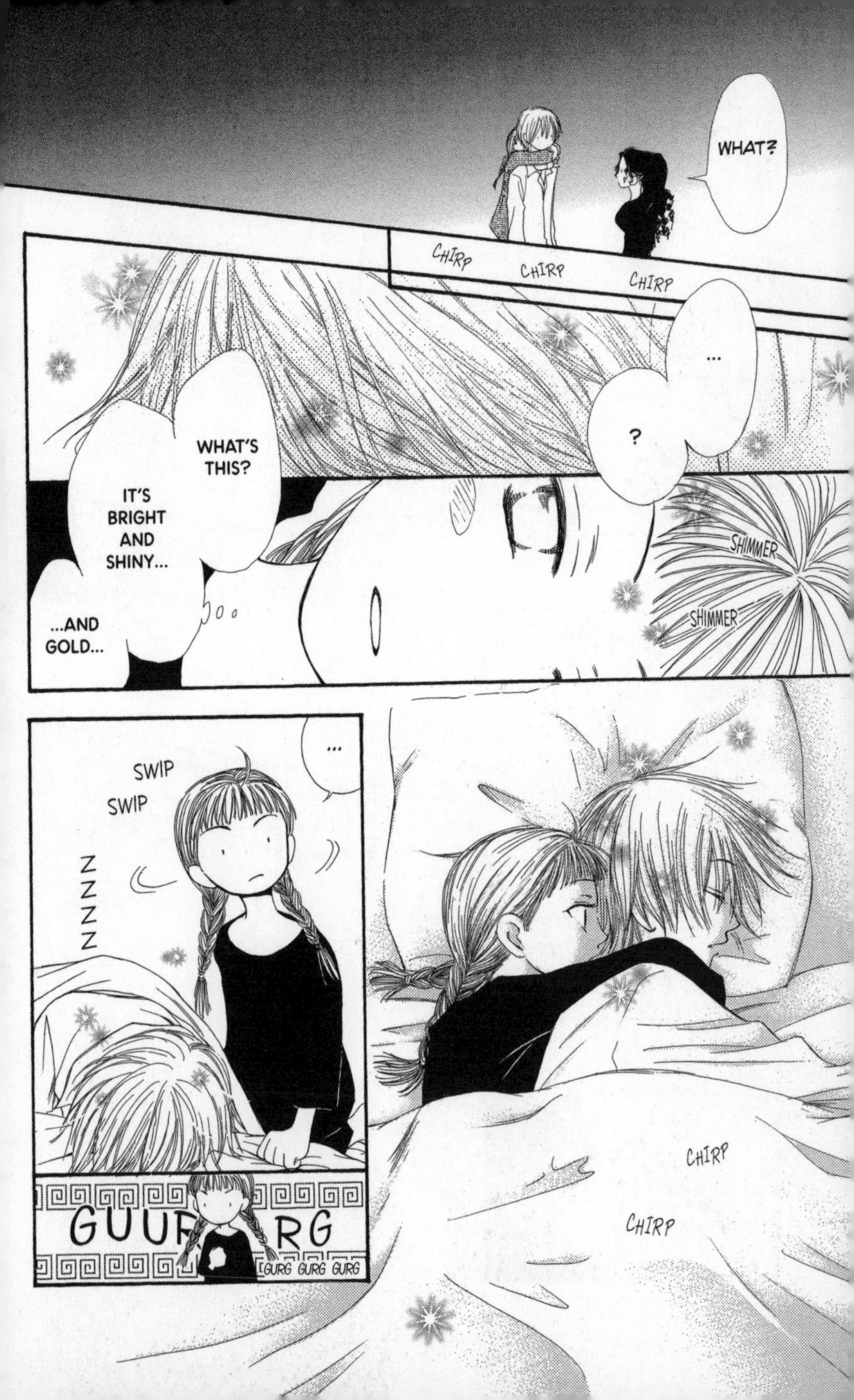

WHAT?
CHIRP
CHIRP
CHIRP
...
?
WHAT'S THIS?
IT'S BRIGHT AND SHINY...
...AND GOLD...
SHIMMER
SHIMMER
CHIRP
CHIRP
...
SWIP
SWIP
ZZZZ
GUUR RG
GURG GURG GURG

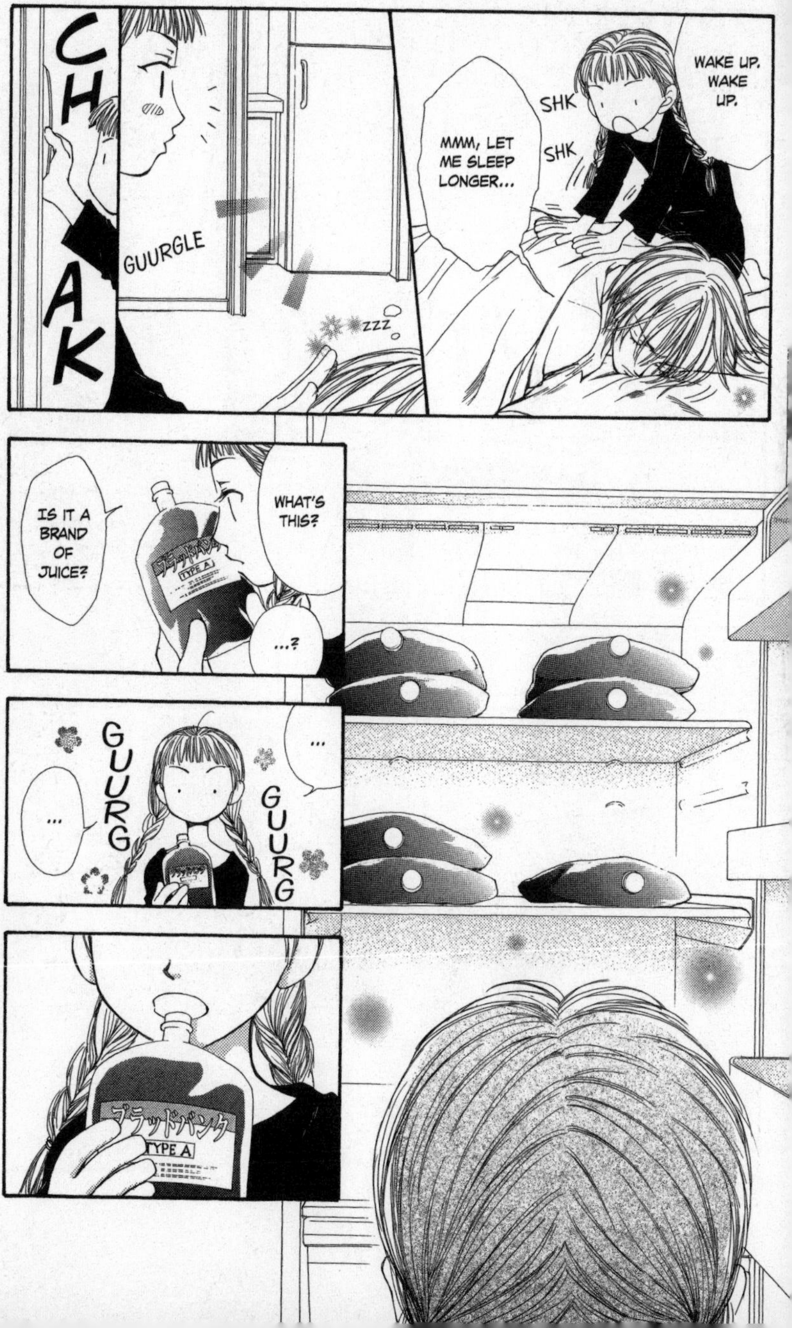
WAKE UP. WAKE UP.
SHK
SHK
MMM, LET ME SLEEP LONGER...
CHAK
GUURGLE
ZZZ
WHAT'S THIS?
IS IT A BRAND OF JUICE?
...?
...
...
GUURG
GUURG
ブラッドバンク
TYPE A

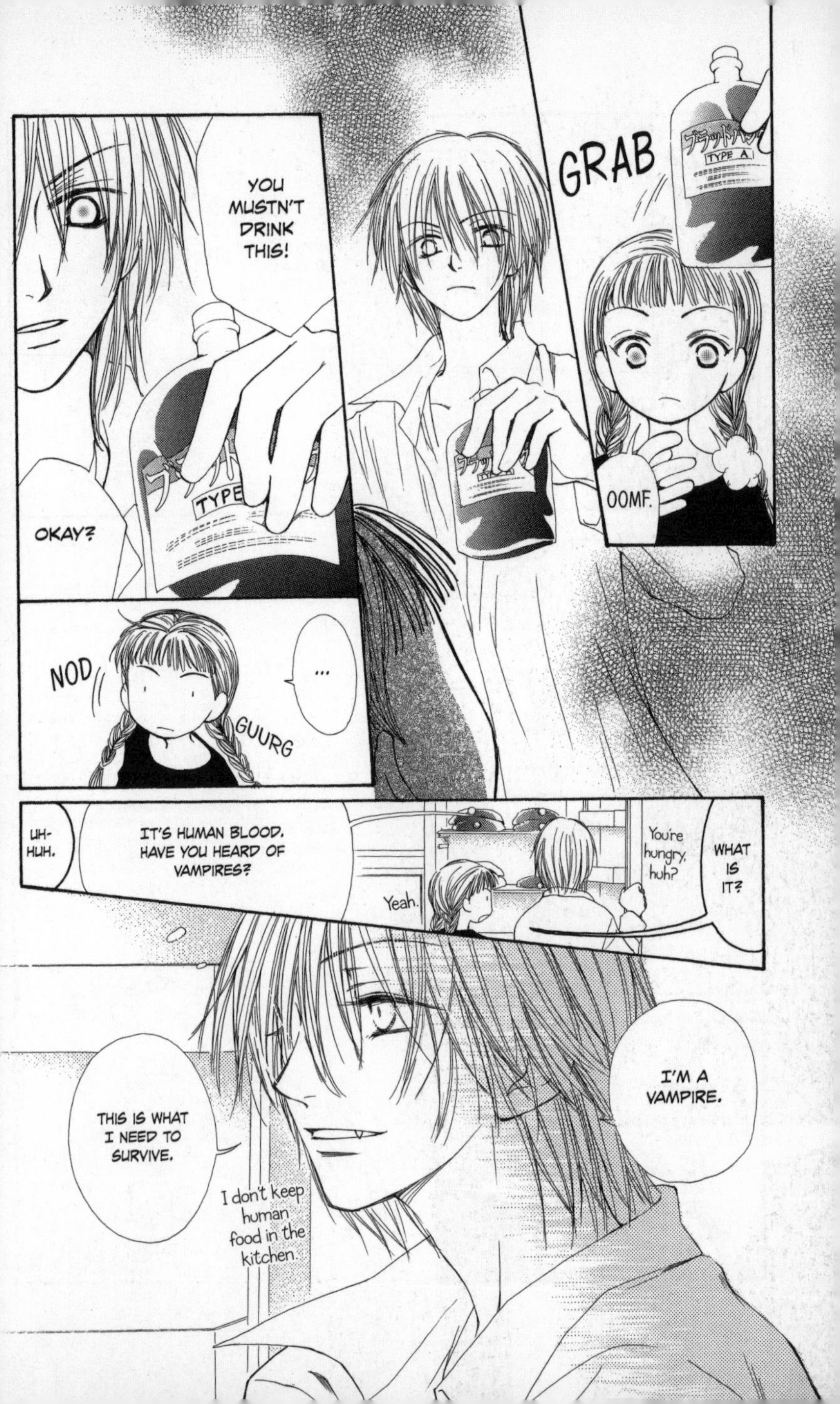
GRAB
TYPE A
OOMF.
YOU MUSTN'T DRINK THIS!
OKAY?
...
NOD
GUURG
WHAT IS IT?
You're hungry, huh?
Yeah.
IT'S HUMAN BLOOD. HAVE YOU HEARD OF VAMPIRES?
UH-HUH.
I'M A VAMPIRE.
THIS IS WHAT I NEED TO SURVIVE.
I don't keep human food in the kitchen.

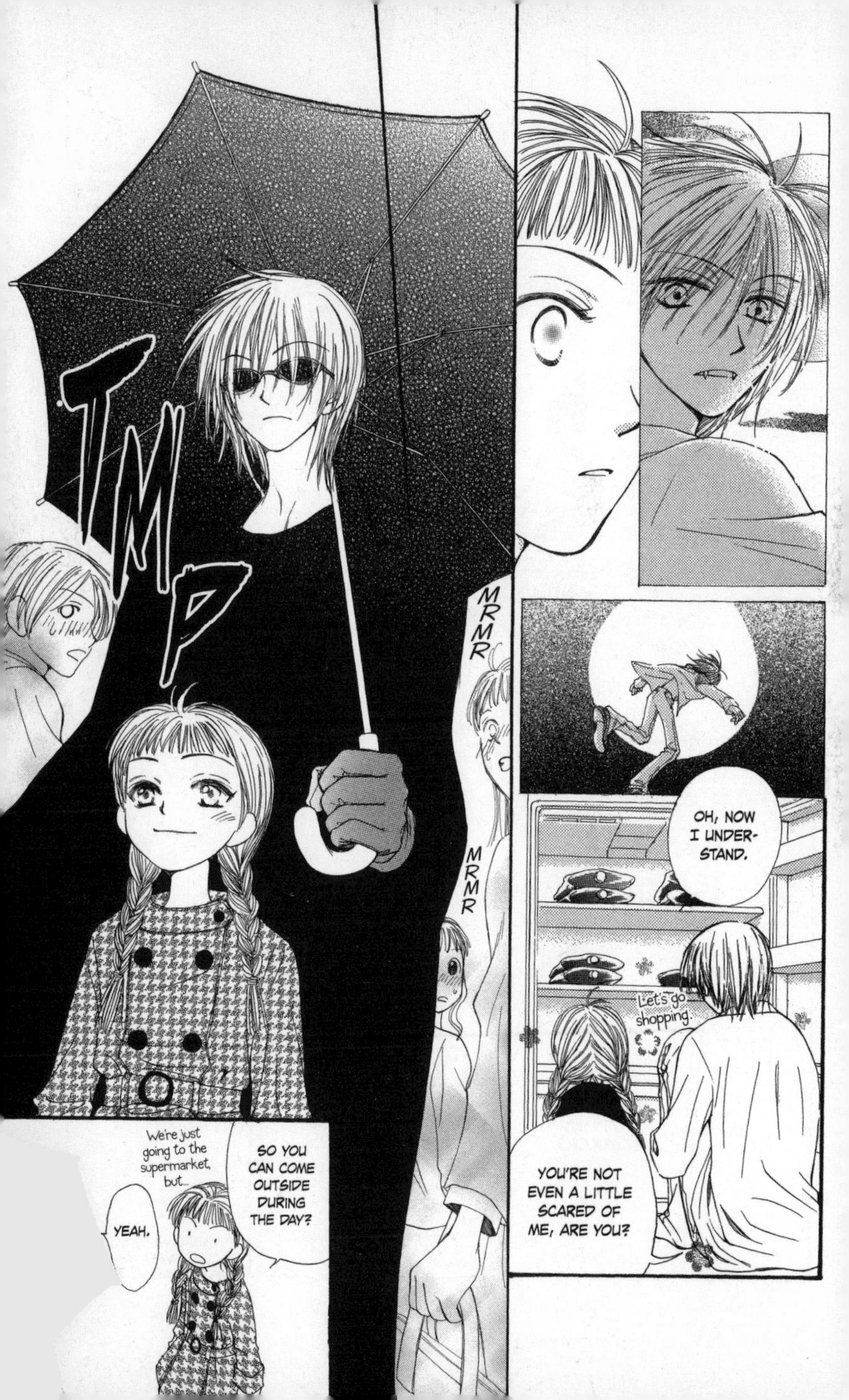
OH, NOW I UNDERSTAND.
Let's go shopping.
YOU'RE NOT EVEN A LITTLE SCARED OF ME, ARE YOU?
TMP
MRMR
MRMR
SO YOU CAN COME OUTSIDE DURING THE DAY?
We're just going to the supermarket, but...
YEAH.

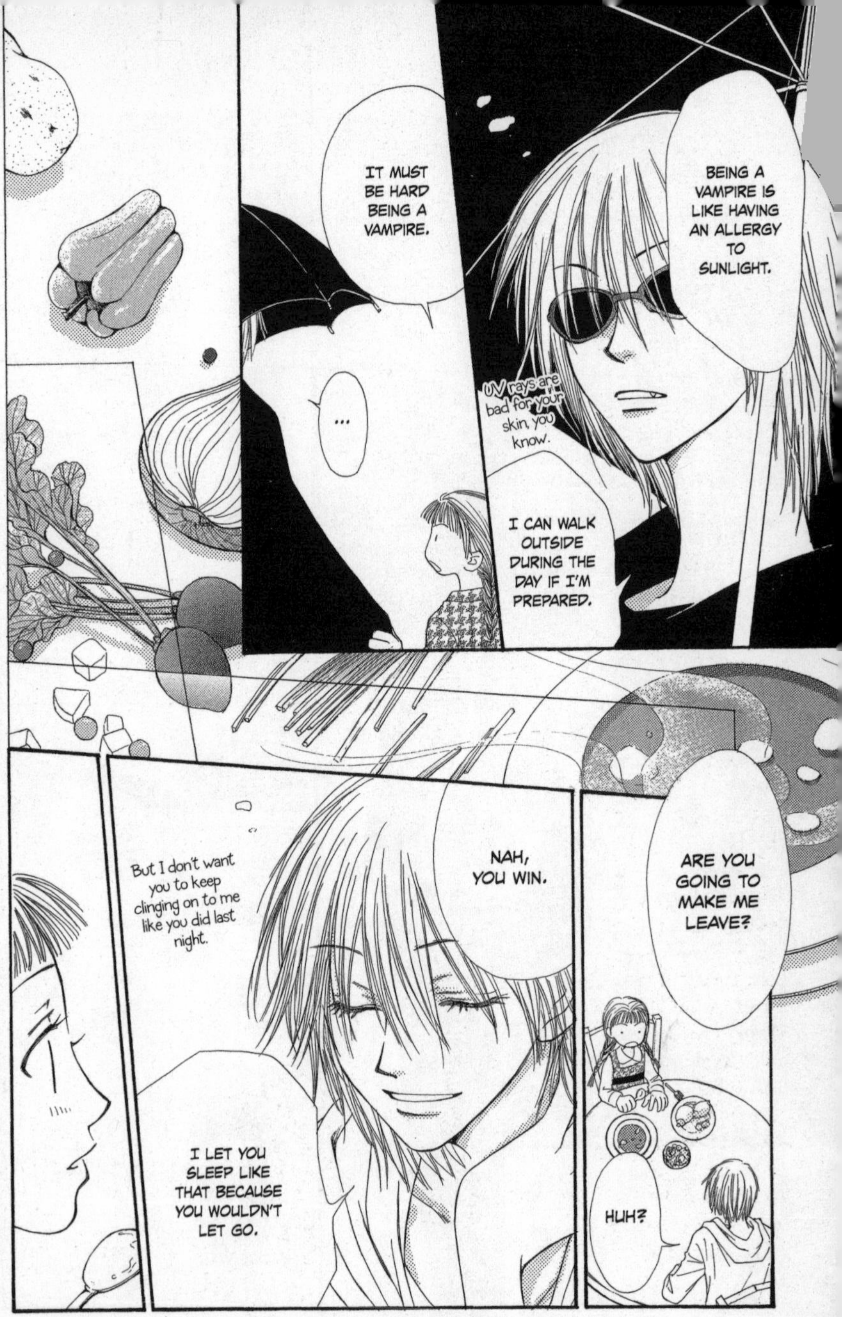
BEING A VAMPIRE IS LIKE HAVING AN ALLERGY TO SUNLIGHT.
UV rays are bad for your skin, you know.
I CAN WALK OUTSIDE DURING THE DAY IF I'M PREPARED.
IT MUST BE HARD BEING A VAMPIRE.
...
ARE YOU GOING TO MAKE ME LEAVE?
HUH?
NAH, YOU WIN.
But I don't want you to keep clinging on to me like you did last night.
I LET YOU SLEEP LIKE THAT BECAUSE YOU WOULDN'T LET GO.

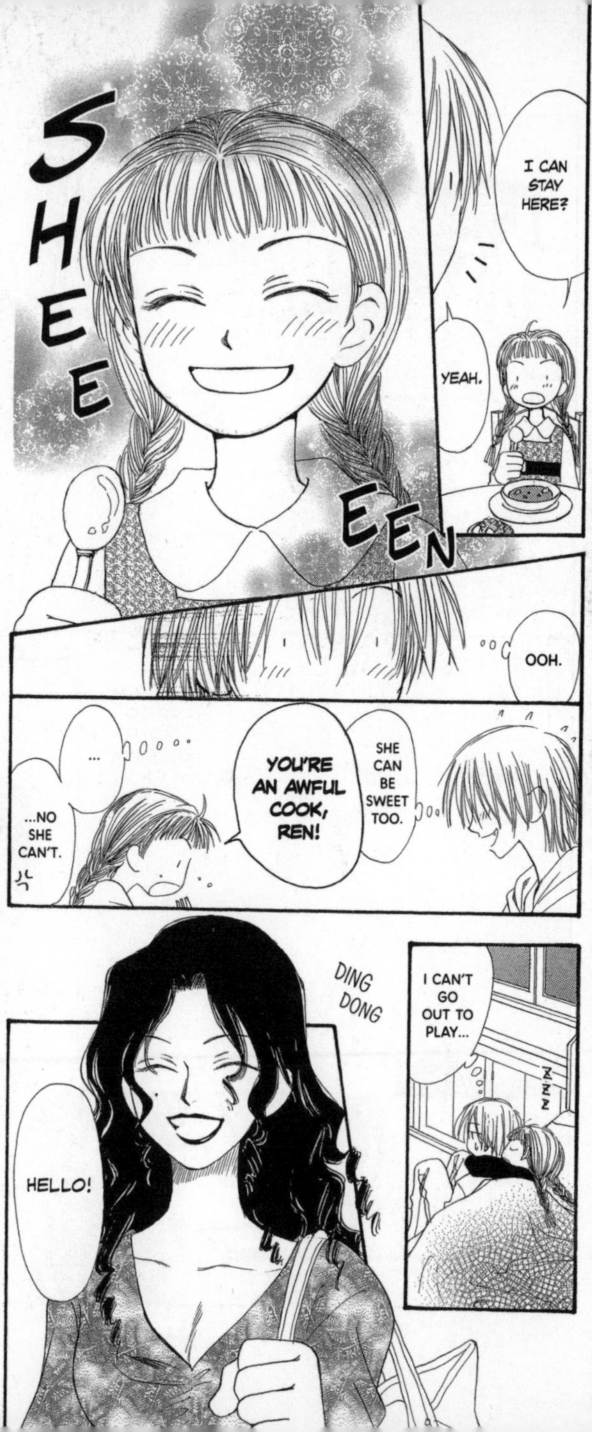
I CAN STAY HERE?
YEAH.
SHEEEEN
OOH.
SHE CAN BE SWEET TOO.
YOU'RE AN AWFUL COOK, REN!
...
...NO SHE CAN'T.
I CAN'T GO OUT TO PLAY...
ZZZ
DING DONG
HELLO!

1/4 Sakura Mail

Part 7

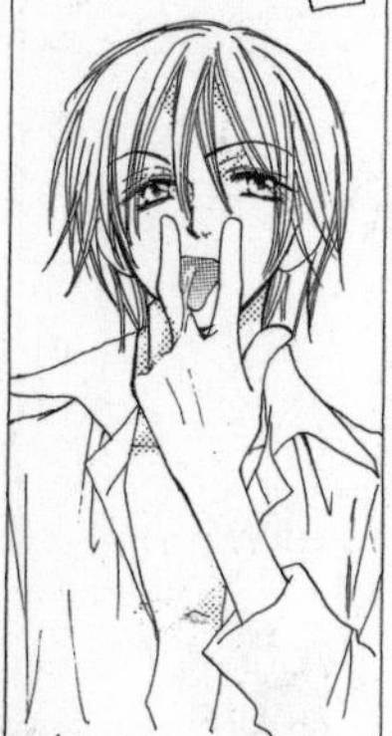

This is "Sweet Bite Mark." It's a vampire story that I've always wanted to write. I wonder why others wouldn't choose to become a vampire if they could be immortal. It would be a pity not be able to walk in the sun anymore, but I've always been a night person, so I'm not very active during the day... And the best thing about vampires is that they're sexy... That's how this story ended up like this. I wanted to draw a vampire sucking blood out of a blood bag. Sorry... By the way, this one-shot was placed in the May issue of *LaLa* magazine.

(Continues)

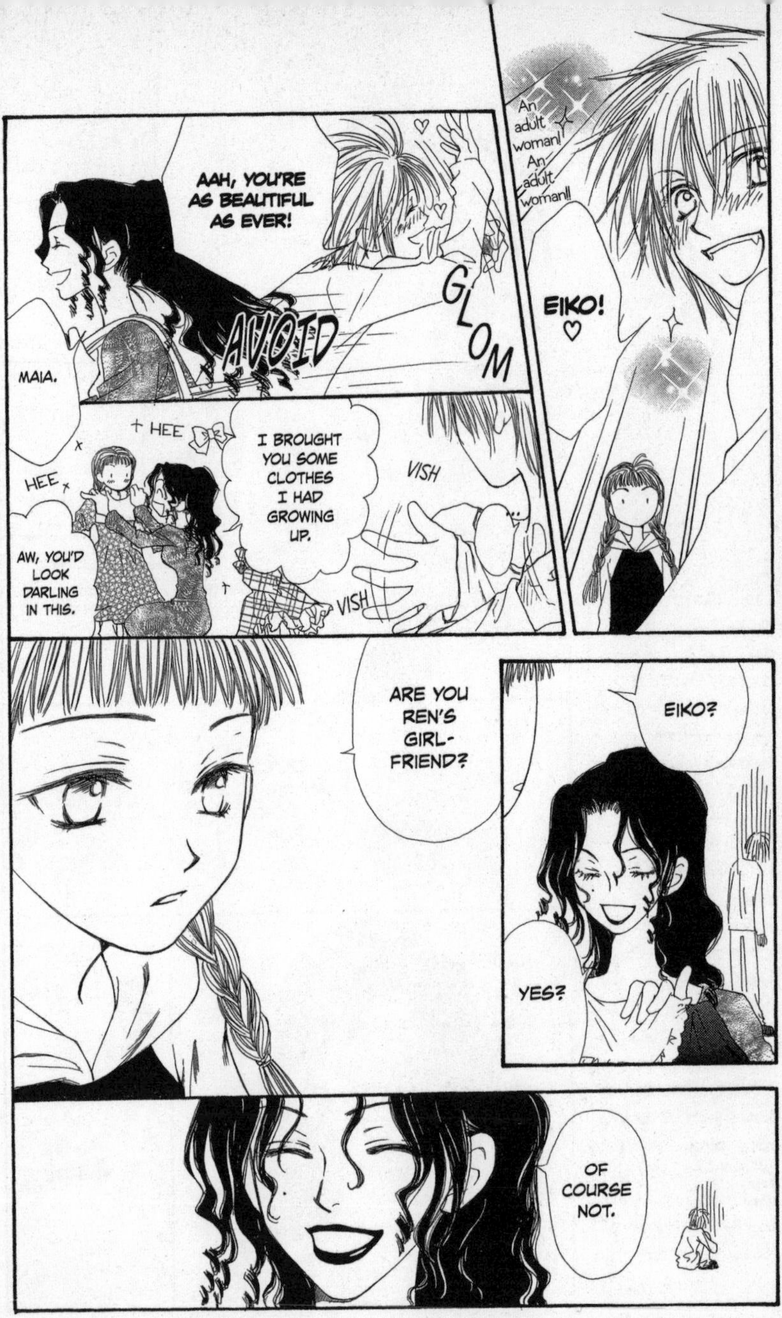
An adult woman! An adult woman!!
EIKO! ♡
AAH, YOU'RE AS BEAUTIFUL AS EVER!
GLOM
AVOID
MAIA.
VISH
VISH
I BROUGHT YOU SOME CLOTHES I HAD GROWING UP.
HEE
HEE
AW, YOU'D LOOK DARLING IN THIS.
EIKO?
YES?
ARE YOU REN'S GIRL-FRIEND?
OF COURSE NOT.

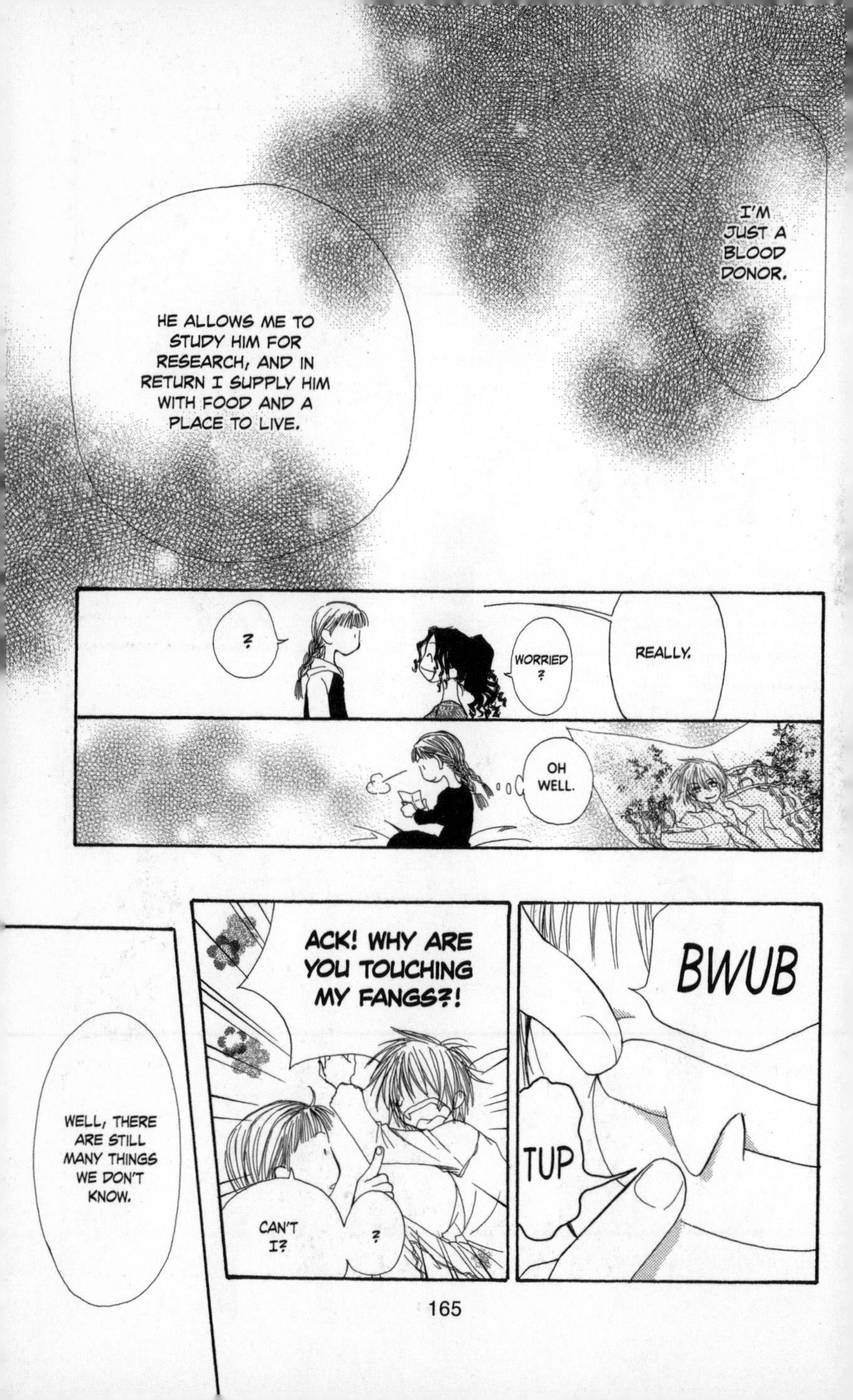
I'M JUST A BLOOD DONOR.
HE ALLOWS ME TO STUDY HIM FOR RESEARCH, AND IN RETURN I SUPPLY HIM WITH FOOD AND A PLACE TO LIVE.
REALLY.
WORRIED?
?
OH WELL.
BWUB
TUP
ACK! WHY ARE YOU TOUCHING MY FANGS?!
?
CAN'T I?
WELL, THERE ARE STILL MANY THINGS WE DON'T KNOW.

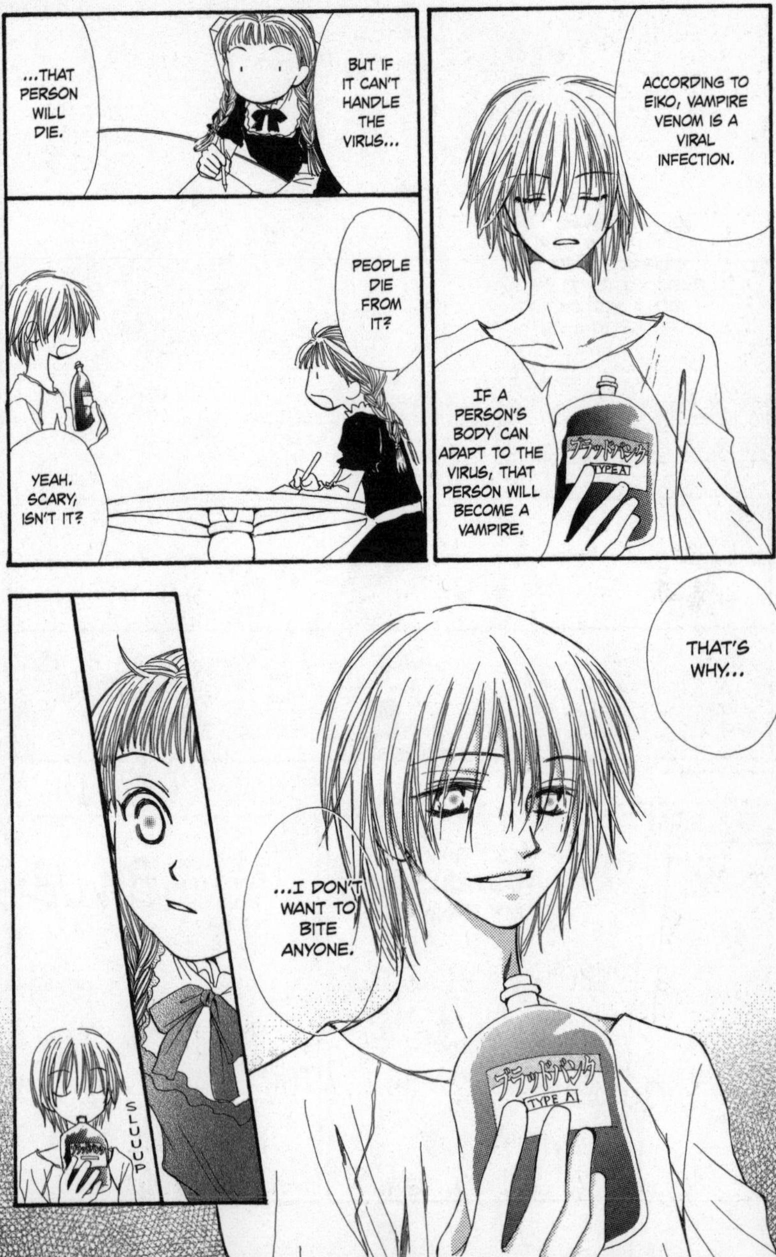
ACCORDING TO EIKO, VAMPIRE VENOM IS A VIRAL INFECTION.
IF A PERSON'S BODY CAN ADAPT TO THE VIRUS, THAT PERSON WILL BECOME A VAMPIRE.
ブラッドバンク
TYPE A
BUT IF IT CAN'T HANDLE THE VIRUS...
...THAT PERSON WILL DIE.
PEOPLE DIE FROM IT?
YEAH. SCARY, ISN'T IT?
THAT'S WHY...
...I DON'T WANT TO BITE ANYONE.
ブラッドバンク
TYPE A
SLUUUP

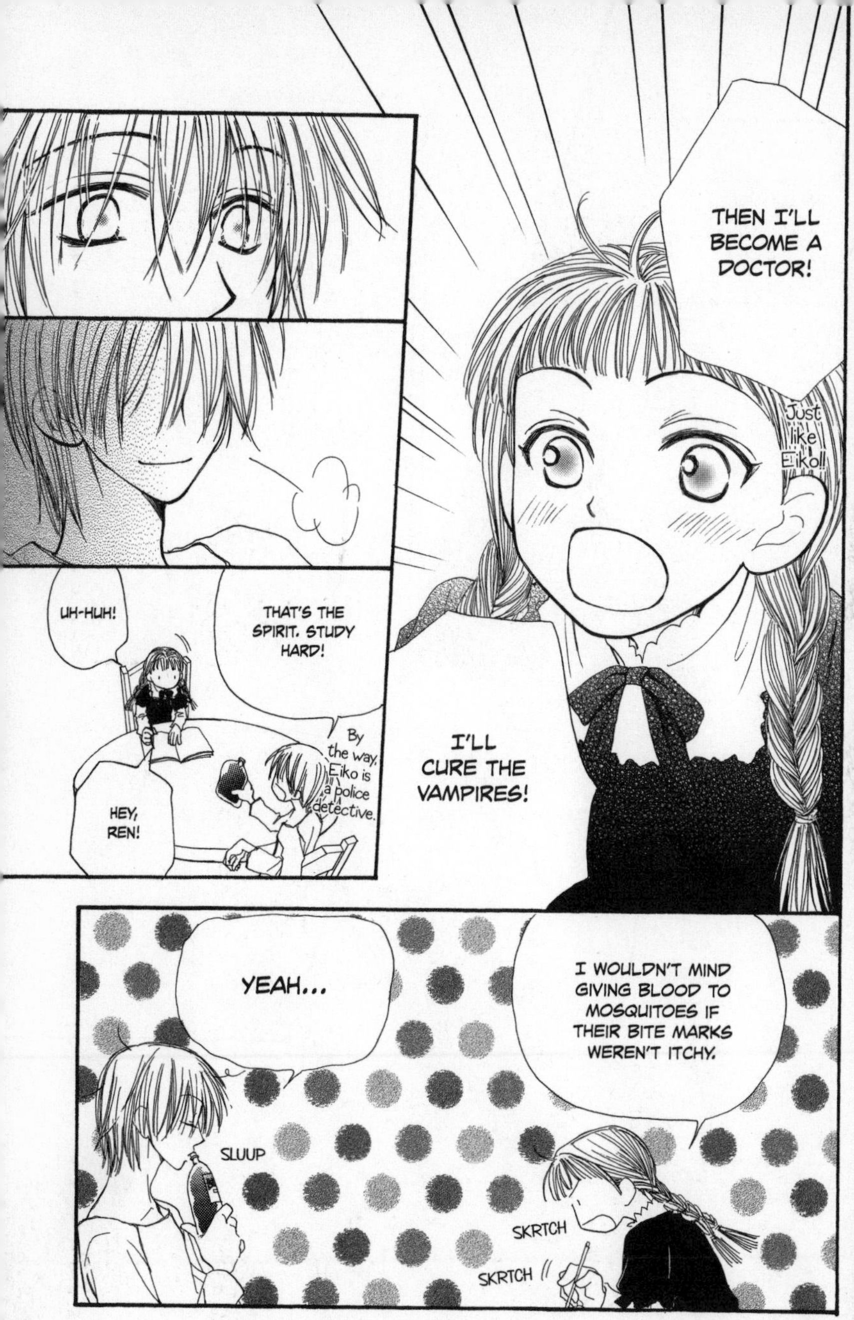
THEN I'LL BECOME A DOCTOR!
Just like Eiko!!
I'LL CURE THE VAMPIRES!
THAT'S THE SPIRIT. STUDY HARD!
By the way, Eiko is a police detective.
UH-HUH!
HEY, REN!
I WOULDN'T MIND GIVING BLOOD TO MOSQUITOES IF THEIR BITE MARKS WEREN'T ITCHY.
SKRTCH
SKRTCH
YEAH...
SLUUP

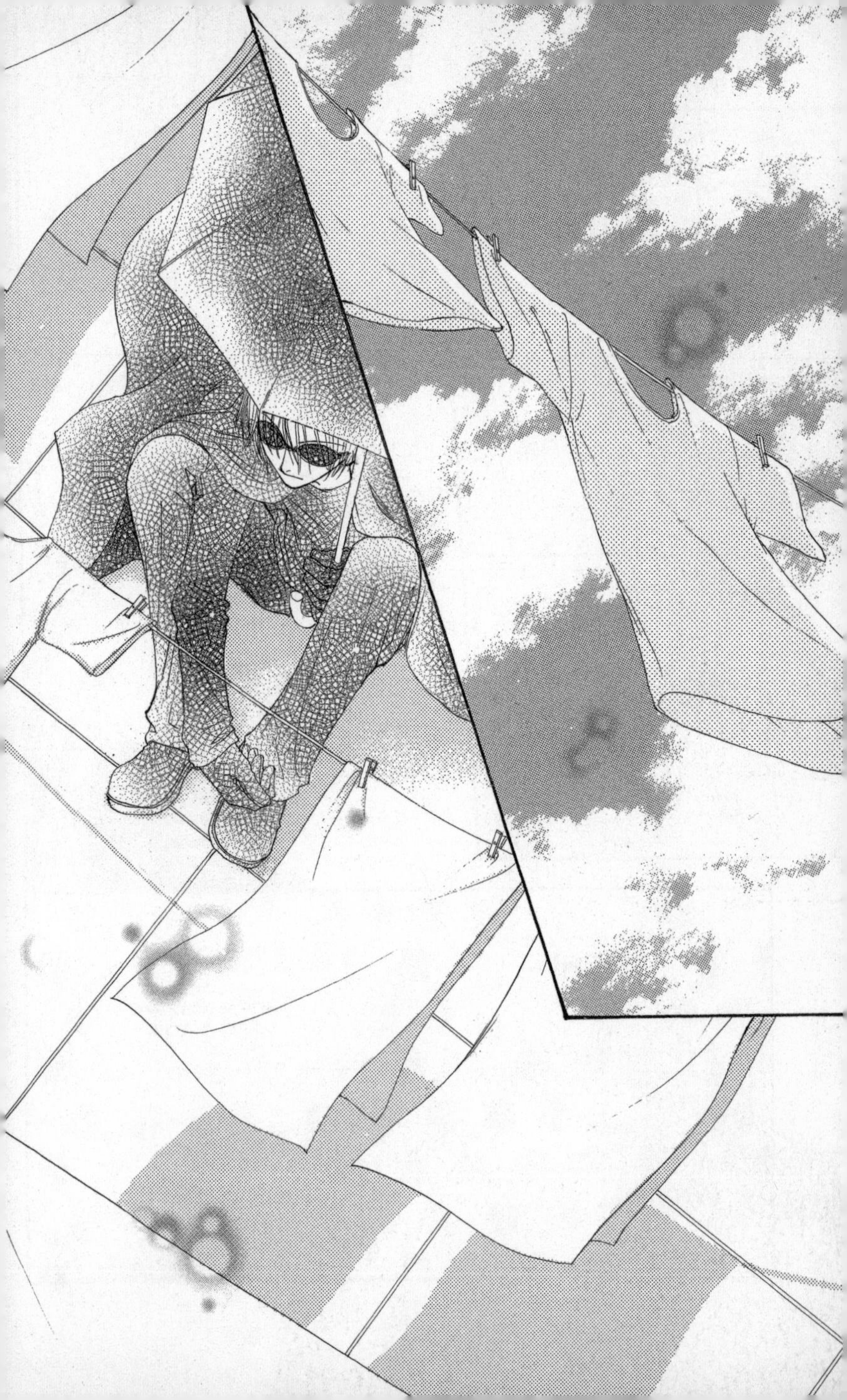

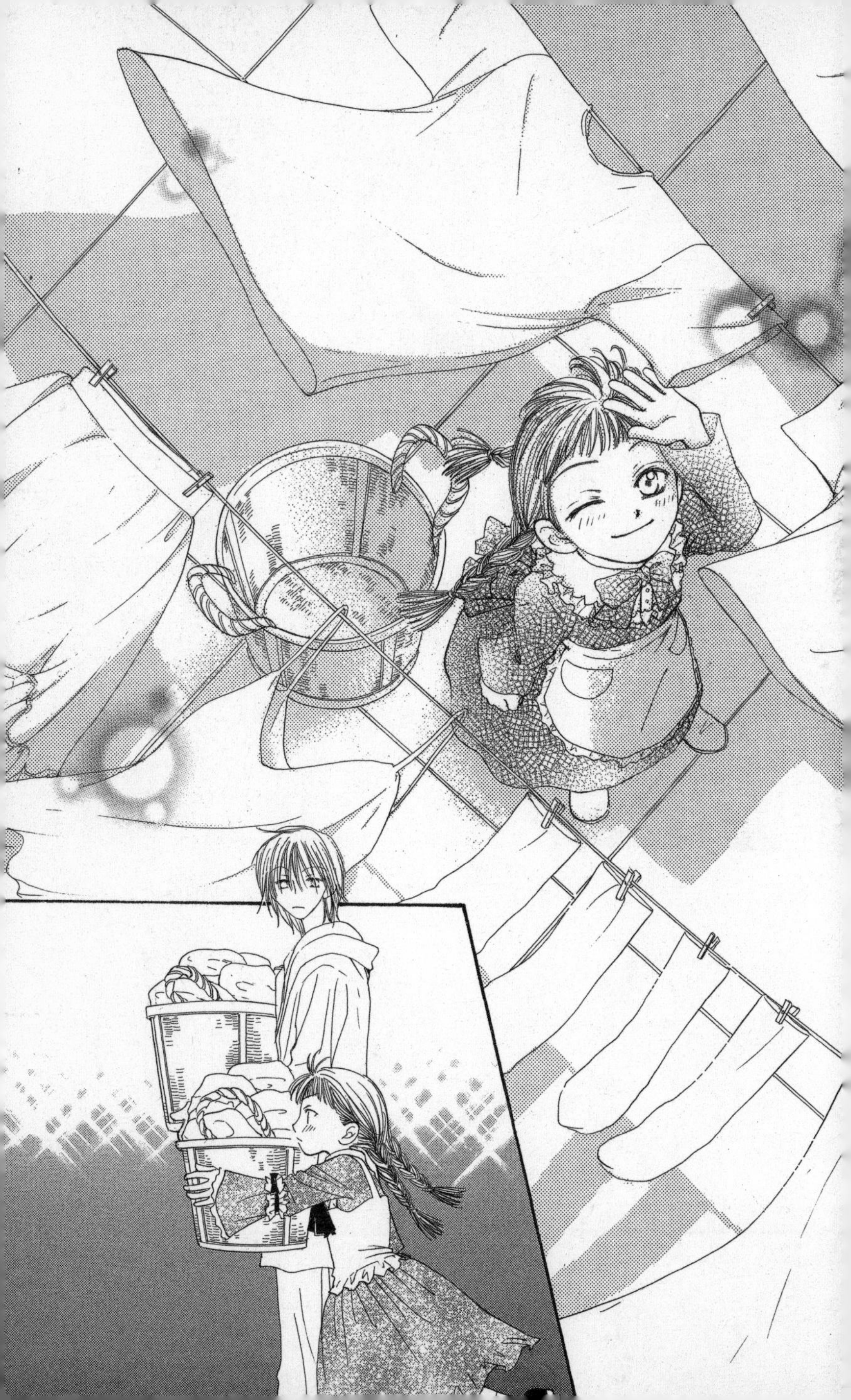

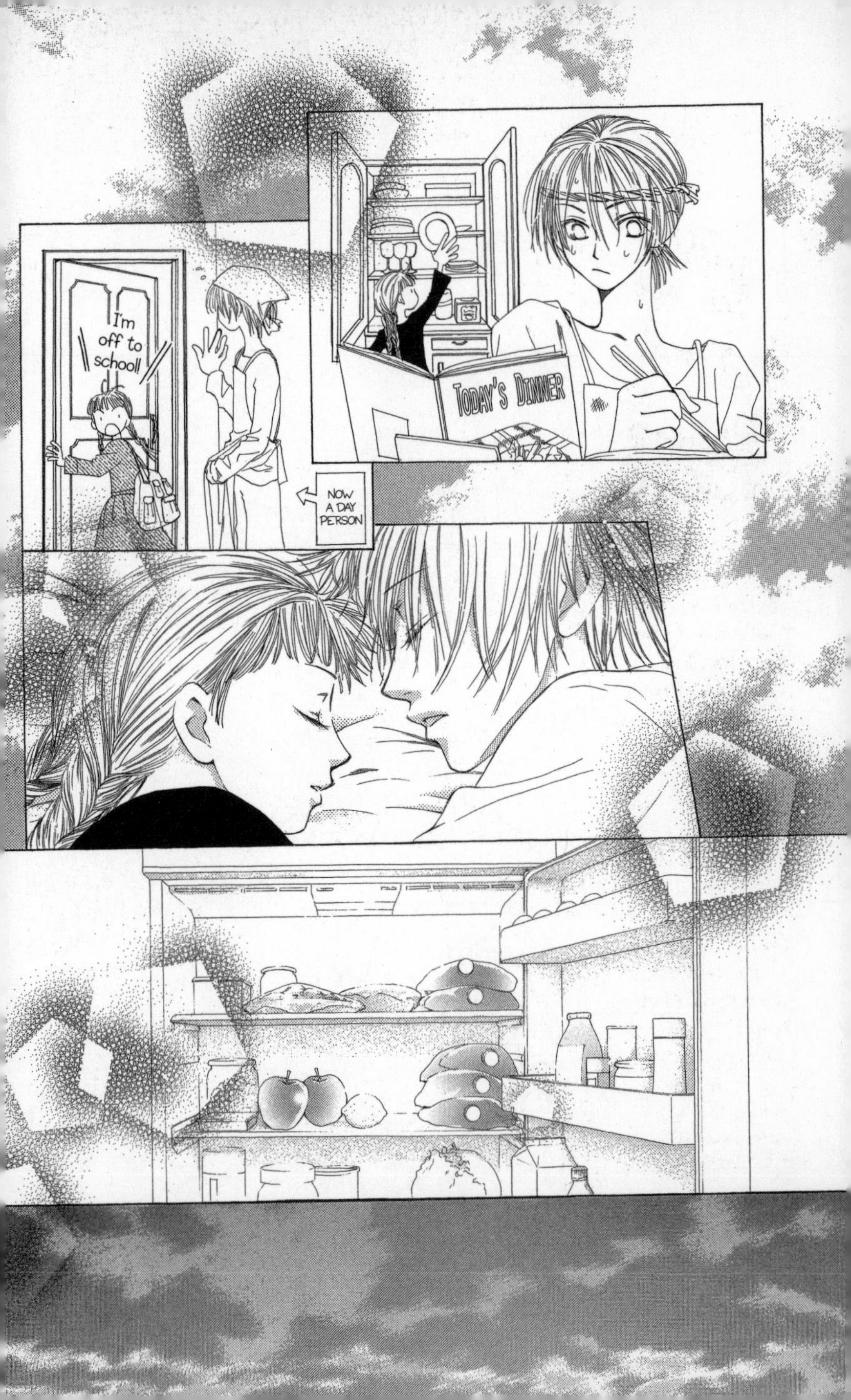
TODAY'S DINNER
I'm off to school!
NOW A DAY PERSON

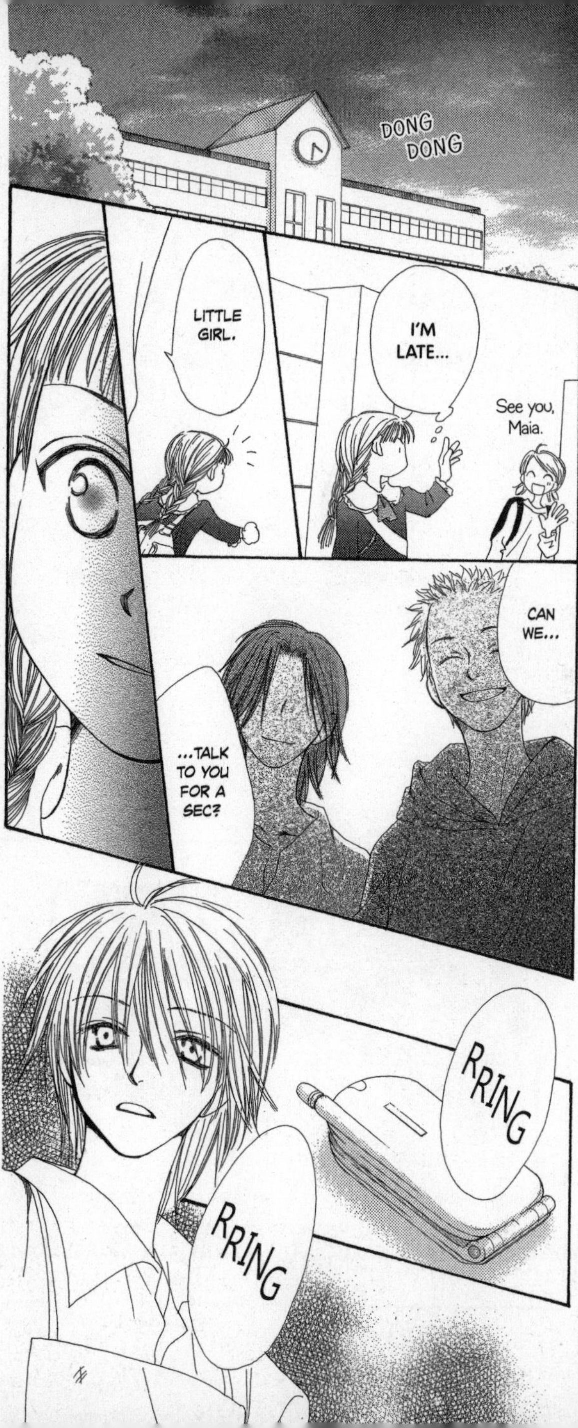
DONG DONG
See you, Maia.
I'M LATE...
LITTLE GIRL.
CAN WE...
...TALK TO YOU FOR A SEC?
RRING
RRING

1/4 Sakura Mail

Part 8

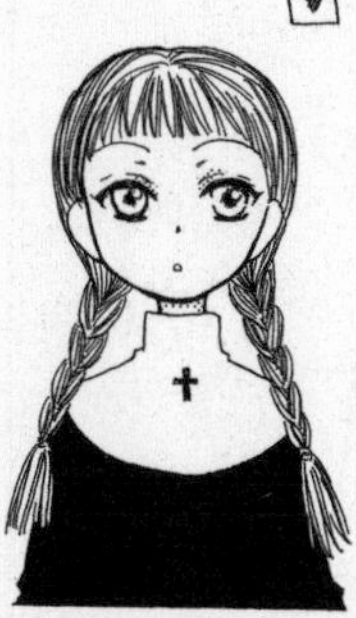

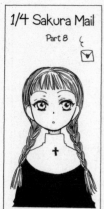

Continued.

When I first drew the color illustration for the title page, the trees in the back didn't have flowers. It was winter. But it didn't seem right, and after much thought, I redrew the illustration. I thought, "This one-shot will be placed in the magazine in spring!!" I also secretly tried to get rid of the winter illustration that I had already sent to the editorial office by post, but my editor had seen it anyway. I was a bit embarrassed...

So there's a winter version that looks exactly like the spring one that was used.
There isn't much space left, so that's all for now!
See you again!!

Sakura Tsukuba

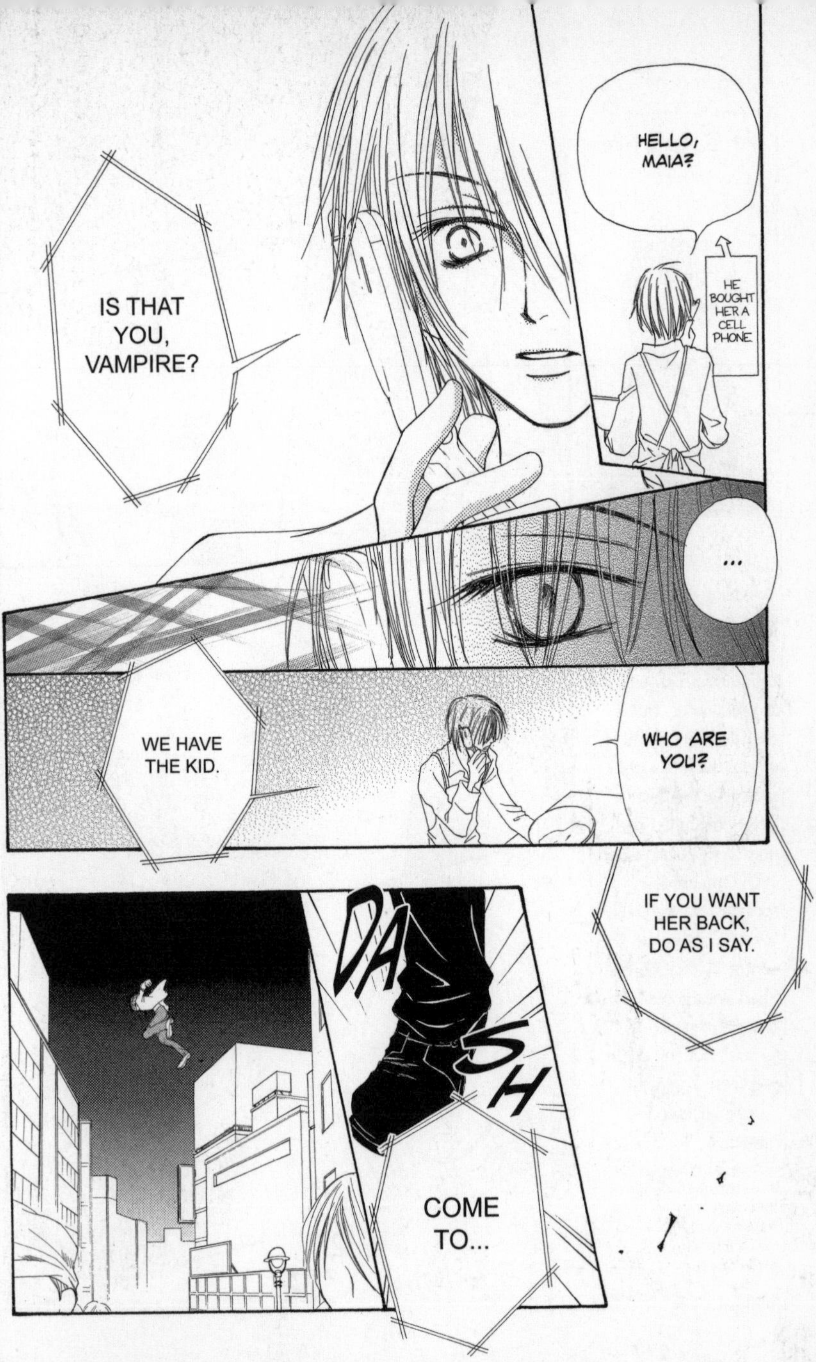
HELLO, MAIA?
HE BOUGHT HER A CELL PHONE.
IS THAT YOU, VAMPIRE?
...
WHO ARE YOU?
WE HAVE THE KID.
IF YOU WANT HER BACK, DO AS I SAY.
DASH
COME TO...

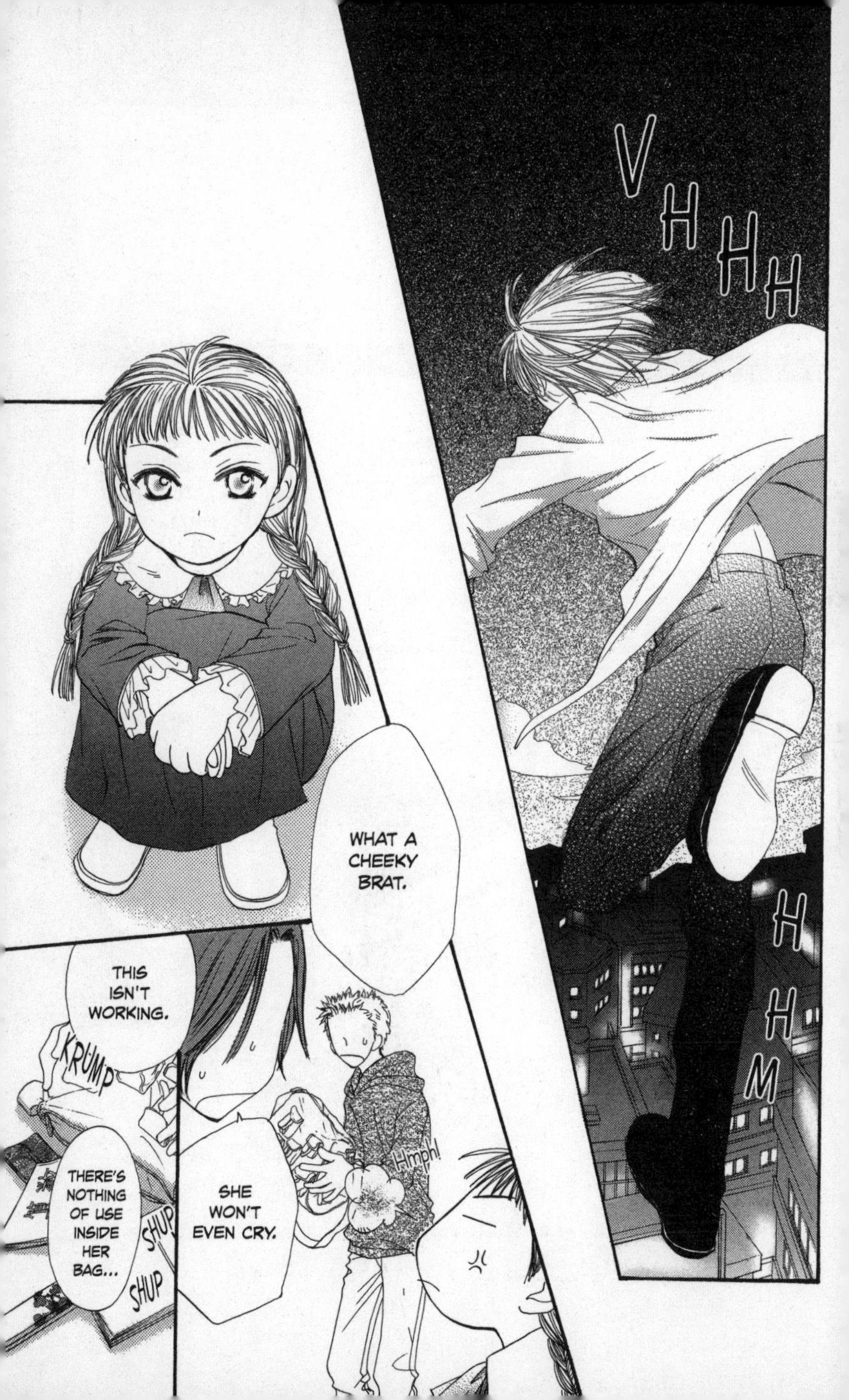
VHHH
HHHM
WHAT A CHEEKY BRAT.
THIS ISN'T WORKING.
Hmph!
SHE WON'T EVEN CRY.
KRUMP
THERE'S NOTHING OF USE INSIDE HER BAG...
SHUP
SHUP

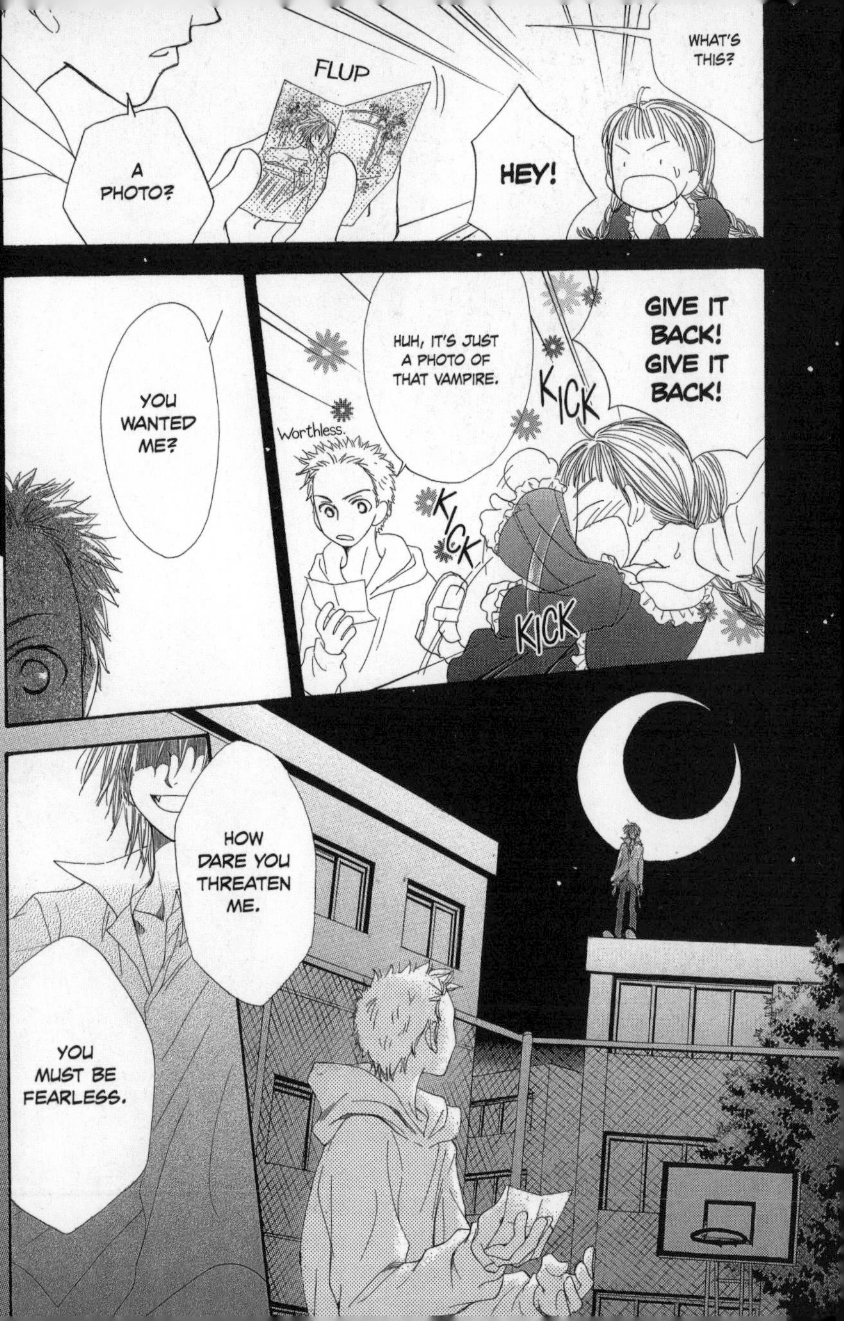
WHAT'S THIS?
HEY!
FLUP
A PHOTO?
GIVE IT BACK! GIVE IT BACK!
KICK
HUH, IT'S JUST A PHOTO OF THAT VAMPIRE.
Worthless.
KICK
KICK
YOU WANTED ME?
HOW DARE YOU THREATEN ME.
YOU MUST BE FEARLESS.

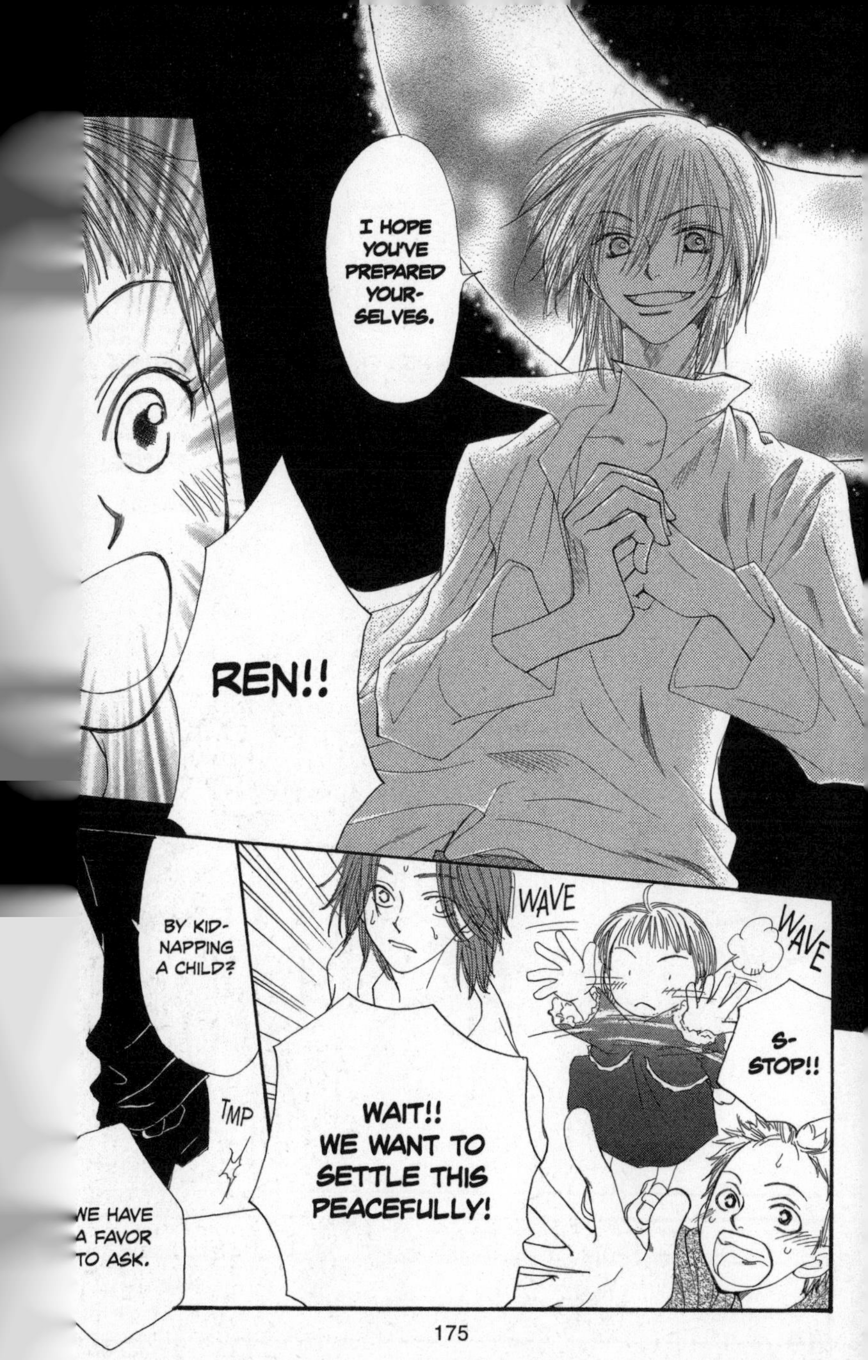
I HOPE YOU'VE PREPARED YOUR-SELVES.
REN!!
WAVE
WAVE
S-STOP!!
WAIT!! WE WANT TO SETTLE THIS PEACEFULLY!
TMP
BY KID-NAPPING A CHILD?
WE HAVE A FAVOR TO ASK.

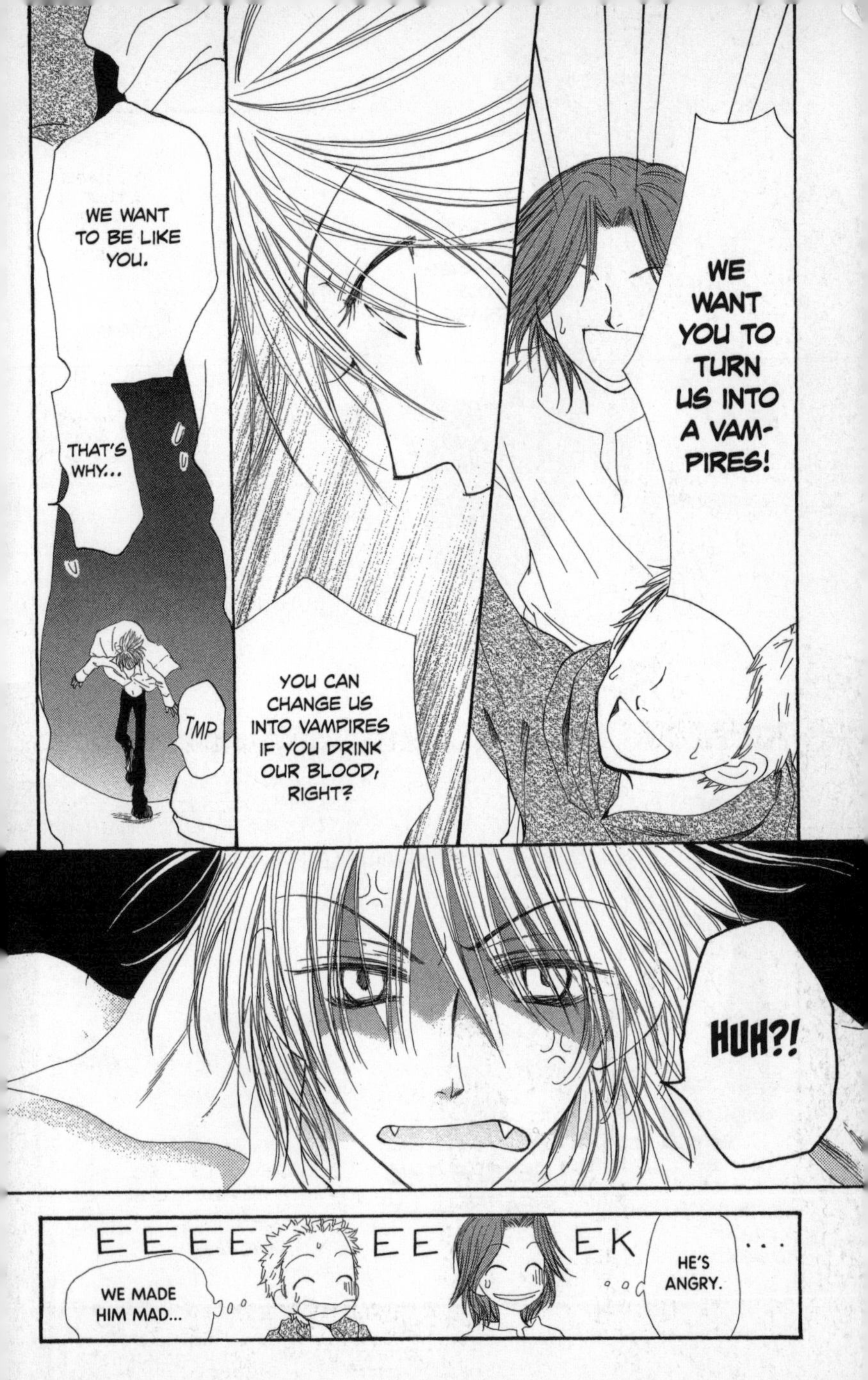

WE WANT YOU TO TURN US INTO A VAMPIRES!
YOU CAN CHANGE US INTO VAMPIRES IF YOU DRINK OUR BLOOD, RIGHT?
WE WANT TO BE LIKE YOU.
THAT'S WHY...
TMP
HUH?!
...
EEEEEEEEK
HE'S ANGRY.
WE MADE HIM MAD...

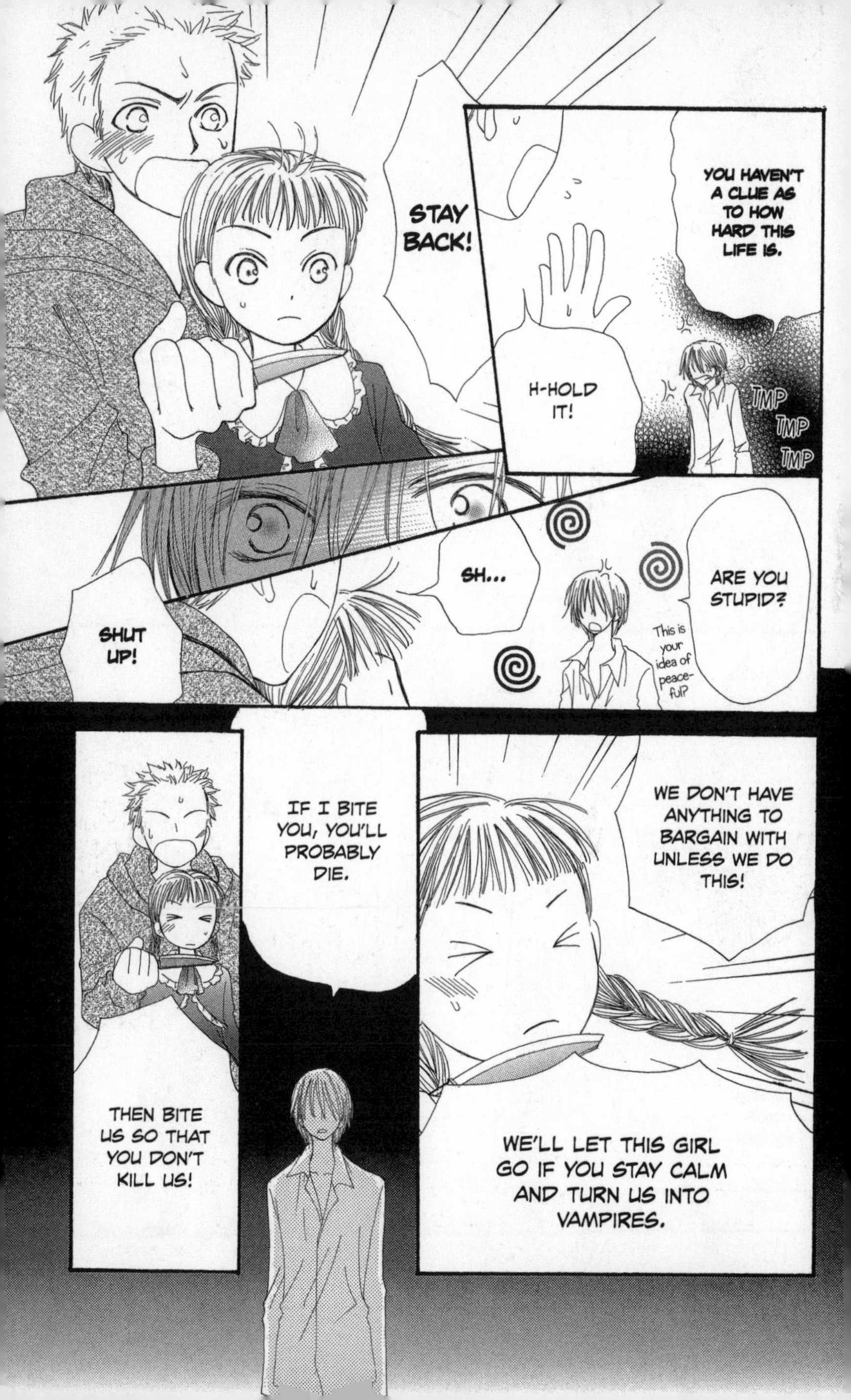
YOU HAVEN'T A CLUE AS TO HOW HARD THIS LIFE IS.
TMP
TMP
TMP
H-HOLD IT!
STAY BACK!
ARE YOU STUPID?
This is your idea of peace-ful?
SH...
SHUT UP!
WE DON'T HAVE ANYTHING TO BARGAIN WITH UNLESS WE DO THIS!
WE'LL LET THIS GIRL GO IF YOU STAY CALM AND TURN US INTO VAMPIRES.
IF I BITE YOU, YOU'LL PROBABLY DIE.
THEN BITE US SO THAT YOU DON'T KILL US!

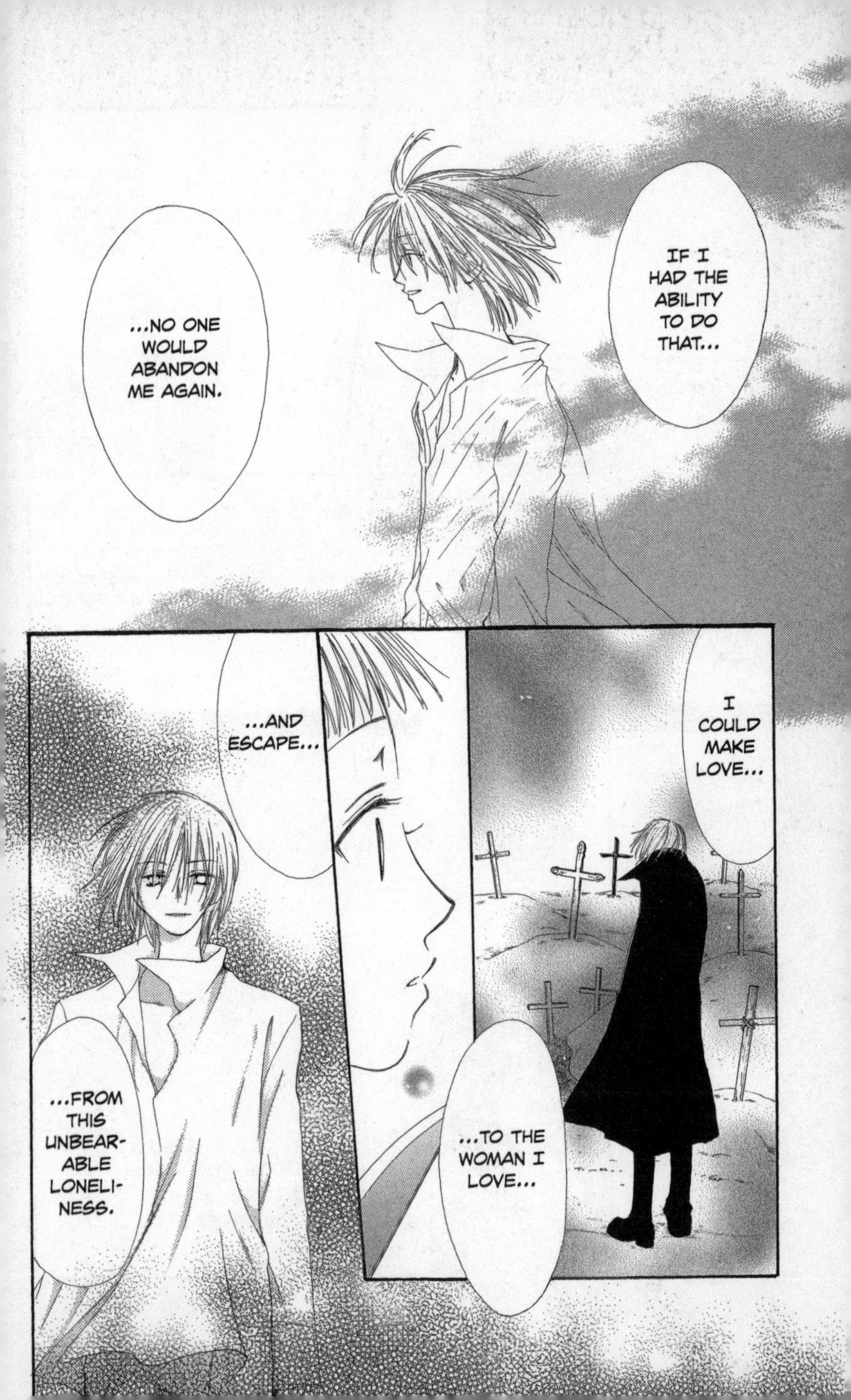
IF I HAD THE ABILITY TO DO THAT...
...NO ONE WOULD ABANDON ME AGAIN.
I COULD MAKE LOVE...
...TO THE WOMAN I LOVE...
...AND ESCAPE...
...FROM THIS UNBEARABLE-ABLE LONELINESS.

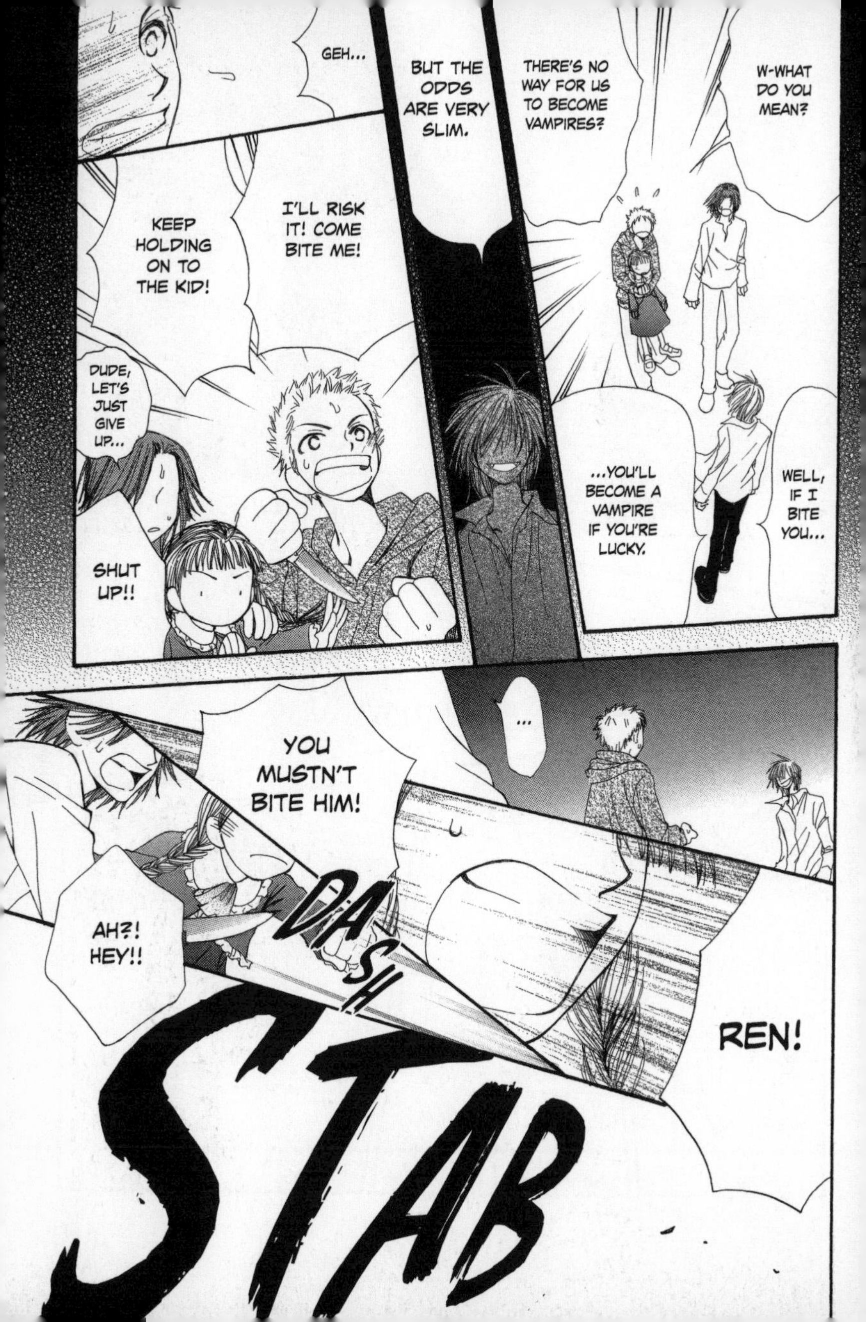
W-WHAT DO YOU MEAN?
THERE'S NO WAY FOR US TO BECOME VAMPIRES?
WELL, IF I BITE YOU...
...YOU'LL BECOME A VAMPIRE IF YOU'RE LUCKY.
BUT THE ODDS ARE VERY SLIM.
GEH...
I'LL RISK IT! COME BITE ME!
KEEP HOLDING ON TO THE KID!
DUDE, LET'S JUST GIVE UP...
SHUT UP!!
...
YOU MUSTN'T BITE HIM!
REN!
AH?! HEY!!
DASH
STAB

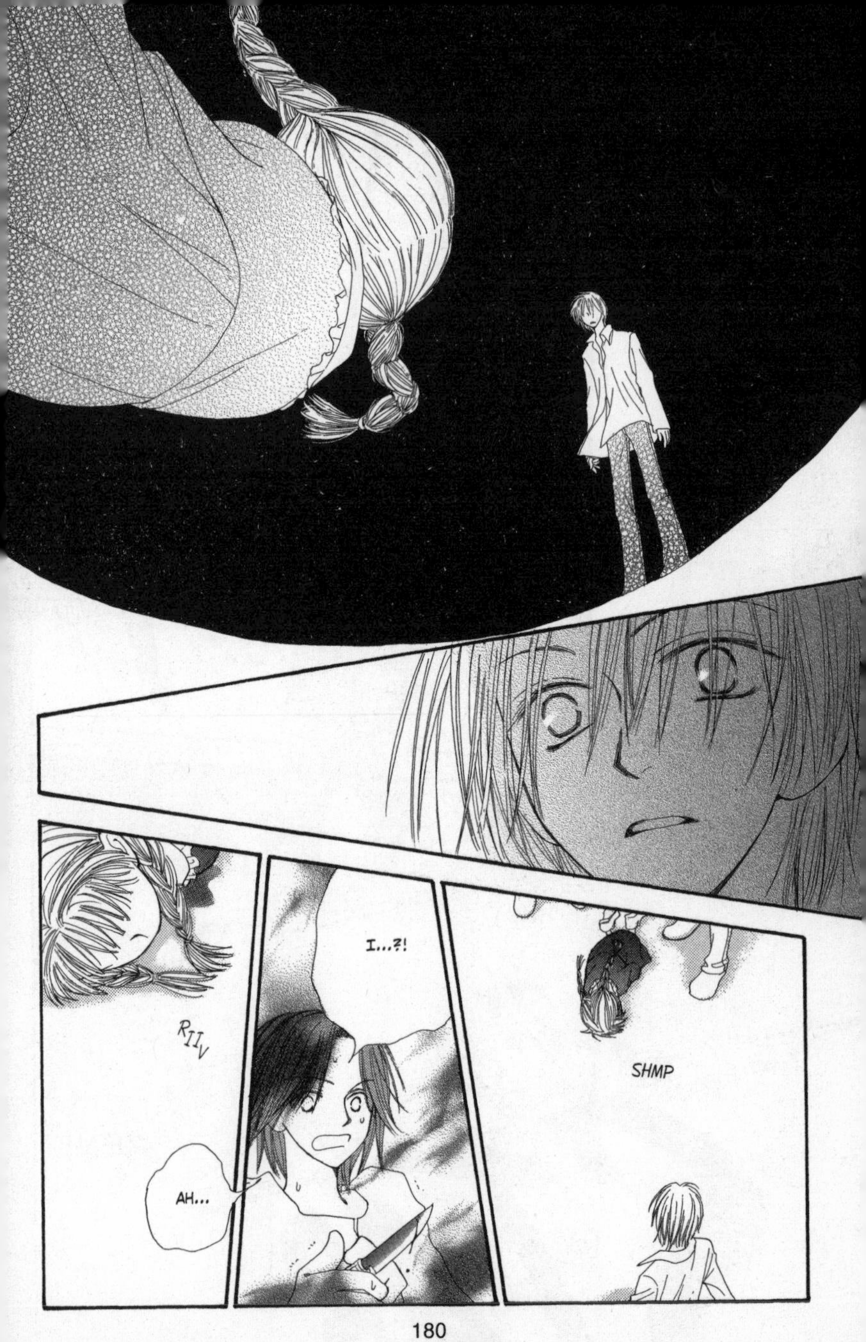
SHMP
I...?!
RIIV
AH...

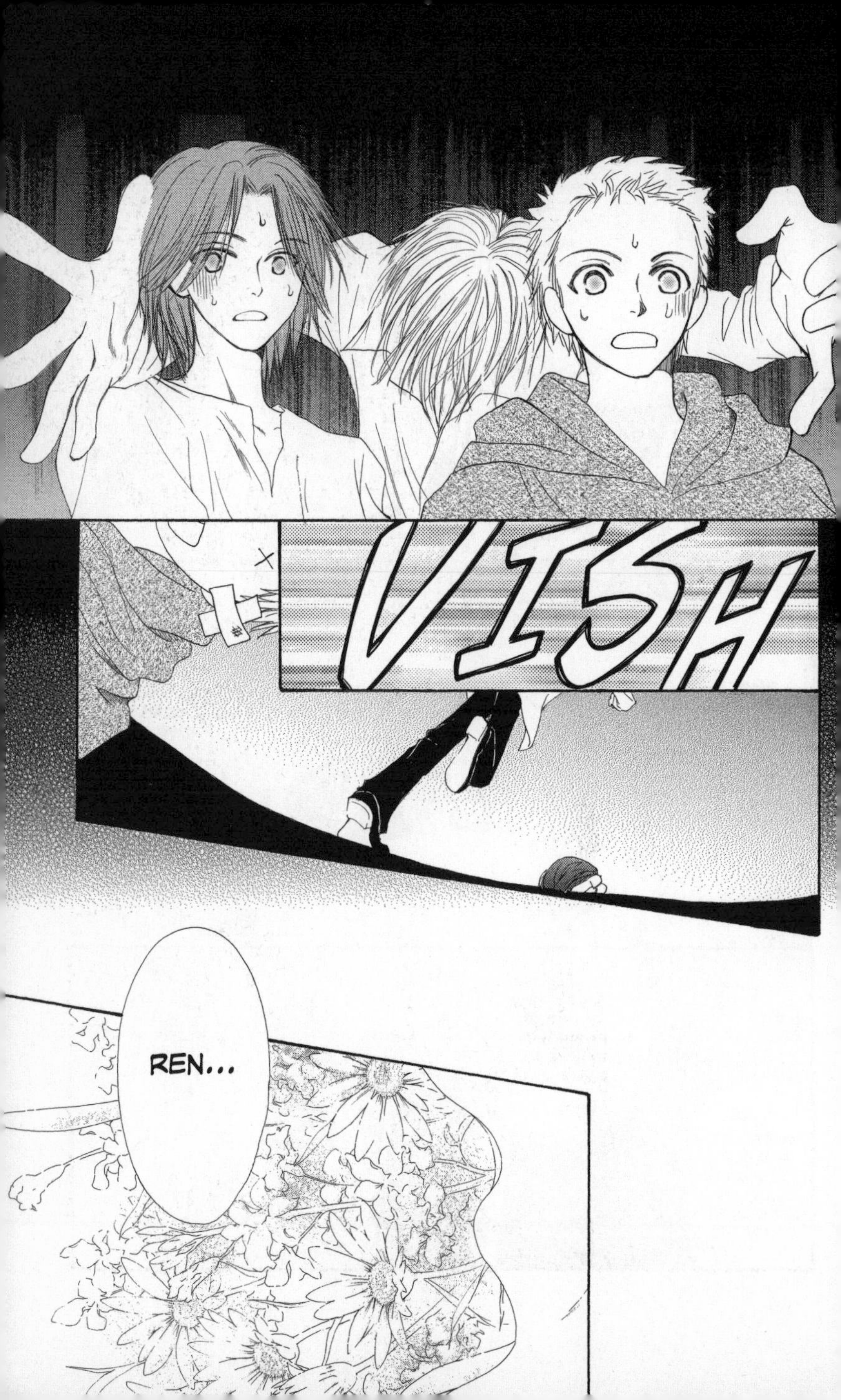
VISH
REN...

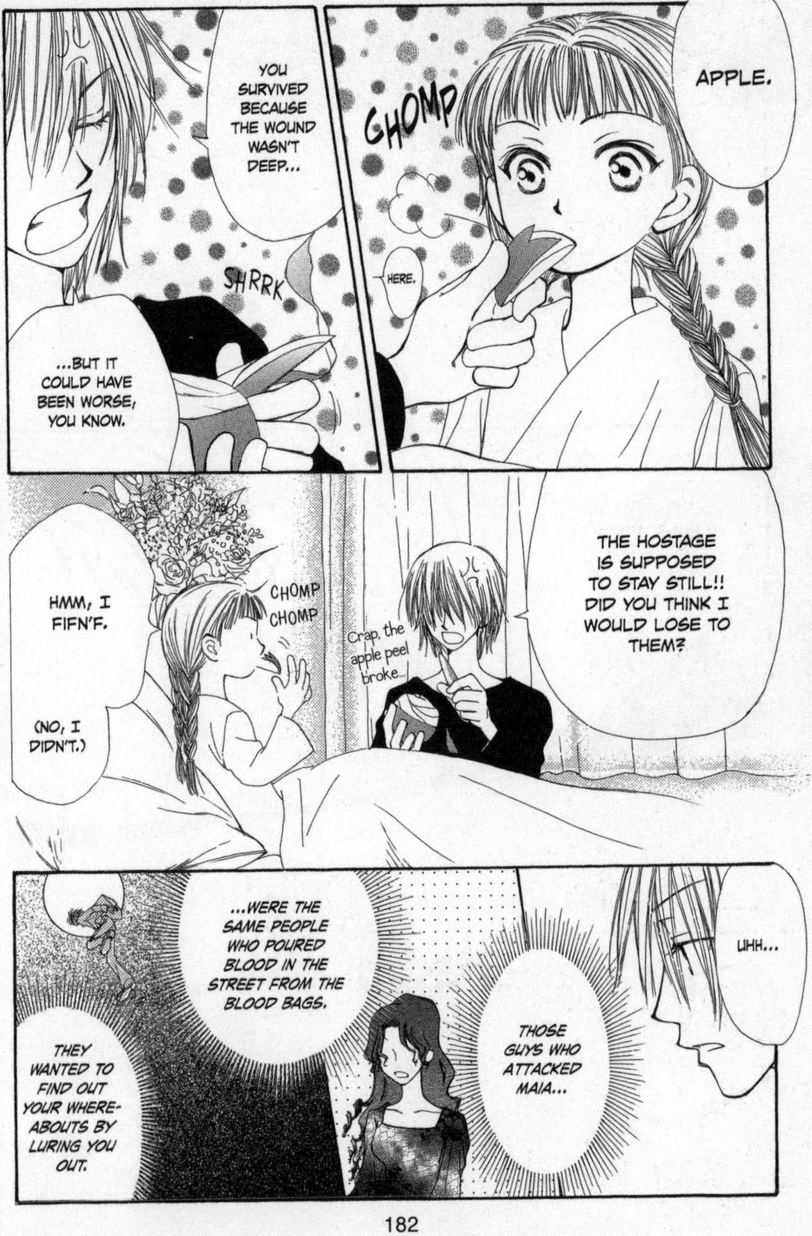
APPLE.
CHOMP
HERE.
YOU SURVIVED BECAUSE THE WOUND WASN'T DEEP...
SHRRK
...BUT IT COULD HAVE BEEN WORSE, YOU KNOW.
THE HOSTAGE IS SUPPOSED TO STAY STILL!! DID YOU THINK I WOULD LOSE TO THEM?
Crap, the apple peel broke...
CHOMP CHOMP
HMM, I FIFN'F.
(NO, I DIDN'T.)
UHH...
THOSE GUYS WHO ATTACKED MAIA...
...WERE THE SAME PEOPLE WHO POURED BLOOD IN THE STREET FROM THE BLOOD BAGS.
THEY WANTED TO FIND OUT YOUR WHERE-ABOUTS BY LURING YOU OUT.

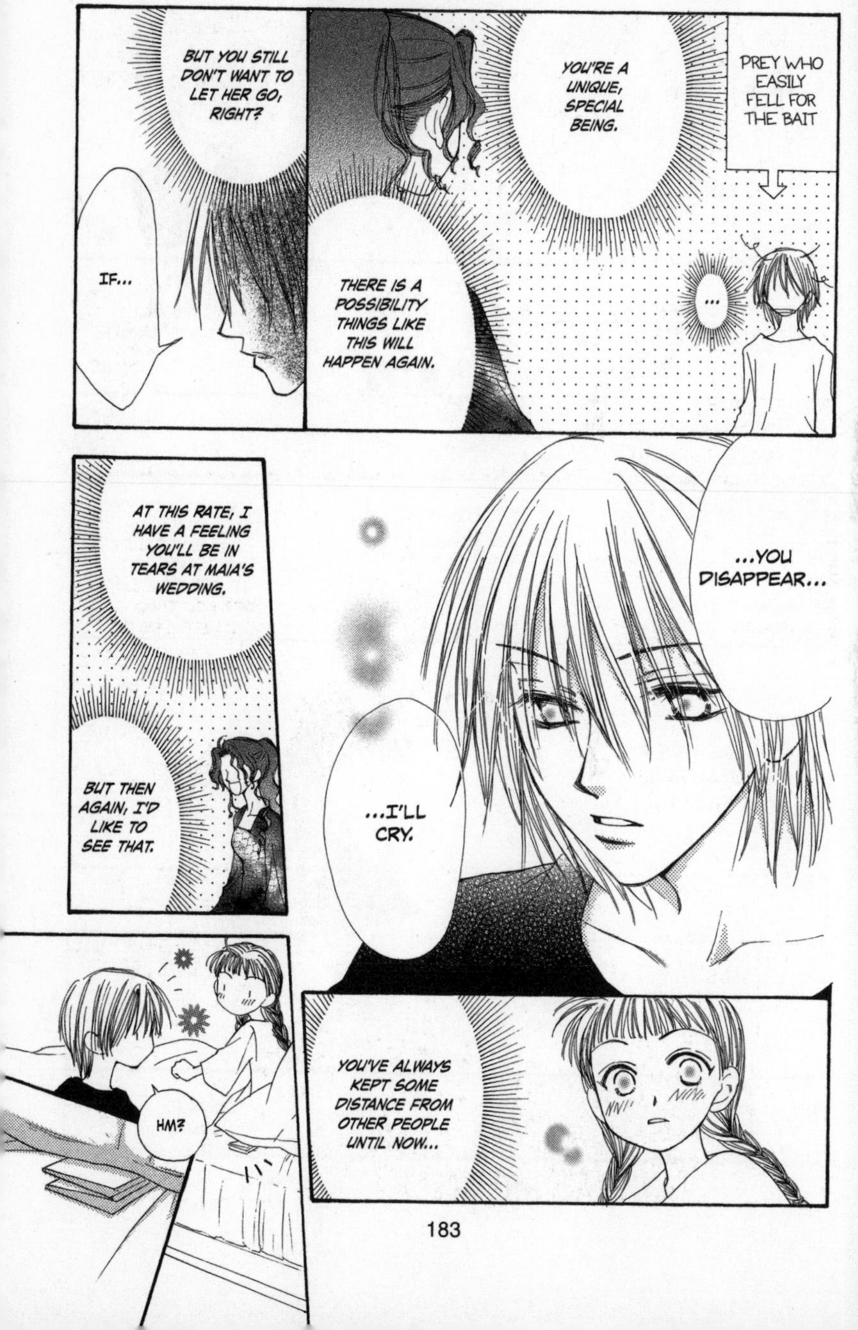
PREY WHO EASILY FELL FOR THE BAIT
...
YOU'RE A UNIQUE, SPECIAL BEING.
THERE IS A POSSIBILITY THINGS LIKE THIS WILL HAPPEN AGAIN.
BUT YOU STILL DON'T WANT TO LET HER GO, RIGHT?
IF...
...YOU DISAPPEAR...
...I'LL CRY.
AT THIS RATE, I HAVE A FEELING YOU'LL BE IN TEARS AT MAIA'S WEDDING.
BUT THEN AGAIN, I'D LIKE TO SEE THAT.
YOU'VE ALWAYS KEPT SOME DISTANCE FROM OTHER PEOPLE UNTIL NOW...
HM?

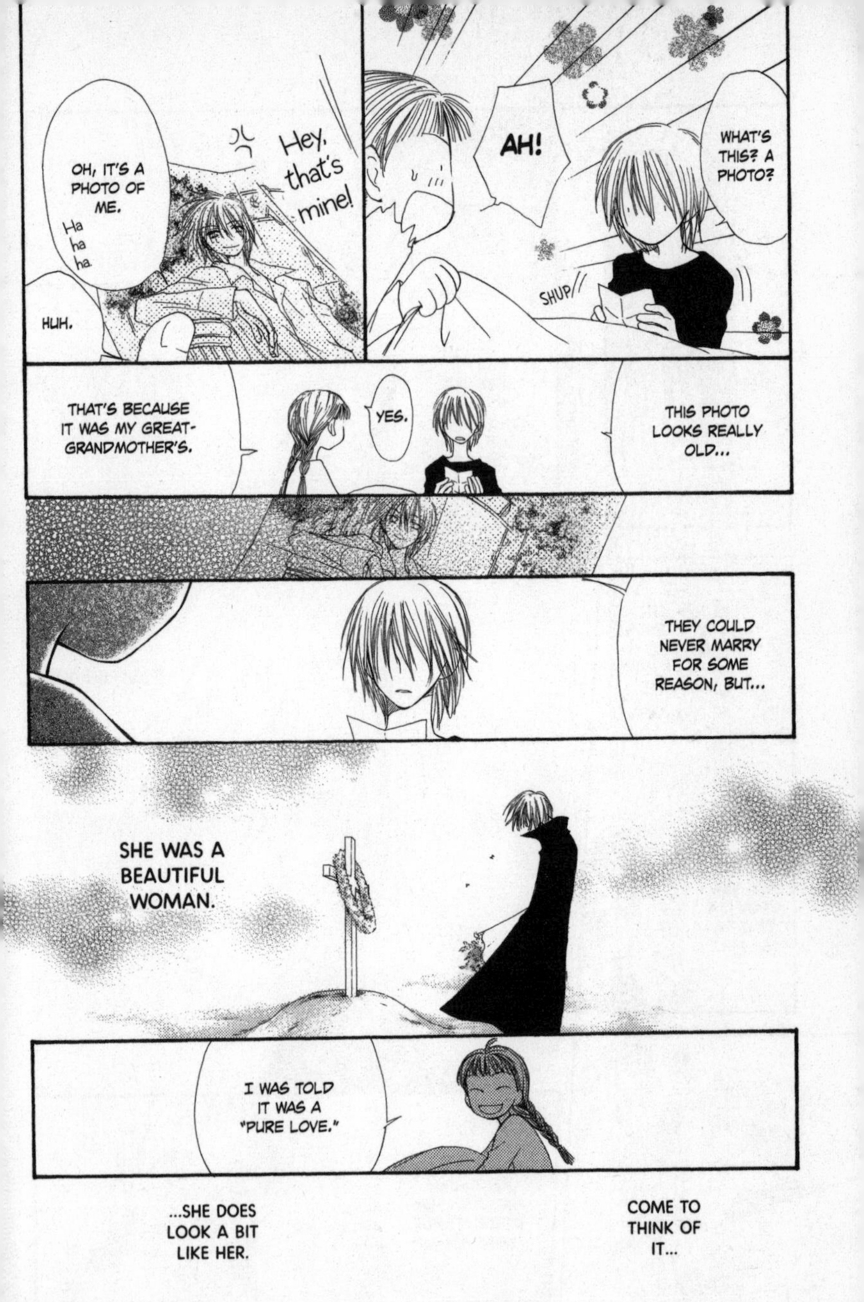
WHAT'S THIS? A PHOTO?
AH!
SHUP
Hey, that's mine!
OH, IT'S A PHOTO OF ME.
Ha ha ha.
HUH.
THIS PHOTO LOOKS REALLY OLD...
YES.
THAT'S BECAUSE IT WAS MY GREAT-GRANDMOTHER'S.
THEY COULD NEVER MARRY FOR SOME REASON, BUT...
SHE WAS A BEAUTIFUL WOMAN.
I WAS TOLD IT WAS A "PURE LOVE."
COME TO THINK OF IT...
...SHE DOES LOOK A BIT LIKE HER.

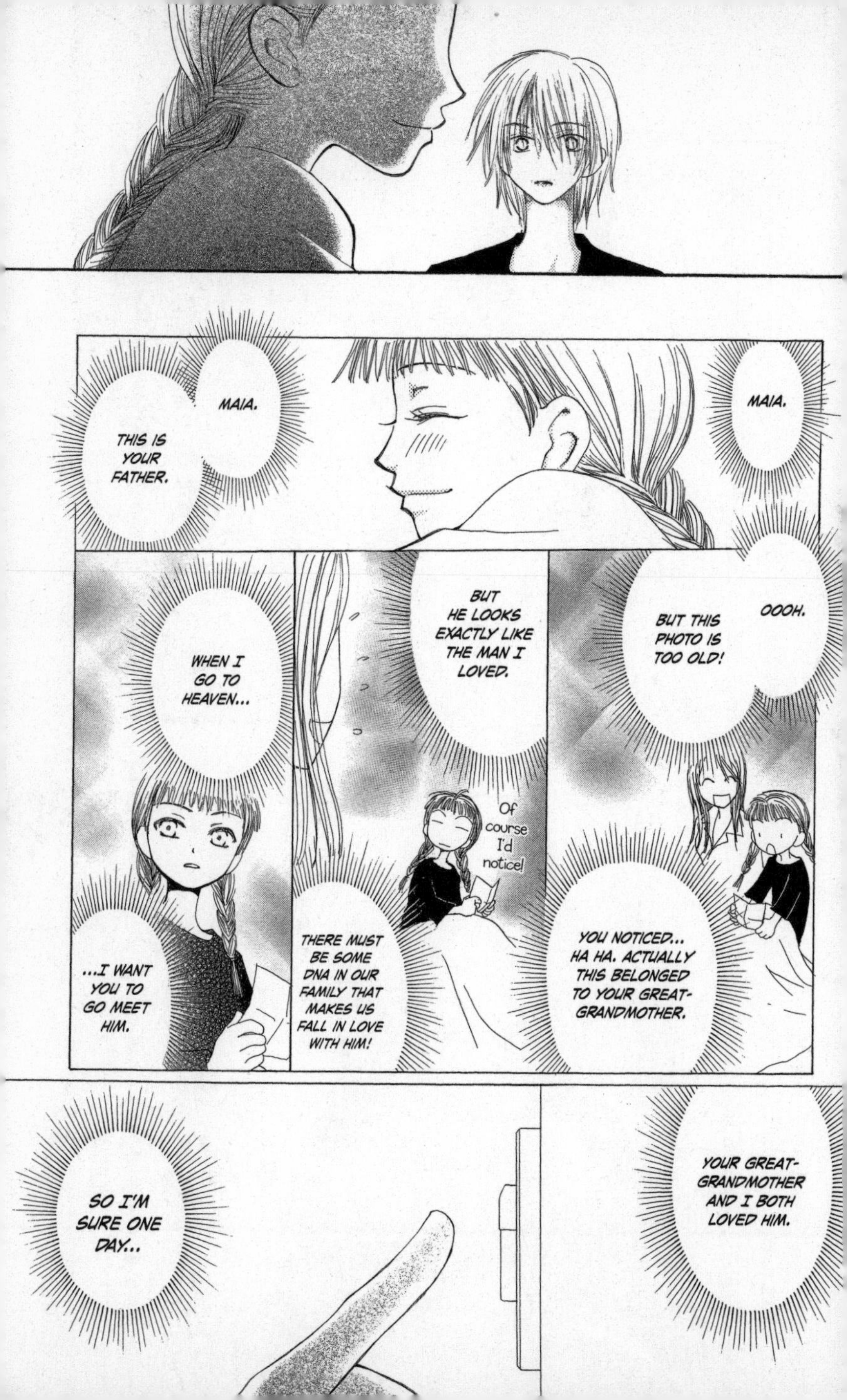
MAIA.
MAIA.
THIS IS YOUR FATHER.
OOOH.
BUT THIS PHOTO IS TOO OLD!
YOU NOTICED... HA HA. ACTUALLY THIS BELONGED TO YOUR GREAT-GRANDMOTHER.
BUT HE LOOKS EXACTLY LIKE THE MAN I LOVED.
Of course I'd notice!
THERE MUST BE SOME DNA IN OUR FAMILY THAT MAKES US FALL IN LOVE WITH HIM!
WHEN I GO TO HEAVEN...
...I WANT YOU TO GO MEET HIM.
YOUR GREAT-GRANDMOTHER AND I BOTH LOVED HIM.
SO I'M SURE ONE DAY...

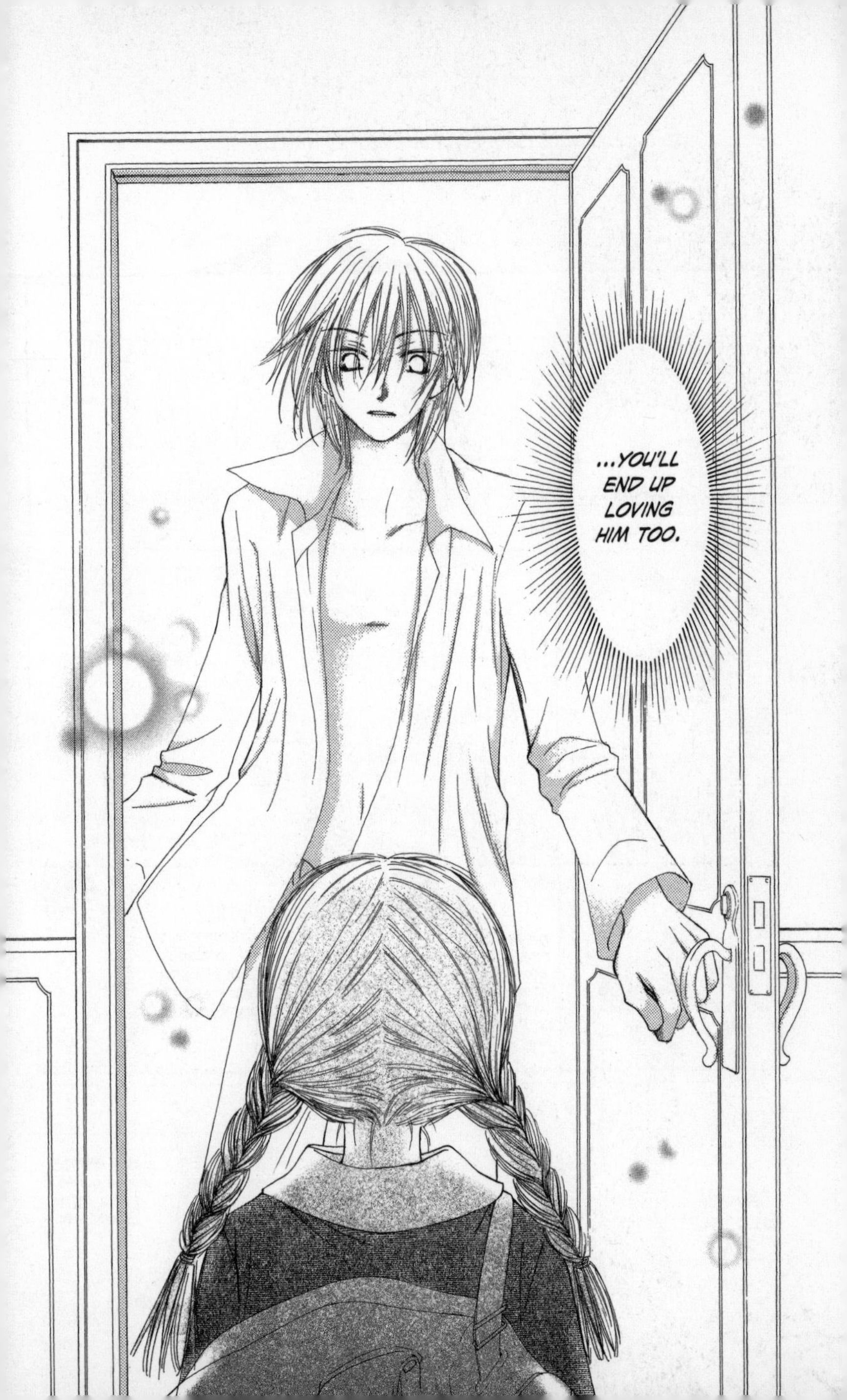
...YOU'LL END UP LOVING HIM TOO.

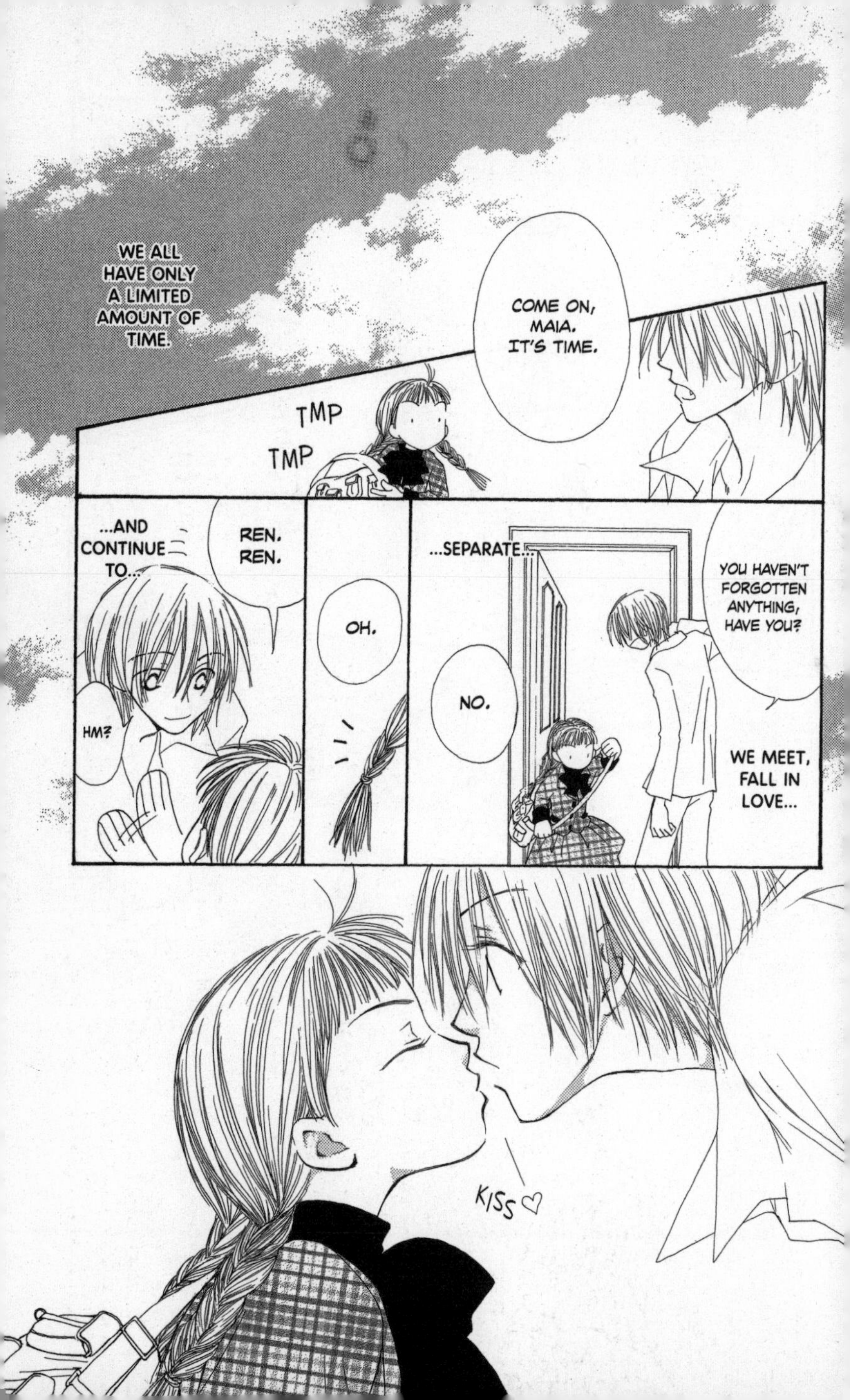
WE ALL HAVE ONLY A LIMITED AMOUNT OF TIME.
COME ON, MAIA. IT'S TIME.
TMP
TMP
YOU HAVEN'T FORGOTTEN ANYTHING, HAVE YOU?
WE MEET, FALL IN LOVE...
NO.
...SEPARATE...
OH.
REN. REN.
...AND CONTINUE TO...
HM?
KISS ♡

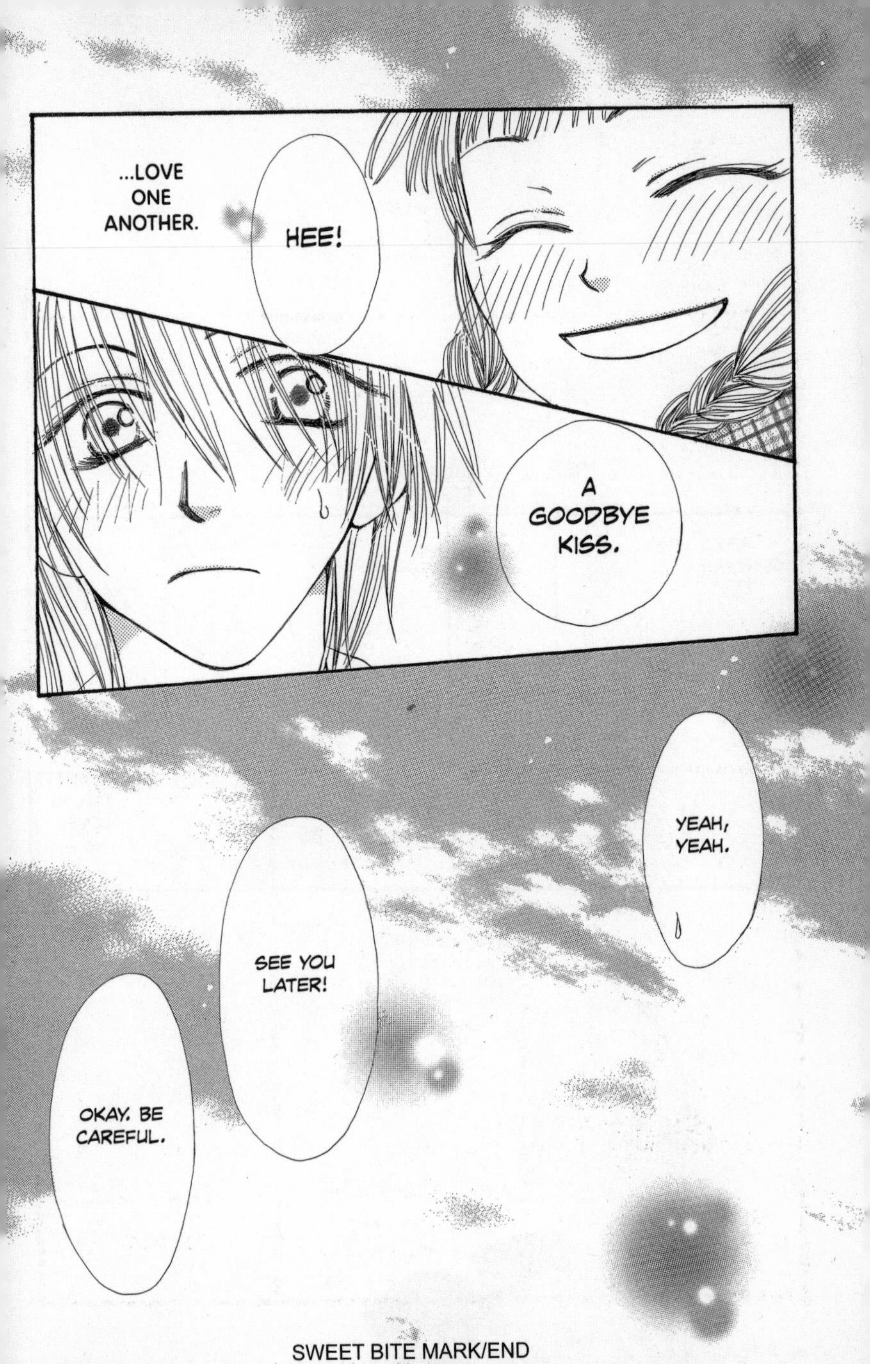
HEE!
...LOVE ONE ANOTHER.
A GOODBYE KISS.
YEAH, YEAH.
SEE YOU LATER!
OKAY. BE CAREFUL.

SWEET BITE MARK/END

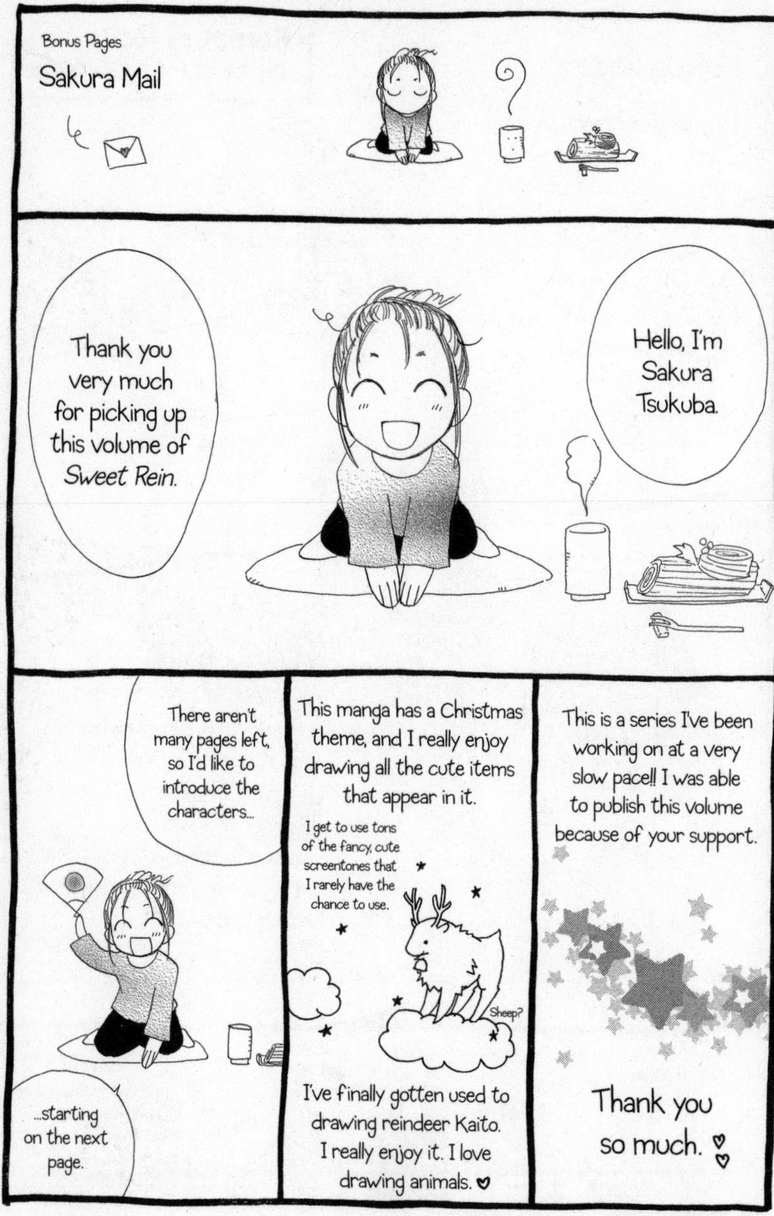

Bonus Pages
Sakura Mail
Hello, I'm Sakura Tsukuba.
Thank you very much for picking up this volume of Sweet Rein.
This is a series I've been working on at a very slow pace!! I was able to publish this volume because of your support.
Thank you so much.
This manga has a Christmas theme, and I really enjoy drawing all the cute items that appear in it.
I get to use tons of the fancy, cute screentones that I rarely have the chance to use.
Sheep?
I've finally gotten used to drawing reindeer Kaito. I really enjoy it. I love drawing animals.
There aren't many pages left, so I'd like to introduce the characters...
...starting on the next page.

Sweet Rein
CHARACTER INTRODUCTION

Kurumi Sagara

I like how she tends to speak bluntly. Kaito is head-over-heels for her, so I think her being a cool person balances things out...
She's a fun character because I can make her wear all sorts of Santa outfits.

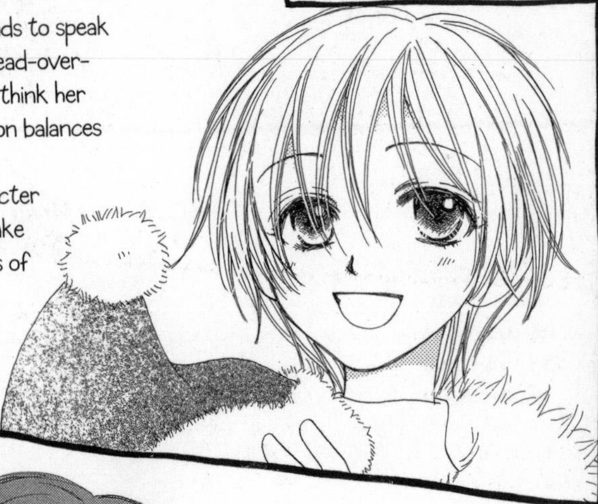

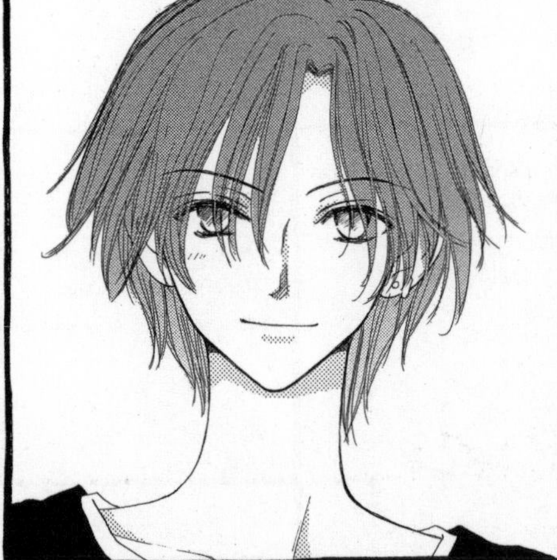

Kaito

It's spelled 魁人 ("best and brightest" or "great leader") in kanji. But his family members and Kurumi use katakana for his name. He seems to get dumber and dumber, but I personally think he's a nice guy. He's popular with the girls. And he often gets lost.

Kaito's Family

The reindeer blood is from the mother's side of the family. Everybody except the father and grandmother are reindeer.

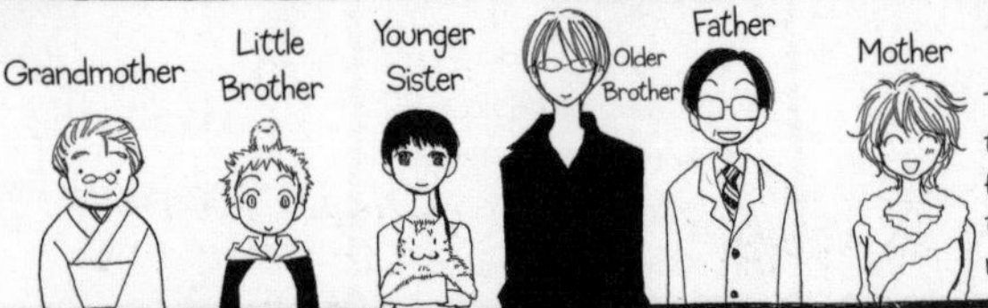
Mother
Father
Older Brother
Younger Sister
Little Brother
Grandmother

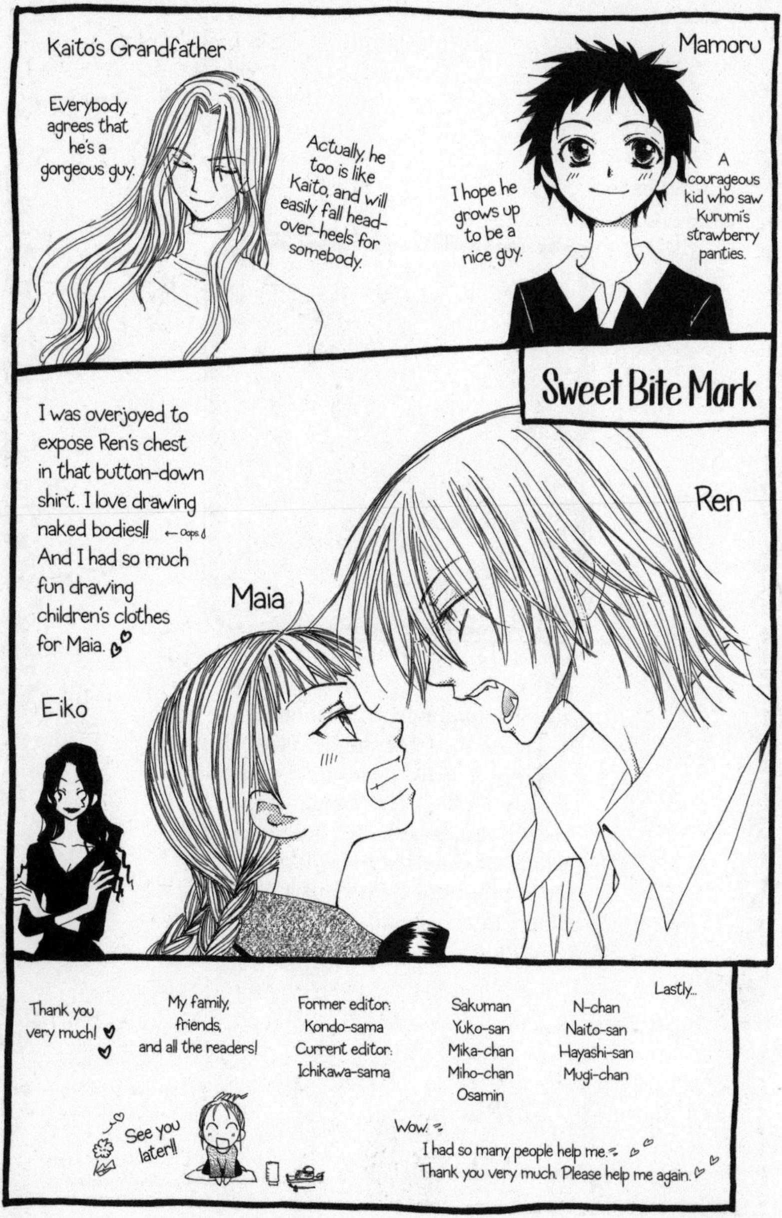

Mamoru
A courageous kid who saw Kurumi's strawberry panties.
I hope he grows up to be a nice guy.
Kaito's Grandfather
Actually, he too is like Kaito, and will easily fall head-over-heels for somebody.
Everybody agrees that he's a gorgeous guy.
Sweet Bite Mark
Ren
Maia
I was overjoyed to expose Ren's chest in that button-down shirt. I love drawing naked bodies!! ← Oops. And I had so much fun drawing children's clothes for Maia.
Eiko
Lastly...
N-chan
Naito-san
Hayashi-san
Mugi-chan
Sakuman
Yuko-san
Mika-chan
Miho-chan
Osamin
Former editor: Kondo-sama
Current editor: Ichikawa-sama
My family, friends, and all the readers!
Thank you very much!
Wow.
I had so many people help me.
Thank you very much. Please help me again.
See you later!!

Sakura Tsukuba is from Saitama
Prefecture. In 1994 she debuted with
Hikari Nodokeki Haru no Hi ni, a title
which won the LaLa Manga Grand
Prix Kasaku Award. Her other works
include *Land of the Blindfolded*
(recipient of the Hakusensha Athena
Shinjin Taisho award) and *Penguin
Revolution*.

Sweet ❤ Rein

Volume 1
Shojo Beat Edition

Story and Art by
Sakura Tsukuba

Translation/Tetsuichiro Miyaki
Adaptation/Nancy Thistlethwaite
Touch-up Art & Lettering/Inori Fukuda Trant
Design/Izumi Evers
Editor/Nancy Thistlethwaite

YOROSHIKU • MASTER by Sakura Tsukuba
© Sakura Tsukuba 2005
All rights reserved.
First published in Japan in 2005 by HAKUSENSHA, Inc., Tokyo.
English language translation rights arranged
with HAKUSENSHA, Inc., Tokyo.

The stories, characters and incidents mentioned
in this publication are entirely fictional.

Printed in the U.S.A.

Published by VIZ Media, LLC
P.O. Box 77010
San Francisco, CA 94107

10 9 8 7 6 5 4 3 2 1
First printing, November 2013

www.viz.com   www.shojobeat.com

PARENTAL ADVISORY
SWEET REIN is rated T for Teen and
is recommended for ages 13 and up.
ratings.viz.com

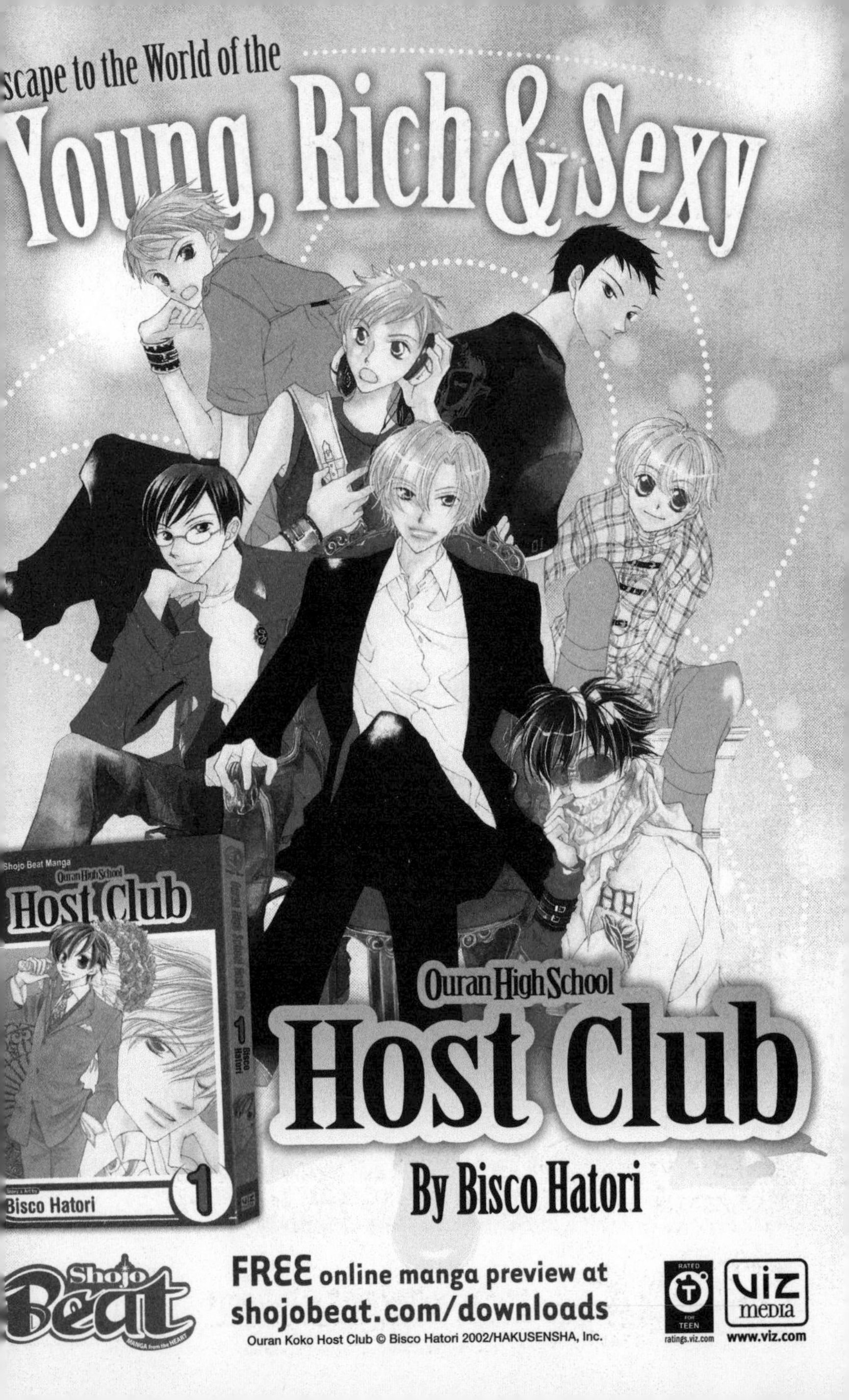

scape to the World of the
Young, Rich & Sexy
Shojo Beat Manga
Ouran High School
Host Club
Bisco Hatori
1
Ouran High School
Host Club
By Bisco Hatori
Shojo Beat
MANGA from the HEART
FREE online manga preview at
shojobeat.com/downloads
Ouran Koko Host Club © Bisco Hatori 2002/HAKUSENSHA, Inc.
RATED T FOR TEEN
ratings.viz.com
VIZ media
www.viz.com